Parents and Grandparents as Teachers

A guide for families in teaching infants through age 8, this insightful book showcases how both parents and grandparents can support greater family success and how creative collaboration can produce benefits for each generation.

Having developed the nation's first curriculum for grandparents and field-tested the intervention program with support from the American Association of Retired Persons, the authors explore topics like trust in infancy, family conversations and child language, praise and encouragement, alone time, peer influence, resilience, and cultural diversity. To bring family members closer together and support child development, each chapter includes principles for application, ten key concepts, and questions for reflection. Readers can benefit from the Generational Perspectives Activities presented at the end of each chapter, and available online, that recommend topics for family conversations and self-evaluation for parents and grandparents.

This book will be invaluable for parent and grandparent readers and may also be of interest to students majoring in family studies and developmental psychology and those preparing to become early childhood or elementary school teachers.

Paris S. Strom is Professor of Educational Psychology at Auburn University in Auburn, Alabama. He currently teaches child, adolescent, and adult development courses to undergraduate and graduate college students and has worked with high school students in the public schools. In addition, he has published over 100 journal articles and books about learning and teaching throughout the lifespan.

Robert D. Strom is Professor Emeritus of Educational Psychology at Arizona State University and Director of the Office of Parent Development International. He taught in public schools of Minnesota and Michigan before becoming Professor of Psychology and Education at Ohio State University. His teaching, writing, and research have focused on the lifespan and mental health. He is the author of over 400 publications.

Parents and Grandparents as Teachers

Supporting Child Development from Infancy through Age 8

Paris S. Strom and Robert D. Strom

NEW YORK AND LONDON

First published 2025
by Routledge
605 Third Avenue, New York, NY 10158

and by Routledge
4 Park Square, Milton Park, Abingdon, Oxon, OX14 4RN

Routledge is an imprint of the Taylor & Francis Group, an informa business

© 2025 Paris S. Strom and Robert D. Strom

The right of Paris S. Strom and Robert D. Strom to be identified as authors of this work has been asserted in accordance with sections 77 and 78 of the Copyright, Designs and Patents Act 1988.

All rights reserved. No part of this book may be reprinted or reproduced or utilised in any form or by any electronic, mechanical, or other means, now known or hereafter invented, including photocopying and recording, or in any information storage or retrieval system, without permission in writing from the publishers.

Trademark notice: Product or corporate names may be trademarks or registered trademarks, and are used only for identification and explanation without intent to infringe.

ISBN: 978-1-032-87828-7 (hbk)
ISBN: 978-1-032-87827-0 (pbk)
ISBN: 978-1-003-53465-5 (ebk)

DOI: 10.4324/9781003534655

Typeset in Galliard
By Apex CoVantage, LLC

Access the Support Material: routledge.com/9781032878270

Contents

About the Authors   vii

Introduction   1

PART I
Emotional and Social Learning   7

1 Parents and Grandparents as Partners   9
2 Infancy: Trust and Social Awareness   24
3 Family Conversations and Child Language   42
4 Play and Child Development   58

PART II
Early Learning at Home   75

5 Young Children Learn About the Internet   77
6 Watching Television With Children and Asking Them Questions   96
7 Child Thinking and Cognitive Development   110
8 The Influence of Media on Children   123

PART III
Motivation and Schooling   139

9 Goals and Priorities During Childhood   141
10 Tutoring for Literacy and School Achievement   155
11 Praise, Encouragement, and Motivation   170
12 Sometimes I Like to Play by Myself   182

PART IV
Mental Health and Development — 199

13 Conflicts and Learning to Get Along — 201
14 Relationships With Parents and Peers — 215
15 Fears of Parents and Children — 230
16 Self-Control, Resilience, and Patience — 247

PART V
The Value of Grandparents — 263

17 Grandparent Goals and Expectations — 265
18 Grandparents Raising Their Grandchildren — 280
19 Grandparents Giving and Seeking Family Advice — 297
20 Grandparent Strengths and Cultural Diversity — 311

Index — *329*

About the Authors

Paris S. Strom (PhD, Arizona State University) is Professor of Educational Psychology at Auburn University in Auburn, Alabama. His career began with teaching public high school students in Arizona. Paris currently teaches child, adolescent, and adult development courses to undergraduate and graduate students. He is the author of over 100 journal articles and books about the learning process throughout the human lifespan. Paris's online polls help secondary educators discover how high school students view conditions of learning at their school. His Teamwork Skills Inventory provides anonymous feedback from cooperative learning teammates in secondary school and higher education regarding their demonstration of collaborative attitudes and skills.

Robert D. Strom (PhD, University of Michigan) is Professor Emeritus of Educational Psychology at Arizona State University. He taught in public schools of St. Paul, Minnesota and Detroit, Michigan, before becoming Professor of Psychology and Education at The Ohio State University. His teaching, writing, and research have centered on lifespan development and mental health to support families, and he is the author of over 400 articles and 25 textbooks. Robert's adult education projects have been presented in *The New York Times* and *The Wall Street Journal*. He received Fulbright awards at the University of Stockholm, Sweden; University of the Philippines, Manila; and Canberra University, Australia. He has been a North Atlantic Treaty Organization scholar at the University of Ankara, Turkey.

Robert's research and development projects have focused on curriculum development for parents and grandparents to improve understanding of younger generations and ways of learning from them. These efforts in the United States have been supported by the American Association of Retired Persons, Danforth Foundation, General Mills Foundation, Motorola, and the National Institute of Mental Health. International sponsors have included the Hitachi Foundation, Japan Ministry of Education, Japan Society for Promotion of Science, International Longevity Center of Japan, Novartis in Switzerland, Swedish National Research Institute, Hong Kong Van Zuiden Foundation, Pacific Cultural Foundation of Taiwan, Werner Reimers Foundation in Germany, and North Atlantic Treaty Organization in Belgium.

We are a father-and-son team whose goals are to improve conditions of learning at home and in school.

Paris S. Strom
Robert D. Strom

Introduction

The purposes of this book are to unite the efforts of parents and grandparents to support child development from infancy through age 8. The reason for focusing on this age group is that longitudinal research by the Annie E. Casey Foundation (2010, 2013, 2024) determined that student reading test scores at the end of third grade are the best predictor of future school success. In addition to parents, the intended readers for this book are grandparents. They have been generally ignored in child development books even though many grandparents devote considerable time and attention to caring for and teaching their grandchildren. College students will also find the book worthwhile, especially if they plan careers related to teaching young children, mental health, and family development.

Parent Education

Parents are responsible for introducing young children to the Internet to guide them in becoming self-directed learners and prepare for cooperative activity with classmates at school. In addition, parents spend more time watching television with their children than other forms of leisure. Accordingly, they should know how to wisely use this context to teach and monitor development of critical and creative thinking. Parents are also expected to teach attitudes and skills that define reading and mathematics readiness expected of students when they arrive at kindergarten. Mothers and fathers want to encourage daughters and sons to become imaginative adults able to solve problems, demonstrate persistence, and show resilience. This goal implicates adult participation with children as fantasy play partners who reinforce the retention of imagination along with other creative abilities.

Many parents realize their education and guidance could be enhanced if grandparents were to contribute some of their talent and time. Being a parent also requires persuading grandparents that their emerging family role will require them to learn from younger relatives. Until recently, parents and grandparents have mostly overlooked the unique experiences of younger generations that qualify them to be an essential source of learning for adults. Formulating an education strategy that allows children to have input to family decisions on what grandparents should learn is a departure from the past.

Adult education that focuses on learning about the life of younger generations will ensure parents and grandparents stay connected, remain well-informed, and in sync with loved ones. Older people are aware of personal assets and limitations, but the education path they choose has been too narrow. The education of grandparents should reveal the current experiences of children, adolescents, and young adults and show how they differ from the way things were when grandparents raised children. This new knowledge cannot be acquired through memory or by intuition.

Grandparent Education

An important goal is to become informed on how communications technology and social media impact parent behavior with consequent implications for what families should expect of older relatives. The success of grandparents depends on finding out how younger generations interpret events, recognize the values they rely on for direction, and appreciate their vision about the future. *Generational reciprocal learning* – generations learning from each other – can make it possible to recognize and understand the feelings, hopes, and concerns of all family members.

Many observers have reported that families seem fragile and require more internal support. There is also recognition that expectations for grandparents are seldom discussed in the family, and so they continue to be poorly defined. Grandparents believe if expectations for them could be modified to fit current conditions, it would be possible to avoid feeling they are being left out of family affairs. The contemporary role should be well-defined, include a sense of purpose, and make wise use of grandparent abilities to improve lives of younger family members (Strom & Strom, 2024).

The Parent and Grandparent Partnership

A parent and grandparent partnership will be essential to create conditions needed to ensure success of families in a longevity society (Strom & Strom, 1983). Both parents and grandparents could gain from a creative orientation that acknowledges their separate strengths and learning needs to be partners. They could benefit from the same mindset to establish a common knowledge base to balance assumptions, opinions, hopes, joys, and worries that can contribute to individual success. Cohesion between parents and grandparents is a key to better mental health for all generations in most families (Strom & Strom, 2021). Building support for this ambitious plan to improve family relationships is unprecedented, demanding, and rewarding. Consider some concepts both generations should try to understand.

Learning During Infancy

The term *infant*, from birth to age 2, comes from Latin and means incapable of speech. Scientific studies of infancy did not occur for many years because babies were unable to report what they could see and comprehend. This language restriction caused adults to speculate that not much learning happened before children start to express their thoughts by using speech during the second year. Another factor accounting for the general underestimate of early mental awareness was a common lack of memory by grownups about their own personal experiences as infants. The assumption was that, if infancy is an important stage of learning, then certainly it would be remembered by at least some people. However, on average, our memories stretch back no farther than age three and a half. Everything that takes place before then appears inaccessible. Because everyone seems to have forgotten their infancy, the consensus among early childhood educators was that experiences during this stage must not be important for mental development. This view was corrected when studies in neuroscience showed that babies are more capable of thinking than was supposed, and they are more emotionally vulnerable (Bortfeld & Bunge, 2024; Garvey, 2023). Attachment, trust, and confidence are recognized as essential conditions to build on as a basis for close relationships, mental health, and well-being.

Early Childhood Learning

During early childhood, from age 2 to age 6, most children spend considerable time in a day care center, a preschool, or a kindergarten; some stay home with mother, grandmother, or a caregiver. After research demonstrated the enormous potential for learning during this early stage, certain environmental factors conducive to teaching and learning were discovered. Some young children learn a lot at home while others do not, largely dependent on the parent-child differences in interaction that characterize low- and middle-income households. Since 1965, the federal government has provided free education for young children and care programs such as Head Start to compensate for the lack of learning opportunities in low-income families. As the proportion of employed middle-class mothers has significantly risen over the past few years, one of their main family concerns has become ensuring access to high-quality education for children that is affordable.

Whether parents are economically poor or qualify as middle class, are employed or stay at home, they are usually the only long-term teachers of their children. Consequently, parents and grandparents wonder what they can do to support readiness for success at school. Young children enjoy being on the Internet, listening to stories, pretending, and watching television. These and other social contexts are examined to improve the quality of family interaction, teaching, and learning.

Elementary School Learning

Lessons that people find difficult often produce frustration. This is the case when trying to foster the acquisition of self-control, self-restraint, demonstrating empathy by caring about the feelings of others, being willing to wait for things that are wanted, ability to delay gratification, and the development of patience. Everyone knows some adults who have yet to learn these important insights. A related problem is knowing how to motivate primary-grade children to do some things that will bring benefits but might not appeal to them. Similarly, performing well in the classroom, persevering when some school subjects are difficult, acknowledging failure, and requesting tutoring are important signs of development. Gaining emotional resilience to continue the pursuit of some goals and doing household chores parents expect are important aspects of growing up. The conditions adults rely on to encourage or praise children can impact social maturity and motivate academic achievement.

Features of the Book

How is the book organized to reflect family experiences of parents and grandparents? The book is divided into five main parts: (1) *Part I Emotional and Social Learning*, (2) *Part II Early Learning at Home*, (3) *Part III Motivation and Schooling*, (4) *Part IV Mental Health and Development*, and (5) *The Value of Grandparents*. This book presents several research studies about parents, grandparents, and children across many cultures. These studies were initiated by Robert D. Strom, Professor and Director of the Office of Parent Development International at Arizona State University, and Professor Paris S. Strom at Auburn University. Together this father-and-son team has taught parent and grandparent classes at numerous facilities including public schools, senior centers, assisted living centers, and the Osher Lifelong Learning Institutes.

Chapters. Aspects of child, parent, and grandparent development are based on research and application of new knowledge. In addition, guidance is proposed for how to build close and durable relationships that enrich the parent-grandparent partnership and ways to support social, mental, and emotional growth for three generations across cultures and ethnicities. Content has been drawn from developmental psychology, educational psychology, social psychology, social work, gerontology, and medicine augmented by the family observations of three generations. Recommendations are offered to guide child social, mental, emotional, and spiritual growth from infancy through age 8.

Key Concepts. The main points explained in each chapter are summarized by ten key concepts. These concepts reinforce knowledge and attitudes to consider as a basis for personal initiatives and to guide family relationships.

Generational Perspectives Activities

How can readers apply relevant information from the text to their own unique family situation? Each chapter concludes with a section called *Generational Perspectives Activities* that presents additional sources of experience and information for consideration. Methods of learning include group discussions, suggestions for conversations with young children, a scenario with reasoning and problem-solving, chapter reviews, storytelling, and self-evaluations.

Group Discussions. Some people will learn alone, and others can learn in small groups. When people form small groups composed of three to five members, they help each other reflect on current issues while also sharing hopes, satisfaction, frustration, doubts, questions, and solutions with peers, relatives, and friends. Benefits of this strategy are learning from peers, gaining their advice, and being able to compare personal impressions with the views expressed by others.

Groups may choose which *Generational Perspectives Activities* they want to complete and choose some that they will ignore. The customary expectation that every task should be finished should be avoided in favor of group judgment about the preferred way to proceed with each chapter. Groups can choose those items that are most relevant to their goals.

Conversations With Young Children. Adults sometimes complete polls to make their opinions, feelings, and concerns known. At times we might feel overinformed regarding their collective outlook. In contrast, grownups cannot accurately claim they understand much about norms and views of young children. Listening to them can reveal their feelings, ideas, values, satisfactions, and worries that should be understood to provide emotional support and practical advice. However, grandparents generally acknowledge that having a sustained conversation with young children can be challenging. Parents express similar frustrations about the meager amount of dialogue many of them have with their children. Structured agenda questions are presented to discover a child's outlook. Adults should be willing to admit how little we know about the youngest generation. Some of the proposed questions are meant for young children, and others are more appropriate for students in the elementary grades.

A Scenario: Reasoning and Problem-Solving. A family decision-making scenario is described along with a listing of some optional solutions. The purposes are to consider the pros and cons for each of the stated choices, generate additional possibilities, listen to how others perceive each solution, and explain reasoning for the advice you consider best.

Chapter Review. The efforts to assess learning of a child, share personal conclusions, offer feedback, and improve quality of instruction are enhanced by a group review. Choose one or two questions to comment on how a chapter influenced your feelings, suggestions you intend to apply in your relationships, aspects of a lesson that would be better understood, and insights you wish were learned earlier.

Parent and Grandparent Self-Evaluation. Participation in self-evaluation is necessary for personal improvement of parents and grandparents. Each chapter includes multiple-choice items for consideration. Sharing results of self-evaluation with the other adult generation in your family will result in a better partnership by increasing reciprocal learning and reliance on common methods of child guidance. The importance of transparency should be understood by parents and grandparents. If you attend a parent or grandparent class, we recommend the self-evaluation be submitted anonymously to a homework box that class leaders tally to let everyone know the group norms for individual comparison with peers. If you do not attend a parent and grandparent class, reflect on each item and share your answers with other peers in a class of college students.

Storytelling. There are many stories throughout this book which were previously told by parents and grandparents in their classes. These stories are used to reinforce a principle, give an example of some behavior, and capture the relevance of a concept. The purposes of a storyteller are to present imaginary or real-life examples showing how some concept or method applies to a particular situation. People like to listen to stories, they pay attention to the procession of events, and usually remember the key elements of a story for a longer time.

Whether storytellers read from a book or a report, describe a movie or television program, reveal an incident someone shared with them, or relate a personal observation, their stories can help others make connections to increase the value of a lesson, grasp concepts that previously seemed unclear, and realize why certain issues require greater attention. The influences of stories on motivation, comprehension, and relationships are difficult to gauge, but the worthwhileness is always there for people who experience it. Parent and grandparent classes usually schedule time during each meeting to share personal stories.

We are grateful to the thousands of parents, grandparents, and children around the world who have participated in our research studies and classes about family development.

References

Annie E. Casey Foundation. (2010, January 1). *Early learning! Why reading by the end of third grade matters [A Kids Count Special Report on the importance of reading by 3rd grade].* https://www.aecf.org/resources/early-warning-why-reading-by-the-end-of-third-grade-matters

Annie E. Casey Foundation. (2013). *Early warning confirmed: A research update on third-grade reading, executive summary.* https://assets.aecf.org/m/resourcedoc/aecf-EarlyWarningConfirmedExecSummary-2013.pdf

Annie E. Casey Foundation. (2024). *2024 Kids Count data book interactive.* aecf.org/interactive/databook?l=502

Bortfeld, H., & Bunge, S. A. (2024). *Fundamentals of developmental cognitive neuroscience.* Cambridge University Press.

Garvey, D. (2023). *Little brains matter: A practical guide to brain development and neuroscience in early childhood.* Routledge.

Strom, R. D., & Strom, S. K. (1983). Redefining the grandparent role. *Cambridge Journal of Education, 13*(1), 25–28. https://doi.org/10.1080/0305764830130107

Strom, R. D., & Strom, P. S. (2021). Learning throughout life about the needs of all generations: Recognizing and counteracting generational isolation. In M. London (Ed.), *The Oxford handbook of lifelong learning* (2nd ed., pp. 183–206). Oxford University Press. https://doi.org/10.1093/oxfordhb/9780197506707.013.9

Strom, P. S., & Strom, R. D. (2024). *Mental health and relationships from early adulthood through old age.* Routledge.

Part I
Emotional and Social Learning

Chapter 1

Parents and Grandparents as Partners

The concepts of parent and grandparent development as partners have not been linked in the past but should become a consideration for achieving family success in a longevity society. Being aware of the common challenges parents and grandparents experience independently and together as teachers can identify ways to improve family relationships and create social harmony. The purposes of this chapter are to (a) explain ways that collaboration could benefit both generations in a longevity society, (b) show how shared learning from a common curriculum for the parents and grandparents can support their adjustment to contemporary family roles, (c) contribute to knowledge about anticipated and unforeseen problems, (d) enlarge the scope of guidance available for children, and (e) monitor the results of parent and grandparent education. Generational Perspectives Activities present topics to discuss with family members and close friends about the concept of parents and grandparents as partners.

Parents as Teachers

Six social contexts are identified where expectations of parents seem to be in transition.

Teach Young Children Before They Go to Kindergarten

Parents have the responsibility for introducing young children to the Internet and helping to acquire digital skills needed for self-directed learning. In addition, parents should devote some time they watch television with children to emphasize development of critical thinking, generate creative ideas, and nurture problem-solving abilities. Children should be taught readiness skills expected by teachers at school. According to the Annie E. Casey Foundation (2010, 2013, 2023, 2024), there is evidence that students in the United States perform poorly on competency tests for the basic subjects of reading and mathematics. Parents should join children as play partners to foster imagination and reinforce the importance of emotional development. Parents should teach self-control and how to resolve peer conflicts. Fears and anxieties of children should be understood by parents. Mothers and fathers should recognize when they should rely on praise or encouragement as their strategy to motivate and guide young children (Morris & Smith, 2022).

Children should be encouraged to set personality goals. When children are allowed to engage in goalsetting, they experience greater control of their lives, develop a sense of personal direction, show additional motivation to succeed, and are more able to avoid distractions that would undermine their purposes. Children require guidance to learn when some self-selected goals are unattainable or too limited and require revision. Becoming involved with teaching basic skills is a continuous task for parents because this enables children to identify their academic weaknesses and overcome learning deficits (Frey et al., 2021).

Child Reliance on Peers and Social Media Increases

There was a time when growing up and assuming adult responsibilities was much the same for successive generations. This similarity of background allowed parents to feel confident that the advice they gave children, based on their memory of what growing up was like, would provide the foundation to ensure child development. Observation was the main reference children depended on to gauge personal growth by comparing themselves with peers. Grandparents were thought to possess wisdom because of lengthy experience (Levine, 2020; Morris & Smith, 2022; Strom et al., 2019).

Most people are not old enough to remember those more stable times although it might seem like yesterday in the memory of older adults. Since then, the revolution in technology and social media has produced significant differences in the attitudes and behaviors of separate generations. Computers, the Internet, iPhones, social media platforms, and satellite television present ideas and values that reflect the evolving norms of youth culture today across the world (Anderson et al., 2023). As a result, the age-segregated students in Los Angeles, Tokyo, London, and Berlin and other cities generally share more goals and concerns with peers than with their parents and grandparents (Kennedy, 2022; Twenge, 2023).

Parents Learn From Listening to Their Child's Experiences

Because of rapid change children are the only group who can accurately describe their unique experiences. In response, adults should realize that, because they are not growing up at the present time, it is impossible to know firsthand about the environment of youth. Consequently, for the first time in history, grownups must learn from children and adolescents before they can be seen by the younger generation as credible advisors (McConnell, 2023; Milkie et al., 2015).

Another complicating factor is that age-segregated conversations are more comfortable because they are based on equivalent status, mutual experiences, greater agreement, and less uncertainty (Jackson, 2023). As peers replace parents and grandparents as the preferred sources of advice and emotional support, adults worry that the mature counsel every young generation needs could be in jeopardy (Bukowski et al., 2019). Dependence of students on peer norms to shape their behavior causes adults to wonder what they can do to remain a chosen source of influence. Learning how youth see situations and interpret events calls for careful listening, a task made more difficult when parents and children do not spend enough time together (Strom & Strom, 2021; Vaterlaus et al., 2019).

Listening to young children is a critical variable because it impacts all aspects of family life. Communication, learning, and emotional support all decline when a family loses control of how time is spent. Some parents assert that moments they are with children is 'quality time.' However, 'quality time' should be defined as any time children need their parents rather than whenever the adults find themselves able to fit children into their busy schedules (Perry, 2023). Quality time is most often mentioned by middle- and higher-income parents but rarely by low-income parents. What seems to happen is that, when professionals return home at the end of a day, they continue checking email or making phone calls as if they were still at the office. In contrast, blue-collar parents typically have a regular work schedule and expect to spend time with their children at the end of the day. Youth in blue-collar families more often describe the relationship with their parents as close than is reported by their peers from affluent families (Luthar et al., 2018). All parents, regardless of social status, should strive to balance their time so it corresponds with personal priorities. The effective way to discover feelings, goals, and concerns of youth is to spend uninterrupted time listening to them (Burkeman, 2021; Collinsworth et al., 1996; Milkie et al., 2015; Minkin & Horowitz, 2023).

Parents Teach the Importance of Time Management

Preparing students to join the workplace means convincing them to abandon some dysfunctional time management habits. Spending many hours a day phoning or texting friends and engaging e-media are distractions from the main responsibility of students which is to spend most of their time on schoolwork (Rothwell, 2023). Polls show that most adolescents admit they have poor time management habits (Strom et al., 2016). Establishing rules that restrict the amount of time youth are allowed to communicate with friends is a practical way courageous parents support self-regulation while also contributing to child academic achievement (Vogels & Gelles-Watnick, 2023).

Most people prefer that their experiences reflect personal decisions. However, in the current environment with competing priorities and information overload, some decisions are based on impulse, stress, and expedience (Krznaric, 2021). Children should be able to observe their parents daily model the benefits of healthy time management. Individuals who possess this ability avoid taking on too many responsibilities, do not break promises to others, and do not ignore the people and activities in their lives that matter most. Instead, they live by a scheduled plan that reflects a reasonable distribution of time. When parents are unable to provide examples of time management, children often repeat the same pattern as adults of overscheduling themselves and experiencing the stressful results of being unable to control their lives (Strom et al., 2004; Strom & Strom, 2024).

Many parents allow children to retreat to their bedroom for hours at a time surrounded by a cell phone, computer, audio devices, and fascination to engage in peer messaging. A related condition is to postpone family conversations about emotional, social, and ethical issues every generation should acquire so they become able to adjust to changing times. Parents should confront the excessive dependence of youth on peer communication that takes them away from academic studies and family relationships (Anderson et al., 2023; Anderson et al., 2024; Turkle, 2015).

Becoming a Caregiver for Aging Relatives

Life expectancy has increased by over 30 years during the past century (McConnell, 2023). Demographic forecasts show that, as the average lifespan continues to lengthen, the population of retirees is increasing more rapidly than younger cohorts (Das, 2024; Locke, 2023). As a result, many parents will need to take care of their aging relatives for a longer time (Mather & Scommegna, 2024).

Protection for fragile retirees will depend on access to caregivers who have patience, show willingness to listen to fears, goals, concerns, and demonstrate self-restraint when certain difficulties of caregiving cause feelings of frustration. The healthy personality attributes that comprise maturity should be nurtured by parents so that all generations are prepared to help when needed. The best methods to ensure relationships with older relatives lead to mutual satisfaction are not fully known, but enough is understood so that education for parents and grandparents can support favorable outcomes.

Greater collaboration within families is bound to become more necessary. The primary caregivers, typically middle-aged daughters, require periodic relief so they remain able to meet their demanding task. This increasingly familiar situation has implications for siblings. Brothers and sisters who do not regularly provide care for their older relatives should step up to provide respite for siblings who are the main caregivers. Financial expenses incurred by the primary caregiver should be shared by all siblings. Relatives who live apart from aging parents should visit or provide travel arrangements so that older adults can come to visit them (Guillén, 2020).

Filial piety is a core virtue of ancient Chinese Confucianism that defines how children should show respect and care toward their parents, ancestors, and elders. The United States does not have a tradition of filial piety. In many East Asian countries, this means that relatives, particularly sons, have been expected to provide respect, economic and emotional support for aging parents. This long-standing custom is reported to be in decline (Yeung & Lee, 2022). China, South Korea, Macao, Japan, Taiwan, and Hong Kong have the lowest fertility rates but also record the world's highest life expectancy (Kaneda et al., 2020). Since Social Security and other nonfamily financial support systems are uncommon in much of Asia, older adults there often suffer poverty and must keep working beyond the normal Western age of retirement. The forecasts of increasing aging populations and shrinking working populations are accelerating more rapidly in Asia than other regions of the world. Accordingly, middle-aged people in these areas more often have concerns about taking care of the elderly than other longevity nations such as the United States.

Parents Encourage Grandparents to Be Active in Family Affairs

Parents believe that bringing up children is becoming more complicated than when they grew up. Also, they recognize that guidance for daughters and sons could be more influential if the lessons they try to teach were reinforced by grandparents. Because of their longer lifespan, grandparents have more active years to offer affection, care, and guidance to their grandchildren from infancy through early adulthood. However, the extent to which individual grandparents remain influential will depend on participation in education that can enable greater understanding and support for younger relatives (Locke, 2023). Grandparent education should orient them to the behaviors, values, and concerns of peer norms for each of their grandchildren's age groups, discover the personal perspective of individual grandchildren, and know the rationale parents rely on to guide the way they bring up their children. Older relatives should acquire this knowledge to become more motivated and able to reinforce lessons parents want children to learn from all relatives (Minkin & Horowitz, 2023; Strom & Strom, 2018a).

Grandparents as Teachers

Parents are not alone in confronting unfamiliar demands that could undermine their influence. Grandparents also have new obstacles to overcome. Six social concerns warrant reflection.

Traditional Norms for Retirees Should Be Replaced by More Mature Goals

An unhealthy state of mind is reflected by retirees who suppose they do not have responsibilities to younger generations or people in their community. This narrow self-impression is widespread even though most retirees in the United States benefit from the most generous and lengthy Social Security financial support system in the history of the world.

The original retirement community norms established during the 1960s centered on the pursuit of self-interests for a much shorter lifespan. Continuing this practice detracts from the mental health benefits generated when a person has a sense of purpose and realizes that efforts to help others represent an important legacy. Ignoring public responsibilities could lead to alienation from younger relatives who are taught that maturity is always shown by concern for the well-being of others. Older citizens who avoid the pursuit of maturity cannot provide younger people with an example of productive aging (Strom & Strom, 2018a, 2018b). Replacing current retirement norms with a more sensible balance of concern for self and for others deserves societal support.

The view that maturity should continue to develop during retirement was acknowledged by Aldous Huxley (1932/2017) in his science fiction novel *Brave New World*. The future society Huxley envisioned had made a scientific breakthrough that delayed most physical evidence of growing old. In this anti-aging environment, looking young and being continually in pursuit of enjoyment had become universal goals. When older adults could no longer hide the effects of their aging, they suffered embarrassment and entered the hospitals that supervised their death.

Huxley's frightening forecast was meant to be a warning about consequences that might happen if the development of technology were to become the greatest priority for society without an equivalent emphasis on the development of human potential for maturity. As Huxley looked ahead, he foresaw that people would come to adore technologies that undo their capacity to think. He recognized that a humane and equitable society would make it possible for retirees to retain a sense of purpose and recognize that feeling useless is the most severe shock the human system can endure.

A major challenge for longevity societies is to convince older adults they are needed by the rest of us and thereby prevent the tragedy of their feeling useless. Education for maturity is a lifelong process that differs from formal learning of shorter duration focused on preparation for work or upgrading job skills. A key condition to remain viable in later life is called *productive aging* (Strom & Strom, 1997, 2020). This concept recognizes most older adults are physically and mentally capable to contribute to society, the time between retirement and frailty is being extended, and most retirees want to remain active, so their life continues to provide purpose and satisfaction.

Grandparents Share With Parents the Obligation to Diminish Family Distancing

George Orwell's (1949/2014) science fiction novel *1984* was meant to be a warning that the communication between generations should never be taken for granted. The main character in the book, Winston Smith, was discouraged because he believed that every aspect of privacy was being eliminated. Everything people did, even within their homes, were observed by Big Brother government-operated telescreens. Winston moreover worried that an additional loss of freedom was presented by a new language that the state had invented as a method to control public thinking. *Newspeak*, a politically correct vocabulary was designed to reverse meanings of words that were used in the past. Consequently, young people could not comprehend nor appreciate the values older generations relied on to establish goals and shape behavior. The only ways these former values could be examined were to search the literature or meet with the few remaining elders.

Modern readers usually interpret George Orwell's Big Brother dystopian vision as a disappointing separation among age groups, a bizarre arrangement meant to guarantee permanent social distancing and prevent the prospect of ever becoming an age-integrated society. A more reflective observation might be that communication between young people and older adults is already so minimal that discovering how to increase interaction and reciprocal learning should become a national goal.

Grandparents Have a Responsibility to Engage in Adult Education About Families

The organizations grandparents affiliate with should persuade federal, state, and local education authorities to provide a curriculum that enables grandparents to remain active members of their family and community (Dede & Richards, 2020). Many grandparents mistakenly suppose that their primary responsibility for learning is to identify topics that interest them without awareness of what younger relatives expect them to learn. However, as people grow older, they should continue to learn. Some education for older adults should focus on obligations in a similar way as curriculum for younger students. Senior citizens are the fastest growing age cohort and the only generation whose learning needs have yet to be defined by society (Mather & Scommegna, 2024). Contradictions in logic are to assert grandparents should have an important role while failing to offer them instruction they need. Further, there is little sense to applauding their capacity for learning without presenting educational opportunities to help them define personal responsibilities and increase their influence (Strom & Strom, 1983).

There are crucial aspects of social development where sources, more mature than same-age peers, are needed by youth to become better able to process doubts, manage anxieties, set goals, and make sensible decisions. The social self is too narrow when defined exclusively by the peer group. Teenagers might believe the only people able to understand them are members of their age group. This premise should be challenged by parents and grandparents as they try to persuade youth that the peer group, at any age in life, should never be the single source of advice about how to behave or actions to be taken. Instead, youth should be taught that caring for older relatives requires sustained contact and keeping elders aware of events in the lives of younger relatives (Strom & Strom, 2024).

Include the Views of Parents and Grandchildren in Grandparent Education

Research has confirmed that people remain capable of learning in old age, but the literature in gerontology rarely includes discussions about what grandparents in longevity societies ought to know and what relatives want them to learn (Strom, 2021; Strom & Strom, 2018a, 2018b). Most retired people are grandparents so education to contribute to their family is considered more important than other topics (Collinsworth et al., 1991; Sadowski, 2020).

Most classes for older adults are available in churches, senior centers, and sometimes online. These groups generally assemble topics they believe will appeal to retirees. In turn, older adults tend to assume that learning should be self-determined, consisting of whatever topics they individually find interesting without regard for societal expectations as the society insists on for younger learners. A sensible strategy to increase family-related classes could be to invite parents and grandchildren of school age, the generations most familiar with grandparent assets and learning deficits, to identify some content they feel grandparents should learn to function well in the modern family and become more responsive to goals and needs of younger relatives.

Support for the preservation of culture and evolution of culture is shown by generational differences of opinion regarding the past and the future (Feder, 2024). The communication of emerging elements of culture relies on algorithms that assign priority to popularity and recency while discounting the worth of ancestral knowledge that is transmitted slowly over many years (Krznaric, 2021). When change interferes with traditional obligations, role expectations become blurred, the scope of older adult influence declines, and their learning needs are overlooked.

Grandparents are aware that many young families appear fragile and need greater internal support. This knowledge motivates older adults to prize education meant to help them strengthen the family. Grandparents typically assign high priority to helping loved ones but agree their impact is declining and acknowledge relatives rarely ask for their advice (Jackson, 2023). Expectations of grandparents should change to reflect their current challenges. Their revised role should be carefully defined, include a sense of mission, and implicate personal talents to help relatives. Adult education that focuses on the lives of younger relatives can keep grandparents connected, well informed, and in sync with family members.

Principles of Child Development Unite Parents and Grandparents

The need to work toward a creative partnership is illustrated by findings from a Mott Children's Hospital national survey completed by 2,016 parents of children under age 18. Clark (2020) asked parents to describe the function of grandparents in their lives and the lives of their children. Parents (40%) stated grandparents were too lenient with grandchildren as often shown by a contradiction of the rules parents had established. Most parents (57%) reported discipline was the greatest source of intergenerational conflict about raising children. Additional sources of generational disagreements were found about child television screen time (36%), snack habits (44%), social manners (27%), and health/safety (25%). The survey highlighted how parenting choices and enforcing rules of parents can be a cause of major strife between generations. When grandparents were unwilling to comply with the requests from parents to adopt their discipline practices, some parents decided to reduce the amount of time grandparents could spend with their grandchildren. Education for grandparents that clarifies the goals of parents and gives reasons to pursue them is necessary to remain in sync with younger family members. In turn, younger relatives should try to understand grandparent aspirations and concerns. Reciprocal learning seems an ideal way to attain the separate goals of parents and grandparents.

Parent and Grandparent Generations: Learning More and Living Longer

Parents and grandparents should realize that if one of their goals is to live longer, they should continue their lifetime role as learners. The positive influence that education has on diminishing all-cause adult mortality was previously recognized in the United States (Albano et al., 2007). However, the relative magnitude was not quantified until an international project at the University of Washington conducted a global systematic review and meta-analysis. The purpose of the investigation was to determine the reduction in all-cause mortality associated with each year of schooling at a global level (Balaj et al., 2024). Data from 1980 to 2023 revealed 603 studies in 59 countries that were eligible for analysis. Results from this analysis determined that education showed a *dose–response relationship*, with an average reduction in mortality risk of 2% for each additional year of education. The effect was greater among younger adults, with an average reduction in mortality risk of 2.9% (2.8–3.0) associated with each added year of education for those aged 18–49 years, compared with a 0.8% (0.6–1.0) reduction for adults older than 70. This study provides compelling evidence regarding the importance of education as a means to increase life expectancy and supports reforms in adult education as a path to reduce inequities in mortality.

A related study by Roy et al. (2020) at Yale University School of Medicine and the University of Alabama at Birmingham assessed the relative impact of two variables most often linked to life expectancy – race and education – by combining data for 5,114 Blacks and Whites in four cities. Among members of a group recruited 30 years earlier for a longevity study, when they were in their early twenties, it was found that level of education, not race, is the best predictor of who will live the longest. Rates of death among the 349 who died reflected racial differences with 9% of Blacks dying at an early age compared to 6% of Whites. Causes of death by race differed with Black men significantly more likely to die from homicide and White men from AIDS. The most common causes of death across all age groups were cardiovascular disease and cancer. But there were also notable differences in the rates of death by education level. About 13% of participants having a high school diploma or less education died compared with only 5% of college graduates. Even after accounting for effects of other variables such as income, level of education was still the best predictor of longevity. The study showed that each education step was related to 1.37 fewer years of lost life expectancy.

Conclusion

Before emergence of the Internet and mobile devices, more of child experiences were governed by adults. Grownups viewed themselves as able to identify personal learning needs and improve their attitudes. There is general agreement that comprehensive education is needed to encourage and clarify greater benefits of reciprocal learning and mutual growth of the adult generations based on respectful consideration of the goals and concerns of one another. Parenting methods should improve to better educate children. Adult education that emphasizes learning of younger relatives can help grandparents become well-informed and more supportive. Grandparents should be aware of how the experiences of children, adolescents, young adults, and parents depart from the circumstances when they raised their children. This knowledge cannot come from memory or intuition but must be told by younger relatives.

A customary assumption has been that the knowledge and skills needed for success should be acquired well in advance. Accordingly, states and communities collaborate to provide curriculum conceptualized to provide adult education that is suitable for longevity societies. Public policy should include learning beyond career preparation to include the responsibilities of parents and grandparents. Such a curriculum can help grandparents become aware of goals parents have for their children so that they can reinforce these goals and arrange time to learn the views of individual grandchildren. Parents should be informed about new ways to support development of children and adolescents. Assuming leadership for the well-being of younger family members is an aspect of maturity that people in early adulthood and middle age should pursue as goals and priorities. This reorientation will be difficult because the nation lacks historical precedent for older people to consider younger relatives as essential sources to learn from. Mutual support by generations should become a national goal reflected by a comprehensive plan to acquaint all age groups with goals and concerns of other cohorts.

In the past, older adults were typically portrayed as the only age group to possess wisdom. This impression was meant to show respect but actually justified ignoring their learning needs. We want young people to value and retain aspects of their heritage, gain benefits from the unique perspectives of older people, pursue the acquisition of maturity, realize the importance of spiritual beliefs as a guide to ethical behavior, and better prepare for longevity. These goals will require intergenerational conversations which should be considered as essential and arranged to ensure that potential benefits occur for all members of families.

Key Concepts

1. Parent responsibility for teaching preschoolers is more complex and demanding than during previous generations. Their obligation includes child introduction to the Internet, teaching reading and mathematics, conflict resolution for getting along with peers, setting goals, establishing priorities, and arranging an unhurried schedule allowing children time for play.
2. Technology continues to present new ideas and attitudes that inform youth and guide the formation of their norms. These norms are not limited to the United States but shared internationally by students from other counties. The growing power of peer norms causes adult relatives to worry that their influence on child development is likely to decline.
3. Learning from children while also teaching them is unprecedented. When adults make an effort to fulfill this task, children are more likely to consider guidance of older relatives as relevant and applicable. There is also recognition that even young relatives have insights that could help adults realize how to better perform their leadership role in the family.
4. Spending time with children is an important expectation for parents. Limiting the amount of time adolescents spend communicating with peers is a way courageous parents teach fundamentals of time management that children will need to be a success in their relationships through life while contributing to the welfare of loved ones.
5. Parents should explain to grandparents the expectations they have for their children. This awareness can guide older relatives to understand and reinforce family norms. In turn, this complementary role enables grandparents to have a more significant

function in helping grandchildren manage the challenges they are bound to face in growing up.
6. The retired population should establish new peer norms that reflect a healthy balance of concern for themselves and meeting the needs of younger generations. One aspect of the new norms should be to prioritize intergenerational communication that sets an example of caring necessary to support the maturity they wish for their relatives.
7. Local and national organizations that serve grandparents should inform them about the education they need and provide family related adult programs for the community. Grandparents share a common need to better understand the younger generations in their family and acquire methods that foster mental health and development of loved ones.
8. Parents and grandchildren should be consulted by adult educators to identify the lessons grandparents should be expected to learn. Reliance on younger generations is appropriate because they are the most relevant observers of how grandparents can improve their contributions to the family.
9. Seeking advice from younger relatives remains uncommon but is needed as a reform in efforts to build family relationships. When all generations can count on reciprocal learning, more suitable expectations can be developed, and everyone has a better understanding of the behavior expected of them by relatives.
10. Parents and grandparents should have access to a common information base about child development so they can harmonize their expectations about suitable instruction, cope with adjustments to emerging challenges, and provide constructive feedback to report on perceived success and failure of individuals.

Generational Perspectives Activities

1.1 Discussion
1.2 Conversations With Young Children
1.3 A Scenario: Reasoning and Problem-Solving
1.4 Chapter Review
1.5 Parent and Grandparent Self-Evaluation
1.6 Storytelling

1.1 Discussion

1. What do you see as advantages of a partnership between parents and grandparents?
2. What are some new things parents should teach young children?
3. What do you regard as the greatest challenges facing contemporary grandparents?
4. Describe the difficult concerns that are commonly experienced by young parents.
5. What lessons have parents and grandparents taught you about time management?
6. How do your relatives motivate grandparents to continue personal development?

1.2 Conversations With Young Children

Adults are often polled to find out their opinions, feelings, and concerns. As a result, there are times when people feel overinformed about the experiences of other adults. In contrast, parents and grandparents know little about the events and challenges faced by young children. Families should invite boys and girls daily to talk about what is happening in their lives.

1. What troubles have you seen other kids experience at the day care center?
2. What are some troubles you have with other kids at the day care center?
3. What do you like most about teachers who work with you at day care?
4. What programs on television do you like to watch most with your family?
5. What things do you enjoy doing most with your mother? your father?
6. What are the qualities you admire most about each of your grandparents?

1.3 Scenario: Reasoning and Problem-Solving

Angela is a widow who lives in a Florida retirement village where she enjoys doing things with friends who look out for one another. Angela's daughter Mandy lives with her husband and their two children, ages 2 and 3, in another state. Mandy wants to go back to work, but the costs of group care are too high. Mandy asks Angela if she would consider moving in with the family so she could provide free childcare. What responses do you suggest?

1. Mandy should homeschool her children without having to pay caregivers.
2. Mandy should choose an employer that provides group care for children.
3. Angela should not relocate because she enjoys her retirement home.
4. Angela should offer to pay Mandy a portion of the cost for childcare.
5. Other _____

1.4 Chapter Review

1. What insights from the chapter will I try to apply in my relationships?
2. What is the most important key concept for me presented in this chapter?
3. Which elements of this chapter do I wish I had known about earlier?

1.5 Parent and Grandparent Self-Evaluation

Directions: For each question, place a check besides statements that describe your feelings. You may give several answers for some items. If your feelings are not on the choices list, write them on the line marked Other.

1. My understanding about learning and development in early childhood is

   a. inadequate and indicate that I should pursue further schooling
   b. as good as most other people and should enable me to get along
   c. poor so I need to take a course to make up for my shortcomings

d. that most adults underestimate the capacity of children to learn
   e. Other _____

2. My views about collaboration among adults in my family are

   a. more of them should share the expenses related to child development
   b. main caregivers should cover expenses for raising their own children
   c. aunts, uncles, and cousins should contribute equally to parent costs
   d. most of us do not feel responsible to support other people's children
   e. Other _____

3. To educate preschoolers in my family

   a. the community could provide more assistance than is available
   b. community agencies provide enough resources for the parents to rely on
   c. religious groups can be counted on to offer help that is needed
   d. government is not concerned enough about education for this age group
   e. Other _____

4. Parents and grandparents should learn from children. In my opinion,

   a. this necessary learning is not seen by most people as a goal
   b. parents do not recognize a need to learn from their children
   c. socialization depends on realizing the potential of peer influence
   d. adults should scrap the idea that they are always the best teachers
   e. Other _____

5. I believe the capacity and desire of most retirees to keep learning

   a. is underestimated by a majority of the American adult population
   b. should become a new context that is emphasized by social media
   c. can be a topic for guided discussion in families of all backgrounds
   d. is potentially a new focus that can unite Americans of all generations
   e. Other _____

6. My observation has been that most grandparents

   a. do not spend enough time getting to know their grandchildren
   b. want to live their lives without being preoccupied by relatives
   c. have their own goals they want to pursue as the main priorities
   d. want to relate mostly to friends from their own age group
   e. Other _____

1.6 Storytelling

Historically, storytelling has been a dominant classic and progressive method of teaching around the world. The purposes of a storyteller are to present imaginary or real-life examples showing how some concept applies to a particular situation. People like stories, they pay attention to the procession of events, and usually remember aspects of a story for a long time. Your stories can reinforce the concepts in this chapter for family members and classmates. Please share your stories with them.

References

Albano, J. D., Ward, E., Jemal, A., Anderson, R., Cokkinides, V. E., Murray, T., Henley, J., Liff, J., & Thun, M. J. (2007). Cancer mortality in the United States by education level and race. *Journal of the National Cancer Institute, 99*(18), 1384–1394. https://doi.org/10.1093/jnci/djm127

Anderson, M., Faverio, M., & Gottfried, J. (2023, December 11). *Teens, social media and technology 2023*. Pew Research Center. https://www.pewresearch.org/internet/2023/12/11/teens-social-media-and-technology-2023/

Anderson, M., Faverio, M., & Park, E. (2024, March 11). *How teens and parents approach screen time*. Pew Research Center. https://www.pewresearch.org/internet/2024/03/11/how-teens-and-parents-approach-screen-time/

Annie E. Casey Foundation. (2010, January 1). *Early learning! Why reading by the end of third grade matters [A Kids Count Special Report on the importance of reading by 3rd grade]*. https://www.aecf.org/resources/early-warning-why-reading-by-the-end-of-third-grade-matters

Annie E. Casey Foundation. (2013). *Early warning confirmed: A research update on third-grade reading*. https://assets.aecf.org/m/resourcedoc/aecf-EarlyWarningConfirmedExecSummary-2013.pdf

Annie E. Casey Foundation. (2023). *2023 Kids Count data book interactive* (34th ed.). https://www.aecf.org/interactive/databook?l=01

Annie E. Casey Foundation. (2024). *2024 Kids Count data book interactive*. https://www.aecf.org/interactive/databook?1=502

Balaj, M., Henson, C., Aronsson, A., Aravkin, A., Beck, K., Degail, C., Donadello, L., Eikemo, K., Friedman, J., Giouleka, A., Gradeci, I., Hay, S., Jensen, M., McLaughlin, S., Mullany, E., O'Connell, E., Sripada, K., Stonkute, D., Sorensen, R., . . . Gakidou, E. (2024). Effects of education on adult mortality: A global systematic review and meta-analysis. *The Lancet Public Health, 9*(3), e155–e165. https://doi.org/10.1016/S2468-2667(23)00306-7

Bukowski, W. M., Laursen, B., & Rubin, K. H. (Eds.). (2019). *Handbook of peer interactions, relationships, and groups* (2nd ed.). Routledge.

Burkeman, O. (2021). *Four thousand weeks: Time management for mortals*. Farrar, Strauss, & Giroux.

Clark, S. (2020, August 17). Mott poll report: When parents and grandparents disagree. *National Poll on Children's Health, 36*(5). C. S. Mott Children's Hospital and University of Michigan Health. https://mottpoll.org/sites/default/files/documents/081720_Grandparents.pdf

Collinsworth, P., Strom, R., & Strom, S. (1996). Parent Success Indicator: Development and factorial validation. *Educational and Psychological Measurement, 56*(3), 504–513. https://doi.org/10.1177/0013164496056003012

Collinsworth, P., Strom, R., Strom, S., & Young, D. (1991). The *Grandparent Strengths and Needs Inventory*: Development and factorial validation. *Educational and Psychological Measurement, 51*(3), 785–792. https://doi.org/10.1177/0013164491513030

Das, S. M. (2024, May 2). Children born now could live 100 years – companies must change their view of age: Andrew J. Scott. *The Economic Times*. https://economictimes.indiatimes.com/news/et-evoke/children-born-now-could-live-100-years-companies-must-change-their-view-of-age-andrew-j-scott/articleshow/99304634.cms?from=mdr

Dede, C., & Richards, J. (Eds.). (2020). *The 60-year curriculum: New models for lifelong learning in the digital economy*. Routledge.

Feder, K. L. (2024). *The past in perspective: An introduction to human prehistory* (9th ed.). Oxford University Press.

Frey, N., Fisher, D., & Almarode, J. (2021). *How tutoring works: Six steps to grow motivation and accelerate student learning*. Corwin.

Guillén, M. F. (2020). *2030: How today's biggest trends will collide and reshape the future of everything*. St. Martin's Press.

Huxley, A. (2017). *Brave new world*. Harper. (Original work published 1932)

Jackson, M. (2023). *Uncertain: The wisdom and wonder of being unsure*. Prometheus.

Kaneda, T., Greenbaum, C., & Kline, K. (2020). *World population data sheet*. Population Reference Bureau. https://www.prb.org/2020-world-population-data-sheet/

Kennedy, B. (2022). *Good inside: A guide to becoming the parent you want to be*. Harper.

Krznaric, R. (2021). *The good ancestor: How to think long term in a short-term world*. W. H. Allen.

Levine, M. (2020). *Ready or not: Preparing our kids to thrive in an uncertain and rapidly changing world*. Harper.

Locke, C. (2023, December 25). Getting old, explained. *Bloomberg Businessweek (Special Issue: The Longevity Issue)*. https://www.bloomberg.com/news/features/2023-12-18/how-to-make-friends-find-love-save-for-retirement-when-you-re-old

Luthar, S. S., Small, P. J., & Cicciolla, L. (2018). Adolescents from upper middle-class communities: Substance misuse and addiction across early adulthood: *Development and Psychopathology, 30*(1), 315–335. https://doi.org/10.1017/S0954579417000645

Mather, M., & Scommegna, P. (2024, January 9). *Fact sheet: Aging in the United States*. Population Reference Bureau. https://www.prb.org/resources/fact-sheet-aging-in-the-united-states/#:~:text=The%20U.S%20population%20is%20older,the%20top%20of%20the%20list

McConnell, T. (2023, February 24). Today's 5-year-olds will likely live to 100. What will their lives be like? *National Geographic*. https://longevity.stanford.edu/wp-content/uploads/2023/03/Todays-5-year-olds-will-likely-live-to-100.-What-will-their-lives-be-like.pdf

Milkie, M. A., Nomaguchi, K. M., & Denny, K. E. (2015). Does the amount of time mothers spend with children and adolescents matter? *Journal of Marriage and the Family, 77*(2), 355–372. http://www.jstor.org/stable/24582757

Minkin, R., & Horowitz, J. M. (2023, January 24). *Parenting in America today: Mental health concerns top the list of worries for parents; most say being a parent is harder than they expected*. Pew Research Center. https://www.pewresearch.org/social-trends/2023/01/24/parenting-in-america-today/

Morris, A. S., & Smith, J. M. (Eds.). (2022). *The Cambridge handbook of parenting*. Cambridge University Press.

Orwell, G. (2014). *1984*. Penguin Books. (Original work published 1949)

Perry, E. (2023, July 10). *How to spend quality time with family (even when you're busy)*. BetterUp. https://www.betterup.com/blog/quality-time-with-family

Rothwell, J. (2023, October 13). *Teens spend average of 4.8 hours on social media per day*. Familial and Adolescent Health Survey. https://news.gallup.com/poll/512576/teens-spend-average-hours-social-media-per-day.aspx

Roy, B., Kiefe, C. I., Jacobs, D. R., Goff, D. C., Lloyd-Jones, D., Shikany, J. M., Reis, J. P., Gordon-Larsen, P., & Lewis, C. E. (2020). Education, race/ethnicity, and causes of premature mortality among middle-aged adults in 4 US urban communities: Results from CARDIA, 1985–2017. *American Journal of Public Health, 110*(4), 530–536. https://doi.org/10.2105/AJPH.2019.305506

Sadowski, M. (Ed.). (2020). *Adolescents at school: Perspectives on youth, identity, and education* (3rd ed.). Harvard Education Press.

Strom, R. D., & Strom, S. K. (1983). Redefining the grandparent role. *Cambridge Journal of Education, 13*(1), 25–28. https://doi.org/10.1080/0305764830130107

Strom, R. D., & Strom, S. K. (1997). Building a theory of grandparent development. *International Journal of Aging & Human Development, 45*(4), 255–286. https://doi.org/10.2190/HAVE-HWKU-6BCG-9EY5

Strom, R. D., Strom, P. S., Strom, S., Shen, Y., & Beckert, T. (2004, Winter). Black, Hispanic, and White American mothers of adolescents: Construction of a national standard. *Adolescence, 39*(156), 669–686. PMID: 15727406

Strom, P. S., Strom, R. D., & Sindel-Arrington, T. (2016). Adolescent views of time management: Rethinking the school day in junior high school. *American Secondary Education, 44*(3), 38–55.

Strom, R. D., & Strom, P. S. (2018a). Education for grandparents in longevity societies. *Journal of Adult and Continuing Education, 24*(2), 208–228. https://doi.org/10.1177/1477971418810652

Strom, R. D., & Strom, S. K. (2018b). Raising expectations for grandparents. In J. Hendricks (Ed.), *The ties of later life* (pp. 133–140). Routledge.

Strom, P. S., Hendon, K. L., Strom, R. D., & Wang, C.-H. (2019). How peers support and inhibit learning in the classroom: Assessment of high school students in collaborative groups. *School Community Journal, 29*(2), 183–202. http://www.schoolcommunitynetwork.org/SCJ.aspx

Strom, R. D., & Strom, P. S. (2020). Productive aging: Peer influence and retirement. *Educational Gerontology, 46*(11), 678–687. https://doi.org/10.1080/03601277.2020.1807085

Strom, P. S. (2021). Grandparents and parents: An essential partnership for longevity societies. *Innovation in Aging, 5* (Issue Suppl. 1), 764. https://doi.org/10.1093/geroni/igab046.2830

Strom, R. D., & Strom, P. S. (2021). Learning throughout life about the needs of all generations: Recognizing and counteracting generational isolation. In M. London (Ed.), *The Oxford handbook of lifelong learning* (2nd ed., pp. 183–206). Oxford University Press.

Strom, P. S., & Strom, R. D. (2024). *Mental health and relationships from early adulthood through old age*. Routledge.

Turkle, S. (2015). *Reclaiming conversation: The power of talk in the digital age*. Penguin.

Twenge, J. (2023). *Generations*. Atria Books.

Vaterlaus, J. M., Beckert, T., & Schmitt-Wilson, S. (2019, June 14). Parent-child time together: The role of interactive technology with adolescent and young adult children. *Journal of Family Issues, 40*(15), 2179–2202. https://doi.org/10.1177/0192513X19856644

Vogels, E. A., & Gelles-Watnick, R. (2023, April 24). *Teens and social media: Key findings from pew research surveys*. https://www.pewresearch.org/short-reads/2023/04/24/teens-and-social-media-key-findings-from-pew-research-center-surveys/

Yeung, W.-J. J., & Lee, Y. (2022, March). Aging in East Asia: New findings on retirement, health, and well-being. *The Journals of Gerontology: Series B, 77*(3), 589–591. https://doi.org/10.1093/geronb/gbab055

Chapter 2

Infancy

Trust and Social Awareness

Some parent responsibilities are unique to the time when they raise their children. Certain obligations also remain constant because they are recognized as enduring priorities. The purposes of this chapter are to: (a) explain why building trust during infancy is essential for developing close relationships, (b) consider the outcomes of maternal deprivation for children in institutionalized settings, (c) examine evidence related to the influence of emotional intelligence, (d) explore how group and family care during early childhood could be improved, (e) illustrate methods to teach young children empathy and social skills, and (f) explain how initial adjustment at school can improve when teachers and parents share their observations of child behavior. Generational Perspectives Activities present topics to discuss with family members and close friends about trust and social awareness during infancy.

Decades of research show that our brains grow faster between the ages 0 and 3 than at any other time (Bortfeld & Bunge, 2024; Calderón, 2023; Garvey, 2023). By the time a child enters kindergarten, these crucial years of early brain development have passed. Nevertheless, some parent responsibilities are unique to the time when they raise their children. Certain obligations also remain constant because they are recognized as enduring priorities. The purposes of this chapter are to (a) explain why building trust during infancy is essential for developing close relationships, (b) consider the outcomes of maternal deprivation for children in institutionalized settings, (c) examine evidence related to the influence of emotional intelligence, (d) explore how group and family care during early childhood could be improved, (e) illustrate methods to teach young children empathy and social skills, and (f) explain how initial adjustment at school can improve when teachers and parents share their observations of child behavior. Generational Perspectives Activities present topics to discuss with family members and close friends about trust and social awareness during infancy.

Trust and Emotional Attachment

Infants (ages birth to 12 months) acquire trust or mistrust of their environment. When caregivers are reliable, can be counted on to provide food, show willingness to change diapers, and consistently show affection, infants learn that adults are dependable and can be trusted. In contrast, when caregivers ignore infant needs, are inconsistent in providing attention, or behave in abusive ways, infants learn fear and conclude that their environment is dangerous and unpredictable (Arterberry & Bornstein, 2024).

The period from 6 months old to 19 months of age is critical for developing the response of love and attachment, the emotional bond that is a basis for later socialization. Attachment is defined as the tie of affection babies establish with someone, typically the mother

DOI: 10.4324/9781003534655-4

or another consistent caregiver. *The Theory of Emotional Attachment* was developed by John Bowlby (1988), a British psychiatrist (1907–1990). He treated maladjusted children during World War II when many had to be evacuated from London to escape the nightly air raids from Germans. At that time England set up the first early childhood centers so that surrogate care could be provided for children whose mothers participated in defense of the nation by working in factories. Bowlby's research on maternal separation confirmed that infants should have a secure relationship with a main caregiver. Otherwise, the normal course of social and emotional development is replaced by dysfunction (Bowlby, 2005).

One of Bowlby's (1944, 1988) research projects examined the long-term effects of maternal separation on juvenile delinquency. He interviewed 44 adolescents referred to his clinic for treatment after they were caught stealing. Another 44 teenagers classified as experiencing emotional problems but not involved with crimes became a contrast group. IQ tests administered to all the teenagers did not reveal differentiation between the two groups. The parents were interviewed to find out whether a separation of mother and child had ever occurred. Separation was not a factor in the non-delinquent group, but half of the adolescent thieves were separated from their mothers for six or more months before 5 years of age. Bowlby diagnosed 12 of the 14 thieves as affectionless psychopaths, unable to feel guilt or sense remorse. All of them had suffered from a prolonged period of maternal separation.

The significance of attachment was confirmed by Moullin et al. (2014) in a longitudinal investigation of 14,000 American children who were born in 2001. Follow-ups found that 60% of these children under 3 years of age developed a secure attachment to parents, a bond formed by being loved, held, spoken to with encouragement, and having expressed needs met when they were upset. These children were more likely to become resilient to adverse effects of poverty, family instability, parental stress, and depression. In addition, when children from low-income families formed strong emotional attachments, they were three times less likely to show behavior problems in school. In contrast, 40% of children did not develop strong bonds with their mothers or fathers. Instead, they were likely to be aggressive, defiant, and hyperactive. These infants showed poor language skills and greater behavioral issues in the classroom. Those with insecure attachment more often quit high school without graduating and less frequently attended any form of higher education or technical training.

Maternal and Social Deprivation

Nonattachment and emotional deprivation are devastating forms of child abuse. The high cost was first discovered by psychologist Harry Harlow (1905–1981), who was President of the American Psychological Association and Professor at the University of Wisconsin. In his well-known experiment, Harlow (1958) deliberately separated two groups of baby monkeys from their mothers. In one group a terrycloth 'mother' provided no food, while another monkey made of wire had an attached baby bottle that contained milk. In the second group a terrycloth mother provided food, but the wire monkey did not. It was observed the young monkeys clung to their terrycloth mother, whether it provided food or not and chose a wire surrogate only when it was the single source of food.

Harlow concluded that nurturing, not just feeding, enables emotional bonding because of intimate contact. However, the cloth monkey was an insufficient replacement for the mother as demonstrated by social isolation of monkeys that grew up with severe emotional and behavioral problems. Even when monkeys were raised in cages where they could see, smell, and hear others but prevented from touch contact, these infants developed an 'autistic like' syndrome including grooming, self-clasping, social withdrawing, and rocking behavior. Harlow's experiments would be unethical according to current standards for research.

Consider an extreme experiment involving maternal deprivation of children. Nicolae Ceausescu, Communist dictator of Romania from 1965 to 1989, wanted to increase the industrial output of his country and believed the solution would necessitate a substantial increase in the national population. He restricted use of contraceptives and made abortion illegal. All young women were ordered to give birth to a minimum of five children. Extra taxes were levied on families that had fewer than five children. Such families were visited regularly by medically trained agents, referred to as 'menstrual police,' to examine women who were not producing their quota of children. Within one year the national population of infants doubled. Ceausescu built institutions for orphans whose parents reported they were unable to take care of the children. In 1989, following a brief public uprising, Ceausescu was executed. At that time observers from outside the country estimated that 170,000 children were living in 700 Romanian orphanages (Nelson et al., 2014; Henderson, 2024).

Significance of Emotional Connection

Mary Carlson (1997), a neurobiologist at Harvard University, studied the impact of child abuse and isolation on cortisol levels. During times of stress, the body secretes adrenaline and cortisol hormones to regulate blood sugar levels. In contrast with the rapid pumping energy immediately provided by adrenaline, cortisol suppresses reaction to stress by shutting down energy-expensive systems normally used to promote growth, digestion, reproduction, and foster immunity against disease. In their experiments with 2- and 3-year-old orphans in Romania, Carlson and Earls (2006) discovered that the children had abnormal cortisol levels, indicating a significant problem in responses to stress. Further study revealed that dysregulation of the cortisol was interfering with physical growth, mental development, and motor activity. Normal 2- and 3-year-olds can perform well on tasks like picture recognition, word repetition, socializing, standing on one foot, and walking up a set of stairs without holding on. However, the Romanian orphans could not do any of these tasks. Most of them scored in the third to tenth percentile on physical growth and were much delayed in motor and mental development. The more abnormal their cortisol levels, the worse the child health and growth outcomes.

Cortisol that can be measured noninvasively by sampling saliva reflects a diurnal pattern. Normally, blood levels of cortisol peak just before people wake up in the morning, then drops abruptly, and remains almost undetectable for the remainder of the day and night until rising again before waking. Carlson examined 30 children, a control group, and discovered that a lack of touch and attention could modify their stress reaction, stunt physical growth, and adversely affect behavior. These results were reinforced by another Romanian sample of children who received poor quality care in day orphanages. Throughout the week at day care centers with understaffed and untrained workers who each had 20 or more infants to look after, child cortisol levels were abnormal but became close to normal on the weekends when they visited relatives. The children who got away from day care part-time to be in more nurturant conditions were compared with peers spending full time at the orphanage. Overall, the part-timers in day care had more normal cortisol indicators (Carlson & Earls, 2006; Konnikova, 2015).

The Importance of Touch

To explore whether stress levels would modify by introducing hugs and other nurturant forms of contact, 30 children were selected to participate in a one-year enrichment experiment organized by Joseph Sparling et al. (2005) from the University of Melbourne in Australia. Unlike typical day care where each adult is responsible for many children, each caregiver in this project had only four children to look after, supervise, and call them by name. Caregiver goals were to cuddle, play with, read to, hug, comb hair, and make sure each child was properly fed and well dressed. Children enrolled in the program uniformly made significant improvements. When the project ended, the children returned to previous conditions of poor care that excluded touching; further tests revealed that the behavioral and physical advantages received by nurturant care faded. Research by Kidwell and Kerig (2023) explained how severely depressed adults as well as military personnel returning from battle conditions with post-traumatic syndrome presented abnormalities in daily cortisol cycles.

Given the predictable relationship between inadequate group care and abnormal cortisol levels, it seems relevant to wonder what might be happening to American children exposed to poor supervision in group care. Carlson (1997, p. 3) explained:

> Clearly, the social networks in which children grow up bear on the development of the neural networks that mediate memory, emotion, and self. As parents, as citizens, and as policy makers, we must ensure that our social policy pathways do not lead to social deprivation. We perhaps cannot prevent a child from experiencing an earthquake, but we can ensure immediate and appropriate intervention when and if one occurs. And when we are faced not with a natural disaster but with choices about children in day care and residential care, we must ensure that our decisions have positive consequence.

Other researchers have found that, when children were denied emotional learning, effects on development were profound. Soon after the extensive neglect in Romanian orphanages was discovered, observations were revealed to the world by television. For example, 1,500 orphans were adopted by American families. Despite the generous affection and loving care provided by these foster parents, Krznaric (2014, 2021) stated that most of the adopted children grew up with permanent social and emotional deficits, particularly a lack of empathy. Many adoptive parents described their children in this way: "My daughter is intelligent, but she does not demonstrate any concern about needs of others."

Harry Chugani, a pediatric neurologist at Wayne State University and Children's Hospital in Detroit, Michigan, conducted brain scans of the adopted Romanians. Chugani et al. (2001) found significant eccentricities within the brain region related to emotional development. The research team discovered there is a limited time frame early in life when children must have healthy emotional stimulation so they can become able to recreate and share these emotions with others throughout life. The Romanian children were prevented from these opportunities at the cost of their potential for caring, compassion, and trusting relationships (Nelson et al., 2014).

Megan Gunnar (2021) and her colleagues at the University of Minnesota identified other pieces of the puzzle. In 1999, she began the International Adoption Project that includes the records of 6,000 children adopted from overseas. Gunnar discovered these children usually had a reduction in brain volume, difficulty with cognitive flexibility, inhibitory control, and working memory. A common behavior pattern that she observed was 'indiscriminate friendliness.' In this syndrome a child who does not know you will throw up his arms and try to hug as though you were a long-lost relative. This dysfunctional pattern persists at all age levels. In her study of 65 toddlers (ages 1–3), Gunnar found that most attached to their new parents relatively quickly, and by nine months after their adoption had formed strong attachments.

Deprivation and Brain Development

Charles Nelson (Neuroscientist at Harvard University), Nathan Fox (Director of Child Development Laboratory at University of Maryland), and Charles Zeanah (Director of Institute on Violence Prevention at Tulane University) saw a unique opportunity to study the lasting impact of neglect during early childhood would have on long-term development (Nelson et al., 2014). Every parent has been awakened at night by a call from an infant seeking help. Parent(s) get up and check on the cause of distress. But, contrary to this familiar experience, the researchers of Romanian children were struck by the continuous silence that was universal in the infant care rooms they visited at the orphanages. There was no noise, the children were quiet having learned that cries for help would not bring support from caregiver adults (Wade et al., 2019, 2022).

Nelson et al. (2014) began the Bucharest Project in 2000 as a randomized control trial of foster care as an alternative to institutional care. Initially, an assessment was made of 136 children ranging in age from 6 months to 36 months, with an average of 22 months. Half the children were randomly assigned to move into Romanian foster families that had been recruited by the researchers and compensated by a continuing plan of monetary assistance. The remainder children remained in institutional care. The team returned numerous times to check on the development of the children in both groups. Members of a control group who had never lived in an institution were also checked at each of the follow-ups.

At the outset of the Bucharest Project, the institutionalized children showed delays in cognitive function, slower motor development, and language deficits. Socio-emotional problems and psychiatric disorders were common. These children revealed changes in electrical activity brain patterns measured by electroencephalography, a noninvasive procedure with electrodes placed alongside the scalp. In contrast, the health profile was more favorable for children who were moved to foster care. They showed improvement in language, IQ, socio-emotional functioning, formed secure attachment relationships with caregivers, and made significant progress in their ability to express emotions.

Even though the foster care group recorded significant improvements, they continued to lag behind a control group who had never been institutionalized. Moreover, some of the foster care children made greater gains with the most progress recorded by ones who left the orphanage before the age of 2. The earlier the age of moving out of the institution, the better the health forecast. These foster care families are no longer compensated by this Bucharest Project, but they receive stipends from the Romanian government. Two decades after the early intervention project began, the team confirmed that assigning children to foster care continued to offer benefits throughout their adolescence (King et al., 2023). The project currently is examining young adults to determine the long-lasting influences on them (Greene, 2020; Wade et al., 2019). The United Nations estimates that eight million children are in institutions worldwide, and their future is in jeopardy because of psychological neglect (Wade et al., 2022).

Evaluation of Home and Group Care

Childcare begins before birth. Healthy mothers are more likely to have normal babies (Cook & Klaas, 2020). Pregnant women should avoid smoking, drinking alcohol, and consuming any non-prescribed drugs. Everything expectant mothers eat and drink goes to the fetus by way of the placenta, a thick wall of tissue through which baby's nourishment comes from the parent's bloodstream. While some substances have difficulty getting past the placenta, other substances such as alcohol and medications pass through quickly and accumulate in greater concentration in the fetus than the mother. Babies are affected by drugs because they lack liver enzymes that do not function until birth (Marcdante et al., 2022). The circadian rhythm is the natural process used by the body to control functions like sleep and appetite. Babies begin to develop their circadian rhythm about 6 weeks of age, and their sleep clock becomes more reliable between three and 6 months of age, which means that parents can count on getting better sleep themselves.

There are 11 million children under the age of 5 who attend group care in the United States. This population is forecast to grow, and quality of the nurture they receive should be improved. Sixty percent of children under age 6 have both parents in the workplace. One aspect of a solution is to ensure that quality supervision of children is made available for families at a reasonable cost. The average annual cost of day care has exceeded tuition at community colleges in most states (Grundy, 2024).

Over the past decade the costs of childcare have risen twice as fast as medium income for families with children. A related concern involves wages of group caregivers. Most of them get minimum wage, leading to high staff turnover. The preschool teacher attrition rate detracts from stability at the time when children most need continuity for care. Two- to four-year-olds should have a predictable routine for sleeping, eating, and adult stability they can count on.

Stranger anxiety is a commonly observed phenomenon. By 8 months of age babies decide their security depends on the main caregivers (Cook & Klaas, 2020; Gross, 2023). Accordingly, these adults continue to get a friendly response while others, including seldom-seen grandparents, may often be treated with apprehension. Even when infants visit unfamiliar places, they insist on being close to the mother. Grandparents should understand stranger anxiety is a temporary condition that will not jeopardize a later positive relationship with their grandchild. Stranger anxiety is linked with the infant developmental task of distinguishing the familiar from the unfamiliar.

Significance of Emotional Intelligence

Theories of learning are unable to explain why some people seem to possess a map for living well, reasons why students with high IQs seldom become wealthy adults, why we feel attracted to some people right away, find others difficult to trust, and how some individuals can withstand adversity and remain resilient while others seem to fall apart when faced with even slight pressure. Psychologist Daniel Goleman (2006, 2015) contended that the answer implicates *emotional intelligence*. Goleman has documented the need for families, schools, and society to pay more attention to this overlooked and needed context of achievement. Some of the attitudes and skills that collectively define emotional intelligence include self-control, persistence, empathy, social concern, resilience, and the capacity for self-motivation. Helping children become proficient with these attitudes and skills contributes to maturity and improves the quality of their relationships.

Goleman and Rinpoche (2022) maintain that moral development depends upon emotional intelligence. Scandals that reveal the greed and lack of ethical behavior by individuals holding prominent positions reflect the need for moral leadership. People who have difficulty with self-control because they are easily swayed by impulses can be considered as suffering from moral deficiency. This description appears accurate because will and character depend on people being able to manage emotions and show restraint when confronted with frustrating conditions. Unless parents and teachers instruct children to become aware of other people's needs, boys and girls will not develop the sense of caring that is needed for them to grow up. Further, Strom et al. (2012) suggested schools should assign priority to self-awareness, self-restraint, and compassion as goals so that bullying and other peer mistreatment and lack of civil behavior will become less common.

A popular misconception is that mental health is served by allowing children to vent their negative emotions. On the contrary, research has found that temper tantrums increase influence and duration of anger. This is a worrisome issue for teachers who report a growing number of misconduct problems are related to student lack of self-control. There are many parents whose busy schedule causes them to want the limited time with their children to be pleasant and free of conflict or discipline. Consequently, they ignore their unique corrective role for helping children learn how to manage feelings of frustration without resorting to temper tantrums. This failure of parents contributes to the emotional dysfunction displayed by children at school long after the age when self-regulation should have been developed (Zinsser, 2022).

A sensible strategy is to encourage children to demonstrate self-restraint when they face conditions that are frustrating for them. Exercising this response helps become more emotionally responsible than when tantrums are allowed without interruption. The reason is continuously stimulating specific groups of brain cells like those required to inhibit the amygdala (brain center of fear and aggression), makes them more sensitive and easier to activate in the future. Children not expected to assume control of the emotional center of their brain become candidates for maladjustment in adulthood because self-restraint was not nourished during a critical stage of development. If children are denied emotional learning, their maturity is bound to be stalled.

Empathy and Social Skills

The way parents, grandparents, and caregivers talk to preschoolers about the feelings of other people, referred to as empathy, has a long-term influence on the acquisition of social skills (Krznaric, 2014, 2021). Social understanding develops based on reflective thinking about how other people see things, considering the way events might be interpreted from someone else's point of view. Henry David Thoreau, author of *Walden* observed "Could a greater miracle occur than for us to look through each other's eyes for an instant?" (Thoreau, 1854/2023).

Researchers Ruffman et al. (2010) and Carr et al. (2018) examined child ability to recognize and appreciate the perspectives of others. A longitudinal experiment tracked 55 children between ages 3 and 11. At the outset, half the mothers were given guidelines for talking to their children about feelings, beliefs, wants, and intentions of others; the other half of the mothers were not provided any recommendations about having conversations with their children. Project staff visited the homes to observe how each mother talked to her children while looking at a series of pictures together. For example, successive pictures of a young girl showed that her favorite toy was broken, she visited swings and slides at a playground, and a high tower she has built of blocks was deliberately knocked over by a bigger boy. Children whose mothers talked with them about the mental state of characters in these and other pictures performed better on social understanding tasks that were administered annually.

The relation between parent-child conversations that focused on mental states and social understanding was strongest during early childhood and independent of mother's IQ or level of social understanding. Mother's influence waned between ages 8 and 11 when their children became less dependent on them and spent greater time with peers and teachers (Ruffman et al., 2010). The main findings determined when the children reached age 8 were: (1) mothers' talk about mental states facilitated children's later social understanding, (2) advanced language in children shapes later parenting styles (rather than vice versa as typically conceptualized), and (3) advanced social understanding of children shown by mental state talk leads to a more cooperative child (Carr et al., 2018).

One measure of social understanding applied with children ages 8 and older involved watching clips from *The Office*, a television comedy series that ran for over a decade. The main character, David Brent, typifies individuals who incorrectly interpret social situations. Adult viewers knew the reason David so often embarrassed coworkers related to his lack of social understanding. Children also detected David's social skill deficits in explaining why he seemed oblivious to the way he continually made others feel uncomfortable. Every parent should take advantage of television viewing to talk with children about how program characters might be feeling because of actions or events as they unfold. Labeling how other people might feel, identifying their mental state, is an important step toward social maturity (Krznaric, 2014, 2021; Segal, 2018).

There are also daily opportunities to reinforce this lesson based on how children interact with companions. For example, when a child grabs a toy from a playmate, the observing parent could use this incident to point out that "When you took the airplane away from Terry, it made him feel sad." This interpretation provides a child with insight and provides greater benefit than saying, "Give it back to him or you will be punished." Relatives should help children develop a vocabulary of feelings so that they become able to express emotions, use words to explain how they suppose other people might feel, and consistently demonstrate empathy (Borba, 2017).

Some mothers are proud to report that they treat all their children the same, regardless of gender. However, observers who have studied parent-child interaction in depth disagree. They found that mothers are far more likely to talk with 2-year-old daughters about feelings than they do with sons. The difference is confirmed by research showing that, by age two and a half years, girls are already more advanced than boys in reading facial expressions and body language. Parents also use more emotion words such as sad, happy, worried, satisfied, and afraid when talking with four-year-old daughters than with sons. In addition, mothers more often talk about emotional experiences with their daughters. "Did you notice how happy grandma seemed when she saw us coming to her house for a visit?" "How do you suppose Barbara felt when Mary grabbed her doll and would not give it back?" Practice involving emotional talk provides girls with an edge in the development of empathy. In contrast, maternal dialogue with boys focuses much more on causes and consequence of emotions than on the nurture of emotional literacy (Levine, 2020).

Children as Social Observers

Young children are egocentric, self-centered, and narcissistic, so they often disregard the feelings of their peers (Turkle, 2021). Teachers of preschool through grade 3 report that the prevalence of self-absorption makes it difficult to teach them about civil behavior. One method a parent can apply to ensure empathy practice and social perceptiveness happens is asking the child to describe observations about daily activities, conversations, and conflicts at school. Instead, it is typical for parents and grandparents to ask, "How was school today?" Children have been gone much of the day, but they have little to say about what happened in class or on the playground.

Social awareness can enlarge personal perspective and increase child's scope of concern to include how others feel and ways they are treated. Setting an expectation for children to become careful observers of behavior encourages them to go beyond reporting only about themselves and acknowledges that the experiences of others are also important. Parents and grandparents should ask questions that invite children to report things they notice and share experiences as an observer.

Child's Concern for Others

The following questions shown in Table 2.1 for children in kindergarten through grade 3 focus on what a child sees during one day at school. We ask parents to keep a record of their questions by checking them in the *Number of Times Asked* column. Then notice how the perception of a child changes as s/he talks about what is noticed through observations over a period of one month.

There is evidence that even by adolescence many students have not yet gained empathy. Surveys of 16,000 students showed they scored 40% lower on empathy than students did three decades ago. Since that time *narcissism*–self-admiration, an all-about-me-centered culture–has increased by 58% (Twenge, 2017, 2021). Daniel Goleman (2015) suggested, "Self-absorption in all its forms kills empathy and compassion. When we focus on ourselves, our world contracts and preoccupations loom large. In contrast, when we focus on other people, our world expands."

Sherry Turkle (2015), Psychology Professor at Massachusetts Institute of Technology, expressed disappointment that her students no longer stopped by to talk during office hours. The usual explanation of students was "I'd rather text than talk." This means

Table 2.1 What Do Young Children Observe at School?

Questions to Ask Children in Kindergarten Through Grade 3	Number of Times Asked
1. Did you see anyone helping someone in your class?	
2. Did you see any bullying on the playground?	
3. What lessons seemed hard for some students to understand?	
4. How did you comfort someone you felt needed help?	
5. What activities did you see your classmates enjoyed doing?	
6. What examples did you see of someone becoming upset?	
7. What fights at school could have been handled better?	
8. What things did the teacher do that helped children like school?	
9. How did you help someone who needed encouragement?	
10. What nice things did you hear kids say to one another?	

Copyright © by Paris S. Strom and Robert D. Strom (2025).

students felt sending and receiving written messages, a transactional view of communication, was preferable to a face-to-face relational view about conversation. Digital conversation can lead to an edited life in which people feel vulnerable unless they can decide ahead of time what they will say. In contrast, face-to-face conversations occur in real time and so the interaction cannot be controlled.

A retreat was held for teachers on the faculty of an elite private middle school to consider their observations of student empathy. The teachers reported that students usually lack patience to listen to others, seem unable to think about anything from the point of view of someone else, avoid eye contact while having conversations, and fail to pay attention to others as shown by not observing body language. The consensus view was that taking turns in a conversation is essential to acquire empathy (Turkle, 2021).

Teacher and Parent Observation of Child Adjustment to School

An adaptable person can adjust to change. Most parents know how difficult it can be to adjust to a new job or move to a different town. Sometimes, adaptability does not involve changing an address but getting used to an unfamiliar environment such as a preschool. For most children, adjustment to being a student begins at an earlier age than when parents started school. Accordingly, some families try to ease adjustment to school by having a child attend only a couple of days a week so that the time with peers is balanced by the time with the mother or another caregiver.

Most teachers realize the limited scope of their own observations. Therefore, they rely on parents to observe a child outside school. When parents are asked to watch for certain behaviors at home, the resulting insight contributes to understanding the individual student. For example, consider the larger perspective that emerges when parents join teachers in looking for success indicators such as "Does your child like school?" Children find it less threatening to share with parents what they dislike. The teacher who assumes children like school unless they complain to her directly overestimates student willingness to confide in nonfamily members. At home, when parents listen to a child's concerns about experiences at school, they can probe to find out "What did you tell the teacher about this problem?" The answer to such questions can make known how comfortable a child is in expressing feelings in class. Teachers and parents consider adaptation to school an important condition for learning, so it is good to share a common observation focus and talk often, at least once a month during the child's first school year. Granted, this takes time and calls for improvisation of faculty schedule. Nevertheless, benefits for children justify a collaborative effort with the teachers a child has at home and in the classroom.

Parents are usually surprised when a teacher informs them their child has self-control issues. How could this be when my child is so well behaved while at home? Adaptation is less difficult at home where a child may get much more attention than s/he does in a group setting with other self-centered individuals who also want to be heard and have situations go their way. Because adaptability requires self-discipline, it is worthwhile to think about this question: What do you suppose the success or failure of a child's beginning days at school should be based on? The usual way to assess child adjustment is teacher observation. Table 2.2 provides a list of questions and considerations to be used by teachers and parents of young children. By carefully watching each child, most teachers and parents will find helpful insights.

Reporting Social Skills to Parents

Most teachers do not report about the social development of students even though skills in this realm of achievement are widely recognized as essential for success. Criteria should be identified that teachers can look for in class and outside during recess as evidence for

Table 2.2 Questions and Considerations About Child Adjustment at School

Questions	Considerations
1. Does the child like school?	Whether the teacher can learn much about how a child feels depends on the teacher-child relationship.
2. Does the child feel comfortable enough to express the full range of feelings at school, including disappointment, anger, and fear as well as pride and satisfaction?	This index of security indicates whether a child believes that the teacher will accept all sorts of feelings.
3. Does the child see the teacher as accessible and willing to help if needed?	Listening is always important but especially during childhood since there are few other resources than the teacher.
4. Does the child demonstrate signs of anxiety such as nail biting, crying, wet pants, fear, or withdrawal from activities involving groups?	Soothing comments can be helpful to reduce anxiety, embarrassment, and stress. Individual teacher attention or referral to school nurse may be needed.
5. Does the child feel a sense of belonging in the school?	This is shown in part by how the child interacts with other classmates, making friends or being rejected by peers.
6. Does the child show willingness to try new activities?	If children see risks of exploration as too high, they avoid participation in situations that can add to learning.
7. Does the child show persistence in trying to do tasks or give up when encountering difficulty?	Adults should admit to children that failure is an important aspect of learning at all ages as each of us fails. Parents differ in the way they interpret lack of success.
8. Does the child feel comfortable enough to be involved with creative play by being an active pretender?	This can be observed on the playground or at recess indicating the child can use imagination for playing with peers.
9. Does the child sit still and listen to a story with pictures?	This shows whether or not a child is easily distracted or is able to pay attention to the teacher.
10. Does the child follow simple directions and carry out the assignments correctly?	Following direction is a sign of paying attention and focusing on teacher-assigned tasks.
11. Does the child know the alphabet, numbers up to 20, and personal information about home address and phone number?	Young children should be able to provide response to this question before they begin school.
12. Does the child respond well to teacher discipline or threaten to tell parents that s/he is being mistreated?	Parents should instruct their children to follow the teacher's directions and tell them about any discipline problems at school.
13. Does the child take care of personal toilet needs?	This is a must. Inability to take care of toilet needs may be a sign of a physical problem.

(*Continued*)

Table 2.2 (Continued)

Questions	Considerations
14. Does the child demonstrate knowledge that is greater than the norm?	An education program for exceptional children (e.g., gifted and talented) may be an appropriate placement.
15. Does the child show any signs of possible physical abuse?	Evidence of repeated bruises should be brought to the attention of the school nurse.

Copyright © by Paris S. Strom and Robert D. Strom (2025).

feedback to students about their behavior, reporting to parents, and initiating interventions with other professionals. Look over this list and add any new criteria that you view as improvements. Elementary school teachers should check each statement that describes the behavior of this student.

1. Accepts suggestions for improvement in a friendly way
2. Provides tutorial help for classmates when it is needed
3. Encourages and recognizes the achievement of others
4. Listens carefully to the feelings and ideas of classmates
5. Waits to talk instead of interrupting a person speaking
6. Acknowledges favorable qualities shown by classmates
7. Uses appropriate language as one way to respect others
8. Asks questions to learn about peer views and impressions
9. Welcomes newcomers without prompting by the teacher
10. Makes known opposition to the mistreatment of anyone
11. Applies self-control of anger in cases of disagreement
12. Avoids use of put-downs, sarcasm, and teasing peers
13. Shares with peers relevant material from the Internet

Conclusion

Emotional attachment and trust are essential conditions for normal infant development. The period from 6 to 18 months of age is a critical time to acquire the human response of love and attachment, ingredients on which socialization is based. Babies who do not have close, intimate, caressing human contact are unable to form attachments and robbed of their humanity. There is a high degree of certainty these infants cannot become fully human because of inability to experience love and affection, joy and empathy, concern, and grief. Helping children become socially aware reduces egocentrism and places them on a path to develop a healthy concern about the well-being of others, a beginning step toward maturity.

Key Concepts

1. Infants acquire basic trust or mistrust of their environment based on ways they are treated. When caregivers are reliable, can be counted on to provide food, are ready to change diapers, and offer affection on a regular basis, babies conclude parents are dependable and can be trusted to provide for them.

2. The time between 6 months and 19 months is a critical period for development of the human response of love and attachment, forming an emotional bond that will be the basis for later socialization. Attachment is the tie of affection babies form with another person, typically their mother or a consistent caregiver.
3. Stranger anxiety is a short-term and common infant experience. By 8 months of age, they decide their security depends on the main caregivers. Therefore, these adults can expect friendly responses while other people might be treated with apprehension.
4. Lack of touch and attention can modify the stress reaction of children, stunt physical growth, and negatively influence behavior. When children attend day care that is supervised by staff with little training, cortisol levels of children can be abnormally high but return to normal again when they are with supportive relatives.
5. Severely depressed adults and military personnel returning from active conflict duty have shown abnormalities in their daily cortisol cycles. The brain images of patients with histories of depression and post-traumatic syndrome show shrinkage in the hippocampus region of the brain that implicates memory as well as regulation of cortisol secretion.
6. There is a limited period early in life when children must experience healthy emotional stimulation to ensure they are able to recreate and share these emotions with others throughout life. When such opportunities are denied, the potential for caring, compassion, and trusting relationships is diminished.
7. Childcare begins before birth. Healthy mothers have normal babies. Pregnant women should avoid smoking, drinking alcohol, or taking non-prescribed drugs. Everything that an expectant mother eats or drinks goes to the fetus via the placenta, a thick wall of tissue through which nourishment comes from the bloodstream of the mother.
8. There are 11 million American children under age 5 who attend group care. This population is forecast to grow, and quality of their care should be improved. One solution is for society to provide quality care and supervision at a reasonable cost to the parents.
9. The way parents and grandparents talk to preschoolers about the need to understand feelings of others, referred to as empathy, has a lasting influence on the development of social skills. Social skills develop by reflection on how others may see things, considering how events might be interpreted from the view of someone else.
10. One method to help children practice empathy and social perspective about feelings of peers is expecting them to tell daily observations about conversations and activities of others. Social awareness diminishes egocentrism and enhances perspectives to include personal concern about how others feel.

Generational Perspectives Activities

2.1 **Discussion**

2.2 **Conversations With Young Children**

2.3 **A Scenario: Reasoning and Problem-Solving**

2.4 **Chapter Review**

2.5 **Parent and Grandparent Self-Evaluation**

2.6 **Storytelling**

2.1 Discussion

1. What are some advantages and disadvantages for the children who go to group care?
2. What arrangements do you favor when parents are unable to care for their children?
3. How can young children become socially aware about the emotions felt by their peers?
4. How can parents and grandparents spend more time together with young children?
5. What should be done to help low-income families better prepare children for school?
6. What relative has influenced you most in how to respond to the needs of other people?
7. Who is someone you know that can always tell when someone needs encouragement?
8. What needs of your parents or grandparents can be met by other family members?

2.2 Conversations With Young Children

1. What things happen at school that make you afraid?
2. Who are the children you feel are your best friends?
3. Who asks more questions of you than anyone else?
4. What do you like to talk with friends about the most?
5. How do parents react when you do something wrong?
6. Who do you enjoy playing with most at your school?
7. Who are you afraid of in your school class? Why?

2.3 A Scenario: Reasoning and Problem-Solving

Melissa is a healthy girl who was born one month ago. Her mother Vicky works as an assistant bank manager, and Melissa's father Ralph is an electrical engineer. Vicky had planned to return to the bank following her 60 days of maternity leave; but being with Melissa has caused her and Ralph to reconsider their options. She is thinking of quitting the job to stay home full-time until Melissa is old enough to go to kindergarten. How do you see some other options of the couple?

a. Vicki staying home will reduce family income but is outweighed by the benefits for Melissa.
b. Remaining at work could lead to Vicki's promotion and increase college savings for Melissa.
c. Going back to work will be less disappointing if a grandma is willing to take care of Melissa.
d. Request reduction to part time, so Vicky can be with Melissa more and still enjoy her career.
e. Other.

2.4 Chapter Review

1. What insights from the chapter will I try to apply in my relationships?
2. What is the most important key concept for me presented in this chapter?
3. Which elements of this chapter do I wish I had known about earlier?

2.5 Parent and Grandparent Self-Evaluation

Directions: For each question, place a check beside statements that describe your feelings. You may give several answers for some items. If your feelings are not on the choices list, write them on the line marked Other.

1. If I were a young mother taking care of my infant, I would

   a. continue working if affordable care could be arranged
   b. stay home and accept the economic sacrifice to be made
   c. remain on the job but feel guilty for not being at home
   d. work part-time so I could devote more time to the baby
   e. Other _____

2. The best thing I can do for parents of relatives with an infant is to

   a. help when mother and baby come from the hospital
   b. offer to pay for some costs to hire a trusted caregiver
   c. learn what I can about infancy before the baby arrives
   d. provide mothers relief occasionally if I live close by
   e. Other _____

3. I believe that helping infants develop a sense of trust is

   a. essential for them to have close relationships
   b. a consideration for the selection of caregivers
   c. encouraging a view that supports mental health
   d. a condition many families do not understand
   e. Other _____

4. My thinking about group care in early childhood is

   a. more mothers should stay home until children attend kindergarten
   b. better prepare caregivers and lower the ratios of adults to children
   c. that this should be a family entitlement that is paid for by the taxpayers
   d. that the focus should be on play, literacy, and getting along with others
   e. Other _____

5. I believe older people should

   a. do more to help families that have young children
   b. expect parents to become more involved with childcare
   c. view children as a resource all of us should invest in
   d. volunteer to do what they can to help with childcare
   e. Other _____

6. The imaginative play of young children has been

   a. an activity I observe without distraction
   b. an activity that I enjoy as a play partner
   c. a context where I have not participated
   d. a behavior that I believe has great value
   e. Other _____

7. I believe children who spend the most time in group care

   a. experience greater stress than those spending less time
   b. become more socialized and capable of getting along
   c. have more language deficits since they imitate peers

d. become less socialized and capable of getting along
e. Other _____

8. When institutionalized orphans move to foster care families

    a. they are more likely to develop normal intelligence
    b. their capacity for caring and compassion increase
    c. their stress levels diminish to become more normal
    d. the age when children are adopted appears crucial
    e. Other _____

9. A parent who stays home with children is a working parent

    a. because caregiving at home is as important as employment
    b. whose labor deserves equivalent status with employment
    c. who can offer better childcare than a group facility
    d. Other _____

10. Empathy and social awareness learning help children

    a. demonstrate concern for the well-being of others
    b. enlarge the perspective about how other people feel
    c. build emotional intelligence for relationships
    d. diminish egocentrism that prevents growing up
    e. Other _____

2.6 Storytelling

Historically, storytelling has been a dominant classic and progressive method of teaching around the world. The purposes of a storyteller are to present imaginary or real-life examples showing how some concept applies to a particular situation. People like stories, they pay attention to the procession of events, and usually remember aspects of a story for a long time. Your stories can reinforce the concepts in this chapter for family members and classmates. Please share your stories with them.

References

Arterberry, M. E., & Bornstein, M. H. (2024). *Development in infancy* (6th ed.). Routledge.
Borba, M. (2017). *Unselfie: Why empathetic kids succeed in our all-about-me world*. Touchstone.
Bortfeld, H., & Bunge, S. A. (2024). *Fundamentals of developmental cognitive neuroscience*. Cambridge University Press.
Bowlby, J. (1944). Forty-four juvenile thieves: Their characters and home-life (II). *The International Journal of Psychoanalysis, 25*, 107–128. https://psycnet.apa.org/record/1945-02692-001
Bowlby, J. (1988). *A secure base: Parent-child attachment and healthy human development*. Basic Books.
Bowlby, J. (2005). *The making and breaking of affectional bonds* (2nd ed.). Routledge.
Calderón, M. (2023, August 10). *Why child care is essential for a healthy start and how we're standing up for babies. Every child thrives*. W. K. Kellogg Foundation. https://everychildthrives.com/why-child-care-access-is-essential-for-a-healthy-start-and-how-were-standing-up-for-babies/?gad_source=1&gclid=EAIaIQobChMIpeXqnqamhQMV_HJ_AB3lPgwqEAAYASAAEgJoWfD_BwE
Carlson, M. (1997). Cortisol kids. *Harvard Magazine (Harvard University)*. https://www.harvardmagazine.com/sites/default/files/html/1997/05/right.kids.html

Carlson, M., & Earls, F. (2006). Psychological and neuroendocrinological sequelae of early social deprivation in institutionalized children in Romania. *Annals of the New York Academy of Sciences, 807*, 419–428. https://doi.org/10.1111/j.1749-6632.1997.tb51936.x

Carr, A., Slade, L., Yuill, N., Sullivan, S., & Ruffman, T. (2018, July 20). Minding the children: A longitudinal study of mental state talk, theory of mind, and behavioural adjustment from age 3 to age 10. *Social Development, 27*(4), 826–840. https://doi.org/10.1111/sode.12315

Chugani, H. T., Behen, M. E., Muzik, O., Juhász, C., Nagy, F., & Chugani, D. C. (2001, December). Local brain functional activity following early deprivation: A study of postinstitutionalized Romanian orphans. *NeuroImage, 14*(6), 1290–1301. https://doi.org/10.1006/nimg.2001.0917

Cook, W. J., & Klaas, K. M. (2020). *Guide to your baby's first years* (2nd ed.). Mayo Clinic Press.

Garvey, D. (2023). *Little brains matter: A practical guide to brain development and neuroscience in early childhood.* Routledge.

Goleman, D. (2006). *Emotional intelligence: Why it can matter more than IQ.* Bantam.

Goleman, D. (2015). *Focus: The hidden driver of excellence.* Harper.

Goleman, D., & Rinpoche, T. (2022). *Why we meditate: The science and practice of clarity and compassion.* Atria Books.

Greene, M. F. (2020, July–August). 30 years ago, Romania deprived thousands of babies of human contact: Here's what's become of them. *The Atlantic.* https://www.theatlantic.com/magazine/archive/2020/07/can-an-unloved-child-learn-to-love/612253/

Gross, D. (2023). *Infancy: Development from birth to age three* (4th ed.). Rowman & Littlefield.

Grundy, A. (2024, January 9). *Rising cost of child care services a challenge for working parents.* United States Census Bureau. https://www.census.gov/library/stories/2024/01/rising-child-care-cost.html

Gunnar, M. R. (2021). Forty years of research on stress and development: What have we learned and future directions. *The American Psychologist, 76*(9), 1372–1384. https://doi.org/10.1037/amp0000893

Harlow, H. F. (1958). The nature of love. *American Psychologist, 13*(12), 673–685. https://doi.org/10.1037/h0047884

Henderson, R. (2024). *Troubled: A memoir of foster care, family, and social class.* Gallery Books.

Kidwell, M. C., & Kerig, P. K. (2023). To trust is to survive: Toward a developmental model of moral injury. *Journal of Child and Adolescent Trauma, 16*(2), 459–475. https://doi.org/10.1007/s40653-021-00399-1

King, L., Guyon-Harris, K., Valadez, E., Radulescu, A., Fox, N., Nelson, C. A., Zeanah, C., & Humphreys, K. (2023, May 22). A comprehensive multilevel analysis of the Bucharest early intervention project: Causal effects on recovery from early severe deprivation. *The American Journal of Psychiatry, 180*(8), 573–583. https://doi.org/10.1176/appi.ajp.20220672

Konnikova, M. (2015, March 4). The power of touch. *The New Yorker.* https://www.newyorker.com/science/maria-konnikova/power-touch

Krznaric, R. (2014). *Empathy, why it matters and how to get it.* Penguin.

Krznaric, R. (2021). *The good ancestor: A radical prescription for long-term thinking.* W. W. Norton.

Levine, M. (2020). *Ready or not: Preparing our kids to thrive in an uncertain and rapidly changing world.* HarperCollins.

Marcdante, K., Kliegman, R., & Schuh, A. (2022). Assessment of the mother, fetus, and newborn. In K. Marcdante, R. Kliegman, & A. Schuh (Eds.), *Nelson essentials of pediatrics* (9th ed.). Elsevier.

Moullin, S., Waldfogel, J., & Washbrook, E. (2014, March 21). *Baby bonds: Parenting, attachment and a secure base for children.* Sutton Trust. https://www.suttontrust.com/wp-content/uploads/2019/12/baby-bonds-final-1.pdf

Nelson, C. A., Fox, N. A., & Zeanah, C. H. (2014). *Romania's abandoned children: Deprivation, brain development, and the struggle for recovery.* Harvard University Press.

Ruffman, T., Slade, L., Devitt, K., & Crowe, E. (2010). What mothers say and what they do: The relation between parenting, theory of mind, language and conflict/cooperation. *British Journal of Developmental Psychology, 24*(1), 105–124. https://doi.org/10.1348/026151005X82848

Segal, E. A. (2018). *Social empathy: The art of understanding others.* Columbia University Press.

Sparling, J., Dragomir, C., Ramey, S. L., & Florescu, L. (2005). An educational intervention improves developmental progress of young children in a Romanian orphanage. *Infant Mental Health Journal: Infancy and Early Childhood, 26*(2), 127–142. https://doi.org/10.1002/imhj.20040

Strom, P. S., Strom, R. D., Wingate, J. J., Kraska, M. F., & Beckert, T. E. (2012). Cyberbullying: Assessment of student experience for continuous improvement planning. *NASSP Bulletin, 96*(2), 137–153. https://doi.org/10.1177/0192636512443281

Strom, P. S., & Strom, R. D. (2025). *Mental health and relationships from early adulthood through old age.* Routledge.

Thoreau, H. (2023). *Walden.* MVP. (Original work published 1854)

Turkle, S. (2015). *Reclaiming conversation: The power of talk in a digital age.* Penguin Press.

Turkle, S. (2021). *The empathy diaries: A memoir.* Penguin Press.

Twenge, J. M. (2017). *iGen: Why today's super-connected kids are growing up less rebellious, more tolerant, less happy and completely unprepared.* Atria.

Twenge, J. M. (2021). *Generations.* Simon & Schuster.

Wade, M., Fox, N. A., Zeanah, C. H., & Nelson III, C. A. (2019). Long-term effects of institutional rearing, foster care, and brain activity on memory and executive functioning. *Proceedings of the National Academy of Sciences, 116*(5), 1808–1813. https://doi.org/10.1073/pnas.1809145116

Wade, M., Parsons, J., Humphreys, K. L., McLaughlin, K. A., Sheridan, M. A., Zeanah, C. H., Nelson, C. A., & Fox, N. A. (2022). The Bucharest Early Intervention Project: Adolescent mental health and adaptation following early deprivation. *Child Development Perspectives, 16*(3), 157–164. https://doi.org/10.1111/cdep.12462

Zinsser, K. (2022). *No longer welcome: The epidemic of expulsion from early childhood education.* Oxford University Press.

Chapter 3

Family Conversations and Child Language

There are 22.4 million children in the United States in the age group 0–5 years (Korhonen, 2024). During these early years, parents, grandparents, and other caregivers represent the most powerful influences on child development and mental health. However, there are substantial differences in the amount of dialogue parents have with children, methods they use for teaching, extent of encouragement given, recognition of child-favorable behavior, and feedback about progress provided to a child. The purposes for this chapter are to (a) describe how conversations between parents and young children can favorably impact later performance in reading and problem-solving, (b) document how the amount of talk between an adult caregiver and child can stimulate or inhibit motivation to learn, (c) examine how to improve the quality of family conversations, and (d) describe research findings about comparative language development of young children made by families of different income groups. Generational Perspectives Activities present topics to discuss with family members and close friends about the importance of conversations with children.

Influence of Parent and Child Conversation

Early Obstacles to Children's Learning

The relevance of parent and early child conversation was initially investigated by Robert Hess, Professor of Education at the University of Chicago. He wanted to explore the relationship between maternal teaching methods and achievement of their children. His main question was this: If children from low-income homes usually arrive at school unprepared for what teachers expect of them, and if middle-class children are usually prepared, what readiness experiences take place in middle-class homes that happen less often in low-income families? Hess recruited 160 Black mothers and their 4-year-old children. Forty mothers qualified as upper middle class; 40 had skilled backgrounds; 40 had unskilled jobs; and 40 were provided welfare. Most mothers came from intact two-parent households. The single mothers on welfare were the exception (Hess, 1965).

The Puzzle Experiment

One way to compare mothers was to observe the methods they used to assist their child in completing a jigsaw puzzle picturing fish of different sizes and colors. Each mother was asked to teach her child to put the puzzle together. Alice defined the task and told her

DOI: 10.4324/9781003534655-5

child how to proceed. Then she spilled the puzzle onto the table, allowed her child to move the pieces, and guided him to success. Alice said:

> This is a jigsaw puzzle. You have never seen one before. We are going to take all the pieces out of the puzzle and then you will try to put them back together again. First, I want you to look carefully at the puzzle picture so you will remember it. Notice the shapes and colors of the pieces so you will remember where to fit them together.

Another mother, Jane, was equally supportive of her child according to staff who had visited her home. She wanted to help her child succeed but was unable to convey the basic concepts needed to solve a simple problem.

Jane began by just dumping the puzzle in front of her child before she said anything. Then she told her child: "Now, I want you to put it back together again." Jane watched while her child picked up pieces and tried to place them where they might belong. Jane's continual directive was "Turn it around, turn it around." She repeated this directive 35 times until, in frustration, the child said, "You do it."

From observations it was soon clear that the ability to convey concepts, share information, and program an uncomplicated task occurred least often in low-income families. But this was not the only significant outcome. Imagine a child who, in repeated conversation with mother, encounters situations that s/he tries to solve but, because maternal guidance is lacking, finds it impossible. The child's reaction of defeat, "You do it," is likely to recur and be magnified many times. This orientation can lead a child to conclude that solutions are lacking for most problems. Compare this response to the conversation of the first parent-child example. That child had no greater knowledge about the puzzle in the beginning but, with the experiences structured by his mother, came to recognize there was a solution. It appears that the way children approach new learning tasks depends on the kinds of conversations they have with a parent (Garvey, 2023; Gross, 2023; Hess, 1965; Hess & Shipman, 1965).

Difficulties arise when a mother is unable to communicate behaviors that are needed for success. When a child is able to solve problems at home because of the favorable motivation, encouragement for learning, then natural curiosity can enable the child to advance through most of the early learning stages. Hess concluded that inner-city low-income mothers were capable of learning skills to provide suitable instruction for their children. However, educators generally did not recognize the potential of low-income mothers to become effective teachers.

Parents' Perceptions of Schooling

The mothers Hess and Shipman (1965) observed also differed in how they perceived school. Responses were compared about how they would handle this situation. Imagine your child is old enough to start school for the first time. How would you get her ready? What things would you say to her? One mother, Lydia, explained:

> First, I would remind her that the reason she is going to school is to learn, the teacher will be taking my place, and students are expected to follow instructions given by the teacher. Also, she should realize that most of her time will be in the classroom with other children, and she should ask the teacher for help whenever she has a question or ask if a problem comes up.

In terms of promoting educability, what did responses of this mother provide her child? Lydia was informative, presenting the school situation as comparable to one already familiar to the child. Second, she provided reassurance and support to help her manage anxiety. Third, she described the classroom as involving a personal relationship between the child and teacher. Fourth, she portrayed school as a place where the child would be expected to learn.

Another mother, Betty, gave a different response because she was concerned about fighting at school (Zinsser, 2022). She said:

> Well, John, it's time for you to go to school. You have to know how to behave in class. The first day you must be a good boy and do exactly what the teacher tells you. Mind the teacher and make sure you don't get in fights with other kids.

What did Betty do differently? She began by defining the student role as passive and compliant. Second, the main issues that she presented involved authority and the institution instead of learning. Third, the expected relationship with the teacher was portrayed in terms of different status and role expectations instead of a personal relationship. Fourth, Betty's message was vague on how to deal with school problems, except by being obedient.

Following his experiments, Hess recommended educational intervention programs for low-income mothers to enable their improvement of parenting skills (Hess, 1965; Hess & Shipman, 1965; Levine & Munsch, 2023).

Project Head Start

Hess's recommendations for intervention programs were overlooked because President Lyndon B. Johnson had been asked repeatedly by Martin Luther King to pass a Voting Rights Act in Congress (LBJ Presidential Library, 1964/2024). The 54-mile Civil Rights march from Selma to Montgomery Alabama that was led by Reverend King was watched by television viewers nationwide as nonviolent protestors were attacked by police.

The United States Office of Education concluded that, rather than helping low-income mothers become more capable teachers as Robert Hess (1965) had suggested, what they needed more was job training since two-thirds of Black families were headed by single mothers. The officials responsible for implementing President Johnson's War on Poverty decided to begin a program that would compensate for early learning that was usually missing in low-income disadvantaged families. This plan to rescue low-income children included a component called *Head Start*. The program continues to operate and currently enrolls nearly a million children at an annual cost of $10 billion. The current participants are Hispanics (37%), Blacks (27%), and Whites (24%) (Head Start, 2023). In terms of benefits, these children have a safe environment and receive free nutritious meals. Decades of longitudinal studies have determined that participants in early childhood intervention who persisted in education until middle age earned higher incomes and committed less crimes than a control group (Heckman & Karapakula, 2019).

Learning to Talk and Vocabulary

There are many compensatory education programs intended to prepare children from low-income homes for kindergarten. One of these efforts was the Juniper Gardens Project in Kansas City, Kansas, directed by Betty Hart and Todd Risley (1995), education professors from the University of Kansas. Their goal was to build language skills of 3- and 4-year-olds attending an inner-city preschool. Language growth was gauged by using a comparison group, which comprised children of professors not provided instruction. Vocabulary of the low-income 3-year-olds initially increased as the members of the staff introduced new words. However, before long, it became obvious their vocabulary could not be accelerated beyond direct instruction at school. Progress slowed further at 4 years of age. By the time children entered kindergarten, previous gains had mostly been lost. Meanwhile, children of professors denied training continued to show rapid increase in their vocabulary.

Hart and Risley (1995) were disappointed their project had failed but did not interpret the result to be a reflection of heredity. Instead, they thought language differences between children of different backgrounds must begin before they arrive in school at age 3. They wondered if providing support during preschool was already too late. To study the origins of verbal differences, it would be necessary to observe family conversations in the home when parents first introduce vocabulary to children. A sample of 7–9-month-old infants was selected. This choice of child age was meant to allow parents time to get used to having observers in their home before the age when children begin to talk. The criteria for recruiting families included a broad range of income, education, and ethnicity, and so the influence of these separate factors on verbal development could be detected. The plan was to follow sample families from the time children were 7–9 months-old until they reached 3 years of age.

To ensure the research sample would be more likely to remain stable over the 30 months scheduled for the project, all families had to be well-functioning and include either a father or some other male who was regularly involved with domestic affairs. The 42 families were White (60%) and Black (40%). Parents of 13 families had attended some college and held professional positions; 23 of the families were led by men who had blue-collar employment, and six families were welfare recipients. A member of staff made monthly visits to each of the homes, observing for one hour while a parent (usually the mother) proceeded with her daily routine. Every word a parent said was tape-recorded. Observers took notes but did not speak to parent or child. These monthly visits continued until the children were three years old (Hart & Risley, 1999).

Parent-Child Language Similarities

Before children are old enough to spend time with peers at a playground or other group activities outside the family, most of what they learn comes from parents, grandparents, or other caregivers. So it was not a surprise that the behavior of the 42 children closely resembled their relatives. However, implications for language development were not fully anticipated. A broad range in vocabulary size was found, but 86% to 98% of the words recorded in each child's vocabulary were also recorded in the vocabulary of their parents. Overall, 1,300 observations of the 42 families were gathered for analysis (Hart & Risley, 1999, 2003).

Hart and Risley (2003) worked several years to complete analyzing their large amount of data. Similar to the children in their earlier project at Juniper Gardens, the three-year-olds from welfare families had smaller vocabularies than their peers from working class and professional families. They also acquired new words at a much slower pace. The vocabulary comprehension gap reflected extensive differences discovered in the earlier project that compared low-income children in a language enrichment program with children of professors denied any instruction.

A follow-up study by Hart and Risley (2003) was conducted involving 29 of the 42 infants when they were in third grade. Researchers were amazed by how measures of language at age 3 could accurately predict verbal skills at ages 8 or 9. For 29 students observed at home before age 3, vocabulary growth rate was strongly correlated with the third-grade performance on the Peabody Picture Vocabulary Test scores and Test of Language Development (TOLD) subtests including listening, speaking, semantics, and syntax. Child vocabulary at age 3 also accurately predicted reading comprehension at grade 3 (age 8) on the Comprehensive Test of Basic Skills. Later studies by Garcia and Weiss (2017) and Levine (2020) confirmed that adequate language skills are essential by grade 3 to perform well in high school and beyond.

The gravity of this situation is underscored by The Nation's Report Card (2024). This assessment of reading is administered every two years to students in grade 4. The most recent results showed that, overall, only 33% of the 4th graders in the United States could read at or above grade level. Further breakdowns indicated that the proportion of Blacks reading at or above grade level was 17%, Native Americans 19%, Asians 58%, Hispanics 21%, and Whites 42%. Low reading proficiency means students are more likely to struggle and more likely to quit school without graduating. The gap between the highest and lowest performing groups is widening, despite $1 trillion sent by the Department of Education to schools over the past 40 years to close the gap (Devos, 2025). These results should be a wake-up call for parents of young children.

Amount and Focus of Parent Talk

The goal of early intervention is to bring greater equality for experiences of children from low-income backgrounds. Determining whether this goal is achieved requires estimates about the amount of experience children from differing income backgrounds bring with them to preschool that usually begins when they are age 3 or 4. One credible basis for arriving at such an estimate is the observation data gathered by Hart and Risley (2003) on children from the time they were 7 months of age until they were age 3. Findings have shown the greatest difference among families was the amount of parent talk. Regardless of income, parents devoted the same amount of talk to making sure the child avoided unsafe activities and were properly fed, dressed, and corrected for behavior that was unacceptable. However, conversations in the welfare families usually concerned little else. In contrast, the extra talk in the professional families and talkative blue-collar families focused on the adult and child getting to know each other with feedback being a natural aspect of doing things together (Garcia & Weiss, 2017; Suskind & Denworth, 2022). This extra talk consisted of more extensive vocabulary, complex ideas, subtle guidance, and positive feedback that is a contribution to mental development (Suskind, 2015).

Some conditions that might annoy adults when they talk with each other are the very things a child needs to hear. The nature of such conversations should consistently draw attention to the obvious, be repetitive, answer questions presented by an adult, and take advantage of observation. For example, while at play a child points to a group of toy animals. In response the adult could say, "Some of these animals are horses. This one is a big horse and that one by the fence is a small horse." During meal preparation a mother who translates her behavior into words might say, "I will slice this cucumber for our salad; I will slice a tomato also for our salad."

The more formal education that a mother had attained, the more often she spoke to her child. On average, professional parents said 2,176 words an hour; working-class mothers

Table 3.1 Child Experience of Language Development Presented by Families

Parent-Child Dialogue	Professional Parents	Working-Class Parents	Welfare Parents
Parent words spoken per hour	2,176	1,498	974
Words heard by child at age 4	45 million	26 million	13 million
Child vocabulary size at age 3	1,116	749	525
Parent comments of encouragement and discouragement ratio per hour	6:1	2:1	1:2

* Adapted from *The Early Catastrophe: The 30 million word gap by age 3*, by B. Hart and T. Risley, *American Educator* (2003). https://www.aft.org/sites/default/files/media/2014/TheEarlyCatastrophe.pdf

spoke 1,498 words an hour; mothers on welfare spoke 974 words an hour, less than a third the amount spoken by professional parents. These patterns remained stable and not attributed to gender, number of siblings, or individuals present during visitor observations. The variations in language experience were converted to the estimates shown in Table 3.1. By age 3, children from the professional homes had heard 45 million words; those from working-class families 26 million words; and welfare children 13 million words (Hart & Risley, 2003; Suskind, 2015; Suskind & Denworth, 2022). The 45 million words heard by children of professionals were not all different words; that would be impossible since dictionaries include less than 300,000 words.

The differences in exposure to language were reflected by the size of child vocabulary. Table 3.1 shows that, according to Hart and Risley (2003), at age 3, children of professional parents, on average, had vocabularies of 1,116 words; children of working-class parents had 749 words; and children of welfare parents had vocabularies of 525 words. These figures underscore the importance of family conversation as the single most important influence on the development of child language. Neuroscience has found that optimal brain development depends on language (Abbott & Burkitt, 2023).

Parent Attention and Feedback

There were other differences than the amount of child exposure to parent speech (Hart & Risley, 2003). The adults who spoke more to children also gave more explanations, raised more questions, and provided greater feedback. Professional parents were attentive to the favorable behavior of their child and made positive comments on this conduct 30 times an hour. "I like the way you are cleaning the playroom; you do a good job in following my directions." This parent reaction to child-favorable behavior was greater than for working class and far more than welfare families.

A corresponding pattern was evident in Table 3.1 for the parent comments of disapproval. Parents of professional backgrounds observed child misconduct and made 5 disapproval remarks per hour, compared to their 30 comments of approval, a 6:1 ratio in favor of the positive comments. By contrast, children in working-class homes heard 12 favorable comments and 7 disapprovals an hour, for a positive ratio of 2:1. Response patterns were reversed in the welfare homes where parents made 5 approval statements and 11 disapprovals each hour for a negative ratio of 1:2. Welfare children heard prohibition statements twice as often as favorable feedback. When low-income parents talked about the behavior of their children, they more often criticized them than praised them. These differences reflect profound lessons. Children of professionals and working-class parents enjoy encouragement that welfare children do not. Instead, welfare boys and girls are mainly taught to follow commands. Parent affection was not a factor contributing to family interaction. Parents who talked with children less often were observed to be as loving as those whose conversations were more extensive and elaborate. Every mother showed concern for her child, but families varied in the amount and type of conversation with a child (Suskind & Denworth, 2022; Suskind, 2015).

The Hart and Risley (2003) results included some good news and some bad news. On the positive side, it appears that poorly educated low-income mothers are capable of providing vocabulary experiences needed to support normal child development. The bad news is that, when parents fail to provide such opportunities, the remedial programs offered at school are unlikely to result in overcoming deficiencies. One promising solution would be to acquaint all parents with their potential for teaching and establish programs showing them ways to become more effective teachers. Parents should know that talking to children often, even about seemingly unimportant topics, contributes to their mental and emotional development. Children become better at doing the things they are encouraged to practice. More conversations, more language tools, and more ability to communicate are important keys to supporting student academic success (Garvey, 2023).

Continued Lag in Child Language

Contemporary studies have confirmed there are significant differences in language skills of children from different income backgrounds. Fernald and Weisleder (2015) at Stanford University followed 48 infants for six months, from the time they were 18 months old until they were 24 months old. She found the same socioeconomic relationship Hart and Risley (2003) reported a decade earlier. In Fernald's study, two-year-olds from low-income homes already suffered a six-month lag in vocabulary size and speech-processing skills when compared to the children from higher-income homes. At age 2, children spoken to the least showed smaller vocabularies and slower language-processing speeds. Children spoken to more often had larger vocabularies and faster processing speeds.

Low-income children, on average, are two years behind peers from middle-income homes when they enter kindergarten and five years behind when they enter high school (Bradley, 2022). Most of this language gap has already been established by age 3, before students go to preschool. This situation suggests the logical time for working on deficit reduction is when children first begin to acquire language and vocabulary. Such teaching takes place at home and is more likely to succeed when there is access to parent education. It is a contradiction to claim that children from all backgrounds are capable of learning, but low-income parents are unable to learn what they should understand to properly prepare children for kindergarten. The potential of parents as teachers has been underestimated, and the consequence is considerable inequity among children. Many infants and toddlers spend most of their days in group care where effective strategies for language building have yet to be established, implemented, and used with homework lessons that parents apply and reinforce their role as a child's long-term teachers (Zinsser, 2022).

Time and Teaching Methods

Milestones of Language Development in Babies

Babies learn to begin speaking at their own pace. According to the Mayo Clinic Staff (2024), the following milestones of baby language development deserve parent attention.

By the end of three months, your child might:

- Smile when you appear
- Make cooing sounds
- Quieten or smile when spoken to
- Seem to know your voice
- Have different cries for different needs

By the end of six months, your child might:

- Make gurgling sounds when playing
- Babble and make a range of sounds
- Use the voice to show likes and dislikes
- Move eyes toward sounds
- Respond to changes in the tone of your voice
- Notice that some toys make sounds
- Notice music

By the end of 12 months, your child might:

- Try copying speech sounds
- Say a few words, such as 'dada,' 'mama,' and 'uh-oh'
- Understand simple commands such as 'Come here'
- Know words for common items such as 'shoe'
- Turn and look toward sounds

By the end of 18 months, your child might:

- Know names of people, objects, and body parts
- Follow simple commands that are given with gestures
- Say as many as ten words

By the end of 24 months, your child might:

- Use simple phrases, such as 'more milk'
- Ask one- to two-word questions, such as 'Go bye-bye?'
- Follow simple commands and understand simple questions
- Speak about 50 or more words
- Speak well enough so that you or another caregiver can understand at least half the time

Electronic Versus Nonelectronic Toys and Language

The early environment effects comprehension of words, development of vocabulary, and readiness for reading. This awareness motivates some parents to purchase electronic toys that manufacturers claim will have a favorable influence on language development. Little is known about how this departure from reliance on traditional playthings is associated with parent-child conversation. To explore this issue, researcher Sosa (2016) studied 26 families, mostly White, well-educated parents. This study was notable because it discovered things about parent-child playtime that occurred without being watched by observers. All the parents were given three sets of toys: First, the battery-operated electronic toys included baby laptops, cell phones, and a talking farm. Each toy had buttons or switches that turned on lights, stated words, phrases, and songs. These toys were chosen because they were marketed as education tools to teach animal names, colors, and shapes. A second set of toys included traditional nonelectronic objects with potential to teach animal names, colors, and shapes. These toys consisted of building blocks, farm animal puzzles, sorter for different shapes, and multicolored rubber blocks with pictures of animals and objects on each side. A third group of toys included board books featuring farm animals, various shapes, and color themes.

Parents and their 10–16-month-old babies engaged in two 15-minute play periods each day for three days using each of the three sets of toys. Parents received an audio-recording device for placement in the pocket of a vest worn by their child during play sessions. Results showed that when babies played with the electronic toys designed for teaching language, their parents spoke to them less and responded less to baby babbling than when children played with traditional toys like blocks or read books. The babies also vocalized less when they played with electronic toys. When electronic toys were used, parents said 40 words per minute, on average, compared to 56 words when using traditional toys and 67 words with books. Parents also used fewer words relevant to content of a toy like saying "this is a big cow" or "that barn is red." Such descriptive words were said four times more often when children's books were the focus than electronic toys and twice as often with traditional toys than electronic ones. Gender results were similar. The conclusion was that, besides allowing electronic toys to talk for them, parents also permitted toys to interact for them (Sosa, 2016).

One mother, a high school English teacher, explained that while cooking she frequently narrated her behavior for the infant to hear. She would say, "I am going to use this red tomato" or "I will put more milk in the pan." In contrast, when using electronic toys, she reflected, "When there is noise going on because of the toy, I didn't feel like I wanted to talk. It was weird to talk over noise of the toy." Then she acknowledged, "The busier I become, the easier it is to let my child play with electronic toys and justify that it is educational when the right thing is to adjust my schedule so I can increase the number of conversations with my child."

Sosa (2016) observed their findings provided a basis for discouraging the purchase of expensive electronic toys advertised as contributing to language formation. Results favor greater potential benefits of reading to children and encourage parents to use interactive speech with traditional toys to enable greater comprehension and vocabulary development.

Parents and Time With Children

Low-income parents generally demonstrate less competence in communicating verbal skills that foster the growth of vocabulary. Accordingly, these families are the ones invited to join federally sponsored early intervention programs. Some affluent families misinterpret this policy by supposing their higher income must mean that they are also more successful parents. However, a more balanced view has emerged about what it takes to bring up healthy children (Levine, 2020). Certain attitudes and skills that parents of all incomes and ethnicities should learn provide the best assurance for elimination of language deprivation. Educators no longer suppose all low-income children are deprived or all affluent families are advantaged. Family research by Levine and Munsch (2023) has determined that parent behavior matters more than the income of parents.

The Australian Government Department of Social Services supports the website *The Australian Parenting Website* for parents at raisingchildren.net.au This important source is for parents to learn about their children beginning with pregnancy and birth, newborns, babies, toddlers, preschoolers, school age, pre-teens, teens, and grownups, autism, and disabilities. Descriptions of child development enable parents to know normative expectations at each age level. Parent and child play activities along with guides and tools, podcasts, and webinars are included for each age group (Raising Children Network, 2024).

Most middle-class and affluent parents have reason to be pleased about how they foster literacy skills of children. At the same time there can be benefit for them in becoming more self-critical. Comparative studies administered the *Parent Success Indicator* by Strom and Strom (2021) to over 5,000 parents of adolescents (ages 10–14). The subjects in China, Japan, and Taiwan and culturally diverse families in the United States including Asians, Blacks, Hispanics, and Whites have identified one factor that appears more influential than all others for raising children. According to Strom et al. (2008), child access to parent time seems the most important gift parents can provide children. This variable is more powerful than access to parent income that, in many affluent homes, takes the form of substitute caregivers who become mainly responsible for educating children throughout the day. A helpful guideline is for parents to spend one hour on weekdays and two hours daily on weekends doing things with your child (Strom & Strom, 2024).

Parents of every income and education level should be generous in spending time with children. Affluent families provide children with many advantages but seldom consider what they might learn from less privileged parents. Our studies have found that blue-collar fathers are often seen as more successful in the estimate of adolescent daughters and sons and themselves than affluent fathers. For example, when blue-collar fathers come home from work, often at an earlier hour than affluent fathers, they do not go to their study to look at messages or make phone calls. Instead, they spend time with the children and ignore distractions. Blue-collar parents rarely talk about "quality time" or other excuses that undermine close family relationships (Strom et al., 2008; Strom & Strom, 2024).

Guidelines for Reading to Children

The best times to read with a child are when you feel fresh and energetic, not times you are fatigued and lack in enthusiasm. When you arrange time for reading it confirms the value that you place on reading as a method for learning and opportunity to share interpretations of events that are read together.

1. Reading books is fun. Make sure that children get to observe you reading alone for pleasure. Otherwise, the lessons you want to teach about the joys and satisfactions of reading have less impact.
2. Reading is more exciting and leads to greater learning when the process includes periodic stopping to ask questions, discuss a story, guessing what is going to happen next, and commenting on how events described in the story are similar to ones that are part of your own experience.
3. Recognize that during reading the adult is in the power position because the child is unable to read. This means the child schedule you should arrange also includes time for play together when a child can share dominance because pretending is a way to honor the greater childhood strength of imagination.
4. Many parents rationalize that after returning home from work they have a need to relax and seem to always choose watching television as the best method. Sometimes try personal reading instead. Children should gain a perspective that reading is a form of enjoyment that can reduce stress in a healthy way.
5. By third grade, sustained silent reading is a better vocabulary builder than textbooks or oral language. Textbooks do not provide the richness of vocabulary as trade books that prepare children for real literature. Half of the 3,000 most commonly used words do not appear in kindergarten through sixth-grade textbooks.
6. Sometimes, parents will read children's books aloud, believing this will motivate child interest in reading. However, there is little benefit if adults use a monotone voice that does not reflect the feelings of characters in a story. In contrast, when an adult expresses emotion similar to the book character, enthusiasm for reading is the typical outcome.

Conclusion

Parents of infants and toddlers should understand that the mental potential of children is related to conversations that take place at home in the first years of life, before preschool. This awareness can motivate parents to use their unique teaching opportunity. Parents love children and want to foster growth and development. However, they vary in the amount of conversation with children, ways they define tasks, extent of encouragement, attention paid to commendable conduct, and attitudes conveyed on solving problems. Since a significant language gap develops between children from low-income and higher-income homes before the age of 3, it is wise for communities to encourage parents to recognize their important role as a child's first teachers.

Affluent children generally identify excessive pressure from their parents for academic achievement as the root cause for many of their coping problems. Also, they feel more distant from mothers and fathers because of adult insistence on adoption of goals that are too narrow. Obviously, parent education must go beyond support for language that is needed to perform well in the classroom. By recognizing all parents can benefit from practical lessons about raising healthy children, an innovative curriculum for them should correspond to ages of their children from infancy through high school.

Key Concepts

1. The vocabulary of three-year-olds closely correlates with their performance in third grade on picture vocabulary scores and measures of language development. Child language at 3 years of age is also predictive of reading comprehension level in the third grade. Possessing grade-level language skills by third grade is seen as necessary for a child to perform well in high school and beyond.
2. The greatest difference among families is the amount of parent talk. Conversations in most professional families and some blue-collar households include more elaborate vocabulary, complete ideas, subtle guidance, questions, and positive reactions. Mothers with higher levels of education talk to their children more often.
3. Certain attitudes and skills that parents of every income and ethnicity should learn provide the best assurance for elimination of deprivation in childhood. We no longer suppose that all low-income children are deprived and that all children from middle class and affluent families are advantaged. Parent income and social class are less important factors to foster child development than behavior of the parents.
4. Affluent parents seldom think about what they might learn from less privileged parents. Many blue-collar fathers are seen as more successful by their children than are affluent fathers. When blue-collar fathers come home from work, they do not go to their study to sort out messages or make calls. Instead, time is devoted to children.
5. Parents who speak more often to their child also provide more explanations, raise more questions, and communicate more positive feedback. Professional parents make positive comments to their child about favorable behavior they observe approximately 30 times an hour. This favorable response is twice as great as the amount of feedback in blue-collar families and five times that of welfare families.
6. Two-year-olds from low-income homes already show a six-month lag in the size of their vocabulary and speech-processing skills when compared to children from higher-income homes. Two-year-olds who are spoken to less often have smaller vocabularies and slower language-processing speeds. Children talked to more often have larger vocabularies and faster processing speeds.
7. To promote language development, parents are encouraged to read to daughters and sons and spend time playing with them. Children vocalize less during play with electronic toys than during play with books. Evidence suggests that electronic toys cause parents to have less meaningful verbal interaction with children.
8. Children and adolescents from affluent households experience mental health risks more frequently than low-income children. They are more likely to get involved with substance abuse, experience sustained anxiety, suffer from depression, and express unhappiness more often than peers. Estimates suggest that at least one-third of affluent children demonstrate some symptoms of psychological problems.
9. Affluent children often identify excessive pressure from their parents for academic distinction as a cause for many of their psychological problems. Many feel distant from parents because of adult insistence on adoption of goals that are too narrow and a failure to pay enough attention to them. Building curriculum for parents must include other issues as well as language development.
10. Studies have found an inverse relationship between income and the emotional closeness of children to their parents. Low-income children are far more likely to report feeling close to their parents than are children from higher-income families. Children who feel distant from parents are less likely to engage them in serious conversations or seek their advice and assistance.

Generational Perspectives Activities

3.1 Discussion
3.2 Conversations With Young Children
3.3 A Scenario: Reasoning and Problem-Solving
3.4 Chapter Review
3.5 Parent and Grandparent Self-Evaluation
3.6 Storytelling

3.1 Discussion

1. What do you think are the best ways to reduce the vocabulary gap among children?
2. What should be done to meet language needs of infants and toddlers in group care?
3. What things have you noticed about parenting practices of low-income families?
4. What are some lessons affluent parents might learn from less privileged parents?
5. How much pressure do children in your family experience because of relatives?
6. Why would you favor or oppose education for families with infants and toddlers?
7. How do you evaluate yourself in terms of the amount of time spent with your child?

3.2 Conversations With Young Children

1. What things do you like to talk about mostly with your mother?
2. What things do you like to talk about mostly with your father?
3. How do you suppose life is different for children in other families?
4. Which of your relatives asks you more questions than anyone else?
5. What do you like to talk to friends about more than to parents?
6. How do parents act when you do something wrong?

3.3 A Scenario: Reasoning and Problem-Solving

Children from low-income families usually have language deficits when they start school. The community wants to overcome this disadvantage, so the city council is asking for suggestions. What options would you propose?

a. Free classes for parents of preschoolers focused on literacy for children
b. Elementary students read to younger children and listen to them read
c. Take children to senior centers, so elders can help build literacy skills
d. Adolescents read children's books and then check on comprehension
e. Other _____

3.4 Chapter Review

1. What insights from the chapter will I try to apply in my relationships?
2. What is the most important key concept for me presented in this chapter?
3. Which elements of this chapter do I wish I had known about earlier?

3.5 Parent and Grandparent Self-Evaluation

1. When I am around young children not old enough to go to elementary school
   a. I ask questions that draw their attention to situations I want them to see
   b. I define words for them as we use imagination while we pretend together
   c. I listen to them and help correct pronunciation when I can tell it is wrong
   d. I frequently imitate their baby talk to resemble an agreeable companion
   f. Other _____

2. Helping children increase the size of their vocabulary
   a. is a task I am motivated to do but uncertain how to achieve it
   b. depends on how much I get to talk as we spend time together
   c. is a goal I want to achieve with the parents of my grandchildren
   d. will help them to prepare for the teacher expectations at school
   e. Other _____

3. During conversations with children
   a. I make more approval comments than disapproval about their behaviors
   b. I ask questions to motivate reflective thinking and problem-solving
   c. I narrate their behavior while I observe whatever they might be doing
   d. I get distracted and miss opportunities to maintain a helpful dialogue
   e. Other _____

4. The goals I have for children
   a. focus mostly on their being able to achieve in the classroom
   b. emphasize emotional, social, mental, and moral development
   c. are the ones parents have for them so I can add to attainment
   d. are mostly social because they live in a social environment
   e. Other _____

5. By the end of third grade, I want children to
   a. request tutoring whenever they need help
   b. be able to read at their grade level or above
   c. read for fun because they find it satisfying
   d. read to me so that we can enjoy it together
   e. Other _____

6. I admire how parents in my family
   a. talk to them about many topics and ask for their opinions
   b. listen to them carefully and are not distracted by devices
   c. read books together and discuss the feelings of characters
   d. encourage them to ask many questions as the way to learn
   e. Other _____

7. My view about electronic toys as a way to teach language is
   a. I do not want to interrupt when s/he is listening to the toy
   b. it further reinforces my goal to sustain more conversation

c. this strategy allows me more time to do something else
   d. I can build child language better than any toy can do
   e. Other _____

8. I think affluent fathers could learn from blue-collar peers

   a. to leave their work behind when they return home
   b. to pay more attention to their children than a cell phone
   c. to do things with their children that are spontaneous
   d. how to become a more successful dad in their family
   e. Other _____

9. My children and I

   a. spend enough time doing things together as a family.
   b. do not spend enough time doing things together.
   c. ignore each other even when we are together.
   d. do not listen well to each other when we talk.
   e. Other _____

3.6 Storytelling

Historically, storytelling has been a dominant classic and progressive method of teaching around the world. The purposes of a storyteller are to present imaginary or real-life examples showing how some concept applies to a particular situation. People like stories, they pay attention to the procession of events, and usually remember aspects of a story for a long time. Your stories can reinforce the concepts in this chapter for family members and classmates. Please share your stories with them.

References

Abbott, R., & Burkitt, E. (2023). *Child development and the brain: From embryo to adolescence* (2nd ed.). Policy Press.
Bradley, K. (2022). *The socioeconomic gap in the US public schools*. Ballard Brief. https://ballardbrief.byu.edu/issue-briefs/the-socioeconomic-achievement-gap-in-the-us-public-schools
Devos, B. (2025, February 6). Betsy DeVos: Shut down the Department of Education. *The Free Press*. https://www.thefp.com/p/betsy-devos-shut-down-the-department-of-education-trump-elon
Fernald, A., & Weisleder, A. (2015). Twenty years after "meaningful differences," it's time to reframe the "deficit" debate about the importance of children's early language experience. *Human Development, 58*(1), 1–4. https://www.jstor.org/stable/26765090
Garcia, E., & Weiss, E. (2017, September). *Education inequalities at the school starting gate: Gaps, trends, and strategies to address them*. Economic Policy Institute. https://www.epi.org/publication/education-inequalities-at-the-school-starting-gate/#epi-toc-24
Garvey, D. (2023). *Little brains matter*. Routledge.
Gross, D. (2023). *Infancy: Development from birth to age 3* (4th ed.). Rowman & Littlefield.
Hart, B., & Risley, T. (1995). *Meaningful differences in the everyday experience of young American children*. Brookes.
Hart, B., & Risley, T. (1999). *The social world of children learning to talk*. Brookes.
Hart, B., & Risley, T. (2003, Spring). The early catastrophe: The 30 million word gap by age 3. *American Educator, 27*(1), 4–9. https://www.aft.org/sites/default/files/media/2014/TheEarlyCatastrophe.pdf

Head Start (2023, June 30). *Head start history*. U. S. Department of Health & Human Services, Office of Head Start, Administration for Children & Families. https://www.acf.hhs.gov/ohs/about/history-head-start

Heckman, J. J., & Karapakula, G. (2019). *Intergenerational and intragenerational externalities on the Perry preschool project*. National Bureau of Economic Research. https://papers.ssrn.com/sol3/papers.cfm?abstract_id=3399272

Hess, R. D. (1965). Maternal teaching styles and educational retardation. In R. D. Strom & E. P. Torrance (Eds.), *Mental health and achievement* (pp. 15–24). John Wiley & Sons.

Hess, R. D., & Shipman, V. (1965, September–October). Early blocks to children's learning. *Children*, 12, 189–194. https://pubmed.ncbi.nlm.nih.gov/14348239/

Korhonen, V. (2024). *Number of children in the U.S. in 2022, by age group*. Statista. https://www.statista.com/statistics/457786/number-of-children-in-the-us-by-age/

LBJ Presidential Library. (2024). *Signing of the 1964 civil rights*. Lyndon B. Johnson. https://www.lbjlibrary.org/object/photo/signing-1964-civil-rights (Original work published 1964)

Levine, L., & Munsch, J. (2023). *Child development from infancy to adolescence: An active learning approach* (3rd ed.). Sage.

Levine, M. (2020). *Ready or not: Preparing our kids to thrive in an uncertain and rapidly changing world*. Harper.

Mayo Clinic Staff. (2024). *Language development: Speech milestones for babies*. https://www.mayoclinic.org/healthy-lifestyle/infant-and-toddler-health/in-depth/language-development/art-20045163

The Nation's Report Card. (2024). *National achievement-level results*. National Assessment Education Progress: Reading. https://nationsreportcard.gov/reading/nation/achievement/?grade=4

Raising Children Network. (2024). *The Australian parenting website*. https://raisingchildren.net.au/

Sosa, A. V. (2016). Association of the type of toy used during play with the quantity and quality of parent-infant communication. *JAMA Pediatrics*, 170(2), 132–137. https://jamanetwork.com/journals/jamapediatrics/fullarticle/2478386

Strom, R. D., Strom, P. S., & Beckert, T. E. (2008). Comparing Black, Hispanic, and White mothers with a national standard of parenting. *Adolescence*, 43(171), 525–545. https://pubmed.ncbi.nlm.nih.gov/19086668/

Strom, R. D., & Strom, P. S. (2021). *Parent Success Indicator*. In J. Carlson, K., Gensinger, & J. Jonson (Eds.), *The twenty-first mental measurements yearbook*. Buros Center for Testing, University of Nebraska.

Strom, R. D., & Strom, P. S. (2024). *Mental health and relationships from early adulthood through old age*. Routledge.

Suskind, D. (2015). *Thirty million words: Building a child's brain*. Dutton.

Suskind, D., & Denworth, L. (2022). *Parent nation: Unlocking every child's potential, fulfilling society's promise*. Dutton.

Zinsser, K. M. (2022). *No longer welcome: The epidemic of expulsion from early childhood education*. Oxford University Press.

Chapter 4

Play and Child Development

Children are entering school at younger ages than was common in the past. This shift has motivated discussions by educators about suitable settings of how high-quality instruction for children ages 3–6 years should be defined. One point of view suggests that early childhood education should focus more on knowledge of language and numbers while reducing the amount of time allowed for recess and play. However, reducing time for the activity children enjoy most in favor of activities preferred by adults discounts the value of child motivation and ignores the research findings of play research. When parents know the relationships between play and mental development, they are interested in methods to improve their teaching. The purposes of this chapter are to (a) examine suitable content of lessons using play with young children, (b) recognize how fantasy play contributes to creative thinking, (c) describe how pretending can be a way to foster the growth of imagination, (d) explore how sharing dominance during pretend play fosters child autonomy and allows for better relationships with playmates, and (e) respond to questions of parents about how they can rely on pretend-type play as a medium for teaching. Generational Perspectives Activities present topics to discuss with family members and close friends about the relationships and benefits of play for child development.

Parent Questions About Benefits of Child Play

Cross-cultural studies by Strom and Strom (2013) about parent-child play began with financial support from the Rockefeller Foundation, General Mills Foundation, and the Toy Manufacturers of America. These support sources helped fund construction for the play lab at Arizona State University and provided contributions of toys for young children. The purpose of the play lab was to provide a place where preschoolers (ages 3–5) could experience play time with parents and peers and an environment that was safe and quiet with few distractions. During this play time, faculty and volunteer graduate students participated in developing and testing theories of parent-child play. Parents considered their time well spent with their children. Several research projects were conducted with over 300 parents and preschoolers representing a wide range of household income and ethnic backgrounds. Our responses to parent questions regarding child play are described for reflection.

How Should I Respond When My Child Asks Me to Play?

When children invite parents to play with them, the best response is to join the play. Even though play is the favorite way children prefer to spend time, adults are reluctant to get involved because pretending causes them to feel silly. Being embarrassed reflects a mistaken assumption that early childhood is the only justifiable time in life for expression of imagination. This view ignores the many forms of fantasy adults rely on to experience a sense of power and escape from the challenges of daily life. A more worthwhile perspective is to think of your child and you as play partners. In a partnership, there is no competition because the strength of each partner is used to the advantage of both. Children have greater imaginative strength while adults possess more developed language, values, and maturity. By combining these assets, both parties benefit.

How Long Can I Stay Interested While We Pretend?

Going shopping with parents has little interest for children. They usually ask mom to go home well before she is ready. Mothers realize that what children complain of as having shopped for 'a long time' is actually only a few minutes. This attention deficit is reversed during family pretend play. For example, parents were invited to come to the play lab with their children. As families arrived, they were greeted by a graduate student who invited them to play with their child using any toys from a large box until a staff member would be ready to talk with them. Parents were unaware that the length of their playtime with children was being measured. Later, parents were told, "We are glad you stayed busy playing until we were able to meet with you. By the way, how long did you play?" Most of the parents guessed they had played for about twenty minutes, even though the actual measured time was just six minutes.

When we say that someone has a short attention span, the length of attention depends on the activity. For many parents and grandparents this means that, in the beginning, they are able to stay involved with pretending for only ten minutes or less without being bored, embarrassed, or distracted. Because it is unwise to play longer than you can maintain interest, tell the child "It is time for me to stop now. I cannot play as long as you can." When you apply this approach, you will experience more satisfaction, become less inhibited, and your attention span for play will lengthen (Jackson, 2018, 2023).

How Important Is My Influence as a Partner During Play?

Some unique benefits of parent-child play do not happen when children play with friends or alone. Whatever play theme a child may choose, adults can help them enlarge their vocabulary by introducing and defining new words in the play context. The more words a child understands and can use because of experience with pretending, watching television, or being on the Internet, the greater the comprehension for important tasks related to reading. Plan to play together when you are energetic and insightful instead of when you are fatigued, impatient, or short-tempered.

Much of what boys and girls learn before elementary school is based on asking questions, playing, and exploring. These activities accord with definitions of the creative process (Siegel & Bryson, 2019). Because children rely on their imagination, parents should assign high priority to the preservation of this valuable asset. Creative thinking is fostered when relatives join children as play partners. Children often tie their self-esteem to the extent to which relatives become involved with activities a child enjoys. It is not surprising that parents who are willing to get involved with pretending are the same ones most likely to develop a close relationship with their child (Goldberg, 2018; Whitebread et al., 2019).

Why Should I Spend Time Watching My Child Pretend?

Given the widespread interest of adults in being spectators of sports, why is that parents find the pretending that occupied them as a child and provided pleasure has little observational appeal as an adult? There is abundant evidence that young children want adults to watch them play. Children will often request parent attention by saying, "Watch this," or "Look at me." Boys and girls experience obvious delight when they are the center of attention. Why are parents distracted when watching a 4-year-old pretend with trucks, action figures, or wooden blocks? Is it because adults do not know what to look for, what to find pleasing, how to identify success, what to say about a form of play that lacks rules, hits, or runs, and cannot be scored?

There is agreement that creativity is a valuable quality and should become a priority at school. However, the dominant form of creativity in early childhood is *fantasy play* and often overlooked. Parents should compare the interaction they have with children of different ages. Playing games that involve motor skills, rules, strategy, and judgment appeal to adults. These kinds of play satisfy us so we can pay attention longer (Abraham, 2018; Bortfeld & Bunge, 2024; Hirsh-Pasek & Hadani, 2020).

In contrast, spending even a few minutes observing young pretenders poses a challenge for most parents and grandparents. When child pretending leads to indifference or inattention of adults, this behavior is bound to diminish. If by avoiding the role of play observers, we convey the impression that imaginative play is unimportant to us, creative expression does not deserve our attention, we prefer to watch only games with rules, it should be expected a child's desire for parent approval would lower the priority s/he attaches to keeping imagination alive.

By watching children pretend, parents communicate the acceptance of creativity that, at this young age, always takes the form of fantasy. Conversely, when we ignore this type of play, children find it difficult to believe their imaginative behavior is considered important. They must feel their actions are worth the time for us to watch before they are able to conclude reliance on pretending is a suitable activity. Because observation takes time, watching represents approval. Remember-time is the most valuable gift parents and grandparents have to give children.

Parents as Partners in Pretending

When parents join children in play, they often present the following questions.

Is It Alright to Multitask While I Play With My Child?

Parent inattention is a major obstacle to nurturing close family relationships This problem is illustrated by the observation of a father about his 3-year-old daughter. He said:

> Whenever she wants to get my attention and cause me to look at something she created, finds interesting, or wants to ask questions especially when I am preoccupied with other matters, I give confirmations such as 'Uh huh,' 'Oh yeah,' or 'That's neat,' without turning my head to look at her. It is during these moments her tone becomes more insistent, and she tells me, 'Daddy, look at me with your eyes.'

It sounds so basic, but this is her method to get my undivided attention in the only way that she knows to confirm it – when I look directly at her." Simone de Beauvoir (2016), the feminist French philosopher, stated, "Attention is the rarest and purist form of generosity."

How Worthwhile Am I as a Model for How to Use Leisure Time?

Children need to observe how parents and grandparents spend leisure time, identify the activities adults enjoy when they are not working. Some parents tell children, "I sacrifice my free time so I can buy things you want and give you opportunities that I did not have as a child." This gratuitous statement implies that a child should be grateful to a parent for doing without leisure. On the contrary, one of the main responsibilities of parents is to model healthy ways to manage time. Parents should recognize that time and conversation shared with children are more valuable than material things that can be purchased for them. Happiness is recognized as one of the most elusive goals in the world. When parents consistently demonstrate how to maintain a life of balance, a schedule that includes adequate time for pleasure as well as for work, their children are rich if not affluent beneficiaries.

Parents whose main goal is to earn a higher income may not be around enough to show children how adults achieve happiness. In these situations, children decide to turn to peers for examples of ways to find satisfaction or arrange time for family sharing. This model is too narrow to foster child development. Recognize it is not what you do for children, but what you have taught them to do for themselves that will help them succeed in life.

Am I Willing to Schedule Time for Pretending With My Child?

Many parents seem to be in a perpetual state of fatigue. They return from work tired or late and usually excuse themselves from playing with children, promising instead to play on the weekend. Nevertheless, a child's need to play with parents is continuous instead of limited to Saturdays and Sundays. A better plan is to amend the schedule, so ten minutes a day can be devoted to play together. Understand that unscheduled play may sometimes also be necessary. Occasionally, every child will try to make demands or provide additional clues that extra attention is needed – "Look what I can do." In such cases, a few minutes of parent-child play can prevent frustration and avoid potential conflict. Successful parents and grandparents share the attitude that family relationships always come first.

Should I Use Praise to Compliment My Child While We Play?

Children seek recognition, but their motivation is less to get praise than to get acceptance. In this sense, acceptance is the greatest reward we offer children because it means they can retain their imagination into adult life. Even though praise may be well-intended, adults generally rely on praise to shape child behavior in ways that undermine development. Normal development is defined as the continuous growth of creative behavior. If praise was the best method to sustain creativity beyond early childhood, schools would not contribute to decline in creativity because teachers spend considerable time praising students. It is when the grownups want to motivate initiative, creativity, and problem-solving that praise fails them most. To liberate these qualities in children, parents should rely on motivation that enables a child to feel free of adult control (Hari, 2022).

Children at play experience the intrinsic satisfaction of play, and so there is no need to praise one another. They may sometimes attempt to control playmates or possess playthings, but praise is not the tool they rely on. In contrast, when grownups praise children they tend to ignore the intrinsic satisfaction of play and instead insist upon behaving as a judge whose function is to verbally reinforce desired behaviors. When parents find pleasure in pretending, they can sustain attention for this activity. On the other hand, if parents lack enjoyment during imaginative play, it shows up as a short attention span and overreliance on praise as an extraneous reward system.

Being an observer implicates praise. Suppose your child or grandchild comes to show you a picture that s/he has colored. You are busy and feel you don't have time to talk right now so you say, "That's wonderful," "Oh, that's great," or "I like that picture more than the one you showed me before dinner." Soon the child returns to present another product and seek praise again. Change your strategy by sitting down and just observing the child engage in coloring. Now, the child knows what s/he is doing is important because it warrants your complete attention so there is no need to seek praise. When children are young, listening to what they say is not all that matters. Recognize that play observation has a powerful effect in helping children identify activities adults consider to be important behavior.

People of any age who become dependent on praise have to look outside themselves for confidence and remain incapable of judging their own behavior. The need for unnecessary praise often occurs when adults impose inappropriate expectations. For example, parents who insist that a four-year-old begin to read usually find it is necessary to give frequent praise. The unintended result is that a child becomes over-reliant on praise in situations that require child ability to stay focused. When my son was in second grade, he asked, "Dad, how come I was good at football right away?" I said, "Probably because we did not start playing football until you were six years old instead of four years old." At age 4 he was less coordinated, and this would have required frequent praise on my part to keep him interested. To support favorable self-concept without the cost of child dependence on continual praise, it is good to emphasize the common motive and unique strength of children, imagination, that is expressed through play. Watch children play with friends to quickly confirm they do not praise one another. Praise discourages independence, a quality that supports perseverance with difficult and lengthy tasks. Should parents ever praise children? Of course, but the purpose of praise should not be to recognize achievement; instead, praise should motivate effort (Duckworth, 2018; Dweck, 2007).

Can Creative Play With My Child Have a Long-term Effect?

The National Child Development Study of Great Britain is a longitudinal effort that has been following over 17,000 people who were born during a single week in 1958. Considerable information has been collected about these 66-year-olds regarding health, physical and cognitive development, social relationships, education, and employment. Gill and Prowse (2021) examined extensive data and determined that creativity of children, measured when they were 7 years old, predicted their labor market and educational success in life. The creative persons earned more in the course of their career, work in higher occupational categories, and reached higher educational attainment. Analysis further suggested that creative persons have acquired practical with so-called soft skills allowing them to thrive in work environments where learning from experience is important. In the quantitative analysis, every standard deviation increase in childhood creativity was associated with a 2% increase in pay and a 2.2% increase in the probability of working in a high-quality managerial or technical job. Evidence clearly indicates there are long-lasting benefits of childhood creativity for results like career earnings, employment rates, and education attainment. Honoring creativity during interactive fantasy play seems a good plan for parents of preschool children (Prowse, 2021).

Relationships of Play to Mental Development

During the 1930s, psychologist Harold Skeels and his assistant Marie Skodak examined two infants at an Iowa orphanage. Both girls had been born to mentally deficient mothers. It was estimated that the girls had IQs of 46 and 35, far below the average of 100. The orphanage was crowded, and so the girls were temporarily placed in a facility that housed mentally deficient women. Eight months passed before Skeels saw them again. He was surprised to find their IQs had risen to 78 and 87. A decision was made to wait and find out whether the unexpected gains would be retained. A year later a re-evaluation found the girl initially scoring 35 and later 87 was now 88; her companion had also made progress from 46 to 78 and then 100. Skeels and Dye (1939) addressed their findings to the American Association of Mental Deficiency.

An effort was made to discover the reason for the unexpected mental improvement. The social environment for children consisted of interaction with 18–50-year-old feeble-minded women whose mental abilities resembled those of 5–9-year-old children. Each of the babies was 'adopted' by an inmate while other women shared affection and companionship. Some of the inmates were mothers so they could bathe, feed, and diaper the infants; the ward supervisor monitored child diet. Women with spending money often purchased toys. Most waking hours for the children were filled with play activity and conversation (Skeels & Dye, 1939).

The House Guest Experiment

Skeels now faced a dilemma. Should he leave the girls who were three years old with the feeble-minded women to whom they appeared to owe their mental ability gains or transfer them back to the orphanage where they would receive less attention? Instead, Skeels decided to have the girls adopted and hoped they would retain their normal intelligence. In addition, he asked the Iowa State Board of Control for permission to take 11 more feeble-minded babies under one year of age, place them in the ward with the mentally deficient women, and label them as 'house guests,' an informal designation so children would still be eligible for adoption. Skeels believed these children would acquire normal intelligence. A contrast group of 12 babies with higher IQs would stay at the orphanage and be a comparison group. The IQs of 11 babies sent to the women's facility ranged from 36, seriously mentally deficient, to 89 or dull normal. In contrast, for babies remaining at the orphanage the lowest IQ was 50; the highest was 103 or normal (Skeels & Dye, 1939).

What previously happened to the two babies happened again to nearly all members of the experimental group. Their progress was phenomenal as the average IQ rose from 64 to 92 by two years of age. Nine of the children were adopted. Three years later, when they were age 5, Skeels visited for evaluation. No child had an IQ below 90; their average was 96. Meanwhile, the group that stayed at the orphanage deteriorated, from an average IQ of 84 when the project began to 66 by the age of 5. This meant that the children who lived with feeble-minded adults attained normal intelligence while the near-normal children staying in the orphanage became feeble-minded.

Skeels described how a group of mentally deficient children in orphanages had attained normal mental ability when they were placed with institutionalized feeble-minded women as their caregivers. When he finished his presentation, prominent scholars came to the podium to denounce him, alleging he must have falsified results. Critics were agreed that intelligence is genetically determined at conception and cannot be altered by environmental intervention. In effect, Skeels was accused of inventing a wandering IQ.

Skeels was disappointed by the reaction of colleagues but remained unshaken. Soon he began a related study of families where parents gave their children little attention. The oldest children from these families generally grew up to have borderline intelligence, or they were mentally deficient. However, their younger siblings often displayed normal mental abilities. This suggested that a younger child lacking parental attention could still benefit from mental stimulation of an older sibling, even though that playmate was not intelligent. Again, play and learning seemed to be linked and challenged the prevailing opinion that intelligence is based entirely on heredity. In each study a common factor seemed to impact mental improvement. That consistent element was a one-to-one relationship with an older person who gave time, affection, and showed willingness to play. Children lacking this ingredient did not make progress (Skeels, 1966).

When World War II began, Skeels joined the United States Air Force. When he returned home in 1945, his research records were missing. He was told that his data had been discarded by administrators who needed filing space. Skeels was depressed, quit his job, and moved to Denver, Colorado. It seemed his work would never be completed, and his innovative efforts would go unrecognized.

Abundant and Deprived Households

Nearly a decade passed before Samuel Kirk (1904–1996), founding director of research for exceptional children at the University of Illinois, published an article reporting that when low-ability children were exposed to a school curriculum that emphasized play, their IQs rose (Harris & Kirk, 1993). Because Kirk (1951) was a respected scholar, his findings about the influence of play on development were taken seriously. Kirk (1996) was also the first scholar to define the term *learning disabilities*. President John F. Kennedy (1960–1963) appointed Kirk as Director of the United States Office of Education's Division of Handicapped Children where he convinced the government to fund the training of teachers for students with learning disabilities (Kirk et al., 2023). In 1963, Martin Deutsch from New York Medical College received nationwide attention when his research produced similar gains using a play-oriented curriculum for Black preschoolers in Harlem, New York (Caldwell, 2003). Within months of the Kirk and Deutsch revelations, there was agreement among educators throughout the nation that low-income children generally had less mental stimulation at home than middle-class children, a disadvantage that should be overcome to prepare children for kindergarten and successful academic achievement.

The terms *abundant* and *deprived* arose in most discussions. Benjamin Bloom (1964), Professor of Educational Psychology at the University of Chicago and President of the American Educational Research Association, testified before Congress describing the hypothetical effects different environments could have on development of intelligence during selected age periods. Bloom illustrated what could happen to two children born with the same mental capacity but raised in dissimilar environments. Further, he explained that the greater environmental influence during the early years reflected the fact that intelligence is a developmental function with more rapid growth taking place in the early years of child life. His contention was that from birth to age 4 a child develops 50% of mature intelligence, from ages 4 to 8 another 30%, and between ages 8 and 17 the remainder 20%. Mature intelligence can be measured at age 17 and does not significantly change thereafter. If as much intelligence develops between birth and age 4 (50%) as during the next 13 years (50%), when children attend school, it would seem reasonable that it would be difficult to compensate for lack of learning during the early years. By age 4 children raised in the two different environments would already be 10 IQ points apart. Between age 4 and 8, another difference of 6 points will occur. Finally, between ages 8 and 17 an additional 4 points would separate them, making a total of 20 IQ points – or the difference between a slow learner (IQ 80) and being at the norm (100 IQ).

In 1965, based on this sobering forecast, President Lyndon Johnson announced a *War on Poverty* (1964–1965) that would include an early childhood component called *Head Start* to make up for readiness experiences missed by preschoolers living in deprived environments. After the introduction of *Head Start* (2023), focusing on play-oriented activities quickly became popular among early childcare centers and parents with young children, believing that this was an acceptable method to contribute to child development.

Few enthusiasts had ever heard of Harold Skeels (1966). One man who did remember Skeels was Robert Havighurst, Professor of Education at the University of Chicago. During a visit to the National Institute of Mental Health, Havighurst saw the name 'Harold Skeels' posted on an office door. He inquired, "Whatever happened to the Iowa children?" Were their mental gains retained, or did they regress to retardation? Skeels was persuaded by Havighurst to conduct a follow-up study supported by the National Institute of Mental Health. Skeels contacted Marie Skodak, his former assistant in Iowa, who had since become Director of Psychological Services for the Dearborn Michigan Public Schools. She agreed to collaborate. There were predictable difficulties because 26 years had passed. Many participants were female and would have changed their names if they got married. Some would have moved away. Nevertheless, after 18 months most participants were located, some as far away as Sacramento, California, and Mesa, Arizona.

Now, it was necessary to devise a strategy to approach them. Should they be sent a letter stating: I knew you when you were mentally deficient and observed you acquire normal functioning. Do you still have normal intelligence? Should the subjects complete another IQ test? It was decided that their current job status was a fair indicator of success, and their children's IQ would confirm parental influence. Given this strategy, 95% of the subjects were willing to participate again.

The 13 original house guests included the two little girls Skeels first examined and the 11 later placed in the experimental group. As adults all of them were self-supporting, having jobs such as nurse, secretary, stewardess, beautician, guidance counselor, and members of the armed forces. Their median education level was grade 12. Collectively, they had 28 children whose IQs ranged from 86–125, with an average of 104. However, a different outcome characterized the contrast group who remained at the orphanage. They had an initial average IQ of 84 compared to 64 for the experimental group. But only one of the 12 was employed; their average education level was third grade. Eight remained residents of an institution. Skeels had challenged the false belief that intelligence is entirely fixed at conception and showed that the cost of institutional care for orphans is five times as great as placing them in foster care. In 1966, Skeels presented results from his follow-up study to the Society for Research in Child Development. This time he received a standing ovation and award for confirming the environment has a significant influence on intelligence (Skeels, 1966).

Differences between abundant and deprived families continue to be a focus for research. Dearing et al. (2024) completed a longitudinal study involving 814 children from low-, middle-, and high-income families. The subjects from across the United States were followed from birth through 26 years old with frequent measurements taken of development and experience documented from early childhood through adolescence; this occurred during the years 1991 to 2017. The National Institutes of Health Study of Early Childhood Care and Youth Development was the first to directly document large differences in opportunities and opportunity gaps between birth through high school that occur at home, in school, after school, and in the neighborhood. Researchers found that two-thirds of children from low-income households experienced no more than one opportunity between birth and high school. In contrast, most youth from high-income families experienced six or more opportunities. Moving from zero to four opportunities increased the odds by 10% to 50% that low-income children would graduate from a four-year college and increase their salaries by $10,000 per year. Eric Dearing, a co-author of the study and Professor at Boston College, explained, "For the first time we were able to directly measure how large opportunity gaps are and how they predict outcomes of students."

Consideration of a Play Curriculum

David Weikart, Director of Special Services for Ypsilanti, Michigan Public Schools was troubled by his observation that many Black preschoolers from poverty families performed poorly when they entered elementary school. Weikart organized a program for preschoolers at Perry Elementary School from 1962 to 1967 (Holmann et al., 2008). Teachers offered students a unique curriculum with a balance of academics and play for low-income 3- and 4-year-old Black students; the child-teacher ratio was 6:1. Children participated in activities that allowed decision-making and problem-solving on weekday morning for 2.5 hours taught by teachers with at least a bachelor's degree. All of the activities were planned, carried out, and reviewed by students with support from adults. Every teacher also engaged in a weekly 1.5-hour home visit to each mother and child, intended to have mothers apply aspects of the curriculum at home.

The program was evaluated using 128 children, 64 from the group who had access to the preschool curriculum and 64 members in the control group who did not. The low attrition rates enabled long-term follow-up studies. During the preschool, attention focused on intellectual and language tests. During the elementary grades, the emphasis shifted to achievement tests, teacher rating of children's social skills and motivation, and school placements. In the high school, interviews with children and parents were added. As adults, the consideration shifted from test performance to life performance (Holmann et al., 2008).

Results were obtained for 90% of the original sample when the children became teenagers. Participants surpassed non-participants at school entry, on achievement throughout schooling, commitment to school, high school graduation, and reduced antisocial behavior, crime, and incarceration. The program's return on investment was estimated to be at least seven times as great as the cost of the operation. Subsequent research follow-ups determined that children in the play-oriented preschool compared with peers who did not attend preschool, had, at ages 16, 23, 27, 40, and 50 higher rates of high school graduation, were more often employed, earned higher incomes, were less likely to receive public assistance, or be arrested for criminal behavior (Heckman & Karapakula, 2019; Heckman et al., 2023; Mark, 2023; Schweinhart, 2005, 2013).

New Pre-Kindergarten Curriculum

Researchers have found that academic gains made by three- and four-year-olds in prekindergarten programs often do not last and disappear by the end of kindergarten. To illustrate, a ten-year Tennessee study by Durkin et al. (2022) about the only randomized control trial of a statewide program showed that 2,990 low-income children in a pre-kindergarten program underperformed a control group that did not attend a pre-kindergarten program on achievement and behavior. Dale Farran, a co-author of the Tennessee report and Professor at Vanderbilt University, worried that pre-kindergarten programs had become too academic, so children don't get enough time for play, to share thoughts and observations, or engage in responsive interaction with caregivers (Mader, 2022). The Vanderbilt team concluded that it would be wise to broaden the scope of pre-kindergarten programs to spend less time on easily learned, simple skills (knowing the alphabet, identifying shapes) and more time on developing complex skills such as listening comprehension and problem-solving even though such skills can be difficult to teach and assess (Dearing & Farran, 2022). Beaver and Wyatt (2023), Hirsh-Pasek and Hadani (2020), and Sahlberg and Doyle (2020) are among the growing number of scholars in the United States to agree with the Tennessee team about the need to improve the educational content and quality of pre-kindergarten programs.

Conclusion

Play is the dominant activity of children, the way they prefer to spend their time. Some adults are misled to believe that child pretending does not provide significant value. The fact is imaginative play contributes to creative thinking and mental health throughout life. Generally, we look to adults as models for most sectors of living, but the children should be the models we should look to for expressing imagination in pretend play. This reciprocal learning is an effective method to build durable relationships that support sharing dominance and creative thinking.

Key Concepts

1. The main strength of children is imagination while adults have more developed language, values, and maturity. By combining these assets, both the adults and children can benefit. Think of your child and you as play partners. In a partnership, there is no competition because the strengths of each partner are used to the advantage of both parties.
2. Children enjoy experiencing the intrinsic satisfaction of play, so they have no need to praise one another. In contrast, adults who praise children overlook the intrinsic satisfaction of play and instead insist upon their being a judge to verbally reinforce behaviors they approve.
3. When the lifestyle parent behavior communicates to children is limited to working hard while excluding examples of how to find satisfaction and arrange for family conversation, this model is too narrow to support healthy child development.

4. Children seek opportunities to share control with their parents. This condition appears most possible during adult-child imaginative pretending. Many grownups are unable to play with young children very long because they cannot tolerate the authority inversion that occurs when they are the less powerful party.
5. Young children prefer play with parents more than play with their peers because then they can be the boss and be in charge. The fact that they prefer playing with a less imaginative partner suggests the desire for play with parents may be motivated in part to redress an imbalance of interpersonal control.
6. When play is driven by the imagination of children, they practice decision-making skills, advance at their own pace, and discover topics of interest. In contrast, when adults control child play, the young must acquiesce to follow adult rules and direction. The consequence is loss of the benefits that unstructured play offers, particularly creativity, leadership, and group skills.
7. Young children are in a stage of development called *identification*. During this stage they acquire moods, feelings, and attitudes of their companions. Pretend play offers chances to invent situations that permit adults to illustrate their values that might seldom be observed in other settings. Parents are more influential illustrating their values than trying to impose them.
8. Fantasy play permits children to share dominance and power with older relatives. The opportunity to share dominance can occur only when child imagination is allowed to enter an effect on interaction with adults. Grownups who engage in child-chosen play themes governed by fantasy can still contribute to learning but must temporarily accept an inversion of authority. The same inversion will happen again when adolescents surpass parents in technological skills.
9. Acceptance of imagination stimulates creativity. Much of what children learn before attending school comes through guessing, questioning, searching, and playing. These activities fit most definitions of the creative process. Since boys and girls prefer using their imagination, our first concern should be to preserve this wonderful asset. Creativity will develop when family members encourage this behavior by valuing fantasy and joining children as play partners.
10. Pretending together respects motivation of children. Parents and grandparents can be seen as a continuing source of guidance when they participate in activities that interest children. Entering the realm of fantasy where abilities of children surpass our own shows a willingness to honor child assets and share dominance. Respect is demonstrated by allowing child strengths to influence your relationship instead of their always being subordinates.

Generational Perspectives Activities

4.1 **Discussion**
4.2 **Conversations With Young Children**
4.3 **A Scenario: Reasoning and Problem-Solving**
4.4 **Chapter Review**
4.5 **Parent and Grandparent Self-Evaluation**
4.6 **Storytelling**

4.1 Discussion

1. How does fantasy help you manage some difficulties you cope with at your age?
2. Why do you suppose adults see play and learning as different activities?
3. What are some things you try to do as a way to support the imagination of your child?
4. What are some skills learned from play that you continue to rely on as an adult?
5. Compare task persistence of children at play with their persistence in other tasks.
6. What themes are you most and least comfortable playing with your children?
7. What problems do you encounter while pretending with young children?
8. Why do children need to spend time at play with other children their same age?
9. What do you recall about spontaneously organized games during childhood?
10. Compare the benefits of games organized by adults and those by children?

4.2 Conversations With Young Children

1. What do you like about playing with your parents?
2. What do you like about playing with your grandparents?
3. What do you like about playing with someone your own age?
4. Why do you like parents to watch while you play alone?
5. What toys do you like to play with the most?

4.3 A Scenario: Reasoning and Problem-Solving

Four-year-old David is waiting for his father to come home from work. As soon as his dad enters the front door David greets him and then he suggests 'Let's play dinosaurs.' How do you think Dad should respond?

a. Change clothes, get on the floor, and let David choose a dinosaur theme.
b. Urge David to seek some other playmate, perhaps one of the neighbor boys.
c. Admit to being tired but promise there will be time for play on the weekend.
d. Suggest instead that they exercise outside by playing catch with the soft ball
e. Other _____

4.4 Chapter Review

1. What insights from the chapter will I try to apply in my relationships?
2. What is the most important key concept for me presented in this chapter?
3. Which elements of this chapter do I wish I had known about earlier?

4.5 Parent and Grandparent Self-Evaluation

Directions: For each question, place a check beside statements that describe your feelings. You may want to give several answers on some items. If your feelings are not on the choices list, write them on the line marked 'Other.'

1. In what ways do you encourage children to develop imagination?

   a. I buy books, toys, and games for them
   b. I observe them during pretend-type play

c. I join them as a play pretender myself
d. We read imaginative stories together
e. Other _____

2. How do you feel when children ask you to join them in pretending?

   a. I am happy to be invited and try to fit into the play situation
   b. I am embarrassed because my imagination is not good enough
   c. I am flattered to be asked but recognize I'm too old to pretend
   d. I feel silly and suggest that they ask someone of their own age
   e. Other _____

3. How do you feel when children choose a bad character for pretend play?

   a. I am bothered and try to discourage this behavior
   b. I am not concerned because it is just pretending
   c. I encourage shifting to a more passive role
   d. I accept whatever role the child decides to play
   e. Other _____

4. Identify the values you would like children to learn during play with adults.

   a. Understanding the needs and feelings of others
   b. Accepting and expressing personal differences
   c. Learning how to cooperate with one another
   d. Sharing our individual fears and worries
   e. Developing the constructive use of power
   f. Other _____

5. What efforts have you made to help children with vocabulary development?

   a. When they use words improperly, I try to correct them
   b. I define certain words we hear while watching TV together
   c. I ask them to define words they don't seem to know
   d. I tell them how pleased I am about their use of language
   e. I introduce new words and their meanings when we play
   f. Other _____

6. When playing pretend themes with my child, I

   a. usually feel silly and embarrassed
   b. find it difficult to stay interested
   c. can't think of ideas to focus play
   d. try to control the level of play noise
   e. Other _____

7. I try to arrange my schedule so there is time to

   a. play cards or other games with friends
   b. participate in competitive electronic games
   c. watch mentally challenging television games
   d. watch sports contests on television or in person
   e. Other _____

8. In reviewing my life as an adult, I

   a. have not spent enough time playing
   b. spent too much time playing
   c. balanced work and play pretty well
   d. ignored play in favor of just working
   e. Other _____

9. In my relationship with children, I

   a. praise them for almost everything they do
   b. seldom praise them for any of their actions
   c. reserve my praise for real accomplishments
   d. use praise as a substitute for involvement
   e. Other _____

10. My feelings about the focus for play of preschoolers is

    a. they should be encouraged early to join a little league team
    b. they should pretend instead of engaging in games with rules
    c. boys and girls should focus on competitive electronic games
    d. boys and girls should play with any toys that appeal to them
    e. Other _____

4.6 Storytelling

Historically, storytelling has been a dominant classic and progressive method of teaching around the world. The purposes of a storyteller are to present imaginary or real-life examples showing how some concept applies to a particular situation. People like stories, they pay attention to the procession of events, and usually remember aspects of a story for a long time. Your stories can reinforce the concepts in this chapter for family members and classmates. Please share your stories with them.

References

Abraham, A. (2018). *The neuroscience of creativity*. Cambridge University Press.
Beaver, N. H., & Wyatt, S. (2023). *Early education curriculum: A child's connection to the world* (8th ed.). Cengage.
Bloom, B. S. (1964). *Stability and change in human characteristics* (2nd ed.). John Wiley.
Bortfeld, H., & Bunge, S. (2024). *Fundamentals of developmental cognitive neuroscience*. Oxford University Press.
Caldwell, B. (2003). Obituaries: Martin Deutsch (1926–2002). *American Psychologist, 58*(1), 75. https://doi.org/10.1037/0003-066X.58.1.75
de Beauvoir, S. (2016). *Memoirs of a dutiful daughter*. Harper Perennial.
Dearing, E., Bustamante, A., Zachrisson, H., & Vandell, D. (2024, September 25). Accumulation of opportunities predicts the educational attainment and adulthood earnings of children born into low- versus higher-income households. *Educational Researcher*. https://doi.org/10.3102/0013189X241283456
Dearing, E., & Farran, D. (2022, March 15). Opinion: What might the future of universal pre-k look like? As researchers, we have some concerns. *The Hechinger Report*. https://hechingerreport.org/opinion-what-might-the-future-of-universal-pre-k-look-like-as-researchers-we-have-some-concerns/

Duckworth, A. (2018). *Grit: The power of passion and perseverance*. Scribner.

Durkin, K., Lipsey, M. W., Farran, D. C., & Wiesen, S. E. (2022). Effects of a statewide pre-kindergarten program on children's achievement and behavior through sixth grade. *Developmental Psychology, 58*(3), 470–484. https://doi.org/10.1037/dev0001301

Dweck, C. (2007). *Mindset: The new psychology of success*. Ballantine.

Gill, D., & Prowse, V. L. (2021, May 28). *The creativity premium*. https://doi.org/10.2139/ssrn.3855808

Goldberg, E. (2018). *Creativity: The human brain in the age of innovation*. Oxford University Press.

Hari, J. (2022). *Stolen focus: Why you can't pay attention-and how to think deeply again*. Random House.

Harris, G. A., & Kirk, W. D. (Eds.). (1993, January 1). *The foundations of special education: Selected papers and speeches of Samuel A. Kirk*. Council for Exceptional Children.

Head Start. (2023, June 30). *Head Start history*. U. S. Department of Health & Human Services, Office of Head Start, Administration for Children & Families. https://www.acf.hhs.gov/ohs/about/history-head-start

Heckman, J. J., & Karapakula, G. (2019). *Intergenerational and intragenerational externalities of the Perry Preschool Project*. National Bureau of Economic Research, U.S. Department of Justice, Office of Justice Programs, NCJ No. 306748. https://www.ojp.gov/library/publications/intergenerational-and-intragenerational-externalities-perry-preschool-project

Heckman, J. J., Pinto, R., & Shaikh, A. (2023, December). *Dealing with imperfect randomization: Inference for the Highscope Perry Preschool Program*. EconPapers. Institute of Labor Economics, IZA DP No. 16675. https://docs.iza.org/dp16675.pdf

Hirsh-Pasek, K., & Hadani, H. (2020, October). *A new path to education reform: Playful learning promotes 21st-century skills in schools and beyond*. Brookings. https://www.brookings.edu/wp-content/uploads/2020/10/Big-Ideas_Hirsh-Pasek_PlayfulLearning.pdf

Holmann, M., Weikart, D. P., & Epstein, A. S. (2008). *Educating young children: Active learning practices for preschool and childcare programs* (3rd ed.). High/Scope Press.

Jackson, M. (2018). *Distracted: Reclaiming our focus in a world of lost attention*. Prometheus.

Jackson, M. (2023). *Uncertain: The wisdom and wonder of being unsure*. Prometheus.

Kirk, S. (1951). *Educating the retarded child*. Houghton Mifflin.

Kirk, S. (1996). *Samuel Kirk*. Illinois Distributed Museum. https://distributedmuseum.illinois.edu/exhibit/samuel_kirk/

Kirk, S., Gallagher, J., & Coleman, M. R. (2023). *Educating exceptional children* (15th ed.). Cengage Learning.

Mader, J. (2022, February 3). Behind the findings of the Tennessee pre-K study that found negative effects for graduates. *The Hechinger Report*. https://hechingerreport.org/behind-the-findings-of-the-tennessee-pre-k-study-that-found-negative-effects-for-graduates/

Mark, G. (2023). *Attention span: A groundbreaking way to restore balance, happiness and productivity*. Hanover Square Press.

Prowse, V. (2021, November 15). The long-lasting benefits of childhood creativity. *Psychology Today*. https://www.psychologytoday.com/us/blog/work-your-mind/202111/the-long-lasting-benefits-of-childhood-creativity

Sahlberg, P., & Doyle, W. (2020). *Let the children play: For the learning, well-being, and life success of every child*. Oxford University Press.

Schweinhart, L. (2005). *The high/scope Perry preschool study through age 40: Summary, conclusions, and frequently asked questions*. High/Scope Educational Research Foundation. https://highscope.org/wp-content/uploads/2018/11/perry-preschool-summary-40.pdf

Schweinhart, L. (2013, December). Long-term follow-up of a preschool experiment. *Journal of Experimental Criminology, 9*(4), 389–409. https://www.ojp.gov/ncjrs/virtual-library/abstracts/long-term-follow-preschool-experiment

Siegel, D., & Bryson, T. (2019). *The yes brain: How to cultivate courage, curiosity, and resilience in your child*. Bantam.

Skeels, H. M. (1966). Adult status of children with contrasting early life experiences: A follow-up study. *Monographs of the Society for Research in Child Development, 31*(3), 1–65. https://doi.org/10.2307/1165791

Skeels, H. M., & Dye, H. (1939). A study of the effects of differential stimulation on mentally retarded children. *Proceedings for American Association of Mental Deficiency, 44*(1), 114–136. https://psycnet.apa.org/record/1940-01422-001

Strom, P. S., & Strom, R. D. (2013). *Thinking in childhood and adolescence.* Information Age.

Whitebread, D., Grau, V., Kumpulainen, K., McClelland, M., Perry, N., & Pino-Pasternak, D. (Eds.). (2019). *The Sage handbook of developmental psychology and early childhood education.* Sage.

Part II

Early Learning at Home

Chapter 5

Young Children Learn About the Internet

Parents have the daunting responsibility of introducing young children to the Internet. Most mothers and fathers have substantial experience with the Internet but admit uncertainty about how to teach their young children the benefits and dangers of being online. The purposes of this chapter are to examine (a) how to acquaint young children with the Internet as the main tool for learning, (b) safety practices that should be consistently applied when parent and child work together online, and (c) guidelines for teaching attitudes and skills. Generational Perspectives Activities present topics to discuss with family members and close friends on how to teach young children about the Internet.

Benefits of Internet Visits for Children

There are 22.5 million children ages 0–5 years in the United States not old enough to be in kindergarten (Korhonen, 2024). Historically, parents have been expected to prepare children for kindergarten by teaching letters of the alphabet and reciting numbers in progression. However, young children lack skills needed for reading to become a learning tool. Therefore, children must rely on observation for much of what is learned. The responsibility for parents is to illustrate attitudes and skills children can observe and adopt as a foundation for online learning and social networking. As child Internet access increases, more learning will occur at home. Three-to six-year-olds are in a development stage known as *identification* that motivates their imitation of attitudes and behaviors of caregivers. Accordingly, parents need help to overcome some unfamiliar obstacles about teaching online (Belsky et al., 2020; Done, 2022).

Parents admit feeling uncertain about the Internet lessons they should teach. Fortunately, just being together can motivate conversations. Visual and audio stimulation urges children to make known feelings, ask questions, interpret images, show curiosity, engage in guessing, detect difficulties, admit and correct mistakes, experience success, and gain self-confidence. There are corresponding chances for parents to share their opinions, arrange discoveries, model curiosity, respond to questions, encourage perseverance, correct mistakes, acknowledge progress, convey attitudes for acceptable behavior, foster empathy about feelings of peers, and build social skills (Haidt, 2024).

Focus on Child Mental Processes

Many adults conceive of the Internet as a huge library that contains infinite knowledge. Easy access to information is a wonderful advance over the way learning was acquired in prior generations. However, rather than expose children to as much information as possible, greater advantage is possible by emphasizing the *mental processes* that enable children to practice creative and critical thinking (Abraham, 2018; Goldberg, 2018; Heitner, 2023). Giving lower priority to teaching factual information may seem strange to parents in the beginning because adults have historically believed that the mission of teachers is to provide lessons students are expected to memorize. This expectation should be left behind because it provides less benefit. Better results are possible by respecting child interest in discovery and getting to practice the Internet search skills that are needed by everyone (Cleese, 2020; Davis, 2023; Garvey, 2023).

The reason for spending time practicing *mental processes* is because this helps children learn to frame questions for online searches, encourages persistence in locating difficult to find data, and motivates critical thinking about truthfulness of messages presented online (Levitin, 2016). The challenge for parents is to model creative thinking by demonstrating curiosity and wonder, generate insightful questions, propose hunches, check out guesses, explore possibilities, decide about credibility of sources, and apply insights for problem-solving (Mayo Clinic Staff, 2023). There is also value in showing that some desired outcomes do not depend on trial and error but instead follow directions when a series of progressive steps is known to complete tasks. This strategy supports cause-and-effect thinking, urges memorization only when it is needed, and enables child satisfaction in attaining personal goals.

Previous generations viewed learning mostly in terms of information students needed to know instead of focusing on the thinking processes needed for engagement with the Internet. By emphasizing how children learn, the ways they think, a new perspective emerges with priority assigned to search skills, processing new ideas, and learning to adapt to an ever-changing social context. Teaching children about thinking is an important responsibility, so they can adjust to a future bound to transcend current ways of looking at events and interpreting situations (Strom & Strom, 2024).

Because some knowledge students acquire on their own goes beyond content of lessons provided by teachers, textbooks, and software programs, and the customary evaluation methods are no longer sufficient indicators to accurately estimate the extent of student knowledge. The shift to reliance on the Internet as the most prominent source of information and discovery enables individuals to decide some of their preferred content for learning and supports motivation to share some of what they learn with classmates. The potential for learning from the Internet is enormous even though uncertainty will continue about what families and schools should independently do to enable this possibility (Khan, 2024).

Support Motivation and Enjoyment

Parents should understand that some of their long-standing habits interfere with digital teaching and should be left behind. First, set aside the assumption prevalent when parents grew up about the relationship between pleasure and learning. Some parents incorrectly suppose that activities students enjoy do not qualify as learning. Instead, educators at home and in the school should know that, besides offering rapid information retrieval, technology tools have appeal to students, can motivate greater participation, encourage intergenerational conversation, increase the length of attention span, and sustain willingness to persist when facing uncertainty. A reason most dropouts give for their decision to leave school before graduation is their experience in the classroom did not provide them any pleasure. All teachers should realize motivation for learning throughout life depends on ensuring student satisfaction that stimulates their continued learning. (Duckworth, 2018).

Early childhood educators are concerned about the lack of parent involvement with teaching. They wish more families would assume greater responsibility to provide instruction. However, encouraging parents to increase participation with teaching presumes that adults are uniformly comfortable with reading, searching the Internet, answering questions, and guiding discussions. On the contrary, many parents, especially among low-income families, feel uncomfortable in the culture of learning. This is because their years in school were disappointing and caused them to gradually withdraw over time. These parents must experience the pleasure of learning online before they become able to motivate enthusiasm in their children. Carefully selected website visits can enable parents to acquire the joy of learning to share with their children. A national survey was conducted with 1,000 low-income parents of 3–13-year-olds. Over 90% of the parents had Internet access and recognized they needed to guide children about digital tools of learning (Rideout & Katz, 2021).

The best way to acquire and apply knowledge is to practice a skill as soon as it is learned, followed by corrective feedback, and further guidance. Situated learning in the family contrasts with how knowledge is usually gained in a classroom where teachers have many students but not enough time to figure out whether everyone has learned the lessons. Consequently, teachers have accepted memorization as sufficient evidence of student comprehension. A more practical form of assessment is to acquire understanding about the context where learning should be applied. Situated learning for children, whose observation is the basis for their formation of concepts, encourages adults to use modeling, the most influential method of instruction (Restak, 2022).

A goal of early childhood education is to provide exposure to different ways of learning. In the future this goal will require greater participation with technology and careful supervision, the one-to-one arrangement that can best be provided by families. Day care and preschool staff have many children to take care of; so they should not be expected to provide individualized instruction for Internet learning (U. S. Bureau of Labor Statistics, 2023). Parents should assume leadership for the initial online instruction to guide young children (Mayo Clinic Staff, 2023).

Caution About Credibility of Sources

Years ago, children were taught that they should believe everything adults told them. This advice is no longer reasonable and, in some cases, could be dangerous. Indeed, deciding what to believe has become a problem that is experienced by people in all age groups. Distinguishing truth from fiction is becoming increasingly more difficult because people are so often exposed to truth distortion. This challenge can be reduced somewhat by checking the origins of a website, background of sources offering information, date of posting, and verification by comparisons with messages from other sites. Searching, verifying, questioning, challenging, and discussing can contribute to better decision-making necessary to evaluate the worth of information presented online (Rideout & Katz, 2021).

Parent Guidance for Teaching

Development of the Search Process

Knowing how to locate desired information is a more important factor for thinking than to memorize information. Practice with the search process is essential to find out things a child wants to know. Conner, age 4, and his mother take turns daily choosing a topic to explore on the Internet. Today, Conner says that he wants to learn more about *dogs*. Some words mother enters for their mutual search are *dogs, puppies,* and *what do dogs eat?* In addition, she enters the words *breed, veterinarian,* and *kennel.* As Conner's mother generates additional search words, Conner becomes more aware of her extensive vocabulary, observes how important key words are to find out things you want to know, and provides more benefit when search words are further defined using additional descriptors like breed (collies, bulldogs, cocker spaniels) or kennel (place dogs are cared for while owners take a vacation or dogs stay while they wait for someone to adopt them). Helping children search while also building their vocabulary should be a goal that is linked with instruction. The reason adults should define words they use during a search is because these words are context relevant, making them key words.

Parents vary in the size of their vocabulary, enabling some of them to draw more connections and appropriate words, especially important for advanced Internet searching. Children learn that knowing words related to a topic they want to learn about is key to better searching. Later, as children grow older, their ability to locate information, organize it, and summarize results provides credible evidence of their problem-solving ability (Strom et al., 2023).

In the past, schools assigned higher priority to student memorization than to thinking (Restak, 2022). One reason was that, until recently, educators thought they knew with a high degree of certainty the knowledge that students would need to secure their future. Consequently, results of tests to evaluate learning were seen as the best predictors of success. Tests showed the extent to which students were able to recall lessons taught by teachers. Memorization was the primary measure of understanding and considered the best evidence of student comprehension.

New conditions of learning emerged when the Internet enabled students to be more self-directed and less dependent on direct instruction from adults. Because some knowledge students gain on their own from searching the Internet is bound to go beyond the content of lessons conveyed by teachers, and tests that measure only what is taught in the classroom can no longer be portrayed as an accurate estimate of student knowledge. Education cannot continue to be limited to the influence of teachers and the curriculum because more of what students learn takes place outside the school. This shift that enables students to govern more of their learning supports individual motivation and increases the amount of information they share as peer teachers. The change implicates revision of the teacher roles and expectations, so students can view their peers as helpful resources for learning and requires innovative formats to evaluate thinking and performance. Teachers should routinely give homework that calls on parents to act as essential sources of learning. Parents should realize their efforts to build healthy attitudes and skills regarding the Internet contributes to child development (Krznaric, 2020; Minkin & Horowitz, 2023).

Schedule Screen Time Carefully

Parents want to protect the health of their children. They recognize the need to limit child consumption of sugar, salt, soda, and exposure to sunlight. However, it is less common to think about screen time as a form of consumption. *Screen time* is defined as all activities that happen in front of a screen, such as watching television, playing electronic games, and using a computer or a mobile device (Auxier et al., 2020; Robertson, 2021). Research on screen time has consistently found that, when viewing time becomes excessive, this inhibits restorative sleep, contributes to attention deficits, encourages unhealthy snack habits, correlates with greater anxiety, depression, anger, and undermines learning (Heitner, 2023; Lauricella et al., 2015).

The Mayo Clinic Staff (2023) recommends that children younger than 18 months old not be allowed any screen time – yes, none. Children from 2–5-years of age should be allowed one hour a day of viewing restricted to high-quality programming, not allowed on the Internet by themselves, and no screens should be located in a child's bedroom. Bear in mind that unstructured playtime is more valuable for the developing brain than is electronic media. Children younger than 2 are more likely to learn when they interact and play with parents, siblings, and other children and adults (Abbott & Burkitt, 2023; Garvey, 2023).

How well do parents implement the guidelines recommended by pediatricians? Madigan et al. (2020) followed 2,440 mothers and their 2-year-olds to examine the prevalence of meeting and exceeding guidelines for screen time. Mothers kept track of how much time their children spent in front of television or computer screen and reported about developmental measures by answering questions about communication skills, behavior, and social interaction of children. Data were collected at the beginning when children were age 2 and again at ages 3 and 5. Results indicated that, on average, children spent 2–3 hours each day in front of screens. Children exposed to the most screen time performed the poorest on all developmental measures. Researchers concluded that parents should know that when a child is watching a screen, s/he is missing out on opportunities to be walking, talking, and engaging in pretend play with friends.

A separate study by McArthur et al. (2021) involved the same 2,440 mothers and their preschool children in the Madigan et al. (2020) research. Given the increasing consumption of digital media, the purpose was to find out if screen use influences offline enrichment activities such as reading and whether reading offsets screen use. The screen time of children and reading activities were assessed by maternal reports at ages 2, 3, and 5 years. Results showed greater child screen time at 2 years of age was associated with lower reading activities at 3 years ($p < .02$) of age. In turn, lower reading at three years was associated with more screen time at age 5 ($p < .02$). Early screen use was associated with less print book reading, resulting in greater screen use at later ages. Findings of these studies suggested that parents should read to children from books as the basis for literacy (Abrams, 2023).

Protection From Social Media Addiction

Students are expected to be at least 13 years old to participate on social media platforms. However, nearly half of 8–12-year-olds reported that they are also involved. Evidence continues to mount about the potential negative effects of this experience. In a longitudinal cohort study of 12–15-year-olds (n = 6,595), Riehm et al. (2019) found that students who spent more than three hours a day on social media doubled their risk of mental health problems that included the symptoms of depression, anxiety, lower self-esteem, and sleep dysfunction. Vivek Murthy (2023), Surgeon General of the United States, published an advisory titled Social Media and Youth Mental Health. Murthy (2024) also wrote an article in *The New York Times* urging Congress to approve the placing of warning labels on social media platforms. To support Murthy's proposal, the Attorney Generals from 43 states addressed members of Congress demanding action to inhibit how social media threatens youth safety. Legislation should protect young people from online harassment, abuse, exploitation, violence, and sexual content (American Psychological Association, 2023; Davis, 2023).

In November 2024, the Australian Parliament approved the world's first social media ban for youth under age 16. According to the law, tech companies could be fined a very large sum if they do not comply to the new law which is expected to go into effect in 2026. This delay time is needed so platforms can test and track ways to verify ages of users. There was strong support for this law shown by 77% of the population who are concerned about online harms to children. The results of the new law are expected to improve the mental health of youth. Australian Prime Minister Anthony Albanese stated, "Platforms now have a social responsibility to ensure the safety of our kids is a priority for them" (Kaye & Pal, 2024; Ritchie, 2024).

California enacted legislation in 2024 to protect youth from powerful addictive strategies tech companies rely on to keep users online (Austin, 2024; Freedberg, 2024). These addictive feeds are generated by automated systems, known as *algorithms*, meant to keep users engaged by suggesting content based on groups, friends, topics, or headlines they may have clicked in the past. The new law makes 'chronological feeds' the default setting for platforms. These feeds are generated only by posts from people they follow based on their order of upload.

Public schools in the United States and other countries have a mental health and safety obligation too. To illustrate, the Norwegian Education Act (§9 A-9) states that each school is responsible for providing a safe environment for children. Smartphone policies and related problems were analyzed by Abrahamsson (2024) utilizing middle school administrative survey data from 529 schools. Baseline data contained 161,371 pupil responses. Results showed that banning smartphones from schools significantly decreased the psychological symptoms among girls; post-ban bullying among both genders decreased also. Girls' academic performance improved and their likelihood of attending academic high school track increased. These effects were larger for girls from low socioeconomic backgrounds. The conclusion is that banning smartphones from schools could be a low-cost policy tool to improve student outcomes.

Parents should create phone-free zones around bedtime, meals, and social gatherings to safeguard child sleep. Moreover, they should wait until later than middle school to allow child participation on social media, a good reason parents should work together to establish shared rules and create healthy new family norms. In this way no family would have to struggle alone or feel guilty when their children complain that they are the only ones who must endure limitations. Youth can support one another, too, by reforming their relationship with social media and building sensible peer norms that avoid excessive time online and help one another transition from narcissism to online exploration experiences that can support the development of maturity.

Video Game Involvement

Video games appeal to a broad age range of users beginning with preschoolers. However, most gamers (70%) are adults (age 18 or older); the average gamer purchaser is 34 years old, owns a home, and is a parent. Most parents (70%) say video games have a positive influence on their child's life (Yanev, 2024). Video games are the most lucrative form of entertainment for the United States, generating more revenue than Hollywood films and the music industry combined (Mitic, 2023; Wolf & Perron, 2023).

Video games include the pleasure of team competition along with a sense of power and control, a place to go to satisfy the personal need to feel in charge. A study to detect stressful conditions experienced by 349 high school students included 172 females and 177 males. In response to a question of how students reduce their stress, 50.8% of males reported playing video games; only 13.4% of females reduced stress by playing video games (Strom et al., 2022).

Because most video games require players to select violent-type responses to score well, critics have questioned whether taking on the role of game characters could result in emotional desensitization about the effects of aggression in real life. Those who oppose video games worry they might encourage aggressive behavior in other sectors of living while also restricting the development of compassion, empathy, and concern for others. The link between exposure to video games and aggressive behavior remains a controversy. Wolf and Perron (2023) reported that video game use is associated with a decrease in prosocial behavior like congenial relationships, moral judgment, and concern for the well-being of others, essential for the development of empathy. These results are relevant for youth since their personality and moral character are being formed (Robertson, 2021; Yanev, 2024).

The good news is that video games specifically designed for young children such as the many LeapFrog products have been around for 20 years and exclude conflict situations, survival, or imitation of aggressive characters. Instead, they present fun tasks that motivate the entire family, provide teaching tools for parents, help children jump ahead in reading readiness activities, select healthy characters to aspire to be like, and practice other qualities of social and emotional development. The more than 2,000 LeapFrog games are categorized according to age, from early childhood, age 3 to 7 (Robertson, 2021).

The 'Shut Up' Toy

Parents consider mobile devices the most effective tools to quiet children, often referred to as 'the shut-up toy.' Mobile media provides multiple modalities of videos, games, and education apps with interactive capabilities. When a family goes to a public place such as a restaurant, their young child may show restlessness and perhaps start to cry. In such cases, parents often pull out their smartphone or media tablet and hand it to the preschooler who momentarily is focused on the app, game, or video. Parents consider mobile devices the most effective tools to quiet children. Visual entertainment from media apps such as Daniel Tiger's neighborhood can distract children from what might cause their fuss. This strategy is convenient in the short term to settle down children, but could it be detrimental later if this has been the main method to teach children about self-control?

Radesky et al. (2015) studied 144 parents of children from 15 to 36 months old to track the frequency with which parents used a smartphone or tablet to calm children down and keep them quiet during the day or at bedtime. Results showed that parents of toddlers who displayed the most difficult behavior were nearly three times more likely to hand them a device to get peace and quiet. In a related study, McDaniel and Radesky (2018) followed 183 couples of newborn children until they were age 5 years. Parents provided information about their child's behavior and reported how often they interrupted parent-child activities by picking up the mobile phone, watching television, or working on a laptop. Results revealed that the parents whose children were exhibiting bad behavior, such as tantrums, hitting, or yelling, showed increased stress and were more likely to turn to devices for relief or avoid confrontation with their child.

Technoference is defined as parent usage of technological devices that interfere with or interrupt everyday normal family relations and interactions including but not limited to face-to face conversations, mealtimes, and leisure time together (Mackay et al., 2022; Sundqvist et al., 2020). Furthermore, technoference also predicts greater behavior problems at a later age. One alternative is to look a child in the eyes when s/he is upset and try to be soothing and reassuring about being able to solve the problem. This approach can help children develop self-control, extend attention span, and lead to better organization of thinking (McDaniel, 2020; McDaniel & Radesky, 2017; Morris et al., 2022).

Radesky et al. (2023) encourage parents to recognize the importance of teaching about self-regulation. Results of their study showed that the use of mobile devices to calm children is associated with long-term difficulties in executive functioning (skills that implicate self-control) and being able to stay focused despite the presence of distractions. A cohort study involving 422 parents and 422 children determined that increased parent reliance on mobile devices to calm 3–5-year-olds is related to decreased executive functioning and increased emotional reactivity. These findings suggest that parent reliance on devices to distract their children should be avoided in favor of instruction about self-regulation of emotions and recognizing that parent overuse of technology that results in ignoring children is poor parenting. Boys and girls who do not learn self-control skills in early childhood are more likely to struggle when they experience additional stress in the school environment (Davis, 2023).

Evaluation of Learning Skills

Parents wonder how effective they are as teachers since they lack evaluative feedback from children. Numerous learning skills that can be identified by parents showing some lessons have been learned, detect deficiencies to focus further instruction, and identify feedback related to the outcomes of instruction should be available. When adults have evidence, their efforts have a favorable effect on child progress, and parent motivation increases for teaching with self-confidence.

Table 5.1 *Parent Observations of Child Internet Learning Skills*, devised by Strom and Strom (2024), is used by parents to evaluate young child learning skills. The left-hand column includes learning skills to be assessed. During occasional observations, parents can write notes in the right column beside the learning skills a child has demonstrated. Parents can enlarge the list to include additional items they want their child to learn.

Table 5.1 Parent Observations of Child Internet Learning Skills

Child Internet Learning Skills	Demonstrates Learning Skill
Asks questions that reflect curiosity	_____
Shows a willingness to keep on trying	_____
Talks about preferences and concerns	_____
Exhibits a sense of accomplishment	_____
Accepts challenges that are unfamiliar	_____
Listens carefully and follows directions	_____
Likes participation in repetitious activity	_____
Explains the difficulties of certain tasks	_____
Demonstrates the willingness to wait	_____
Makes guesses for experimentation	_____
Attention and concentration to a task	_____
Displays carefulness along with caution	_____
Reflects, takes time to make decisions	_____
Manages frustration without getting mad	_____
Views failure as an aspect of learning	_____
Requests help whenever it is needed	_____
Uses vocabulary terms of the Internet	_____
Predicts what is going to happen next	_____
Accepts time limits on the computer	_____
Recalls sequence of steps in a process	_____
Able to accurately interpret symbols	_____
Risks mistakes and accepts correction	_____
Summarizes a lesson that was learned	_____

Source: P. S. Strom and R. D. Strom (2024, p. 56).

Internet Safety Practices

Adults generally consider the Internet to be a wonderful resource but fear that exposure to unhealthy messages could endanger children. These fears decline in families where efforts are made to carry out the following practices to foster greater child safety (Davis, 2023; Oh, 2024).

Always Sit Beside a Child

Non-stop supervision is essential for guidance and protection of young children while on the computer. Most boys and girls ages 10 and younger do not possess the critical thinking skills that are needed to be online alone. Most 7-year-olds and older will disagree with this recommended age restriction, but parents should not relent. A good practice is to support child independence but only if adults are there to provide supervision. Generally, by age 10 a child can be allowed online alone.

Conversations About Privacy

Children know the frustration when peers intrude on their play space or fail to respect their wish to spend time alone. In contrast, children generally trust adults and rarely challenge their authority. Preschoolers should be told an important family rule is never share information about us with anyone outside the family. If a website parents believe is worthwhile invites children to submit their name(s) to personalize content, create an unrelated nickname (Oh, 2024).

Keep a List of Child's Favorite Websites

Restrict a child to the websites that the parent has approved and listed as favorites. Young children are dependent upon adult relatives to locate favorite websites. This practice allows a child to recognize that returning to familiar and safe Internet sites is easier when parents keep a word file on the desktop listing the preferred addresses to quickly access for a return to fun experiences.

Adult Supervision Is Always Necessary

Knowing whether certain situations are unsafe might not be evident to children. A child should be taught to always tell an adult if s/he has any doubts or worries about being online. When children are urged to share their concerns, adults can provide information needed to assess whether certain conditions pose a risk or require help. Respond to child reports by reinforcing positive statements such as "I am glad you told me about that situation because I would not have known otherwise." Software enables parents to block some inappropriate content and prevent requests for personal data. Besides being reliant on protective software, adult supervision is always necessary.

Encourage Questions About the Right Thing to Do

The decision of children to proceed with Internet responses by themselves should be based on certainty that parents would approve of the actions they choose. Inviting children to ask questions about the Internet should be continually encouraged as the right thing to do and represents the best procedure to gain greater knowledge that will ensure self-protection (Oh, 2024).

Social Networking for Young Children

Young children are not mature enough to engage with the social networks that interest adolescents, such as Snapchat, Instagram, Facebook, Twitter, and YouTube. Networks that motivate young children – such as Club Penguin, Webkinz, LeapFrog, and ABCmouse – compete for this growing market of young consumers (Heitner, 2023; Oh, 2024; Strom & Strom, 2020).

Internet Skills

Parents welcome insights about how to enrich child guidance online. The following guidelines can help define aspects of this important and complex responsibility for families.

Respect Child Desire for Repetition

Playing a game or repeatedly participating in any satisfying activity is more appealing to children than to adults. These repetitive experiences foster confidence that, in certain situations, children know in advance what is going to happen next. Being able to predict some things will remain the same as a daily schedule for meals and going to bed at the same time satisfies a need for order and consistency that is far stronger in early childhood than later stages.

Allow the Child to Use the Mouse

This experience allows a greater sense of control than watching a parent always be the sole control agent. Certainly, control by adults is easier for they can make the pace of events proceed more quickly. Nevertheless, sharing control in most situations is more helpful than constant dominance by an adult. Recognize that being able to move a mouse is difficult in the beginning, particularly since young children lack muscle control. Encourage their practice. Responses such as "You can do it," and "You did it correctly" are better to confirm progress than praises, such as "You are amazing," "You are awesome," or "You are really smart."

Following Directions Is Essential

Parents who read aloud directions that are given online and follow them present a far more effective method to get things done than resorting to random trial and error owing to their impatience. Children should be asked to explain directions in their own words to confirm their understanding about proper sequence of steps that should be taken (Abbott & Burkitt, 2023).

Asking Questions Is Part of Self-Directed Learning

When parents reveal their uncertainty by asking questions, children adopt this behavior to confront unfamiliar situations. Premature conclusions and impulsive responses can be prevented with questions that motivate reliance on reflective thinking. When the child asks a question that the adult is unable to answer, it is recommended to support curiosity and wonder by sometimes searching together to find out more about a particular topic on the Internet.

Schedule Unhurried and Uninterrupted Time

A comfortable pace for learning avoids feeling hurried and confirms the priority a child has in the parent's life. In the beginning, 15 minutes seems to be a good length of time for Internet visits together. Devote complete attention to the child; this means turning off all distractors such as a cell phone or other devices that could intrude and capture your attention.

Allow Child Time to Explore Possible Alternatives

Parents who develop this strategy support creative thinking and critical thinking. Having enough time to examine possibilities motivates children to learn the importance of deliberation as an essential aspect of the thinking process for reaching decisions about what they will do or say. In contrast, expecting rapid responses without giving time for reflection fosters impulsive behavior (Abraham, 2018; Strom & Strom, 2024).

Listen Carefully to Child Feelings and Opinions

This practice recognizes the value of curiosity and confirms for a child s/he has undivided attention. When adults multitask, try to do more than one thing at the same time such as texting on the cell phone and talking with a child, it is difficult to remain attentive, and distractions can cause grownups to miss comments made by a child. Boys and girls who feel repeatedly ignored often seek advice from peers who show greater willingness to listen (Levine, 2020).

Correct Mistakes to Motivate Continued Effort

Acknowledging failure is necessary because it helps identify learning needs and amend goals. Detection of failure should be followed by remedial instruction, urging further effort to increase success and provide feedback on progress. Persistence is needed to become competent and attain personal goals. Giving up when a task becomes difficult can avoid further mistakes but also prevent success that can follow the correction of behavior. Willingness to keep trying while also getting help is essential for achievement (Duckworth, 2018; Kellerman & Seligman, 2023).

Children Control Pace of Learning

The Internet allows users to return to a task, begin consideration of the task again, and retrace steps required in a sequence to solve some problems. In this way, Internet activities promote practice needed to build comprehension, problem-solving skills, and self-confidence.

Conclusion

A hundred years ago, parents and children read books together. As time passed, they were able to listen to the radio and still later watch television. Visits to the Internet can also become enjoyable as parents communicate their values during the stage when children are most inclined to adopt them. Getting children ready for the expectations of a digital environment means parents should provide a continuous orientation related to learning online and becoming self-directed. Technology encourages children to question, challenge, and disagree, behaviors that can increase their potential to become critical thinkers.

Day care and preschool staff are responsible for the safety of many immature children. This means their student-to-adult ratio is too high to offer one-to-one supervision children need to be on the Internet. Parents should take leadership for online learning at a time when children are easily directed to discovery tasks, search skills, and formation of attitudes to develop healthy social networking. As more children have Internet experiences, their potential grows. Elementary schools should help families of preschoolers prepare to meet digital readiness expectations by offering workshops on supervision, corrective feedback, safety practices, and encouragement.

Key Concepts

1. The Internet focus of young children should be mental processes that offer practice in creative and critical thinking. This may seem strange in the beginning because most adults suppose the mission of teachers is to communicate lessons students should memorize. However, greater learning emerges from respecting the interests of children in discovery and search skills.
2. Encouraging a child to navigate the mouse alone allows greater control than observing a parent always act as the sole control agent. Recognize that being able to move a mouse is difficult in the beginning, so practice is required. Responses like "You can do it" and "You did it correctly" are more suitable ways to confirm progress than reliance on praise.
3. When parents demonstrate uncertainty by asking questions, this behavior is usually adopted by children as the method they prefer to confront unfamiliar situations on the Internet. If a child asks a question the grownup cannot answer, support child curiosity and wonder by searching online together to find out some of what is known about the topic.
4. Day care workers and preschool staff typically must supervise many children. Therefore, it is unreasonable to expect them to provide one-to-one attention needed to offer instruction about the Internet. Parents are the teachers who should assume leadership for introducing children to the Internet and help them to eventually become self-directed learners.
5. Searching the Internet while also learning vocabulary are complementary goals. Parents should define the words they use during a search process because these words are context relevant, making them key words. As children get older, the ability to find information, organize it, and summarize results in a rational way is credible evidence of their problem-solving ability.
6. Video games for preschoolers such as the Leapfrog products avoid conflict situations, survival strategies, or imitation of aggressive characters. Instead, they present tasks that can motivate family involvement, provide teaching tools, help children with readiness skills for reading, select healthy characters to imitate, and practice healthy social and emotional attitudes.
7. Young children are self-centered and have few responsibilities, but they should be expected to remain in contact with older relatives, especially grandparents. This practice can begin with children dictating messages the parents send by email. Relatives want to learn from children about activities that excite them, worrisome situations, and opportunities they want to explore.
8. Always sit beside a child while s/he is doing anything on the computer. Before age 10, most children do not have critical thinking skills needed to be online alone. Generally, children will disagree with this assessment, but parents should not relent. They can support independence of children best when continual supervision is offered by the adults.
9. Children are inclined to trust grownups, so they rarely challenge the authority of adults. Young children should be told an important rule is to never share family information with anyone else online. If a website that parents feel is worthwhile invites children to submit their name to personalize content, use an unrelated nickname.

10. Playing a game repeatedly is often more appealing to children than to adults. These repetitive experiences provide confidence that, in some situations, children know in advance what will happen next. Being able to predict some things will remain the same as mealtime and going to bed satisfies a need for order and consistency that is far stronger during early childhood.

Generational Perspectives Activities

5.1 Discussion
5.2 Conversations With Young Children
5.3 A Scenario: Reasoning and Problem-Solving
5.4 Chapter Review
5.5 Parent and Grandparent Self-Evaluation
5.6 Storytelling

5.1 Discussion

1. Why should parents be the teachers to introduce preschoolers to knowledge about the Internet?
2. What aspects of a child's social development can be nurtured by instruction about the Internet?
3. How could the Internet enable parents to become more involved as educators of their children?
4. How should kindergarten readiness be redefined to include some Internet orientation at home?
5. How does teaching preschoolers on the Internet differ from traditional methods of instruction?
6. How will Internet learning that is acquired at home affect the school evaluation of knowledge?
7. How should homework for students include instructional tasks clearly defined for the parents?
8. Speculate about the motivational value of including self-directed learning for young children.
9. What amount of screen time have you established as the daily limitation for your children?
10. What challenges do you anticipate as you attempt to teach children about the Internet?

5.2 Conversations With Young Children

1. What are some favorite websites that you like to visit on the Internet?
2. What rules do parents want you to follow when you are on the Internet?
3. How much time each day do parents spend with you on the Internet?
4. How has the Internet been helpful in finding things you want to know?
5. How do you stay in contact with your grandparents on the Internet?
6. What dangers on the Internet have parents said that you must avoid?

7. How do you think your mom is doing teaching you about the Internet?
8. How do you like searching the Internet to learn what you want to know?
9. How do parents let you know they are pleased with your Internet learning?

5.3 A Scenario: Reasoning and Problem-Solving

Problem-solving scenarios present an opportunity to look at situations that might happen for a family and think about possible solutions. Your task is to look at pros and cons of choices that are stated, think of additional options, identify relevant information that might be missing, find out how teammates view options, and defend your reasoning on advice you consider best.

Richard is 6 years old and likes to play games on the Internet. When 20 minutes that parents have set for his daily limit have passed, Richard complains that his friends are given more time by their parents. What suggestions do you have for Richard's parents?

a. Do not cave in about the sensible time restriction you have established.
b. Explain to Richard that you want exercise to also be a priority for him.
c. Allow more time for games if Richard agrees he will stop crying about it.
d. Remind him about the possible dangers related to child media addiction.
e. Other _____

5.4 Chapter Review

1. What insights from the chapter will I try to apply in my relationships?
2. What is the most important key concept for me presented in this chapter?
3. Which elements of this chapter do I wish I had known about earlier?

5.5 Parent and Grandparent Self-Evaluation

Directions: For each question, place a check beside the statements that describe your feelings. You may want to give several answers on some items. If your feelings are not on the choices list, write them on the line marked 'Other.'

1. Introducing my child to the Internet

   a. is a task I accept and will try to do my best
   b. scares me because I do not feel prepared
   c. can be a learning experience for both of us
   d. should be expected of schools, not families
   e. Other _____

2. The biggest Internet problem I anticipate is

   a. making sure that my child is safe online
   b. being patient and allowing child exploration
   c. knowing the attitudes and skills to focus on
   d. conveying the importance of privacy and safety
   e. Other _____

3. I want to schedule time so my child

   a. does not spend too long a period on the computer
   b. is involved with regular physical exercise outside
   c. has time every day to also engage in solitary play
   d. dictates email messages to relatives that I will send
   e. Other _____

4. As an Internet teacher of my child, I hope to

   a. let my child explore while I watch
   b. provide correction and support self-confidence
   c. prevent distraction so I listen to child questions
   d. illustrate how learning from failure is necessary
   e. Other _____

5. My feeling about being an Internet teacher is

   a. having a one-to-one ratio for tutoring is necessary
   b. that it is a family obligation, not day care or preschool
   c. everyone in the family should help educate preschoolers
   d. healthy attitudes established at this early age will pay off
   e. Other _____

6. Readiness for kindergarten means families should recognize

   a. they alone have the teacher-child ratio needed to introduce the Internet
   b. there is a need to orient children to the Internet as a source of learning
   c. the Internet offers a basis for conversation to support mutual learning
   d. teaching letters and numbers is only part of the family responsibility
   e. Other _____

7. Families can take advantage of the childhood stage of *identification* by

   a. teaching attitudes and skills needed for communication on the Internet
   b. serving as mature examples for children about civil treatment of others
   c. providing feedback to children on their progress in social development
   d. illustrating the sense of caution necessary to ensure online safety
   e. Other _____

8. When I think about the amount of my child's screen time,

   a. I feel the family needs to guard against excessive viewing
   b. we all need to set an example of more balanced activities
   c. the need for physical exercise must become a daily activity
   d. being online or watching television prevents trouble
   e. Other _____

9. Keeping in touch with grandparents is an obligation that

   a. more parents should teach their children
   b. has not been well taught to children in our family
   c. I want to teach this obligation to my children

d. doesn't matter very much to me
e. Other _____

10. The importance of having safety rules online is a lesson

    a. I intend to reinforce continually to my children
    b. that won't matter much with increase in hacking
    c. my children should learn to value their safety
    d. schools should encourage for all students
    e. Other _____

5.6 Storytelling

Historically, storytelling has been a dominant classic and progressive method of teaching around the world. The purposes of a storyteller are to present imaginary or real-life examples showing how some concept applies to a particular situation. People like stories, they pay attention to the procession of events, and usually remember aspects of a story for a long time. Your stories can reinforce the concepts in this chapter for family members and classmates. Please share your stories with them.

References

Abbott, R., & Burkitt, E. (2023). *Child development and the brain: From embryo to adolescence* (2nd ed.). Policy Press.

Abraham, A. (2018). *The neuroscience of creativity*. Cambridge University Press.

Abrahamsson, S. (2024, February 22). *Smartphone bans, student outcomes and mental health.* NHH Department of Economics Discussion Paper No. 01. http://dx.doi.org/10.2139/ssrn.4735240

Abrams, Z. (2023, August 3). *Why young brains are especially vulnerable to social media*. American Psychological Association. https://www.apa.org/news/apa/2022/social-media-children-teens

American Psychological Association. (2023, May). *Health advisory on social media use in adolescence*. American Psychological Association. https://www.apa.org/topics/social-media-internet/health-advisory-adolescent-social-media-use.pdf

Austin, S. (2024, September 20). *California governor signs law to protect children from social media addiction.* https://apnews.com/article/california-social-media-addiction-children-law-bc649326701f892a16be1159bc008d71

Auxier, B., Anderson, M., Perrin, A., & Turner, E. (2020, July 28). *Parenting children in the age of screens*. Pew Research Center. https://www.pewresearch.org/internet/2020/07/28/parenting-children-in-the-age-of-screens/

Belsky, J., Caspi, A., Moffitt, T., & Poulton, R. (2020). *The origins of you: How childhood shapes later life*. Harvard University Press.

Cleese, J. (2020). *Creativity: A short and cheerful guide*. Crown.

Davis, K. (2023). *Technology's child: Digital media's role in the ages and stages of growing up*. The MIT Press.

Done, P. (2022). *The art of teaching children: All I learned from a lifetime in the classroom*. Simon & Schuster.

Duckworth, A. (2018). *Grit: The power of passion and perseverance*. Scribner.

Freedberg, L. (2024, September 23). *California acts to protect children from 'addictive' social media*. EdSource. https://edsource.org/2024/california-acts-to-protect-children-from-addictive-social-media/719340#:~:text=The%20bill%20will%20prohibit%20online,hours%20and%20late%20at%20night

Garvey, D. (2023). *Little brains matter (little minds matter)*. Routledge.

Goldberg, E. (2018). *Creativity: The human brain in the age of innovation*. Oxford University Press.

Haidt, J. (2024). *The anxious generation: How the great rewiring of childhood is causing an epidemic of mental illness.* Penguin.

Heitner, D. (2023). *Screenwise: Helping kids thrive (and survive) in their digital world* (2nd ed.). Routledge.

Kaye, B., & Pal, A. (2024, November 28). *A social media ban in Australia for children under 16 is first in the world.* The Associated Press/NPR. https://www.npr.org

Kellerman, G. R., & Seligman, M. (2023). *Tomorrowmind: Thriving at work with resilience, creativity, and connection – now and in an uncertain future.* Simon Element/Simon Acumen.

Khan, S. (2024). *Brave new words: How AI will revolutionize education (and why that's a good thing).* Viking.

Korhonen, V. (2024, July 5). *Number of children in the U.S. in 2022 by age group.* Statista. https://www.statista.com/statistics/457786/number-of-children-in-the-us-by-age/#statisticContainer

Krznaric, R. (2020). *The good ancestor: A radical prescription for long-term thinking.* The Experiment.

Lauricella, A., Wartella, E., & Rideout, V. (2015, January–February). Young children's screen time: The complex role of parent and child factors. *Journal of Applied Developmental Psychology, 36,* 11–17. https://doi.org/10.1016/j.appdev.2014.12.001

Levine, M. (2020). *Ready or not: Preparing our kids to thrive in an uncertain and rapidly changing world.* Harper.

Levitin, D. J. (2016). *A field guide to lies: Critical thinking with statistics and the scientific method.* Dutton.

Mackay, L. J., Komanchuk, J., Hayden, K. A., & Letourneau, N. (2022, March). Impacts of parent technoference on parent-child relationships and child health and developmental outcomes: A scoping review protocol. *Systematic Reviews, 11*(45). https://doi.org/10.1186/s13643-022-01918-3

Madigan, S., Racine, N., & Tough, S. (2020). Prevalence of preschoolers meeting vs exceeding screen time guidelines. *JAMA Pediatrics, 174*(1), 93–95. https://doi.org/10.1001/jamapediatrics.2019.4495

Mayo Clinic Staff. (2023). *Screen time and children: How to guide your child.* Children's Health. https://www.mayoclinic.org/healthy-lifestyle/childrens-health/in-depth/screen-time/art-20047952

McArthur, B., Browne, D., McDonald, S., Tough, S., & Madigan, S. (2021, June 1). Longitudinal associations between screen use and reading in preschool-aged children. *Pediatrics, 147*(6), e2020011429. https://doi.org/10.1542/peds.2020-011429

McDaniel, B. T. (2020, December 5). Technoference: Parent mobile device use and implications for children and parent-child relationships. *Zero to Three, 41*(2), 30–36. https://www.zerotothree.org/resource/technoference-parent-mobile-device-use-and-implications-for-children-and-parent-child-relationships/

McDaniel, B. T., & Radesky, J. S. (2017, May 10). Technoference: Parent distraction with technology and associations with child behavior problems. *Child Development, 89*(1), 100–109. https://doi.org/10.1111/cdev.12822

McDaniel, B. T., & Radesky, J. S. (2018, June 13). Technoference: Longitudinal associations between parent technology use, parenting stress, and child behavior problems. *Pediatric Research, 84,* 210–218. https://doi.org/10.1038/s41390-018-0052-6

Minkin, R., & Horowitz, J. M. (2023, January 24). *Parenting in America today.* Pew Research Center. https://www.pewresearch.org/social-trends/2023/01/24/parenting-in-america-today/

Mitic, I. (2023, July 4). *Video game industry revenue set for another record-breaking year.* https://fortunly.com/articles/video-game-industry-revenue/

Morris, A. J., Filippetti, M. L., & Rigato, S. (2022, March). The impact of parents' smartphone use on language development in young children. *Child Development Perspectives, 16*(2), 103–109. https://doi.org/10.1111/cdep.12449

Murthy, V. H. (2023). *Social media and youth mental health.* The U. S. Surgeon General's Advisory. https://www.hhs.gov/sites/default/files/sg-youth-mental-health-social-media-advisory.pdf

Murthy, V. H. (2024, June 17). Surgeon general: Why I'm calling for a warning label on social media platforms. *The New York Times.* https://www.nytimes.com/2024/06/17/opinion/social-media-health-warning.html

Oh, E. W. (2024, June 12). *Help kids practice smart internet habits and stay safe online.* Common Sense. https://www.commonsense.org/education/articles/23-great-lesson-plans-for-internet-safety

Radesky, J. S., Kaciroti, N., Weeks, H. M., Schaller, A., & Miller, A. L. (2023). Longitudinal associations between use of mobile devices for calming and emotional reactivity and executive functioning in children aged 3 to 5 years. *JAMA Pediatrics, 177*(1), 62–70. https://doi.org/10.1001/jamapediatrics.2022.4793

Radesky, J. S., Schumacher, J., & Zuckerman, B. (2015, January). Mobile and interactive media use by young children: The good, the bad, and the unknown. *Pediatrics, 135*(1), 1–3. https://doi.org/10.1542/peds.2014-2251

Restak, R. (2022). *The complete guide to memory: The science of strengthening your mind.* Skyhorse.

Rideout, V., & Katz, V. (2021). *Learning at home while under-connected.* Rutgers University.

Riehm, K. E., Feder, K. A., Tormohlen, K. N., Crum, R. M., Young, A. S., Green, K. M., Pacek, L. R., La Flair, L. N., & Mojtabai, R. (2019, September 11). Associations between time spent using social media and internalizing and externalizing problems among US Youth. *JAMA Psychiatry, 76*(12), 1266–1273. https://doi.org/10.1001/jamapsychiatry.2019.2325

Ritchie, H. (2024, November 28) Australia approved social media ban on under-16s. *BBC.* https://www.bbc.com/news/articles/c89vjj0lxx9o

Robertson, A. (2021). *Taming gaming: Guide your child to healthy video game habits.* Unbound.

Strom, R. D., & Strom, P. S. (2020). Learning throughout life about the needs of all generations: Recognizing and counteracting generational isolation. In M. London (Ed.), *The Oxford handbook of lifelong learning* (2nd ed., pp. 183–206). Oxford University Press.

Strom, P. S., Hendon, K., Strom, R. D., & Wang, C.-H. (2022). High school student stress and school improvement. *School Community Journal, 32*(2), 205–228. https://www.schoolcommunitynetwork.org/SCJ.aspx

Strom, P. S., Hendon, K., & Strom, R. D. (2023). Assessment of Internet learning for high school students. *Journal of Educational and Developmental Psychology, 13*(1), 17–28. https://doi.org/10.5539/jedp.v13n1p17

Strom, P. S., & Strom, R. D. (2024). *Mental health and relationships from early adulthood through old age.* Routledge.

Sundqvist, A., Heimann, M., & Koch, F. S. (2020, June). Relationship between family technoference and behavior problems in children aged 4–5 years. *Cyberpsychology, Behavior, and Social Network, 23*(6), 371–376. https://doi.org/10.1089/cyber.2019.0512

United States Bureau of Labor Statistics. (2023). *Occupational outlook handbook: Preschool teachers.* https://www.bls.gov/ooh/education-training-and-library/preschool-teachers.htm

Wolf, M. J. P., & Perron, B. (Eds.). (2023). *The Routledge companion to video game studies* (2nd ed.). Routledge.

Yanev, V. (2024, January 2). Video game demographics – who plays games in 2024? *Tech Jury.* https://techjury.net/blog/video-game-demographics/#gref

Chapter 6

Watching Television With Children and Asking Them Questions

More family conversation is possible when parents and their children watch television together. Asking questions allows everyone to express their own opinions, make known how characters are seen, interpret situations of a story, and stimulate expression of personal feelings, thoughts, values, and concerns. When parents emphasize asking questions as a way of learning, children are motivated to retain curiosity as an asset for finding solutions to problems. Children can also find out the things they want to know about by framing questions for the Internet.

The purposes of this chapter are to (a) explain how being a spectator encourages curiosity and creativity; (b) recognize that asking questions is an effective procedure for teaching and learning; (c) increase conversations to better understand child feelings, thoughts, hopes, and interpretations; (d) improve personal ability to be a more careful listener; and (e) establish a strategy for asking questions that can ensure mutual learning and satisfaction between children and their parents. Generational Perspectives Activities present topics to discuss with family members and close friends about watching television with children and asking them questions.

Family Challenges of Television

Most families spend more time watching television together than other leisure activities. Television presents three major challenges. First, parents must decide on the programs they will allow children to watch. Second, adults should encourage critical thinking by helping children interpret the messages communicated by media. Third, adult willingness to ask questions and listen to answers increases the prospect that children will continue to regard older relatives as valued sources of guidance (Garvey, 2023; Heitner, 2024; Holman, 2024).

Unstructured playtime is more valuable for a young child's brain development than is electronic media. Children younger than 2 are more likely to learn when they interact and play with parents, peers, and adults (Mayo Clinic Staff, 2024). At age 2 and older, children benefit from screen time that includes music, movement, and stories. When adults and children watch television together, everyone sees the same pictures and hears the same words. However, because parents and children have dissimilar backgrounds of experiences, they do not interpret media messages in the same manner and may reach different conclusions. These differences in perception mean there is much to gain when generations share their observations (Garvey, 2023; Heitner, 2024).

Questions to Stimulate Parent-Child Conversation

These open-ended questions can stimulate conversation. Consider two reminders. First, these questions are not meant to be presented in a particular sequence. Instead, parents should ask questions when they seem to fit events in a story or program the family watches together. Second, do not expect every question must be answered. Instead, focus on the questions you choose. The purposes and rationale of these open-ended questions are explained.

1. *How would you handle this situation? Purpose: Identify alternatives.*
   Being able to generate options is valuable at every age. Individuals who can see many possibilities in a single situation are more able to negotiate, get along with others, and identify solutions for problems. These strengths can help manage conflicts and preserve mental health. Sharing interpretations means everyone makes known the limitations of their individual thinking. This knowledge enables parents to gauge child comprehension and identify issues that require further instruction and practice.
2. *What do you suppose will happen next? Purpose: Anticipation of events.*
   Ask children to guess, think about it, imagine what is unseen, and express a futuristic perspective. Such an approach encourages children to talk more because there is no single correct answer for open-ended questions. This strategy also approves children expressing differences of opinion from older relatives. When parents become aware a child has created ideas the grownup was unable to generate, respect for child thinking increases. In addition, parents who ask guessing-type questions become comfortable admitting uncertainty and more willing to discuss topics for which they do not know a full range of appropriate answers.
3. *What parts of this program did you like most? Purpose: Expression of interest.*
   This question invites a statement of personal interest. An important condition for nurturing relationships is striving to remain aware of things that please or disappoint the other person and, in turn, make your choices and preferences understood. The mutual expression of likes and dislikes provides information needed to make sensible decisions about compromise and sacrifice. Sharing enjoyable experiences is the easiest context for dialogue.
4. *If you were a friend, how could you help? Purpose: Responding to needs.*
   Children should learn to care about others and be motivated to help when needed. The combination of loyalty, willingness to offer support, and ability to recognize when a friend needs help can be taught through conversation and example. Relatives benefit from telling each other about their friendship difficulties and methods relied on to maintain relationships. Children frequently ask for advice about how to preserve and build friendships while at the same time trying to establish independence. This topic arises early and is most prominent by age 8 or 9 when peer pressure becomes a strong force that influences all members of a peer group. Some parents tell children, "If some kids do not treat you right, forget about them and find new friends who will be nice to you." This advice suggests that withdrawal is the way to handle insensitivity of peers who, at this age, are most likely to participate in mistreatment. Children want to get along with classmates, even the ones who treat them poorly. They are eager to know how to transform difficult relationships to satisfying ones. When parents show they do not share a similar goal, they disqualify themselves as advisors preferred by children (Levine, 2020).

5. *What does* _____ *(a word you heard on television) mean? Purpose: Vocabulary development.* The building of vocabulary should be a lifelong goal and valuable for conversation with other generations. Some words on television cannot be understood by young children and should become a focus for questions. Adults are usually amazed at the number of words they could define that would otherwise remain unknown to children. There are also words children may understand that adults do not and can be shared while watching shows preferred by children. The most effective method of learning new words is in social context. Therefore, conversations that take place while watching television should augment the vocabulary lessons taught at school. This strategy calls on whomever is the more informed viewer to define words and bring new meaning for others who are watching.

We recommend that for a mutually selected program, everyone repeat aloud any words they do not understand when spoken by characters on an episode. At the end of the program share the meanings of identified words by looking them up and talking about them. Vocabulary is more easily acquired when words can be visually defined. For example, what is fairness? Go to YouTube and enter *Two Monkeys Were Paid Unequally* – to consider how obvious the concept of fairness becomes for you. Children learn the importance of this concept early and use it often in discussions with parents about equity.

6. *Do you think s/he is making the right decision? Purpose: Evaluation of judgment.*

The goal is to evaluate judgment about actions taken by a character on television. Parents want children to learn good judgment so they will be more able to avoid serious mistakes. Sometimes, harmful consequences happen before important lessons are learned. This is sometimes referred to as learning the hard way. By responding to stories on television that resemble real-life dilemmas, families can simulate predictable problems and explore the worth of individual judgment without experiencing disappointment or other undesirable consequences (Goldberg, 2018).

7. *What kind of person does s/he seem to be? Purpose: Assessment of character.* Parents want children to evaluate situations so they can decide on their own whether being with certain people is in their best interest. One way to learn to assess character is compare how an adult and child evaluate television characters early in a program and again at the end of an episode. Parents and grandparents may not always understand what is best, but children usually conclude adults have something of value to teach when it comes to knowing how to size up situations.

8. *What has happened in the story so far? Purpose: Sequence of events.*

The need to recognize sequence begins in early childhood, around ages 3 to 5. The purpose for learning to read is comprehension, understanding what has been read. This skill calls for more than memorizing the alphabet or recognizing words. Understanding the progression of events is necessary. In the books from which children learn to read, words are simple, and the storyline can be uneventful. In contrast, most television programs have a beginning, middle, and end. Television programs are well suited for teaching about sequence of events and are a valuable medium to improve comprehension (Haidt, 2024).

At the end of a program or while reading a children's book, ask your child to describe the main events that have taken place so far. This will enable you to figure out what was understood, details a child considered most important, and elements that were overlooked. These insights enable you to call attention to missing events or concepts. Urging children to summarize what they observe is a much more important skill than commonly recognized. Students with opportunities to practice summarizing become more able to describe ideas, feelings, and events in their own words (Borba, 2017).

9. *How do you want this story to end? Purpose: Explain the preferred ending.*

Expressing personal preferences is a way to make individual values known. Public polls report on opinions and priorities of grownups covering a variety of topics. However, the likes and dislikes of children and adolescents are seldom identified or considered by educators at school. Strom and Strom (2024) have developed and administered polls to secondary school students; the results indicate polling can improve school policies and practices. Polling allows students to be involved and contribute to making their school a better place for learning.

10. *What was learned from this situation? Purpose: Evaluation of learning.*

Television offers a chance to observe difficulties that others encounter and witness how they try to solve their problems. Parents and children can identify with issues portrayed by describing related events and struggles in their own lives. The most beneficial way to gain moral learning is in the role of an observer. If the misconduct of someone else is the focus of attention instead of our behavior, we are less defensive and more able to consider possible changes in personal conduct.

Talking with children about right and wrong decisions made by television characters can support learning. There is growing concern that the moral development of children is not keeping pace with the growth of mental abilities. One method of teaching morals that deserves consideration originated with the Ancient Greeks, who were provided their moral education at the theater. They realized that, unlike other forms of instruction, a theatrical production can hold people's attention and convey a profound influence. How does this reliance on the theater for moral education relate to the current society? Children are daily exposed to dramatic productions on television. Parents should take advantage of this appealing context by exploring child values and sharing their own during mutual televiewing (Belsky et al., 2023).

More Exploration of Primary Grade Child Thinking

Develop a justification for asking a child (ages 5–8 years) about the following concerns. The purpose of each question is provided in Table 6.1, but the motivation for asking will depend on your own rationale and anticipated benefits.

Table 6.1 Television Questions for Conversations With Children Ages 5 Through 8[*]

Questions to Ask Young Children About Television Programs	Purpose
1. What did you like about some character in the story?	*Perception of potential*: The child will see and talk about added possibilities because children are more optimistic.
2. Why did this person do what s/he did?	*Recognize motivation*: The child can identify the motivation of the characters.
3. How will that person's behavior affect others?	*Influence on others*: The child can recognize consequences of behavior.

(*Continued*)

Table 6.1 (Continued)

Questions to Ask Young Children About Television Programs	Purpose
4. How do you think that person should be punished?	*Scale consequences:* The child recognizes the difference between a little mistake and a big mistake.
5. Has anything like this ever happened to you?	*Identify similarities:* The child recognizes connections and relationships.
6. What choices does that person have in this story?	*Generate options:* The child can express alternatives in situations.
7. How are you like any of these people?	*Personal identification:* The child can move from egocentrism to empathy.
8. Why do you think that person made that decision?	*Evaluate goals:* The child can identify the obvious and the possible.
9. How do the people in this story differ from us?	*Note differences:* The child observes ways people are alike or different.
10. What is an important lesson in this story?	*Describe the main events:* The child talks about and understands the main message.

*Strom, P. (2024). Parents learn>parent questions. Auburn University. https://parentslearn.auburn.edu

Curiosity and Creativity

In describing himself, Albert Einstein (1879–1955) explained he did not have a special talent beyond a passionate curiosity. This observation suggests parents can promote creative thinking by encouraging curiosity in early childhood. Another icon who revealed clues about his own creative thinking was Leonardo Da Vinci (1452–1519). His scope of competencies included painting, sculpture, engineering, and anatomy. The core skill Da Vinci relied on was observation, as shown by the extensive notes and drawings he kept of nature and portraits of people he saw in Rome, Florence, and Milan, Italy. These examples of people recognized for extraordinary abilities reinforce the necessity for children to retain curiosity. This is especially important because the less people are self-absorbed, the more able they are to notice things beyond themselves. In Da Vinci's opinion, "Many people look, but few see – and mindful seeing is a foundation of experience, itself the base of direct knowledge" (Hoque & Baer, 2022).

The passion to figure things out shows the impact that curiosity has on initial motivation of children to learn. Yet, in only a few years, even before they complete the elementary grades, many students stop asking questions. What is it that happens between early childhood and the onset of adolescence that undermines interest in discovery of new knowledge, causes students to give up on exploring how the world works, and eliminates fascination about mysteries of the unknown? There are no answers that completely explain the reason for this common decline on such a grand scale. However, it seems clear that when someone ceases to be curious, s/he gives up the prospect of being a self-directed learner. The concept of self-directed learning should be a prominent education goal because of the Internet. One premise is that individuals are naturally curious and want to search for knowledge of interest to them while also developing academic skills that are needed by everyone. However, individuals who abandon curiosity are unlikely to continue a search for knowledge. Accordingly, preservation of child curiosity should be given high priority by families, schools, and the nation.

Restricting Time for Child Televiewing

In this social context, parents should recognize the importance of limiting the time that children are allowed to watch television. Landhuis et al. (2007) conducted a longitudinal study of 1,000 children at Dunedin University in New Zealand. Researchers found that children who watched the most television at ages 5 and 7 were more likely to show signs of attention deficit at ages 13 and 15. Attention deficits in adolescence were compared to the amount of time parents reported their children watched television at ages 5, 7, 9, and 11. Psychologists independently rated the children's attention span and ability to concentrate at ages 3 and 5.

Even after gender, cognitive ability, socioeconomic status, and amount of viewing time during adolescence were factored in, results showed that students who watched three or more hours of television per day between ages 5 and 11 had greater attention problems at ages 13 and 15 than their peers who watched two hour or less a day. Over a decade later, at age 26, children were reexamined. Robertson et al. (2013) found those who spent more time watching television in childhood and adolescence were significantly more likely to have a criminal conviction, diagnosis of antisocial disorder, and more aggressive traits compared to peers who saw less television.

Retention of Curiosity and Creativity

Families should recognize the need to help children keep their curiosity and creative behavior alive. E. Paul Torrance (1964, 1974, 2017), considered to be the 'Father of Creativity,' developed the *Torrance Tests of Creative Thinking*. Early in Torrance's research career on creativity, he recognized that children from all racial and economic backgrounds have creative potential. Professor Torrance's lifetime achievements were recorded by Garnet W. Millar (1995) in a book titled *E. Paul Torrance: "The Creativity Man", an authorized biography*. In addition, a helpful resource for educators has been provided by Alabbasi et al. (2022) regarding what they need to know about the *Torrance Test of Creative Thinking*. Longitudinal studies of the Torrance creativity tests include extensive work by Cramond et al. (2005) and Runco et al. (2010).

Kyung Hee Kim (2011), Professor of Educational Psychology at William and Mary University, completed a meta-analysis of all the articles on creativity and intelligence that were published between 1965 and 2005. Kim found a negligible relationship between creative thinking and intelligence, indicating that these two aspects of ability originate from a different realm of cognition. Kim hypothesized that if IQ scores are continually rising, referred to as the Flynn effect, then creativity might not be rising because research had confirmed their unrelated origins. Kim's (2019) studies found that creativity scores had risen steadily in a similar way as IQ scores, but progression for creativity ended in 1990. During the following two decades, creativity scores declined for all age ranges with kindergarten through sixth-grade students recording the greatest losses (Bronson & Merryman, 2014; Kim, 2024; Plucker, 2022).

Kim (2019, 2021, 2024) believes the foundation of creative thinking is expertise. Her reviews of studies determined not all Nobel Prize winners and other innovation thought leaders have high IQs. Instead, each had expertise within a specialized field. The foundation of creative thinking seems to be expertise that develops by devoting significant amounts of time to deep exploration. The way to value originality is to appreciate imaginative thinking. Individuals are unique in having imagination, a wonderful attribute that enables us to look beyond the moment and current circumstance. Imagination allows us to go back in time, revisit the past, look ahead, and envision ways to create a more desirable future.

No one can predict what is going to happen tomorrow, but actions motivated and shaped by imagination can influence what life will become. Mankind might be evolving biologically at a similar rate as other living organisms. However, according to de Waal (2016, 2022), people must change and adjust more rapidly. As far as we can tell the cats and dogs that we cherish are not changing socially at a corresponding rate. When left to themselves, they keep on doing what has always been their behavior and concern themselves with the same things as in the past. There is no need to keep checking up on them to find out what is new. Something will always be new for humanity because the imagination of people triggers creativity.

Parents and grandparents who teach young children should understand they can count on a valuable resource that will become less available in the upper elementary grades. Strom and Strom (2021b) explain that beginning students are eager to ask questions and suppose teachers know almost everything. No one understands what happens between early childhood and early adolescence (about age 10), but peer norms that emerge during middle school diminish the questioning that was a prominent student behavior a few years earlier. Recognize middle school students will do anything to avoid being seen as different from peers, so admitting ignorance by raising questions declines since it might result in being teased, ridiculed, and rejected. These peer norms inhibit creative thinking. Such norms are dysfunctional and should be a priority for replacement.

Evaluating Creativity of Parent Questions

Young children often introduce something they want to share by asking older relatives, "Guess what?" Unfortunately, most parents and grandparents do not respond as requested. Instead of generating hunches or speculating the adults commonly reply "What?" In effect, they make it known that guessing is not the method they prefer to learn something new. Instead, they choose to learn by being told. The seriousness of this mistake is typically overlooked. To explore some aspects of questioning, we observed the family play of 60 parents and their preschoolers (ages 3–6 years). A family fun jet, accompanied by colorful wooden passengers and their suitcases focused the play. Time sampling of interaction for each home was audio-recorded (Strom & Strom, 2021a, 2021b).

As a group, the parents asked over 800 questions. A close examination of the questions showed 57% were of a classification type. For example, "Where is the blue toy in the group?" Another 33% were descriptive questions. To illustrate, "How many of the airplane passengers are children?" Together, the classification- and description-type questions comprised 90% of the total parent questions. Every parent had expressed a desire to support creative thinking; yet less than 2% of the questions asked by parents invited the children to guess.

Hypothesis-type questions are open-ended and motivate children to go beyond what is directly seen and instead to imagine what is possible and acquire a positive outlook about the future. Hypothetical questions urge children to talk more, because there is not a single correct answer. For the same reason, these questions allow children to express differences from adult opinions. Parent questions should legitimize guessing because children like to practice creative thinking. Descriptive questions are also important, particularly when a teacher and students view things together on a field trip or in class. Questions can disclose what children see and what escapes their notice. By calling to their attention the details children do not see, teachers can provide a broader perspective. This is important for children in preschool and the primary grades whose perception is otherwise limited by *centration*, the term for being able to focus on only one aspect of a situation at a time, and *egocentrism*, the inability to consider the view of someone else.

Parents were disappointed with the analysis of their questions. They asked for help to improve their behavior. The guidance offered to parents is available for you on the Strom (2024) Website at Auburn University, Parents Learn https://parentslearn.auburn.edu and then click the tab *Parent Questions*. Here you will find 20 links containing 20 different pictures, each accompanied by six types of questions. The types of questions are (a) hypothesis, (b) classification, (c) comparison, (d) definition, (e) illustration, and (f) origin. Young children can be asked these questions by parents and grandparents. They will enjoy answering these questions, and you will gain insights about their mental capability.

Wait for Children to Respond to Questions

Waiting for children to respond is another factor to consider in asking them questions. Adults who undervalue the importance of deliberation often misjudge its silent process as being a sign of child misunderstanding. Consequently, often an adult tends to quickly amend questions or resorts to clues. However well-intended, efforts to motivate quick responses disrespect pace of thinking or what is called cognitive tempo. Children who have an impulsive tempo are inclined to act on first impressions without pausing to evaluate their merit. So they are prone to respond quickly but make more errors. Reflective tempo children take more time, and, because they think before they act, make less mistakes. Even though society declares reflective thinking is valued, children are expected to provide immediate answers to parent questions. Strom and Strom (2021b) observed that mothers waited a minimum of five seconds for their child to answer a question 60% of the time. Fathers, whose need for closure was higher, waited five seconds in only 40% of cases. In contrast, children were the most respectful of the deliberation process, waiting five seconds or more in 86% of the cases. Teachers should avoid inviting students to answer because they are the first to raise their hand. Delay selecting someone to provide an answer until the whole class has had sufficient time for reflection. A rush-oriented environment does not support healthy child thinking.

Conclusion

Parents and grandparents should monitor the content of television programs seen by children. Otherwise, children could be exposed to scenes involving sex intimacy or violence. Some of what children could watch is inappropriate because of age and unsuitability of subject matter. Parents should forbid watching some programs, even when children plead their friends are permitted to see them. Adult relatives can be comfortable when the role they give themselves goes beyond censorship to include responsibility for guidance, helping children interpret what they see.

By talking about what the family sees together, familiar topics and seldom-considered issues are shared. A continuing dialogue can help everyone know the opinions of others and share a broader outlook. Many parents and grandparents are disappointed that it is difficult for them to get the child to share thoughts and feelings. This is less often a problem when watching television – this can be a time to share together. Asking questions while seeing a program motivates self-disclosure, reveals how people view situations, and enables students to express feelings, thoughts, and values.

Presenting questions while watching television disturbs some adults in the beginning. They consider this behavior distracting and liken it to the conduct of others who make watching a movie at a theater disappointing. They believe observers should watch quietly to avoid interrupting the concentration of others. However, parents and children can easily follow a story and talk at the same time. Adults underestimate child capacity to manage two simple concurrent tasks. Adults also show this ability when watching television and reading a message that runs across the bottom of a screen. Children and parents readily keep up with the flow of content and can talk about changing events as they unfold. When parents and grandparents make this shift in habit, they experience the satisfaction of having children express themselves more. Adults also recognize the benefits of conversation are greater than the entertainment offered by a program. Seeking child opinions influences the amount of attention they pay to comments from adult relatives.

There is much to learn about using television to support thinking and observational skills. Parents should set new expectations for themselves that enable them to contribute to their child's education. Specifically, watch television together – this requires time. Next, ask questions during mutual observations – this takes practice. And, just as children are expected to express personal impressions, parents and grandparents should share their own experiences – this requires self-disclosure. Finally, children should select some of the programs the family watches, showing acceptance of child interests. When adults accept these expectations, they communicate more easily and establish themselves as a lasting source of guidance. If adults convey the importance of questions, their children are likely to adopt an attitude that helps retain curiosity so they can find solutions to problems throughout life.

Key Concepts

1. Adults who ask guessing-type questions approve of speculation and guessing. They become more comfortable with uncertainty and willing to discuss issues for which they may not know the full range of possible answers.
2. Children begin asking for parent advice about preserving and building friendships while also trying to establish independence. This topic arises early and becomes influential by 8 or 9 years of age when pressure from peers emerges as a strong force that implicates behavior of everyone in a peer group.
3. By reacting to televised versions of real-life dilemmas, families simulate predictable problems and can explore the merits of individual judgment without having to experience disappointment, embarrassment, or other undesirable consequences.
4. There can be benefit in comparing how an adult and child see characters at the beginning and end of a program. Adults may not always know best, but children usually conclude grownups have something of value to teach them in terms of being able to size up situations.
5. At the end of a program or when reading a children's book, ask the child to summarize the main events that have happened. You will learn what was understood, the details a child considered important, and elements that were overlooked.

6. The most beneficial way for children to acquire moral learning is in the role of an observer. When someone else's behavior is the focus of children's attention instead of their own conduct, they are less defensive and more able to consider making personal changes that are suitable.
7. Critical thinking should have high priority for education at home and the classroom because students must be prepared to distinguish between fact and opinion, determine quality of judgment, and evaluate reasons that govern decision-making.
8. During the past two decades creativity scores of students have declined, with kindergarten through sixth-grade students recording the greatest losses. This is worrisome because business leaders identify creative thinking as an important competence needed for the future.
9. Some of what children might watch on television is inappropriate because of their age and unacceptability of the subject matter. Parents should forbid children from seeing some programs, even when children plead that their friends are allowed to watch it.
10. Asking questions at the same time you observe a program with children motivates self-disclosure, reveals how individual family members interpret situations, and elicits feelings, thoughts, and values.

Generational Perspectives Activities

6.1 Discussion
6.2 Conversations With Young Children
6.3 A Scenario: Reasoning and Problem-Solving
6.4 Chapter Review
6.5 Parent and Grandparent Self-Evaluation
6.6 Storytelling

6.1 Discussion

Each team member answers one question.

1. What are some favorite television shows of children that you also enjoy?
2. What television programs do your children like you do not care to watch?
3. How do caregivers monitor the television viewing of your children?
4. What changes would you like in television viewing habits of children?
5. What are your impressions about the children's programs on television?
6. How do you feel about television commercials directed to children?
7. What are some benefits your children gain from watching television?
8. What are your favorite programs and why do you like watching them?
9. What programs are on television you do not want the children to watch?
10. How is speech of children influenced by being in day care or preschool?

6.2 Conversations With Young Children

1. What kinds of television programs do you dislike and choose not to watch?
2. What television programs do you and your parents like to watch together?

3. While watching television, what does your family talk about?
4. Who are some of the favorite characters you like to watch on television?
5. What are the cartoons you enjoy seeing more than any of the others?
6. What rules do parents have about programs you are not allowed to see?
7. How are Mom and Dad different from you in programs they like most?

6.3 A Scenario: Reasoning and Problem-Solving

Problem-solving scenarios present an opportunity to look at situations that might happen for a family and think about possible solutions. Your task is to look at the pros and cons of choices that are stated, think of additional options, identify relevant information that may be missing, find out how others view the alternatives, and defend your reasoning about the advice that you consider best. Grandparents can learn and teach while watching television with grandchildren. But a familiar problem is that many older adults do not recognize their potential for influence when they join children as spectators. How can reluctant grandparents be motivated to apply their creativity?

a. Use an agenda of questions while watching television with a child.
b. Identify and build skills that are essential for doing well in school.
c. Become an interpreter of story events and define vocabulary words.
d. Share personal failures like those portrayed by actors in programs.
e. Show you value asking questions as a way for children to learn more.
f. Other

6.4 Chapter Review

1. What insights from the chapter will I try to apply in my relationships?
2. What is the most important key concept for me presented in this chapter?
3. Which elements of this chapter do I wish I had known about earlier?

6.5 Parent and Grandparent Self-Evaluation

Directions: For each question, place a check beside statements that describe your feelings. You may want to give several answers on some items. If your feelings are not on the choices list, write them on the line marked 'Other.'

1. How could you improve your television viewing habits?

   a. spend less time watching television just for something to do
   b. plan better for what programs are worth watching
   c. concentrate more instead of channel switching
   d. turn television off when doing other things
   e. Other _____

2. In what ways does television contribute to your education?

   a. stimulates new ideas and interests for me
   b. helps me reduce the stress of everyday life
   c. keeps me informed about news of the day
   d. supports my involvement with imagination

e. causes me to be curious and ask questions
   f. Other _____

3. What methods can help children improve television viewing habits?

   a. limit the amount of time allowed for watching television
   b. parental censorship of the child's choice of programs
   c. observing good spectator behavior by family members
   d. media courses at school that include television literacy
   e. Other _____

4. When I watch television with my child,

   a. we mostly talk about other things
   b. we share interpretations of a show as we watch
   c. we pay attention but interact during commercials
   d. we mostly watch and don't interrupt the program
   e. Other _____

5. My views about watching television with a child

   a. have changed from being a spectator to learning together
   b. recognizes that asking questions is a way to inform us both
   c. is a context where each of us can share interpretations
   d. allows me a guidance role I did not previously recognize
   e. Other _____

6. Asking questions as a method to motivate curiosity

   a. is a procedure I will use to support creative thinking
   b. encourages my child to be a self-directed learner
   c. shows children that inquiry is basic for learning
   d. is a behavior I want to adopt for relating to children
   e. Other _____

7. Helping a child learn how to process failure is an important lesson that

   a. I can teach by drawing attention to failure of characters on television
   b. can be conveyed by revealing some of my own failures
   c. I feel is overlooked as many families deny failure experiences
   d. they learn from setbacks instead of becoming defensive
   e. Other _____

8. Waiting for children to respond after I ask a question

   a. allows an opportunity to reflect before giving a response
   b. is a behavior I should adopt instead of encouraging hurry
   c. lets them know I respect processing ideas before answering
   d. is a habit I must check myself on to contribute to thinking
   e. Other _____

9. My schedule of television shows I watch on a regular basis

   a. reflects a well-rounded selection of programs
   b. emphasizes domestic and international news

c. relates to sports, comedies, and documentaries
   d. features ballet, concerts, nature, and religion
   e. Other _____

6.6 Storytelling

Historically, storytelling has been a dominant classic and progressive method of teaching around the world. The purposes of a storyteller are to present imaginary or real-life examples showing how some concept applies to a particular situation. People like stories, they pay attention to the procession of events, and usually remember aspects of a story for a long time. Your stories can reinforce the concepts in this chapter for family members and classmates. Please share your stories with them.

References

Alabbasi, A. M. A., Paek, S. H., Kim, D., & Cramond, B. (2022, October 25). What do educators need to know about the Torrance tests of creative thinking: A comprehensive review. *Frontiers in Psychology, 13*, 1000385. https://doi.org/10.3389/fpsyg.2022.1000385

Belsky, J., Caspi, A., Moffitt, T., & Poulton, R. (2023). *The origins of you: How childhood shapes later life*. Harvard University Press.

Borba, M. (2017). *Unselfie: Why empathetic kids succeed in our all-about-me world*. Touchstone.

Bronson, P., & Merryman, A. (2014, January 23). The creativity crisis. *Newsweek*. https://www.newsweek.com/creativity-crisis-74665

Cramond, B., Matthews-Morgan, J., Bandalos, D., & Zuo, L. (2005). A report on the 40-year follow-up of the Torrance tests of creative thinking: Alive and well in the new millennium. *Gifted Child Quarterly, 49*, 283–291. https://doi.org/10.1177/001698620504900402

de Waal, F. (2016). *Are we smart enough to know how smart animals are?* W. W. Norton.

de Waal, F. (2022). *Different: Gender through the eyes of a primatologist*. W. W. Norton.

Garvey, D. (2023). *Little brains matter: A practical guide to brain development and neuroscience in early childhood*. Routledge.

Goldberg, E. (2018). *Creativity: The human brain in the age of innovation*. Oxford University Press.

Haidt, J. (2024). *The anxious generation: How the great rewiring of childhood is causing an epidemic of mental illness*. Penguin.

Heitner, D. (2024). *Screenwise: Helping kids thrive (and survive) in their digital world* (2nd ed.). Routledge.

Holman, C. (2024, August 20). The serious work that free play can do. *Bloomberg*. https://www.bloomberg.com/news/articles/2024-08-20/kids-need-room-for-risky-play-enter-the-adventure-playground

Hoque, F., & Baer, D. (2022). *Everything connects: Cultivating mindfulness, creativity, and innovation for long-term value* (2nd ed.). McGraw-Hill.

Kim, K. H. (2011). The creativity crisis: The decrease in creative thinking scores on the Torrance tests of creative thinking. *Creativity Research Journal, 23*(4), 285–295. https://doi.org/10.1080/10400419.2011.627805

Kim, K. H. (2019, May 8). Demystifying creativity: What creativity isn't and is? *Roeper Review, 41*(2), 119–128. https://doi.org/10.1080/02783193.2019.1585397

Kim, K. H. (2021, January 25). Creativity crisis update: America follows Asia in pursuing high test scores over learning. *Roeper Review, 43*(1), 21–41. https://doi.org/10.1080/02783193.2020.1840464

Kim, K. H. (2024). *Persistence: The key to creativity and innovation*. Idea to Value. https://www.ideatovalue.com/crea/khkim/2017/05/persistence-key-creativity-innovation/

Landhuis, C. E., Poulton, R., Welch, D., & Hancox, R. (2007, September). Does childhood television viewing lead to attention problems in adolescence? Results from a prospective longitudinal study. *Pediatrics, 120*(3), 532–537. https://doi.org/10.1542/peds.2007-0978

Levine, M. (2020). *Ready or not: Preparing out kids to thrive in an uncertain and rapidly changing world*. HarperCollins.
Mayo Clinic Staff. (2024). *Screen time and children: How to guide your child*. https://www.mayoclinic.org/healthy-lifestyle/childrens-health/in-depth/screen-time/art-20047952
Millar, G. (1995). *E. Paul Torrance: "The Creativity Man", an authorized biography*. Ablex Publishing.
Plucker, J. A. (Ed.). (2022). *Creativity and innovation: Theory, research, and practice* (2nd ed.). Routledge.
Robertson, L. A., McAnally, H., & Hancox, R. (2013, March). Childhood and adolescent televiewing and antisocial behavior in early adulthood. *Pediatrics, 131*(3), 439–446. https://doi.org/10.1542/peds.2012-1582
Runco, M. A., Millar, G., Acar, S., & Cramond, B. (2010). Torrance tests of creative thinking as predictors of personal and public achievement: A fifty-year follow-up. *Creativity Research Journal, 22*(4), 361–368. https://doi.org/10.1080/10400419.2010.523393
Strom, P. S., & Strom, R. D. (2021a). *Adolescents in the Internet age: A team learning and teaching perspective* (3rd ed.). Information Age.
Strom, R. D., & Strom, P. S. (2021b). Learning throughout life about needs of all generations: Recognizing and counteracting generational isolation. In M. London (Ed.), *The Oxford handbook of lifelong learning* (2nd ed., pp. 183–206). Oxford University Press.
Strom, P. S. (2024). *Parents learn>Parent questions*. Auburn University. https://parentslearn.auburn.edu
Strom, P. S., & Strom, R. D. (2024). *Polling student voices for school improvement: A guide for educational leaders* (2nd ed.). Information Age.
Torrance, E. P. (1964). Identifying the creatively gifted among economically and culturally disadvantaged children. *Gifted Child Quarterly, 8*(4), 171–176. https://doi.org/10.1177/001698626400800401
Torrance, E. P. (1974). *Torrance tests of creative thinking*. Scholastic Testing Service.
Torrance, E. P. (2017). *Torrance test of creative thinking: Norms technical manual, figural streamlined forms A & B*. Scholastic Testing Service.

Chapter 7
Child Thinking and Cognitive Development

Historically, teachers have been expected to provide most of the knowledge students will need for success. However, the Internet has altered the conditions of learning that favor helping students think for themselves, become less dependent on direct teacher instruction, and share what they learn independently with peers. Insights from neuroscience on brain functioning urge schools to consider adding thinking as a new basic subject to join a customary focus on reading, mathematics, and science. Students who acquire these skills can find information by searching the Internet, process and organize data from multiple sources, generate creative and practical ideas, convey ideas with people across generations and distances, and collaborate with peers in teams. These abilities enable students to adapt to shifts in technology and social media. The present situation is better understood by recognizing how previous efforts are linked to contemporary conditions of learning. The purposes of this chapter are to (a) examine intelligence as a quantitative concept, (b) consider intelligence in terms of qualitative levels for thinking, (c) describe the potential and limitations of thinking during childhood, and (d) identify appropriate expectations for tasks in the classroom, at home, and the community. Generational Perspectives Activities present topics to discuss with family members and close friends about child thinking and cognitive development.

Why Start School Early

The American inclination to push children and introduce them ever earlier to academic expectations is illustrated by a story about Jean Piaget (1896–1980), the Swiss psychologist whose influence on child development is unmatched (Piaget, 1954). Even today, much of his work remains in our school curriculum decisions. After a lecture at Harvard University, Piaget consented to reflect on his experiences in the United States. A newspaper reporter began questioning Piaget, "Is it true, as Harvard Professor Jerome Bruner (1960/1976) asserts, that if we try hard enough, we can teach almost any child at any age to do almost any task in some reasonable way?" Piaget's short reply was, "Only an American would ask." In his later writings Piaget (1963, 1969) called this 'The American Question.' Let's assume Piaget is correct in doubting the appropriateness of our academic expectations for young children. In that case, the guiding question changes from "What can children learn?" to "What kinds of learning are best in early childhood?"

This shift in concern is overdue according to former kindergarten teachers whose disappointing experience with forcing academic goals led many of them to seek a reassignment for teaching at a higher grade level. For parents the answer to our question is a recommendation. To enroll your child in kindergarten at the earliest age might be a good idea if the experiences provided there include a generous portion of time for play, conversation, and expression of curiosity. If such experiences are not available, then the child is better off at home with the family, in a socially oriented preschool or with a caregiver who respects imagination and will accept the child's preference for learning through play (Dearing & Farran, 2022).

Intelligence and Thinking

People might suppose that educators and psychologists would have agreed on the meaning of intelligence a long time ago. Even though many definitions of intelligence have been proposed, none have universal acceptance. The reason is because no intelligence test measures the full range of known mental abilities. Nevertheless, student scores on intelligence tests and achievement measures greatly influence how they are perceived by educators. The way students are classified, by ability and achievement, impacts decisions about their placement for instruction, whether they qualify for regular classes, special education, or gifted and talented acceleration (Abbott & Burkitt, 2023; Ginsburg & Opper, 1987).

Quantitative Assessment of Intelligence

Education officials in Paris, France, were uncertain about how they could identify students who lacked sufficient mental ability to benefit from classroom instruction. Alfred Binet (1857–1911) was commissioned to develop a screening test that would detect mental deficiencies. The inventory Binet (1916) devised in 1904 was the world's first measure of intelligence. He found that a good test item is solved more readily as students become older. Therefore, he arranged test items based on the age when about 50% of students could perform them correctly. This allowed the most capable students to differentiate themselves. The same method of test item selection continues as standard practice for achievement testing. Lewis M. Terman (1877–1956) of Stanford University devised a related measure he named the Stanford-Binet Intelligence Scale to credit Binet as the originator. The Stanford-Binet is still administered to individuals by school psychologists when a faculty considers it necessary to evaluate the ability of a student to learn in a regular classroom (Terman, 1916/2007; Roid, 2005). An alternative source of assessment is the Wechsler Preschool and Primary Scale of Intelligence (Park & Demakis, 2020).

Qualitative Differences in Thinking

Jean Piaget was the first to explore how children think and observe the ways they process information to be able to interpret their environment. During the 1920s, Piaget was employed to work on test development. His tasks required using standardized measurement tools until three observations caused him to take a different path for assessing mental abilities. First, instead of identifying correct answers of students, the most common method applied to examine student responses, Piaget inspected the incorrect responses to detect limitations students of the same age had in common. He concluded the way older children think is qualitatively different from younger children. This decision led Piaget (1954, 1963, 1969, 2001; Miller, 2016; Piaget & Inhelder, 1972) to abandon his search for a quantitative measure of intelligence.

A second observation led to a novel technique to study intelligence. Some strategy was needed to give interviewers more freedom than the methods required in standardized testing. Besides having students answer questions as best as they could, Piaget had them manipulate objects that credited actions as evidence of thinking instead of demonstrating knowledge only by using words (Piaget, 1963). Years later, it was found that verbal facility is generally greater among students from higher-income families (Eysenck, 2022).

A third way Piaget (1969) departed from other childhood researchers was his recognition that the way for schools to educate students is to provide a curriculum they comprehend at their current level of thinking. His terminology is important for understanding information processing. Piaget used the term *schemas* to describe how children make sense of their experiences. Schemas are temporary cognitive structures that govern how information is processed and situations are organized. As students encounter unfamiliar experiences, their schemas must either enlarge or change to allow for adjustment (Piaget, 1963).

Information Processing of Children

Piaget's theory described the way students develop their own meaning for events based upon personal experience. Initially, teachers resisted the idea that students could learn on their own and felt this notion depreciated their classroom function. The emergence of the Internet has further justified Piaget's views.

Elements of Schema Adjustment

According to Piaget and Inhelder (1972), everyone relies on two methods for information processing. First, the *assimilation* process requires integration of new conceptual, perceptual, or motor information into already existing schemas. To illustrate, Don is a first-time visitor to the French Impressionist Exhibition at the Metropolitan Museum of Art in New York City. Before coming to the museum Don has looked at many magazines with pictures by Monet and Van Gogh. During Don's observation at the museum, his *Impressionist art schema* must expand to include art that has been produced by Manet, Toulouse-Lautrec, Cezanne, Gauguin, Seurat, Sisley, and Matisse – all artists of the late nineteenth century who explored visual analysis of color and light. Assimilation enlarges the size of a schema, as in Don's case, but does not result in a schema change.

A second process relied on for adaptation is *accommodation* that requires alteration or replacement of a schema so novel conditions can be accepted (Piaget & Inhelder, 1972). When Don left the Impressionist gallery, he took the elevator to the next higher floor of the museum where the modern art is located. In this new context, Don was obliged to accept a different set of criteria to appreciate the work of abstract expressionists whose representations are more symbolic than literal. This artistic group includes icons such as Braque, Picasso, Calder, Kandinsky, Miro, Nevelson, and Pollock. The schema Don relied on to enjoy *Impressionism* did not enable him to appreciate *Modern Art*, so a new schema had to be adopted. Imbalance between the familiar and novel creates tension until new categories are formed (Pulaski, 1980).

Self-Organized Learning Environment

Sugata Mitra (1952–) is a computer scientist and educational innovator from India who has become a worldwide leader in cyber constructivism. His original focus of research on peer-oriented teaching and learning methods emphasizes the view that students can learn best when they work together (Mitra, 2003, 2013, 2015, 2018, 2019). Mitra's theory of child learning describes how students can build their own knowledge, rely on the computer as a main source of information, and recognize the potential of peers whose similar experiences motivate them to work in cooperative teams to solve complex problems. His first experiment involved children being given free access to a computer embedded in a wall between his office and a New Delhi slum. Mitra's experiments demonstrated that groups of kids could learn to navigate computers and the Internet by themselves. Research has continued to support his initial observations that groups of children, with access to the Internet, can learn almost anything by themselves. His emphasis on peer support using technology led him to conclude that public schools should be reformed to prepare students for a better future.

Piaget's Stages of Cognition

Parents and grandparents should recognize progressive changes in the way normal children view and interpret situations as they grow older. This knowledge helps establish reasonable expectations for child thinking and schoolwork, prevents imposition of undue stress, and takes advantage of opportunities for growth. Piaget (1963; Piaget & Inhelder, 1972) discovered mental abilities emerge in a predictable sequence, in stages roughly associated with chronological age. One stage is called *preoperational*, referring to thinking from ages 2 to 6, before children develop logic.

Thinking of Preschoolers

The elements of preoperational thinking for two–six-year-old children are shown in Table 7.1. An explanation for each of the thinking abilities follows Table 7.1.

Language. Meaningful words people outside the family can understand are initially spoken by infants around 12 months of age. Most words acquired between ages 1 and 2 years identify a child's favorite objects or *situations* such as doggie, cookie, milk, and toys. Some two-word phrases like 'all gone,' 'big truck,' and 'more water' become evident. The basic information is there but verbs are not. During the third year the number of words children comprehend increases to nearly a thousand. The vocabulary children understand is far larger than their spoken vocabulary. At this age they experiment with three- and four-word

Table 7.1 Piaget's Preoperational Thinking Stage of Young Children*

Ages	Thinking Abilities	Achievements and Limitations
2 to 6	Language	Speech is becoming socialized
	Classification	Organizes using a single factor
	Perception	Judgment is based on senses
	Centration	Focuses on one aspect at a time
	Egocentrism	Unaware of how others see things

*Adapted from J. Piaget, 1969. *Psychology of Intelligence*. Littlefield, Adams.

sentences like "I want more milk." A typical 4-year-old asks 300 questions a day, leading parents to temporarily feel omniscient. Four-year-olds begin to grasp rules of grammar but falsely suppose they are consistent. So they sometimes say things parents consider funny and awkward like, "Mama telled me," or "I drinked my milk." At age 5, most irregular verbs of grammar are in place, and by age 6 all the letter sounds including *s*, *r*, and *th* can be spoken (even by those who lisp). First graders are capable of conversation with any age group.

Young children are more likely to have poor speech models than during the past. This is because they spend more time with their peers in day care settings. A far higher rate of maternal employment changed interactive conditions. Because language is learned mostly through imitation, children in group care or preschool naturally copy speech of immature peers and reinforce poor communication habits.

Classification. The ability to classify is necessary to organize things and to solve problems. Preschoolers can sort objects into groups based on a single factor like color, size, or function. Limitations can also be recognized. When four-year-olds are asked whether there are more boys or children in their preschool class, they say "there are more boys than girls." This response shows a lack of understanding that a person can belong to two groups at the same time. This will not be a difficult task to understand by age 7, when children recognize Gregory classifies as a boy and a child. In one day, preschoolers can see a few short, tall, thin, and fat Santa Clauses at different shopping malls yet not have their belief about Santa shaken because they consider every Santa Claus to be one and the same.

Perception. Preschoolers rely on sight more than they can on the ability to reason, and so they can be easily misled by problems of conservation. The term *conservation* means that unless something is added or taken away from an object, quantitative aspects of that object remain the same despite changes that might occur in appearance. Consider the conservation of substance. Before age 6 a child will observe that two balls of clay are of equal size and then, several moments later, declare the piece that they have just seen transformed into a long, thin strip has more clay than the ball-shaped clay. In a similar way, preschoolers believe the same amount of liquid is greater when in a tall, narrow glass than when in a short, wide container.

Centration. Failure to understand conservation of volume attributes to another limitation of thinking in early childhood. Centration limits attention to only one aspect of a situation at a time. Thus, the preschooler tends to focus on either height or width of a container and fails to notice the other also changes in a compensating way, so the volume remains the same. Centration is also evident while watching television, as a child misses some things that are noticed by adults. Grownups can enlarge the scope of what children see by asking questions that draw attention to details they would otherwise overlook. When parents realize children can focus on only one thing at a time, the directions they are given should be simple, clear, and repeated as often as necessary.

By age 6 some children attain the concept of conservation, but by age 7 one-third of students still have not acquired the concept. Even by age 10, there may be 15% of children who do not comprehend that quantity remains the same regardless of altered appearance (Piaget, 1969). This means it is probable that slow learning children do not understand school assignments but simply go through the motions when given rote tasks that involve habit and repetition. Instruction can go beyond a child's level of thinking, so s/he counts and writes without grasping lessons. This is why tutoring is important and can lead to higher achievement.

Egocentrism. The thinking of preschoolers is limited by *egocentrism*. This is not a derogatory term; instead, it describes an excessive reliance on personal views with a consequent inability to be objective. Egocentric people of all ages find it difficult to understand how anyone can look at things from a different perspective than their own. Therefore, in their mind, they are always right. This outlook ensures there will be continuous conflict in day care centers, preschools, and other childhood group settings.

Egocentric children lack the ability to distinguish between their own views and views of someone else. A preschooler may shake his head indicating yes or no while on a cell phone as if the caller who may be many miles away can observe these gestures. First-grade teachers report that when a child is at the front desk speaking to her, another student may come and begin a conversation, disregarding the other child who is talking at the same time. A mother complains, "When I try to get Michelle ready in the morning, she dresses slowly and does not understand the urgency for me to get to work on time." It is this insensitivity that adults try to banish when they urge children to show empathy for playmates who are crying or feel left out. However, young children are unable to demonstrate desirable qualities beyond their level of maturity.

Nearly half the speech of preschoolers is egocentric (Singer & Revenson, 1997). Collective monologues can be observed in situations where children are expected to engage in a similar activity. Each describes what they are doing, but none seem to listen to others. Everyone is talking aloud to themselves in front of their peers. The same behavior can be seen in the backyard as young children are engaged in parallel play. Most kindergartners and first graders are egocentric, so they need help to enlarge their perspective. These students can benefit from daily dramatic play requiring role taking, identifying alternatives, and listening to others share their feelings. Such activities are better for developing empathy than urging children to feel guilty for being self-centered.

Adults view child egocentrism as a selfish behavior that presents inconvenience to caregivers. While this assessment is accurate, it is important to realize egocentrism also makes young children (ages 2–7) more vulnerable to experiences of family crisis. For example, children who are mistreated seldom recognize lack of self-control by an abusive adult is the cause of their harm. Instead, they are likely to feel at fault, to interpret a spanking as something that must have been deserved. This inclination to credit self as the cause of most events can also account for young children feeling they are the reason for parent separation or divorce, even though the adults have told them, "It was not your fault." Because there is a potential for crisis in any family, children should be urged to share feelings and talk about things that bother them.

Thinking of Students in Primary School

Table 7.2 shows Piaget's Concrete Operational Stage of Thinking for children of ages 6–11. During this stage, thinking is restricted to direct experience or tangible materials because students are unable to solve abstract problems.

Reversibility. The most important mental ability that differentiates elementary students from preschoolers is reversibility. Having the capacity to carry thought backward as well as forward is a requirement for arithmetic reasoning because addition and subtraction are the same operation carried out in opposite directions. Second graders can learn that 4 + an unknown number = 7 and use reversibility to find out the answer (7 − 4 = the unknown). As early as third-grade children can play the hand bean game in which a student counts

Table 7.2 Piaget's Concrete Operational Thinking Ages 6 to 11*

Concrete Operations	
6 to 11 Years Old	Achievements and Limitations
Reversibility	Carries thought forward and backward
Logic	Solves problems on tangible things or involving familiar situations
Decentration	Attends to several aspects of a problem at once
Classification	Uses multiple factors to organize or categorize; class inclusion
Seriation	Arranges things in order by sequence or according to some quantitative aspect

*Adapted from Piaget, J. (1969). *Psychology of Intelligence.* Littlefield, Adams.

out a required number of beans. The teacher puts these beans in both her hands. Then she closes one hand, hiding some of the beans while opening the other hand to show beans that are there. Regardless of the bean combinations, children know the total will always be the same. This is not magic but reversibility. When faced with a liquid conservation task where children must judge whether a tall slender vessel contains more liquid than a wide short container, elementary students are able to rely on reversibility by pouring the liquid back into the original container to see whether the two quantities take up the same amount of space. In this way they try to solve problems by retracing conclusions.

The concepts of reversibility and conservation take on additional meaning as children mature. In the upper elementary grades (4–6), students apply reasoning to specific problems. When faced with a discrepancy between thought and perception as in conservation tasks, they make logical decisions instead of perceptual (based on appearance) decisions. As students acquire logic they move away from egocentric thinking toward greater objectivity. They no longer perceive the world exclusively from their own view and become capable of looking at situations from the perspective of others. When this ability is exhibited with regularity, typically by age 9 or 10, children are ready to shift from doing schoolwork alone to also working in small cooperative teams and develop teamwork skills needed for success in the workplace and at home.

Logic. Beginning logic becomes more evident as students can solve story problems in mathematics by choosing the right arithmetic process to apply instead of computing answers by rote or asking the teacher for direction on how to proceed. By fourth grade (age 9), students learn to figure percentages and can understand that parts of an object make a whole. Fifth graders are expected to predict story endings. Logic is needed for this activity because the ending is a rational extension of events that have been presented.

Decentration. The ability to decenter, focus on more than one aspect of a situation at a time, is observed during play. 'Battleship' has long been a favorite table game with an electronic version calling for locating and destroying enemy ships. Players find their opponent by guessing and deduction using board grid numbers and letters in combination such as B6 or G4. Children can recite numbers and letters before third grade but usually cannot handle them simultaneously. This is why the package in which this board games come indicates a recommended mental age (not chronological age). For Battleship, a mental age of 8 is the suggested minimum for players. Often, adults want to play games like Monopoly with children well before the age children are ready to participate.

When seven-year-old Kathy plays checkers, she knows positions for each of her pieces. Because she can focus on more than one set of circumstances, Kathy can devise a strategy for winning the game. Playing the piano or another musical instrument also calls for decentration, as the musician must pay attention to several aspects of a situation, including reading of notes and taking the timing into account.

Classification. As children move ahead in the elementary grades, they improve in ability to classify objects and events. When second graders are given eight pictures of animals that contain slight differences, most students can identify two pictures that are alike. An increasing need for competence in this connection is tested by assignments at school, such as recognizing vowels in a word, deciding whether each has a short or long vowel sound, and determining which ones are silent. By the third grade, students learn to group animals into classes such as mammals and reptiles. Fifth graders can subdivide by classes and tell which numbers are divisible by 5 (out of, e.g., 15, 19, 12, or 20) and which numbers are divisible by 3 (e.g., 15, 19, 21, or 33).

Seriation. Primary school students can seriate. In reading they may be expected to examine separate events in a story and place them in proper sequence or arrange pictures in correct order. Third graders have learned to place groups of five words that all begin with the same letter into alphabetical order. They can apply the seriation concept of 'more' and 'less' and the symbols for 'greater than' (>) and 'less than' (<) when comparing groups of numbers. When asked to seriate the states by size, as determined by square miles, they correctly indicate Alaska is biggest, then Texas, and California.

Tutoring, Home Schooling, and Mental Health

Tutoring allows the ability of an individual rather than cognitive level of the peer group to become the focus for instruction. The benefits of one-on-one tutoring have been confirmed by the majority of peer-reviewed studies (Ray, 2024). Overall, 78% (35 of 45 independent studies) reported by the *Journal of School Choice* found that home-schooled students performed significantly better than peers from public schools in academic achievement, social and emotional development, and success into adulthood including at college or university.

The United States Census Bureau (2024) *Household Pulse Survey: Measuring Emergent Social and Economic Matters Facing U.S. Households* reported that, as of 2023, 85% of students are enrolled in public schools, 9.6% of them attend private schools, and 5.4% are home schooled. Parents of home-schooled young children often rely on free lessons available online at *Khan Academy Kids* (2024) [ages 2–8] that represent multiple levels of ability. Parents are not surprised that home-schooled students outperform peers because they have an ideal student-teacher ratio to detect errors and are able to follow-up immediately with correction to a greater degree than classroom educators working with groups. Parents often need greater confidence in their ability to teach children and to learn from them (The Connection Academy, 2022; Hattenstone & Lawrie, 2021; Jacobs & Jack, 2024; Ray, 2024; Weaver, 2022).

Conclusion

Intelligence testing, originated by Alfred Binet in France, is the main method used to assess mental deficiency for decisions about student placement at school in special education. The determination of readiness for learning also implicates the level of cognitive development students should be expected to perform at different ages. Jean Piaget's qualitative view of intelligence has been the dominant influence on curriculum that corresponds with student stages of thinking. His orientation emphasized that individuals build their own knowledge instead of limiting learning to what they are told by the teacher.

The main reason for Piaget's continued eminent standing in developmental learning and practice is because his methods to evaluate thinking abilities enable educators to rationally determine suitable assignments. He emphasized the wisdom of using each child stage as a basis to guide curriculum. Children should get to perceive, talk about, and manipulate objects so they gain the experience needed to develop their mental abilities. First-hand experience, however, time-consuming, is essential for stable learning. Therefore, a fundamental responsibility of adults in school and at home is to offer tasks that enable children to acquire understanding. What matters more than verbalizing rules or memorizing without understanding is involvement in activities that require problem-solving, critical thinking, and creativity.

Parents and schools collaborate to identify the child's test performance as determined by the National Assessment of Educational Progress (2024) and provide for the tutoring needed. Parents should teach children that going to school and studying are their main responsibilities. Accordingly, children will not be permitted to spend unreasonable amounts of time communicating with friends and involvement with excessive screen time (Haidt, 2024; Heitner, 2023).

Key Concepts

1. The initial purpose for intelligence tests was to identify students who could not benefit from instruction provided in regular classrooms because of limited mental abilities. In the 1970s, the government began to provide education for the disabled.
2. Students are administered an individual intelligence tests (IQ) when considered necessary to assess their ability to participate in a regular classroom. Therefore, the IQ of most students is never known by them or their parents.
3. There are 14 criteria to qualify for special education that include learning disabilities, speech and language impairment, autism, mental disability, and health issues. About 14% of students in public schools attend special education.
4. Students in gifted and talented programs do not qualify based on intelligence testing. Instead, they are chosen because of higher scores on commonly taken achievement tests than their age group or ethnic peers.
5. Jean Piaget explored how children think and the ways they process information to interpret their environment. He abandoned the notion of quantitative intelligence in favor of studying qualitative differences in the way children think at various chronological ages.
6. Many of the instructional principles that teachers rely on are based on observations of Piaget. Some lessons students learn on their own from the Internet rather than only from teachers implicate comprehension and transfer of training.
7. Students from other nations are expected to perform well so they devote most of their time to academic study. This orientation should become more common for American

students who, by comparison, have poor study habits illustrated by excessive time communicating with friends and social media.
8. Piaget's emphasis on self-directed learning has become prominent because the Internet allows students to be guided by curiosity as they try to acquire information not presented at school. Achievement testing reflects only school curriculum, so some learning is not covered by testing.
9. Parents need to be informed about how their student performs on the National Assessment of Educational Progress (2024) tests, ensure they receive suitable tutoring, and monitor the amount of time spend on homework and communicating with peers.
10. Piaget described specific potential and limitations of thinking at cognitive development levels roughly associated with chronological age. His qualitative view of intelligence has been influential in shaping curriculum, so tasks in school reflect the stage of student thinking.

Generational Perspectives Activities

7.1 Discussion With Parents and Grandparents
7.2 Conversations With Young Children
7.3 A Scenario: Reasoning and Problem-Solving
7.4 Chapter Review
7.5 Parent and Grandparent Self-Evaluation
7.6 Storytelling

7.1 Discussion With Parents and Grandparents

1. What do you know about the inclusion practices applied in public schools?
2. What are the advantages and disadvantages of people not knowing their IQ?
3. How should students who are gifted and talented be educated differently?
4. How do you think teachers feel about variance of abilities among students?
5. Provide an example of how parents expect too much or little of children.
6. What would you like to know of child performance than report cards tell?
7. What do you know about friends in school that your child likes the most?
8. What is your reasoning about having one set of expectations for everyone?
9. What are some reasons for students taking tests difficult for most of them?
10. During your schooling, how did teachers deal with students who were slow?

7.2 Conversations With Young Children

1. What assignments do teachers give that you do not understand?
2. Do you think the schoolwork you have is hard or easy to do?
3. How do teachers react when you report a schoolwork problem?
4. How often do you ask for parent help to do school assignments?
5. How does the teacher think you are doing in the classroom?

7.3 A Scenario: Reasoning and Problem-Solving

Janice and Tom wonder how daughter Jennifer gets along with classmates. How should they find out about Jennifer's social relationships with peers?

1. Ask Jennifer to describe her relationships with individuals in her class.
2. Ask the teacher to share her observations of Jennifer's peer relationships.
3. Request the opportunity to become a class observer for a morning.

7.4 Chapter Review

1. What insights from the chapter will I try to apply in my relationships?
2. What is the most important key concept for me presented in this chapter?
3. Which elements of this chapter do I wish I had known about earlier?

7.5 Parent and Grandparent Self-Evaluation

1. The expectations I have for my child are based on

    a. comparative observations of the child's friends
    b. books on child development at different ages
    c. observations of the child's abilities and limits
    d. discussions with neighbors who are parents
    e. Other

2. I believe my academic expectations for my child are

    a. reasonable and based upon grade level
    b. reinforced by meetings with the teacher
    c. above average for students in the same grade
    d. to be a leader among students in the same age
    e. Other _____

3. The orientation program for parents at my child's school should

    a. provide information on social behavior expected of the students
    b. give a list of milestones to guide child expectations at home
    c. identify student misbehaviors that are considered unacceptable
    d. recommend curriculum parents are expected to teach at home
    e. Other _____

4. If my child has difficulty completing assignments, what are the options?

    a. sign up for free tutoring help that should remediate academic deficits
    b. meet with a school counselor to consider possible courses of action
    c. try assignments at home to find out if the child can do the work
    d. talk with my child to learn if issues like bullying could be the cause
    e. meet with the teacher to find out her explanation of the problem
    f. Other _____

7.6 Storytelling

Historically, storytelling has been a dominant classic and progressive method of teaching around the world. The purposes of a storyteller are to present imaginary or real-life examples showing how some concept applies to a particular situation. People like stories, they pay attention to the procession of events, and usually remember aspects of a story for a long time. Your stories can reinforce the concepts in this chapter for family members and classmates. Please share your stories with them.

References

Abbott, R., & Burkitt, E. (2023). *Child development and the brain: From embryo to adolescence* (2nd ed.). Policy Press.
Binet, A. (1916). *The development of intelligence in children (the Binet-Simon scale)*. University of California Libraries.
Bruner, J. S. (1976). *The process of education*. Harvard University Press. (Original work published 1960)
The Connection Academy. (2022, July 15). *Homeschooling*. Pearson. https://www.connectionsacademy.com/support/resources/article/9-biggest-myths-homeschooling/
Dearing, E., & Farran, D. (2022, March 15). Opinion: What might the future of universal pre-k look like? As researchers, we have some concerns. *The Hechinger Report*. https://hechingerreport.org/opinion-what-might-the-future-of-universal-pre-k-look-like-as-researchers-we-have-some-concerns/
Eysenck, M. W. (2022). *Simply psychology* (5th ed.). Routledge.
Ginsburg, H., & Opper, S. (1987). *Piaget's theory of intellectual development* (3rd ed.). Pearson.
Haidt, J. (2024). *The anxious generation: How the great rewiring of childhood is causing an epidemic of mental illness*. Penguin Press.
Hattenstone, A., & Lawrie, E. (2021, July 18). Covid: Home-education numbers rise by 75%. *BBC*. https://www.bbc.com/news/education-57255380
Heitner, D. (2023). *Screenwise: Helping kids thrive (and survive) in their digital world* (2nd ed.). Routledge.
Jacobs, E., & Jack, A. (2024, October 14). The boom in home schooling. *The Financial Times*. https://on.ft.com/4fcesyZ
Khan Academy Kids. (2024). *Joyful learning*. https://learn.khanacademy.org/khan-academy-kids/
Miller, P. H. (2016). *Theories of developmental psychology* (6th ed.). Worth.
Mitra, S. (2003, June). Minimally invasive education: A progress report on the "hole in the wall" experiments. *British Journal of Educational Technology*, 34(3), 367–371. https://doi.org/10.1111/1467-8535.00333
Mitra, S. (2013, February 27). *Build a school in the cloud*. TED. https://www.ted.com/talks/sugata_mitra_build_a_school_in_the_cloud?language=en&delay=2m&subtitle=en
Mitra, S. (2015, January). Minimally invasive education: Pedagogy for development in a connected world. In P. Rothermel (Ed.), *International perspectives on home education: Do we still need schools?* (pp. 254–277). Palgrave Macmillan. https://doi.org/10.1057/9781137446855_18
Mitra, S. (2018). New systems for children's learning: Changes required in education. In K. C. Koutsopoulos, K. Doukas, & Y. Kotsanis (Eds.), *Handbook of research on educational design and cloud computing in modern classroom settings* (pp. 22–33). IGI Global.
Mitra, S. (2019). *The school in the cloud: The emerging future of learning*. Corwin.
National Assessment of Educational Progress. (2024). *The NAEP long-term trend assessment results for reading & mathematics are here*. https://nces.ed.gov/nationsreportcard/
Park, S. E., & Demakis, G. J. (2020). Wechsler preschool and primary scale of intelligence. In V. Zeigler-Hill & T. K. Shackelford (Eds.), *Encyclopedia of personality and individual differences* (pp. 5757–5760). Springer.
Piaget, J. (1954). *The construction of reality in the child*. Basic Books.

Piaget, J. (1963). *Origins of intelligence in children*. Norton.
Piaget, J. (1969). *Psychology of intelligence*. Littlefield, Adams & Co.
Piaget, J. (2001). *The psychology of intelligence* (Vol. 92, 2nd ed.). Routledge. (Original work published 1969)
Piaget, J., & Inhelder, B. (1972). *The psychology of the child*. Basic Books.
Pulaski, M. (1980). *Understanding Piaget: An introduction to children's cognitive development*. Harper Collins.
Ray, B. D. (2024, May 29). *Home schooling: The research*. National Home Education Research Institute. https://www.nheri.org/research-facts-on-homeschooling/
Roid, G. H. (2005). *Stanford-Binet intelligence scales for early childhood (early SB-5)* (5th ed.). Western Psychological Services.
Singer, D. G., & Revenson, T. (1997). *A Piaget primer: How a child thinks*. International Universities Press.
Terman, L. M. (2007). *The measurement of intelligence: An explanation of and a complete guide for the use of the Stanford revision and extension of The Binet-Simon intelligence scale*. Houghton Mifflin. (Original work published 1916). https://www.gutenberg.org/files/20662/20662-h/20662-h.htm
United States Census Bureau. (2024, December 19). *Household Pulse Survey: Measuring emergent social and economic matters facing U. S. households*. https://www.census.gov/data/experimental-data-products/household-pulse-survey.html
Weaver, L. (2022, April 22). *8 Myths about homeschooling debunked*. Moms for America. https://momsforamerica.us/blog/8-myths-about-homeschooling-debunked/

Chapter 8

The Influence of Media on Children

The impact of media is a focus of researchers worldwide who explore screen addiction and the excessive time youth devote to this aspect of their lives. However, more attention should be given to the influence media has on young children whose ability to think critically and make decisions has yet to develop (Lemish & Jordan, 2024). The social context of media is one in which protection by parents and child education are essential. The purposes of this chapter are to (a) summarize conditions that have implicated child marketing, (b) show ways parents can help young children learn how to interpret advertisements directed to them, (c) illustrate how children can become more informed about truth distortion, and (d) suggest questions parents can ask children about their experiences with advertising. Generational Perspectives Activities present topics to discuss with family members and close friends about the influence of media on children.

Evolution of Advertising to Children

Young children do not understand why some of the products they find appealing are not purchased by parents. This cognitive limitation exposes their vulnerability that advertisers are willing to exploit. A growing child parade of commercials means parental guidance is needed to teach critical thinking skills with long-term application. Lessons should start before kindergarten (Blades et al., 2020; Bowell et al., 2020). Most parents agree their children encounter too much advertising pressure. As a result, some families resent sponsors of child programs. Other parents believe their best response is to help children acquire interpretation skills to be intelligent consumers. "*Critical thinking* is the intellectually disciplined process of actively and skillfully conceptualizing, applying, analyzing, synthesizing, and/or evaluating information gathered from, or generated by, observation, experience, reflection, reasoning, or communication, as a guide to belief and action" (James, 1983; Scriven & Paul, 1987).

Children should be educated to evaluate events and understand situations they see on screens, which will help them become more discerning decision-makers and less susceptible to misinformation. Many adults recognize that children today require guidance due to having more options and making decisions at younger ages compared to the past. Traditional indicators of success, such as memorization, are being replaced by a more comprehensive approach that emphasizes reflective thinking and critical analysis (Garvey, 2023; Kellerman & Seligman, 2023).

Angelina is 4 years old. She likes to watch cartoons sponsored by the fun fruit candy company. After seeing a commercial, Angelina asks her mother, "Can I have it?" Mother

DOI: 10.4324/9781003534655-11

says, "No Angelina, it will spoil your dinner." The little girl looks at her mother in a reflective way and then concludes, "TV makes you want things, doesn't it?" Parents can count on children to solicit them to buy products seen on child programs. Mothers and fathers can choose to dislike advertisers, shun their products, and dislike television stations. Alternatively, they can see these situations as chances to support instruction about how commercials influence us to buy things (Jackson, 2023).

Young children lack awareness about the purposes of commercials, so they should watch advertisements critically with parents, learn ways that other people try to influence behavior of families and persuade them to buy things. The parent goal is to interpret concepts, ideas, events, and situations that children see on television. This guidance function includes clarifying the values by the family. Education to motivate thinking is better understood when parents know how companies make their pitch to young children (Heitner, 2023; Lemish et al., 2018).

The Beginnings of Character Licensing

In anticipation of the St. Louis World's Fair in 1904, the Brown Shoe Company purchased rights to use the image of the Phantom, a comic book hero whose identity was not known because he always wore a purple mask (Fraser, 1966; Saint Louis Art Museum, 2024). The idea was to replicate the Phantom's image in a paper cutout form as a way to motivate world fair customers to buy shoes. This was the origin of character licensing. Customers would buy a product and receive a free toy they wanted, usually an inexpensive object that portrayed the image of the famous hero (Wu, 2016).

Charlie Chaplin, a well-known actor of the silent screen era, was the first individual to benefit from character licensing. He was made into paper doll cutouts and given away free with the purchase of household goods such as sugar, salt, and flour. Every family bought these products, so getting a Charlie cutout as a bonus favored companies that gave away his cutout. The benefit for Charlie was additional fame and recognition. Twenty years later Walt Disney foresaw the potential of character licensing when he introduced Mickey Mouse in a film called *Steamboat Willie*. Character licensing was essentially free advertising. No money was paid to the person whose likeness was replicated and given away. But then, during the 1930s and 1940s, actress Shirley Temple attracted an unprecedented international audience (Biography.com Editors, 2021). Her appeal was so great it changed the nature of character licensing. The companies that manufactured Shirley dolls were financially obligated to share some of their profits with her. Other heroes in the 1940s who advertised on the radio and in movies included Buck Rogers, Flash Gordon, Tarzan, and Little Orphan Annie (Jacobson, 2004). These popular characters became beneficiaries of character licensing.

Advertising on Television to Children

Television was not available to the public until the 1950s. Initially, there were not many programs, so most were presented as variety shows in the evening. Turning a television set on in the daytime would show test patterns including circles and number of the channel. However, shortly before dinner, children from across the nation would get together with friends in front of a television to hear Buffalo Bob ask, "What time is it, kids?" The young audience would reply in unison, "It's Howdy Doody Time." Howdy Doody was the first children's program that remained on the air from 1947 to 1960. Buffalo Bob was the host and responsible for advertisements. He told kids, "Make sure your Mom takes you to the store where you can buy Poll Parrot shoes and ask the clerk for your free Howdy Doody cutout." In the 1960s, heroes of Western movies were also franchised. Hopalong Cassidy was a cowboy whose mission was to ensure justice prevailed on the prairie. Companies competed to sell Hopalong pajamas, tee shirts, candy bars, and toothpaste (Kunkel & Castonguay, 2011). Duke University Libraries Exhibits (2011) provide a look back at advertising to children during the 1950s–1980s showing examples of persuasive approaches.

Jim Henson was a puppeteer on television with his endearing Muppet characters such as Kermit the Frog, Miss Piggy, Fozzie Bear, Big Bird, and others from 1956 to 1981. His famous quote was, "Life is like a movie, right your own ending. Keep believing. Keep pretending. Watch out for each other" (Jones, 2016). The marketing procedure then was that a toy company, cereal manufacturer, or fast-food restaurant would approach a television producer. For example, Wendy's market surveys found that 85% of parents consulted with their children about where the family should go out for dinner. So a happy meal at McDonald's and getting a toy treat with the meal made certain restaurants more likely places where families chose to eat out. Advertisers purchased image rights to the character(s) of a program and manufactured paper cutout to give away as gifts to the customers (Roberto et al., 2010).

The Revolution of Franchising

The franchising tradition was revolutionized as film director George Lucas (1977) prepared to release his highly anticipated movie *Star Wars*. Lucas had popularizing characters like Luke Skywalker, Hans Solo, Princess Lela, Obi wan Kenobi, and Darth Vader before the release of his movie. He also signed an exclusive agreement with Kenner Products, a toy company owned by General Mills, to be the sole producer of space doll characters. These dolls were instantly popular. To ensure the likenesses were acceptable to boys, all the doll characters were identified as action figures. Soon G. I. Joe and Johnny West led a crowd of action figures children wanted to own (Schor, 2005).

The new marketing orientation George Lucas introduced was soon adapted by other media outlets in the 1980s. Companies that previously paid television programs for licensing image rights decided to create their own characters instead of sharing profits with television companies. The idea was to create a fantasy background for characters and advertise them on a program-length commercial catering to children that featured these characters. This is how a colony of blue dwarves called the Smurfs became popular (Schneider, 1987). They ate smurfberries and engaged in continual conflicts to overcome Gargamel, the evil wizard. The Smurf dwarfs became the most watched child program on Saturday mornings with profits of more than $1 billion in annual sales. Other previously unknown characters such as Pac Man and Donkey Kong took a similar path to find their way onto spaghetti cans and bubble gum (Wulffson & Keller, 2014).

Objections to Child Advertising

Objections to child advertising practices started in the 1970s by a parent group called Action for Children's Television. Their presentations were successful in persuading the

Federal Communications Commission to remind the media industry about its responsibility to serve the welfare of children by adopting codes to limit the amount of advertising time, level of violence in cartoons, and offer a more comprehensive menu of content that offered education value for the viewers. These efforts were achieving some success until President Ronald Reagan, in 1980, maintained the federal government was too intrusive, and deregulation was needed so businesses could flourish. Reagan's point of view was, "Television is just another appliance, a toaster with pictures" (Wu, 2016). Instead of regarding broadcasters as trustees of public welfare, the new concept was that television should be treated like any other business trying to make a profit. Accepting this change, in 1984, the Federal Communications Commission removed guidelines that had been in place for over a decade (Linn, 2005). The change permitted television stations to run as many commercial minutes as they wanted, thereby allowing program-length commercials for children to reemerge (Haidt, 2024).

The major networks quickly eliminated the children's programs they had presented to meet their public service commitment. Some prominent programs terminated included Captain Kangaroo and all the prime-time after-school specials. From 1985 to 1990, stations shrunk the time for children's shows from 12 hours a week to four hours a week. As a replacement, the time on Saturday morning for program-length commercials increased from two hours to seven hours. Profits rose quickly for television stations as the sponsoring toy companies collectively reported sales of more than $15 billion a year. For example, Prince Adam was transformed into He-Man as he would announce, "I have the power to defend the universe against the evil Skeletor." His heroic behavior was widely recognized, as He-Man presented himself onto the screen for 120 domestic stations and 30 stations in other countries. The resulting sales for Mattel Toy Company, producers of He-Man and Masters of the Universe characters, represented over 100,000 figurines sold every day. These characters reflected polling of 3- to 7-year-old boys who reported they spent a lot of time imagining conflicts between the forces of good and evil (Schor, 2005; Heitner, 2023).

By 1988, Congress was receiving frequent complaints from parent organizations insisting on legislation to reduce advertising pressures on children and resulting family conflict about family spending. The emerging legislation required television stations to restrict advertisements to children below age 10 to ten minutes an hour on weekends and 12 minutes an hour on weekdays. This shift returned previously operating guidelines and renewed the argument about whether television had ethical obligation to young viewers (Cross, 1999).

Channel One and School Curriculum

The responsibility to consider educational benefits for young viewers was emphasized by entrepreneur Chris Whittle (2005), founder of Channel One. Whittle maintained that students growing up in a global environment should have a curriculum that would include daily access to world news. Whittle thought the news should be presented in a format similar to CNN but tailored to a youth audience. A decision was made to offer the expensive technological service free to subscribing schools, including all necessary equipment and programming. Part of the arrangement with each school district was that two minutes of the 15-minute daily news would be devoted to advertising of fashion products targeting youth such as jeans.

Opponents of Channel One argued that the schools could not waste two minutes a day. This was exploiting education as a platform for commercial advertising. However, before long 40% of all middle schools and high schools across the nation adopted the news program. Channel One remained on the air for 28 years, from 1990 to 2018. Young reporters were sent across the globe to gather stories of interest. Some of the announcers like Anderson Cooper of CNN went on to become well-known journalists to serve adult markets. From the mid-1990s, Channel One was frequently commended for stories about vital issues, received many awards for reporting, and was popular with students (Whittle, 2005).

Child Health and Nutrition Concerns

According to the Mayo Clinic Staff (2024), too much screen time and regular exposure to poor-quality programming have been linked to:

- Obesity
- Inadequate sleep schedules and insufficient sleep
- Behavior problems
- Delays in language and social skills development
- Violence
- Attention problems
- Less time learning

Child obesity is defined as a body mass index (BMI) at or above the 95% of CDC sex-specific growth charts. According to the Centers for Disease Control and Prevention (2024), obesity rates have nearly tripled since the 1970s. The prevalence rate of obesity in 2020 was 12.7% among children ages 2–5 and rises to 20.7% among 6–11-year-old children. The minority groups have even higher rates; the prevalence is 26% among Hispanic children and 24% for Blacks. Obesity-related health conditions include high blood pressure, high cholesterol, type 2 diabetes, and breathing problems like asthma and sleep apnea.

To acquire some perspective of child obesity, the Kaiser Family Foundation examined the websites of 77 major U.S. food companies (Cheadle et al., 2018). Media regulators lacked the authority to require change on these sites because information was considered to be editorial rather than advertising. Kaiser research determined that 85% of the food brands that targeted children also used branded websites that could increase the influence because there were no time limits for exposure as there was on producing short commercials. In addition, Packer et al. (2022a, 2022b) conducted a meta-analysis of 39 studies that confirmed a strong association between increases in advertising for non-nutritious foods and childhood obesity.

Legislation for Child Protection

Parents are concerned about the family consuming too much sugar and calories which are linked to obesity and heart disease. However, regularly eating too much salt is also a public health issue for children and adults. Recommendations in the United Kingdom are that adults consume no more than 6g of salt a day; but on average they consume 40% more than this (8.4g/day). Reducing salt is one of the quickest and most effective ways to reduce blood pressure. It is a challenge to accurately gauge how much salt we are eating because most of it is already in the food we buy. Salt use accelerates when parents take children out to eat at fast food restaurants. Blood pressure in children is rising, and parents need to monitor the salt intake of children when they are eating both at home and going out to a fast-food restaurant (Pombo, 2024).

To prevent child exploitation from advertising, the Canadian province of Quebec has implemented legislation, called the *Consumer Protection Act*, which prohibits commercial advertising to children under the age of 13 (Office de la Protection du Consommateur, 2012). The ban applies to all merchants including those who request the promotion of goods or services as well as those involved in the advertising process. Target formats involve radio, television, the web, mobile phones, newspapers, and other printed materials such as comic books, signs, and promotional items. Should the United States consider adoption of this type of child protection legislation that has been enacted in Quebec?

Big Business Advertising

The desire for instant gratification is common among all age groups, as people generally feel they should not have to wait for the things they want. Risky attitudes lead to poor consumer decisions. Current estimates are that children watch more than 40,000 advertisements a year. The United States has only 3% of the world's minor-age population, but families in this country purchase over 40% of toys, mobile devices, and playthings in the world. The annual cost of these products exceeds $20 billion (Ferguson, 2020).

Raffoul et al. (2023) conducted a simulation analysis to determine the number of U.S. youth users of social media and annual advertising revenue. The six major platforms in the 2021–2022 study included Facebook, Instagram, Snapchat, TikTok, Twitter, and YouTube. The estimated results in the study were that these sites collectively derived $11 billion revenue in U.S.-based users ages 0–17. As concerns about child and adolescent mental health increase, more policymakers want legislation to curtail social media platforms that may stimulate depression, anxiety, and disordered eating habits in young people.

Ways to Limit Child Screen Time

Here are some suggestions for limiting child screen time (Balzar, 2023; Centers for Disease Control and Prevention, 2024; Mayo Clinic Staff, 2024; Strasburger et al., 2013).

- Organizations such as Common Sense Media have programming ratings and reviews to help parents determine what's appropriate for children of different ages.
- Remove screens from the child's bedroom. Those with a television watch more than children who do not.
- Talk with your child about the video games they play and the content they engage with online.
- Eat without electronics. Families who dine together are healthier.
- Develop a family screen time schedule and no screen time before bedtime.
- Discuss ideas for family activities including exercise, take a walk together, ride a bike, or play an outside game.
- Build in time for reading together from children's books.
- Show healthy habits like turning off the phone during family time and dinner.

- Have a contest to see who can do the most push-ups or jumping jacks during commercials.
- Enjoy watching television on the weekend as a family versus weekdays. Ideally, your family should watch two hours or less of television each day.
- Do not utilize media viewing (television, iPhones, and computers) with children younger than two years.
- Limit total media time for children 2 years old to not more than 30 minutes a week.
- Use screen media with children ages 2 years and older only for educational purposes or physical activity.
- Parents should be aware that during the middle childhood (ages 9–12 and older) children will begin to spend an increasing amount of time on social media, and it will likely continue as they grow older (Annie E. Casey Foundation, 2024).

Truth Distortion and Critical Thinking

Americans are disappointed by their daily exposure to fake news and the distortion of truth. We wonder how to avoid being gullible or developing a cynical pattern of thinking. Daniel Levitin's (2017) book *Weaponized Lies: How to Think Critically in the Post-truth Era* provides many examples about the ways people misuse information to deceive others into adopting inaccurate opinions and become wary about our own decisions. Levitin states that truth matters no matter how much the media might distort facts. The individual ability to distinguish between truth and what is false demands adults to maintain a continuous commitment to logic and reliance on the scientific method (Levitin, 2019). Yoon and Templeton (2024) contended this plan should begin early and parents should insist critical thinking be emphasized during early childhood education. Early learning can ensure that curriculum enables young children to develop accurate and balanced views to interpret the media messages they are bound to encounter.

People of all ages experience frustration when they see how television advertising distorts the truth. Consider a short story, *The Sunday Zeppelin* by William Saroyan (1948). In this tale, 10-year-old Luke tells his younger brother Mark that he and friend Ernest West are saving money so they can buy a Zeppelin they had seen in *Boys World* magazine. The magazine illustration shows two boys high above the earth, standing in the basket of their airship. The price to get a Zeppelin is one dollar, and Luke believes that it would probably be sent to him by a freight train. Dad tells Luke if he cleans the garage and takes care of the yard for a week and does other errands, he will be given a dollar next Saturday – provided his brother Mark is allowed to ride in the Zeppelin with Ernest West. Luke finished the chores and a letter, including the dollar from the post office to the people in Chicago.

Now, Luke said, "All we have to do is wait." For ten days the boys anxiously waited and talked about all the places that they would travel in their Zeppelin. Then the package arrived with Boys World stamped on the box. The package was small and did not seem to weigh much. The box contained a letter with directions for how to operate the Zeppelin and stated that the toy will quickly rise and can stay up for 20 seconds. Luke started to assemble the airship, but the paper tore and this caused the shape to collapse. Luke was mad as he recalled out loud that the picture he had seen was of two boys' way up in the air. He tore up the remainder of the toy, went to the garage, and began to nail boards together. All Mark could do was say to himself, "Them people in Chicago are sons of bitches, that's what they are" (Saroyan, 1948). This zeppelin story usually causes adults to laugh and attribute unreasonable expectations of the boys to the fact that they were young and naive.

Similar distortions of truth are conveyed to adults who seem easily misled as well. A classic film example was *Crazy People* (Bill & Young, 1990), starring Dudley Moore and Daryl Hannah. An advertising executive suggests that a new approach would be, "Let's not lie to people, let's level with them." His boss responds by placing him in an insane asylum where, along with fellow inmates, their products appeal to advertisers and makes them famous.

In another story of truth distortion, one grandmother recalls that her brother wanted to get a coded ring that would unlock secrets. When he applied, the coded message said, "Drink Ovaltine." Yes, he was angry.

Children's Food Preferences

The example parents set for how they choose foods can impact decisions children make about nutrition. Generally, adults tend to ignore food shopping as a context that offers rich opportunities to teach and illustrate healthy lifestyle lessons. Wanting children to be healthy begins with helping them choose what to eat.

Roberto et al. (2010) studied 40 children from 4 to 6 years old. The children tasted three pairs of identical foods (graham crackers, gummy food snacks, and carrots) that were presented in packages with or without a popular cartoon character. Children tasted both food items in each pair and told whether the two foods tasted the same or one tasted better. Boys and girls then chose which of the food items they would prefer for a snack. Results showed children preferred the taste of foods with popular cartoon characters on the packaging compared to the same foods without the characters. It was concluded branding food packages with licensed characters can influence children's taste perceptions and their preferences for junk foods. Since millions of dollars are spent on advertisements featuring character licensing, the use of characters on junk food advertising should be restricted (Gantz et al., 2007; Gunter, 2016).

In a related study, Packer et al. (2022a, 2022b) conducted a systematic review and meta-analysis of over 20 studies carried out for more than a decade to evaluate the impact on dietary outcomes of licensed and brand equity in marketing unhealthy foods high in fat, salt, and sugar to children. Under experimental conditions, use of characters on food packaging compared with packaging without characters resulted in a significantly higher taste preference for characters. Narrative findings supported this with participants reporting the impact of both character types on product preferences including food liking and snack choice. These findings are supportive of policies that limit exposure of food marketing using characters to children.

Teaching Children About Commercials

Parents have responsibility for teaching children to think critically about advertisements they will be exposed to that seek to shape spending habits. As children grow older, the products they are invited to buy or ask relatives to purchase for them become more expensive. One way to provide critical thinking practice and reinforce good judgment is to establish a continuing dialogue that draws attention to motives, methods, and consequences of commercials. Consider a homework assignment we prepared for parents of kindergarten through third-grade students. This activity consists of questions about commercials.

Choose questions you will talk about while watching commercials with a child. Remember, the purpose is to help children become more critical consumers. Explain to the child that the reason television has commercials is to get viewers to buy things companies make like junk foods, toys, or cereals.

1. What is your favorite breakfast cereal?
2. What cereal characters and boxes make you want to buy the cereal and why?
3. What kind of cereal would you like to try that you never had before?
4. What commercials do you enjoy, and why do you want to watch them?
5. Why do you suppose the sound of commercials is louder than the program?
6. What songs can you remember from hearing advertising jingles on television?
7. What are some commercials that you think do not tell the truth?
8. What do you think about advertisements about cereals that have lots of sugar?
9. Who are some famous people you have seen in commercials on television?
10. What food commercials make you feel hungry and want to eat?

Parental Guidance for Child Critical Thinking

Some suggestions are offered to parents for carrying out their difficult guidance role.

- Discuss advertisements together to identify both truthful and misleading messages. Parents recognize their duty to teach children the importance of honesty, so they can be reliable as family members, friends, and teammates. The most effective moral learning for children occurs when they observe others. When the focus is on another person's behavior rather than their own, children are less defensive and more open to understanding the personal significance of a lesson.
- Watch advertisements with your child and highlight how companies attempt to influence us. Children often lack the experience needed to identify the motives of others, making them susceptible to unrealistic suggestions and advertising tactics. By pointing out how advertisers try to persuade, parents can help children gain valuable insights without the disappointment of discovering these tactics on their own. Children can be easily influenced by commercials to want to buy something simply because it has been advertised as there is a 'Free Toy Inside.'
- Verbalize the decision-making process before taking any action. This involves reflective thinking, where options are considered to determine the most appropriate response. Reflective thought guides better decision-making. Teaching a child to move from impulsive to reflective thinking is an essential and valuable lesson.

Conclusion

Television and Internet advertising directed to young children is going to require greater attention from parents and necessitate better guidance. The Internet presents a more comprehensive challenge for families. The perspective we encourage as the way for parents to protect children from exploitation is teach them to become critical thinkers. In this way, parental guidance helps children get ready for their lifelong role as consumers who learn decision-making skills that are essential for a media-driven environment.

Parents are often in a position of having to convince children to do things they might not want to do, such as going to the dentist, cleaning their bedroom, avoiding junk foods, and eating vegetables. This persuasion role is reversed when a child observes appealing products advertised on television and tries to convince mom and dad to purchase them. This common situation is one where children make an effort to discover the methods that are effective in causing parents to behave in a desired way. When parents view these family conversations as opportunities to practice critical thinking, children come to recognize that sometimes the family does not buy products when we believe they are not good for us or we cannot spend that much money at this time. There are also times when we purchase things because they are good for us, and we want them. Each choice to buy something is different and calls on us to think about it. The way children are taught to become consumers will carry over to how they respond to advertiser persuasion as they grow older, and the costs of being a vulnerable consumer rise.

In the future, advertisers can be expected to continue motivating children to want certain products and asking their parents to purchase them. The parent challenge to remain vigilant in providing healthy food guidance is reinforced by the comedy movie *Unfrosted*, co-written, directed, and starring Jerry Seinfeld (2024). The film (rated PG-13) is set in 1963 in Battle Creek, Michigan, the company headquarters of two rival cereal makers, Kellogg and Post. Looking back to his childhood at age 10, Seinfeld recalled his first taste of a Kellogg's Pop-Tart and was convinced it was so good that it would no longer be necessary to eat anything else (Seinfeld, 2012).

Key Concepts

1. Children are being targeted as consumers at ever younger ages. Most parents believe there is too much advertising pressure on children, so they resent sponsors who exploit young consumers. Other parents have concluded that the best way to protect their children is teach media interpretation skills that contribute to becoming wise consumers.
2. Most families recognize that critical thinking, exercising good judgment, is necessary for children because they have more choices and are allowed to make decisions at an earlier age. For the same reason, teachers of all grades assign priority to teaching critical thinking skills essential to reach good conclusions and solve problems.
3. Most parents dislike watching advertisements, but young children often enjoy them. Children should be able to view commercials critically, become aware of how advertisers strive to influence their behavior, and persuade them to want things. An important aspect of parent teaching is to be an interpreter of concepts, events, and situations and clarify family values.
4. Help children practice critical thinking skills by interpreting advertisements with them. Asking questions about commercials that both of you observe can draw the child's attention to factors s/he might otherwise overlook and encourage use of reflection to process information.
5. Public concern continues to grow about marketing directed to younger audiences. Cereal companies encourage children to persuade parents to buy unhealthy sugary and salty snacks featured in online games. At the same time, foods that contribute to obesity in childhood are identified by warnings from the Centers for Disease Control and Prevention.

6. An epidemic of child obesity exists partly because poor eating habits are common, and advertisements encourage consumption of unhealthy foods. Families and schools need to collaborate to ensure children are well-informed about their nutritional needs and understand the consequences of choosing risky lifestyles.
7. Parents feel they need to protect their children from the incessant barrage of advertising that encourages poor eating habits. They are always playing defense trying to resist a wide range of bad influences in raising their children. Many parents also realize they need to do a better job teaching healthy eating habits.
8. The desire for instant gratification is a common goal as people of all ages are unwilling to wait for things they want. This combination of risky attitudes translates into poor decisions by consumers. The United States has a small fraction (3%) of the world's child population, yet we purchase over 40% of all toys in the world market (Blades et al., 2020).
9. Children are misled because of their cognitive limitations, but adults should show greater ability to recognize distortions of the truth. Parent-child conversations should focus on television advertisements that appear untrue or exaggerated and discuss the implications for families.
10. One way to allow practice and reinforce good judgment is by conversations focused on questions that draw attention to motives, methods, and consequences of commercials. The result can be reciprocal learning as children gain media interpretation skills, and parents become aware of their child's thinking limitations.

Generational Perspectives Activities

8.1 Discussion
8.2 Conversation With Young Children
8.3 A Scenario: Reasoning and Problem-Solving
8.4 Chapter Review
8.5 Parent and Grandparent Self-Evaluation
8.6 Storytelling

8.1 Discussion

1. What products shown on television has your child tried to persuade you to purchase?
2. What likenesses or other child gifts contained in products have led you to buy them?
3. To what extent does your child pay attention to advertisements that target children?
4. How are you preparing children to interpret media advertising they are bound to face?
5. What are some foods with poor nutritional value you will not buy for your children?
6. What do you think children should be taught about becoming intelligent consumers?
7. How do you provide a good and poor example of eating habits for your child?
8. What changes would you suggest in how companies present child advertising?
9. How can families protect children from health concerns like obesity and diabetes?

8.2 Conversation With Young Children

1. What are the advertisements that make you feel hungry and want to eat?
2. What are the favorite commercials that you have watched on television?

3. What commercials make you want to buy the product being advertised?
4. What songs can you remember from listening to jingle advertisements?
5. How do you like advertisements for breakfast cereals with lots of sugar?

8.3 Reflection Scenario

Five-year-old Jim is staying for the weekend at his grandmother's house. The only cereal he can find in the pantry is Quaker Oats, used to make Oatmeal. What should Jim say to his grandma?

a. Can we go to the store and get another kind of cereal for me?
b. I am not used to this kind of cereal for breakfast at our house.
c. My choice of morning cereal is usually fruit loops or cheerios.
d. I'll give oatmeal a try even though we don't have it at home.

8.4 Chapter Review

1. What insights from the chapter will I try to apply in my relationships?
2. What is the most important key concept for me presented in this chapter?
3. Which elements of this chapter do I wish I had known about earlier?

8.5 Parent and Grandparent Self-Evaluation

1. My job in deciding about food choices at our house is to

   a. make sure my family gets meals that are balanced
   b. restrict the amount of sugar that the children consume
   c. educate children about how to define good nutrition
   d. let everyone decide on their own choice of meals
   e. Other _____

2. In my opinion, young children

   a. are pressured too much by advertising on television
   b. should learn the basics about nutrition at an early age
   c. are not being respected by the television industry
   d. should shop for groceries often with their parents
   e. Other _____

3. I believe obesity during early childhood

   a. can be reduced if parents are advised by dieticians
   b. calls for education by the food and drug administration
   c. is a disease that could be the cause of an earlier death
   d. can be managed by daily exercise and attention to diet
   e. Other _____

4. Unhealthy eating patterns among young children require

   a. a focus on less sedentary lifestyles
   b. more family exercise and weight planning

c. reducing the amount of media screen time
   d. parent insistence on less social media
   e. Other _____

5. Learning about commercials and how they influence us

   a. should occur at home with parents as teachers
   b. should be part of consumer education in school
   c. can become part of critical thinking curriculum
   d. could have lifelong consequences for health
   e. Other _____

6. Television advertising directed to children

   a. takes advantage of their mental limits
   b. should result in not buying the product
   c. offers adults chances to teach thinking
   d. should result in not buying the product
   e. Other _____

7. When a box of cereal contains a toy gift my child wanted

   a. I would usually purchase that product
   b. I would buy it if the product was healthy
   c. I would disregard a request by the child
   d. I would buy another better product
   e. Other _____

8. When children cry to get their way in a store,

   a. I feel sorry for the embarrassed grownup
   b. my reason for saying no should be given
   c. the wishes of the child should be ignored
   d. making a better choice could be explained
   e. Other _____

9. When I buy food products for children,

   a. I check the amount of sugar and salt
   b. I look at the nutritional values
   c. I will not buy junk food
   d. I emphasize fresh vegetables
   e. Other _____

10. My observation is that most parents

   a. do a poor job educating their children about food
   b. allow children to develop bad eating habits
   c. provide a poor model for children to imitate
   d. ignore their obligation to teach about foods
   e. Other _____

8.6 Storytelling

Historically, storytelling has been a dominant classic and progressive method of teaching around the world. The purposes of a storyteller are to present imaginary or real-life examples showing how some concept applies to a particular situation. People like stories, they pay attention to the procession of events, and usually remember aspects of a story for a long time. Your stories can reinforce the concepts in this chapter for family members and classmates. Please share your stories with them.

References

Annie E. Casey Foundation. (2024, June 23). *Social media and teen mental health*. https://www.aecf.org/blog/social-medias-concerning-effect-on-teen-mental-health?gad_source=1&gclid=EAIaIQobChMI3qCzjsLriQMVCJ1aBR2qES8dEAAYASAAEgKdwfD_BwE

Balzar, D. (2023, May 23). *Mayo Clinic minute: How much screen time is too much time for your kids?* https://newsnetwork.mayoclinic.org/discussion/mayo-clinic-minute-how-much-screen-time-is-too-much-time-for-your-kids/

Bill, T., & Young, B. L. (Director). (1990). *Crazy people* [Film]. Paramount Pictures.

Biography.com Editors. (2021, April 20). *Shirley Temple*. https://www.biography.com/actors/shirley-temple

Blades, M., Oates, C., Blumberg, F., & Sinclair, M. (Eds.). (2020). *Media marketing to children*. Wiley. https://doi.org/10.1002/9781119171492.wecad292

Bowell, T., Cowan, R., & Kemp, G. (2020). *Critical thinking* (5th ed.). Routledge.

Centers for Disease Control and Prevention. (2024, February 21). *Screening for child obesity*. https://www.cdc.gov/obesity/child-obesity-screening/index.html

Cheadle, A., Atiedu, A., Rauzon, S., Schwartz, P. M., Keene, L., Davoudi, M., Spring, R., Molina, M., Lee, L., Boyle, K., Williamson, D., Steimberg, C., Tinajero, R., Ravel, J., Nudelman, J., Azuma, A. M., Kuo, E. S., & Solomon, L. (2018, May). A community-level initiative to prevent obesity: Results from Kaiser Permanente's healthy eating active living zones initiative in California. *American Journal of Preventive Medicine, 54*(5 Suppl. 2), S150–S159. https://doi.org/10.1016/j.amepre.2018.01.024

Cross, G. (1999). *Kids' stuff: Toys and the changing world of American childhood*. Harvard University Press.

Duke University Libraries Exhibits. (2011). *Look boys and girls! Advertising to children in the 20th century: Children's commercials*. https://exhibits.library.duke.edu/exhibits/show/childrenads/comm

Ferguson, G. (2020, January 31). *Talking advertising and youth with U of M*. University of Minnesota. https://twin-cities.umn.edu/news-events/talking-advertising-and-youth-u-m

Fraser, A. (1966). *A history of toys*. Delacourte Press.

Gantz, W., Schwartz, N., Angelini, J., & Rideout, V. (2007). *Food for thought: Television food advertising to children in the United States*. The Henry J. Kaiser Family Foundation. https://www.kff.org/wp-content/uploads/2013/01/7618.pdf

Garvey, D. (2023). *Little brains matter: A practical guide to brain development and neuroscience in early childhood*. Routledge.

Gunter, B. (2016). *Food advertising: Nature, impact, and regulation*. Palgrave Macmillan.

Haidt, J. (2024). *The anxious generation: How the great rewiring of childhood is causing an epidemic of mental illness*. Penguin Press.

Heitner, D. (2023). *Screenwise: Helping kids thrive (and survive) in their digital world* (2nd ed.). Routledge.

Jackson, M. (2023). *Uncertain: The wisdom and wonder of being unsure*. Prometheus.

Jacobson, L. (2004). *Raising consumers: Children and the American mass market in the early twentieth century*. Columbia University Press.

James, W. (1983). *The principles of psychology* (Vols. 1–2). Harvard University Press. (Original work published 1890)

Jones, B. J. (2016). *Jim Henson: The biography*. Ballantine Books.

Kellerman, G., & Seligman, M. (2023). *Tomorrowland: Thriving at work with resilience, creativity, and connection – now and in an uncertain future*. Simon & Schuster.

Kunkel, D., & Castonguay, J. (2011). Children and television advertising. In D. Singer & J. Singer (Eds.), *Handbook of children and the media* (2nd ed., pp. 375–394). Sage.

Lemish, D., & Jordan, A. B. (2024). The invisible children, adolescents, and media and the future of our research. In D. Lemish (Ed.), *The Routledge international handbook of children, adolescents, and media* (2nd ed.). Routledge.

Lemish, D., Jordan, A. B., & Rideout, V. (2018). *Children, adolescents, and media: The future of research & action*. Routledge.

Levitin, D. (2017). *Weaponized lies: How to think critically in the post-truth era*. Dutton.

Levitin, D. (2019). *A field guide to lies: Critical thinking with statistics and the scientific method*. Dutton.

Linn, S. (2005). *Consuming kids: Protecting our children from the onslaught of marketing & advertising*. Anchor.

Lucas, G. (Director). (1977). *Star wars* [Film]. 20th Century Studios.

Mayo Clinic Staff. (2024, June 19). *Screen time and children: How to guide your child*. https://www.mayoclinic.org/healthy-lifestyle/childrens-health/in-depth/screen-time/art-20047952#:~:text=If%20you%20introduce%20digital%20media,day%20of%20high%2Dquality%20programming

Office de la Protection du Consommateur. (2012). *Advertising directed at children under 13 years of age: Guide to the application of sections 248 and 249 consumer protect act*. https://cdn.opc.gouv.qc.ca/media/documents/consommateur/sujet/publicite-pratique-illegale/EN_Guide_publicite_moins_de_13_ans_vf.pdf

Packer, J., Russell, S., McLaren, K., Siovolgyi, G., Stansfield, C., Viner, R., & Croker, H. (2022a, July). The impact on dietary outcomes of licensed and brand equity characters in marketing unhealthy foods to children: A systematic review and meta-analysis. *Obesity Reviews, 23*(7), e13443. https://doi.org/10.1111/obr.13443

Packer, J., Croker, H., Goddings, A., Boyland, E., Stansfield, C., Russell, S., & Viner, R. (2022b, December). Advertising and young people's critical reasoning abilities: Systematic review and meta-analysis. *Pediatrics, 150*(6), e2022057780. https://doi.org/10.1542/peds.2022-057780

Pombo, S. (2024, May). *Are children's meals worth their salt? Research into the nutritional quality of children's meals in the out of home sector*. Action on Salt. https://www.actiononsalt.org.uk/media/action-on-salt/awareness/saltweek24/Are-Children's-Meals-Worth-Their-Salt_.pdf

Raffoul, A., Ward, Z. J., Satoso, M., Kavanaugh, J. R., & Austin, S. B. (2023, December 27). Social media platforms generate billions of dollars in revenue from U.S. youth: Findings from a simulated revenue model. *PLoS One, 18*(12), e0295337. https://doi.org/10.1371/journal.pone.0295337

Roberto, C. A., Baik, J., Harris, J. L., & Brownell, K. D. (2010, July). Influence of licensed characters on children's taste and snack preferences. *Pediatrics, 126*(1), 88–93. https://doi.org/10.1542/peds.2009-3433

Saint Louis Art Museum. (2024). *1904 St. Louis World's Fair*. https://www.slam.org/teachers-students/educator-resources/art-along-the-rivers/art-on-display/1904-st-louis-worlds-fair/

Saroyan, W. (1948). *The Saroyan special: Selected short stories*. Harcourt Brace Jovanovich.

Schneider, C. (1987). *Children's television: The art, the business and how it works*. National Textbook Company.

Schor, J. B. (2005). *Born to buy: The commercialized child and the new consumer culture*. Scribner.

Scriven, M., & Paul, R. (1987). *Defining critical thinking. The foundation for critical thinking*. Presented at the 8th Annual International Conference on Critical Thinking and Education Reform. https://www.criticalthinking.org/pages/defining-critical-thinking/766

Seinfeld, J. (2012, December 20). Jerry Seinfeld interview: How to write a joke [Video]. *The New York Times*. https://www.youtube.com/watch?v=itWxXyCfW5s&t=11s

Seinfeld, J. (Director). (2024, May 3). *Unfrosted* [Film]. Columbus 81 Productions.

Strasburger, V., Hogan, M., Mulligan, D., Ameenuddin, N., Christakis, D., Cross, C., Fagbuyl, D., Hill, D., Levine, A., McCarthy, C., Moreno, M., & Swanson, W. (2013, November). Children, adolescents, and the media. *Pediatrics, 132*(5), 958–961. https://doi.org/10.1542/peds.2013-2656

Whittle, C. (2005). *Crash course: Imaging a better future for public education*. Riverhead.

Wu, T. (2016). *The attention merchants: The epic scramble to get inside our heads.* Alfred Knopf.
Wulffson, D., & Keller, L. (2014). *Toys! Amazing stories behind some great inventions.* Square Fish.
Yoon, H. S., & Templeton, T. N. (2024). Reflecting, representing, and expanding the narrative(s) in early childhood curriculum. *Urban Education, 59*(8), 2269–2299. https://doi.org/10.1177/00420859221097893

Part III

Motivation and Schooling

Chapter 9

Goals and Priorities During Childhood

Learning to set goals and priorities is an expected outcome of education and recognized as being common among people we consider wise. However, this asset seems increasingly difficult for many people to achieve in a society characterized by over-choice and continuous distraction. Given regular parental teaching and guidance, young children can learn to set goals and priorities. The purposes of this chapter are to (a) examine the benefits of encouraging children to set some goals and acquire the confidence that comes from self-reliance, (b) urge children to think about personality goals before considering possible career goals, (c) explore the link between parent trust and child decision-making, (d) consider how setting goals and experience in planning during early childhood can increase student motivation for academic achievement, and (e) acknowledge the importance of teachers setting high expectations for students. Generational Perspectives Activities present topics to discuss with family members and close friends about children setting goals and priorities.

Teach Children to Set Goals

When we know the goals of another person, it is easier to understand them and to provide feedback on the progress they are making. There is less inclination to misinterpret their purposes or reach unfair conclusions. Accordingly, it can be helpful to find out as much as possible about the motives and goals that guide child behavior (Jackson, 2023). Most parents and grandparents recognize that setting goals and amending some of them are common elements of growing up. However, many children are denied these experiences when their parents choose all of the goals they are expected to pursue. Parents usually justify their takeover of decision-making and claim that a child's poor choices could have disappointing consequences. So, "I am doing this for your own good." A more promising method to reduce the chances for harm is prepare children to make well-informed choices (Levine, 2020). Those who learn to set goals are able to gain experience in making choices, setting priorities, and recognizing personal failures and success. Parents should know the factors that contribute to good decision-making. In particular, consider the importance of self-reliance, being trusted, and having opportunities to set personal goals.

Trust, Decision-making, and Self-Reliance

David McClelland (2010, 2015), Professor of Psychology at Harvard University, studied successful adults to explore the origins of their motivation. In one study, he invented a game to determine whether the parent-child relationship was implicated. A group of

DOI: 10.4324/9781003534655-13

preschool children were blindfolded and assigned the task of building as high a tower of blocks as possible. An additional obstacle was that the children were restricted to using only one hand. They were allowed to ask a parent for advice, but the parent could not touch the blocks. If a child's pile fell down, the game was lost. When asked to guess how high a pile of blocks their child could build, parents whose children scored poorly on this task and other indicators of what McClelland identified as *achievement motivation* usually gave low estimates. These parents often demonstrated dominance and shifted from giving advice to taking over and directing a child's activity.

In contrast, parents of children who possessed high achievement motivation behaved differently. They gave high estimates of what their child would be able to achieve, offered encouragement throughout the task, and left decision-making up to their child. These parents favored early self-reliance. Other studies of high achievers have also found that parents favored early involvement in decision-making, goal setting, and self-evaluation (Ferguson & Robertson, 2019; Greene, 2000).

Importance of Parent Trust

There is a link between trust and decision-making. Sooner or later parents discover that their children want to be trusted. Since trusting someone calls for relinquishing control of their behavior, we can claim to trust only those who are allowed to reach some of their own conclusions and make their decisions. It follows that parents fail to demonstrate trust when they regularly insist upon making most decisions for their children. Further, without parent trust, children have fewer opportunities to practice the decision-making abilities that are needed for success. This means parents should begin to show trust before their children ask them to do so. A good way to begin is by allowing children to make decisions that match their mental abilities. When the emphasis is on making intelligent choices instead of directing children on what to do, the message of a parent is, "You are capable, and I trust you. Life is complicated but there is not enough danger to prevent you from getting practice needed to set some of your goals" (Strom & Strom, 2011).

Another unreasonable practice among parents is to decide what their children will do during the summer when school is not in session. By overscheduling and dominating choices, parents render their children less capable of critical thinking and making their own decisions. In many homes, the entire summer schedule is planned for children, supposedly for their welfare and protect them from getting in trouble. When child confusion and uncertainty are substantial, the risk of overdependence on parents rises. There can be no autonomy without self-direction (Jackson, 2023).

Besides enjoying the trust of parents, children need opportunities to practice setting goals in low-risk settings. Some people might suppose such chances are plentiful at school. After all, educators understand the rapid pace of change, minimal social constraints, and growing range of choices that make mental health reliant on setting goals and establishing reasonable priorities. However, teachers find it hard to arrange such experiences for students because they themselves are assigned lengthy lists of goals by the school administration that all students are expected to reach. High standards of performance are commendable and should be encouraged. Still, in the quest to make public schools accountable, the need for students to become self-directed learners must be assigned greater prominence than is the current norm (Strom & Strom, 2024).

What happens when child learning is limited to carrying out goals determined by adults? Such students lack their own goals so they cannot look ahead; instead, they live for the present and typically complain about boredom. They are unable to evaluate themselves properly because they lack appropriate self-selected goals to use as criteria. Generally, they do not know what to do when other people with higher status do not direct their behavior or assign tasks they are expected to complete. They are not self-directed learners. To support child independence and responsibility, most parents believe three goals should be nurtured: students should practice goal setting, be permitted to amend goals as needed, and be free from unreasonable expectations imposed by others (Strom & Strom, 2024).

Personality Goals Before Career Goals

Goals are an essential aspect of identity, so parents wonder about how they can arrange opportunities that allow children to set some goals without sacrifice to academic progress. At school, students are not allowed to decide whether to study mathematics, English, or science. Around third grade they begin to decide what their values and ambitions are and persons they want to become like in the future. One effective method to support this step in emotional development is encourage the adoption of personality goals before selection of career goals. This sequence of setting personality goals first before setting goals about occupations motivates the initial direction of the kind of person boys and girls wish to become, ways they want to behave, and influence they hope to have on others. These aspects of maturing can be observed long before there is evidence on jobs that a person may one day be qualified to perform. Adopting goals related to the "kind of person I want to become" contributes to success no matter what career path or occupation an individual may choose (Ali & Chin, 2023; Strom & Strom, 2024).

Students Select Personality Goals

By motivating children to choose personality goals and provide them feedback about their progress, everyone in the family acknowledges the importance of this achievement context. Otherwise, if students adopt a definition of achievement that is too narrow, their prospects to attain maturity, resilience, mental health, and long-term occupational success are in jeopardy. Major problems of getting along with others, such as abuse, divorce, crime, racism, and being fired, are more often a result of emotional dysfunction and lack of maturity than getting poor grades in the classroom. Reading, writing, and mathematics are fundamental skills; they are also the easiest lessons for children to learn. In addition, the education needed should support learning about how to manage unfamiliar conditions, cope with adversity, and demonstrate resilience. Here are four personality goals young children might consider. Progress can be observed by parents and grandparents who also identify child needs for further development.

- *Get along with others.* An eight-year-old girl told her grandmother Marie, "I want to be just like you when I grow up." Marie replied, "Why? I have so little and never made much of myself." The granddaughter said, "Grandma, you have more friends than anyone I know." What a nice compliment that reflects child recognition of adult compassion and kindness to others. This is what growing up and maturity are about, shifting from being a self-centered egocentric person in favor of showing concern for others.

- *Treat people fairly.* Children often report learning values from relatives indirectly by how they respond to characters on television and how they react to stories about neighbors or people described on news programs. Concerns about perceived unfairness and inequity are lifelong.
- *Show acceptance and tolerance of others.* Being able to accept people who are from a different background of race, creed, or color is an important aspiration for democracy. Intolerance shows up early as children call one another unfriendly names. This behavior is taught mostly at home and by peers. Intolerance jeopardizes the quality of relationships as well as maturity.
- *Be honest in what you say and do.* Learning how to reach these goals begins early in life and grows stronger through experience and age – it doesn't happen easily or quickly. This behavior is seen as an accomplishment that reflects who you are for your whole lifetime. Parents and grandparents need to reinforce the significance of this asset as a condition for adapting to social changes in society.

Personality goals individually chosen by children are a more appropriate long-term focus for self-evaluation than academic subjects such as reading and mathematics where tests scores can provide the necessary evaluation. A focus on personality emphasizes observational feedback from adult relatives. Personality is the key to *identity*, the way we see ourselves and are seen by others. Personality and identity are linked because both are concerns throughout life. Family and school support for long-term personality development conveys a message that child emotional and social development requires the same level of attention as development of academic abilities (Jackson, 2023; Kellerman & Seligman, 2023).

When parents are asked to identify the personal qualities they want to be remembered for, they typically mention nonintellectual characteristics that can endear individuals to one another. These personality goals could become more common if chosen as goals in elementary school. The example set by parents and grandparents is important. They can share some of their own goals and limitations to younger relatives, describe their plans to overcome deficiencies, and ask for observational feedback to help them evaluate progress. In addition to enabling children to set short-term and long-term goals, older relatives can share stories about personal goals with loved ones. Everyone should make a continual effort to improve personality as long as they live (Kellerman & Seligman, 2023; Krznaric, 2020).

Adults Make Known Personal Goals and Limitations

One grandmother wanted to have a conversation with her eight-year-old granddaughter that could be fun for them both and invite sharing of observations. After reading the list of personality goals together in Table 9.1, Personality Goals and Achievements for Consideration, the grandmother said, "Everyone should keep trying to improve their personality at every age. Could you identify two of the goals on this list you would suggest I should work on?" The granddaughter recommended two goals for consideration. Grandmother then asked, "Now, can you identify two goals on the list you would like to work on to improve yourself?" Reciprocal sharing of shortcomings and motivation enabled both relatives to later provide relevant feedback about individual progress.

When you talk to a child, ask whether s/he would like to add any goals to the list. For example, some additional goals might include – willingness to keep on trying when school homework is difficult or asking for tutoring in some school subject when it is needed. Then, encourage the child to work toward the personality goals s/he has chosen. You can

Table 9.1 Personality Goals and Achievements for Consideration*

Goals for Individual Consideration	Achievements Perceived by Parents, Teachers	Achievements Perceived by Self
1. Getting along with others		
2. Treat people around me fairly		
3. Show willingness to help others		
4. Look at the bright side of things		
5. Make time for what is important		
6. Develop a healthy sense of humor		
7. Make feelings known to relatives		
8. Be a better listener		
9. Understand how other people feel		
10. Ask questions if I don't understand		
11. Avoid unkind remarks about others		
12. Keep trying when things get difficult		
13. Ask for help when it is needed		
14. Be patient in dealing with others		
15. Be a person who others can rely on		
16. Keep mind and body healthy		
17. Reflect on behavior to improve self		
18. Seek and accept criticism of others		
19. Have self-control and self-discipline		
20. Become a self-directed person		
21. Learn to work well in teams		

* Adapted from *Becoming a Better Grandparent: Viewpoints on strengthening the family*, by Robert D. Strom and Shirley K. Strom, 1991. Copyright © 1991 by Robert D. Strom and Shirley K. Strom.

also share some goals you are still trying to reach. Such conversations can help everyone to enlarge their definition of achievement. The recognition of progress in personality development is ignored in many families even though it is a central asset in building maturity (Evans et al., 2023).

After reviewing the personality goals chosen by his grandson, one grandfather admitted, "All my life what I really wanted was to become someone. Now it is clear to me I should have been more specific." Conversations about personality goals should redefine the scope of achievement and identify ambitions beyond academic performance for children to expect of themselves.

Consider a simple illustration. In the springtime, I went to my son's house to observe the cleaning of his septic tank by a service company. A man was already there using an electronic instrument to detect location of the tank. After he determined the position, his little boy started to jump up and down on the spot as a way to confirm the yet-unseen worksite was directly beneath him. Soon another man went down the driveway in a big truck required for processing waste. Next, the dirt covering was removed. The leader introduced the team as a grandfather, father, and son. During several hours on the job, their three-way conversations were continuous as the little boy observed tasks necessary to complete the work. The boy said that he was 5 years old and glad to be on the septic tank team. His dad mentioned that last week he had to leave early in the morning for a distant job, so decided not to take his son with him and let him sleep in. When he got home that night, his son met him at the front door and was upset as he told him, "Dad, you forgot to take me to work with you."

As the grandfather listened to this story he smiled, reflecting the joy that he felt in having three generations work together on the septic installation. No one knows whether this boy will one day continue the same kind of work as his dad and grandpa. But, for now, the two men are building a close relationship, so the boy will know that he can count on their support for whatever occupation he might choose. A reminder is that grandparents can have an influence on getting grandchildren to consider the pursuit of personality goals that contribute to growth and maturity.

Sibling Rivalry and Pursuit of Autonomy

Adults who are younger sisters or brothers have memories about how their status of being in the shadow of an older sibling influenced their autonomy and goal setting while growing up. Five-year-old Sherry was four years younger than sister Marie. This meant that getting new clothes were actually hand-me-downs, not having a bedroom to herself was another disappointment, and having to sleep in the same bed with her sister was not a choice. When Marie had an opportunity to take dancing lessons and be part of theatrical performances in Detroit, the only comments relatives made to Sherry were that she should try to be like her older sibling.

However, Sherry also wanted to pursue her own goal of autonomy and fulfill her personal dreams. She thought that one way to reach these ambitions was to set up an outdoor tent that would provide a private space for her only. She took an old sheet her mom said she could use and tied one end to the fence in the backyard. When the task was finished, Sherry sat inside her new tent with a sense of autonomy, a feeling of pride because this was her own private place, and only she would decide who else was allowed to come in. Having an outside tent may not seem like a big deal for most people, but for Sherry it was a healthy beginning that enabled her to set goals and feel comfortable following her own path.

Sibling rivalry is common in families where children compete for parent attention and privilege. Instead of using behavior of an older child as criteria to judge the progress of younger siblings, parents should set the sibling relationship on a proper course when the children are young. This means all relatives should take pride in the progress of one another. Such an inclusive noncompetitive way of defining success is healthier than someone resenting achievement of a sibling as if it detracts from personal recognition. Parents should teach children to know their expected family role includes encouraging siblings to do well and support them in setting and achieving goals. The usual outcome of this expectation is a loving and mutual pride that describes the sibling relationships as adults.

Many parents do not teach their children they will have to amend some of their goals. The processes to enable amendment should be better understood. This issue is becoming more important as students are increasingly exposed to over-choice. The wise amendment of goals is essential for adjustment to previously unrecognized requirements, underestimated difficulties, and opportunities that may have been overlooked.

Influence of Expectations

Self-Fulfilling Prophecy

Robert Merton (1910–2003) was Professor of Sociology at Columbia University in New York. He introduced the concept of *self-fulfilling prophecy*, defined as setting an expectation for others that might affect behavior toward them in a way that causes the anticipation to be fulfilled. Merton suggested that, once an expectation has been set, even if it is inaccurate, people are likely to behave in a way that is consistent with the anticipation conveyed to them. The consequence is that, as if by magic, the expectation and resulting goals often turn into reality (Merton, 1967).

The Roman poet, Ovid (43 BC–AD 18), was the first to illustrate how the self-fulfilling prophecy works in his mythology poem called *Metamorphoses* (Britannica, 2024). This story is about a lonely sculptor who had given up hope of getting married. While Pygmalion carved an ivory figure of his ideal woman, he became attracted to the clay figure that he named Galatea and talked to her as though she was alive. When he went to the Venus festival, Pygmalion prayed, "If the gods can give what they wish, grant me a wife like her." After returning home, Pygmalion's prayer was answered. Galatea was transformed into a human being who became his lifelong partner.

George Bernard Shaw (1856–1950), a Nobel Prize winner for literature, published his own version of *Pygmalion* (Shaw, 1913). *Pygmalion* was filmed (1938), won an Academy Award for Shaw for his screenplay, and was adapted into a popular musical, *My Fair Lady* (Cukor, 1964) motion-picture version. In the play *Pygmalion*, Professor Henry Higgins made a bet that he could transform a young Cockney flower girl with little formal schooling into a lady who would be accepted by the status group of the social elite in London. Henry won his wager and fell in love with the person that the young woman had become. The sequence was the same again – high expectations were set and conveyed to the person treated accordingly. In turn, the person reciprocated, thus transforming the original expectation into a reality (Stewart & Weintraub, 2024).

Results of Setting High Expectations

How does the self-fulfilling prophecy apply to the goals of children and quality of their education? Kenneth B. Clark (1914–2005) was Professor of Psychology at City College in New York, the first Black person to receive a doctorate in psychology at Columbia University in 1940. One year later his wife Mamie (1917–1983) became the second Black scholar to earn a doctorate at Columbia University. Together the Clarks designed their *Doll Study* as a test to measure the psychological effects of segregation on the self-esteem of Black children (Keppel, 2002; National Park Service, 2024).

The subjects in the Doll study were 3–7-year-old African American children who were asked questions about their racial perceptions and preferences regarding two white and two black plastic-diapered dolls. The experiment was repeated multiple times with the same results. The Black children preferred the white dolls and attributed positive characteristics to them while they also attributed negative characteristics to the black dolls. The conclusion by the Clarks was that prejudice, discrimination, and segregation caused Black children to develop a sense of inferiority and self-hatred. Clark believed that if society says it is better to be White, not only White people but Negroes also come to believe it. A child may try to escape the trap of inferiority by denying the fact of his own race (Clark, 1955, 1965, 1974).

In the early 1950s, the legal landscape facing the National Association for the Advancement of Colored People (NAACP) looked grim. The segregation of schools was practiced in 17 states and the district of Columbia. Nevertheless, Thurgood Marshall as lead attorney for the NAACP was hopeful he could convince the Supreme Court that the separate but equal educational practices that had been in place for more than 50 years was unconstitutional and should be overturned. The Clark (1955) baby doll experiments were entered as evidence in the case and played a key role in what was one of the most important legal rulings of the twentieth century. In Brown v. the Board of Education in May 1954 the Supreme Court, led by Justice Earl Warren, unanimously overturned the separate but equal doctrine and ordered desegregation of public schools with all deliberate speed. This decision created a national goal for school policy. Thurgood Marshall joined the Supreme Court as the first Black Justice in 1967 (City University of New York, 2019).

Kenneth Clark became President of the American Psychological Association in 1966. In that position he argued that the low expectations common among inner-city teachers represented a threat to achievement of minority students. Many of his colleagues agreed with Clark, and several projects were initiated to support more reasonable expectations of teachers for inner-city children (Strom, 1965, 1966, 1967; Strom & Strom, 2024).

Teacher Expectations and Student Progress

Lenore Jacobson, the principal of an elementary school serving low-income families in San Francisco, read an article by Robert Rosenthal (1964) of Harvard University, in which he described his studies about the experimenter effect on behavior of animals. Specifically, he misled college students to suppose the randomly chosen rats they would be training were genetically superior or inferior. Depending on what students were told, they treated their rats differently. Those who believed the rats they cared for were highly capable handled them gently, talked to them often, observed them with careful attention, expressed encouragement, and portrayed their rodents as pleasant and likable. They set high expectations for their rats to solve maze puzzles (Rosenthal, 1971).

Another group of students in the study were led to believe rats they were responsible for did not have much of a chance for success. They tended to handle these rats roughly, seldom spoke to them, gave meager encouragement, referred to the rats as being unpleasant, and held low expectations for their maze performance. When the experiment ended, it was determined that the rats provided a supportive environment and exposed to high expectations performed better than those with similar capabilities to learn but seen by their caretakers as dull and treated in less nurturing ways. Rosenthal's work on the Experimenter Bias Effect encouraged psychologists to conduct their experiments in a double-blind fashion where neither the subjects nor the assistants testing them were aware of the hypothesis under tests (Hooley et al., 2024). In his conclusion, Rosenthal wondered whether the teachers who expected students to be slow were contributing to a self-fulfilling prophecy (Rosenthal & Jacobson, 1968).

Principal Jacobson was intrigued by the premise that what you expect is what you get, so she wrote to Rosenthal proposing, "If you ever graduate to working with children, let me know if I can help." Soon the principal and researcher agreed to collaborate. Jacobson pointed out it would be naive to suppose her teachers could be told that certain students had previously unrecognized potential. Instead, a test that teachers were unfamiliar with had to be taken by the students. So the faculty was informed Rosenthal had invented a new measure called the *Harvard Test of Inflected Acquisition*. His test, administered to all of the students, would identify those *about to blossom* and show surprising growth over the next eight months. In fact, Rosenthal did not have such a test but instead administered a nonverbal intelligence measure not recognized by the teachers. Then, 20% of all the students in grades K-6 were chosen at random and identified as an *about to blossom* group (Rosenthal & Jacobson, 1968).

At the end of the school year, students were reexamined using the same test. Considering the school as a whole, students from whom teachers were led to expect greater gains improved achievement scores to a higher degree than a control group of similar age, sex, and ability but not labeled as *about to blossom*. In Rosenthal's experiment, there was no intervention, no special projects, no unique challenges for identified students. The only distinction was a favorable shift in teacher outlook – a change in their expectations that Rosenthal and Jacobson (1968) called the *Pygmalion Effect* or more technically called *interpersonal expectancy*. When the expectations of teachers rose, the students made better use of their mental capacities.

Establishing high expectations for children is an important way parents and grandparents can show they recognize child potential. However, wishful thinking about the future of a child is never enough to achieve the desired result. Relatives must also establish high expectations for themselves because they are the only long-term teachers of children. The *Pygmalion Effect* and the *Blossom Experiment* should motivate all relatives to increase the amount of time spent with children, listen to their feelings, ideas, and opinions, learn with them and from them, help them acquire attitudes and skills for resilience, overcoming failure, and becoming successful (Kellerman & Seligman, 2023; Rosenthal & Jacobson, 1968).

Family Principles for Monitoring Success

Maintain an Optimistic Attitude

The way parents and grandparents look at people and interpret situations is an important aspect of current influence and their future legacy. By focusing on possibilities of people and situations more than on limitations, you give a positive perspective to support mental health and build resilience whenever setbacks occur that should be overcome.

Couples Should Adjust to Social Change

People who accept social change are seen as living in the present and are considered as potential sources of advice. More older adults need to think about how changes in gender role expectations from past generations implicate their behavior. Grandparents can contribute to strengthening the family by building intergenerational relationships (Strom & Strom, 1992).

Broaden Your Goals for Self-Improvement

Physical exercise, playing games, and having hobbies are worthwhile activities. Time should also be spent on acquiring education that enables grandparent and parents to become more successful (Strom & Strom, 1991). By balancing what you want to learn with the things you need to know, you can become a more favorable influence on your relatives and the larger community.

Raise Expectations of Peers

Grandparents should establish high standards for their peer group. These expected behavior norms should include a commitment to personal development, concern for the welfare of others demonstrated by volunteering, and taking an active role in community affairs to support a better future for everyone.

Goal Setting Is Needed for Adult Success

Defining the grandparent role in cooperation with younger relatives clarifies expectations, provides a sense of direction, and determines priorities. Grandparents are able to judge personal progress better when their self-evaluation centers on how well goals set previously are met. Children and grandchildren should give feedback.

Treat Children as Individuals

When children are treated as individuals, they will have a greater impact on you, cause you to understand them better, and stimulate you to remain in touch with them. Resolve to experience the joys and difficulties of getting to know each grandchild as a separate person and make sure you self-disclose so they can get to know you better as well.

Conclusion

Children can improve self-evaluation when they are given opportunities to set some of their own goals, find out how they think they are progressing, and get feedback from parents. Without goals that are clearly stated, there is nothing for children to evaluate because adults who set the goals are always the judges. Goals should be age-appropriate, but this is often not the case. Therefore, helping children modify goals that might be too ambitious is one of the first steps in self-evaluation. To amend plans, children should recognize some particular goal was unattainable or too limited and should be amended. The advice of parents and grandparents about goals is more acceptable when adults reveal their own goals and share stories about how they have coped with setbacks.

Learning to set personality goals, modify aspirations, and leave unreasonable dreams behind are necessary aspects of growing up. Unfortunately, many children do not have such experiences because parents make most of their decisions for them. In contrast, when children are allowed to set some of their goals, they feel more in control of their lives, develop a sense of personal direction, show more motivation to succeed, and avoid distractions that could contradict their goals. Children need guidance to reflect on whether some of their goals are unattainable or too limited and therefore should be revised.

Key Concepts

1. When someone's goals are known, it is easier to understand them and to provide them with feedback on how well they are doing toward reaching personal aspirations. There is less of a tendency to misinterpret their intentions or risk unfair conclusions on how well they perform.
2. Parents and grandparents should recognize that learning to set goals and amend them are necessary aspects of growing up. Yet many children are denied such opportunities by adults who insist on deciding all the plans for younger relatives. Adults justify the takeover of decisions by claims that a child's poor choices could result in disappointing consequences.
3. One way to support child development is encourage students to choose personality goals before having deliberations about possible career options. Personality goals focus on the kind of person a student wishes to become.
4. Personality goals are a more appropriate long-term focus for self-evaluation than is performance in academic subjects. Family and school support for personality

development communicates the message that emotional and social development is seen as achievement.
5. Resilience is an outlook that motivates efforts needed to overcome personal limitations. Early development of this ability enables children to see setbacks as a failure to reach some self-determined goals. When children are not allowed to set some of their goals but expected to reach only goals set by parents, they may deny failure or lack the motivation to do anything about it.
6. Parents of high achievers insist their children, from an early age, learn to plan some things by themselves. They give high estimates of what their child can accomplish, provide encouragement, and leave most decisions up to the child. These parents favor early self-reliance for accountability.
7. Because trusting someone means relinquishing control of their behavior, we can claim to trust only those who are allowed to reach their own conclusions and make some of their own choices. This means parents fail to show trust if they regularly insist on making decisions for their children.
8. The way to show trust is permitting children to make decisions that match their mental abilities and stage of development. When the emphasis is on making intelligent choices rather than always telling children what they should do, parents convey the message, "You are capable. I trust you."
9. When children are restricted to carrying out goals established for them by others, they lack their own goals and often express boredom. They cannot evaluate themselves because they lack suitable purposes to use as criteria and do not know what to do when they are not assigned tasks by others. They lack self-motivation.
10. High achievers in all age groups share the ability to accurately detect their personal limitations. They know how to self-evaluate, a skill everyone needs to acquire to identify personal learning needs. Parents and teachers judge behavior of children daily but seldom arrange opportunities for youngsters to judge themselves.

Generational Perspectives Activities

9.1 Discussion
9.2 Conversations With Young Children
9.3 A Scenario: Reasoning and Problem-Solving
9.4 Chapter Review
9.5 Parent and Grandparent Self-Evaluation
9.6 Storytelling

9.1 Discussion

1. How do you feel about the over-choice experienced by many students?
2. Compare your self-reliance at the age as your children; grandchildren.
3. How supportive were your parents in letting you set some of your goals?
4. What were some goals you set but later found necessary to amend?
5. What are some personality goals you are striving for at your present age?
6. Explain how your goals for children seem well-balanced or too narrow?

9.2 Conversations With Young Children

1. What was an unreasonable goal you tried to achieve and had to amend?
2. What do you think about overscheduling in the lives of many children?
3. How supportive are parents in letting you decide some of your own goals?
4. What are some personality goals you are trying to achieve at this time?
5. What goals would you try at school if you did not have to get a grade?
6. What opportunities do parents provide you to judge your own behavior?

9.3 Reasoning and Problem-Solving

Becoming self-reliant requires opportunities to set goals and later gauge how well the goals have been met. Unfortunately, many parents set most goals for children and fail to recognize the best time for practicing this important skill is when stakes are low. What advice do you have for this large group of parents?

a. Setting goals is a fundamental aspect of autonomy needed to build independence.
b. If students lack practice in setting goals, they remain overly dependent on adults.
c. One benefit of setting personal goals is later realizing a need to amend some goals.
d. Urging persistence to attain goals of others denies quitting can be a good option.
e. Other _____

9.4 Chapter Review

1. What insights from the chapter will I try to apply in my relationships?
2. What is the most important key concept for me presented in this chapter?
3. Which elements of this chapter do I wish I had known about earlier?

9.5 Parent and Grandparent Self-Evaluation

1. In my family, parents

    a. seem to make most decisions for children
    b. try to plan the whole summer of children
    c. favor early self-reliance by their children
    d. give them experience in learning to plan
    e. Other _____

2. Parents who make most decisions for children

    a. do so because the children are immature
    b. deprive children of learning about planning
    c. ignore that child goals motivate the most
    d. feel they know what is best for children
    e. Other _____

3. The way for children to learn from poor decisions is to

    a. let them experience the consequences
    b. make sure there is a low cost for failing
    c. point out long-term mistakes by others

d. amend goals when they are not suitable
   e. Other _____

4. I have shared with children

   a. some foolish goals of mine that had to be changed
   b. the goals I pursued despite having to face difficulty
   c. goals other people had for me that I did not want
   d. the benefit of talking to mature people about goals
   e. Other _____

5. My conversations with children about goal setting

   a. include a need to become aware of personal limitations
   b. is pursue any goal you want as long as you don't give up
   c. is identify your strengths in relation to goals you set
   d. is tell parents, relatives, and teachers about your goals
   e. Other _____

6. My own goals at this time are focused on

   a. preservation of my health
   b. managing money wisely
   c. pursuit of personal interests
   d. helping younger relatives
   e. Other _____

7. When I compare myself with the children in our family,

   a. I was more self-reliant
   b. I was more responsible
   c. I was on my own more
   d. I was less peer-driven
   e. Other _____

8. I would like children in our family to have

   a. more instruction and practice with goal setting
   b. more knowledge about goals of older relatives
   c. lessons at school about how to amend goals
   d. more opportunities to make low-cost mistakes
   e. Other _____

9.6 Storytelling

Historically, storytelling has been a dominant classic and progressive method of teaching around the world. The purposes of a storyteller are to present imaginary or real-life examples showing how some concept applies to a particular situation. People like stories, they pay attention to the procession of events, and usually remember aspects of a story for a long time. Your stories can reinforce the concepts in this chapter for family members and classmates. Please share your stories with them.

References

Ali, S., & Chin, M. M. (2023). *The peer effect. How your peers shape who you are and who you will become*. NYU Press.

Britannica, The Editors of Encyclopedia. (2024, October 10). *Metamorphoses*. Encyclopedia Britannica. https://www.britannica.com/topic/Metamorphoses-poem-by-Ovid

City University of New York. (2019). *Brown v. the Board of Education: The desegregation of America's schools. The legacy of Dr. Kenneth B. Clark toward humanity and racial justice*. https://kennethclark.commons.gc.cuny.edu/brown-v-the-board-of-education/

Clark, K. B. (1955). *Prejudice and your child*. Wesleyan University Press.

Clark, K. B. (1965). *Dark ghetto*. Harper & Row.

Clark, K. B. (1974). *Pathos of power*. Harper & Row.

Cukor, G. (Director). (1964). *My fair lady* [Play]. Warner Bros.

Evans, S. W., Owens, J. S., Bradshaw, C. P., & Weist, M. D. (Eds.). (2023). *Handbook of school mental health: Innovations in science a Teach your children well: Parenting for authentic success* (3rd ed.). Springer.

Ferguson, R. F., & Robertson, T. (2019). *The formula: Unlocking the secrets to raising highly successful children*. BenBella Books.

Greene, R. (2000). *The 48 laws of power*. Viking.

Hooley, J. M., Langer, E. J., Lenzenweger, M. F., Rubin, D. B., & McNally, R. J. (2024). Robert Rosenthal, 90: Memorial minute-faculty of arts and sciences. *The Harvard Gazette*. https://news.harvard.edu/gazette/story/2024/10/memorial-minute-for-robert-rosenthal-90/

Jackson, M. (2023). *Uncertain: The wisdom and wonder of being unsure*. Prometheus.

Kellerman, G., & Seligman, M. (2023). *Tomorrowmind*. Atria Books.

Keppel, B. (2002). Kenneth B. Clark in the patterns of American culture. *American Psychologist, 57*(1), 29–37. https://doi.org/10.1037/0003-066X.57.1.29

Krznaric, R. (2020). *The good ancestor: A radical prescription for long-term thinking*. The Experiment.

Levine, M. (2020). *Ready or not: Preparing out kids to thrive in an uncertain and rapidly changing world*. Harper.

McClelland, D. C. (2010). *The achieving society*. Martino Fine Books.

McClelland, D. C. (2015). *The achievement motive*. Martino Fine Books.

Merton, R. K. (1967). *On theoretical sociology*. Free Press.

National Park Service. (2024, April 11). *Brown v. board of education: Kenneth and Mamie Clark Doll*. African American Experience Fund of the National Park Foundation. https://www.nps.gov/brvb/learn/historyculture/clarkdoll.htm

Rosenthal, R. (1964). Experimenter outcome-orientation and the results of the psychological experiment. *Psychological Bulletin, 61*(6), 405–412. https://doi.org/10.1037/h0045850

Rosenthal, R. (1971). Teacher expectations and pupil learning. In R. D. Strom (Ed.), *Teachers and the learning process* (pp. 33–60). Prentice-Hall.

Rosenthal, R., & Jacobson, L. (1968). *Pygmalion in the classroom: Teacher expectation and pupils' intellectual development*. Crown House.

Shaw, G. B. (1913). *Pygmalion* [Play]. Wikipedia. https://en.wikipedia.org/wiki/Pygmalion

Stewart, J. I. M., & Weintraub, S. (2024, October 23). *George Bernard Shaw: Irish dramatist and critic*. Encyclopedia Britannica. https://www.britannica.com/biography/George-Bernard-Shaw

Strom, R. D. (1965). *Teaching in the slum school*. Charles E. Merrill Books.

Strom, R. D. (Ed.). (1966). *The inner-city classroom: Teacher behaviors*. Charles E. Merrill.

Strom, R. D. (1967, August). *The Preface Plan: A new concept of inservice training for teachers newly assigned to urban neighborhoods of low income*. The Office of Education, U. S. Department of Health, Education and Welfare and the Ohio State University [Contract No. OEC-3-6-061365-0711]. https://files.eric.ed.gov/fulltext/ED017596.pdf

Strom, R. D., & Strom, S. K. (1991). *Becoming a better grandparent: Viewpoints on strengthening the family*. Sage.

Strom, R. D., & Strom, S. K. (1992). *Achieving grandparent potential: Viewpoints on building intergenerational relationships*. Sage.

Strom, R. D., & Strom, P. S. (2011). A paradigm for intergenerational learning. In M. London (Ed.), *The Oxford handbook of lifelong learning* (pp. 133–146). Oxford University Press.

Strom, P. S., & Strom, R. D. (2024). *Mental health and relationships from early adulthood through old age*. Routledge.

Chapter 10

Tutoring for Literacy and School Achievement

Parents worry about undesirable lessons that students might learn from classmates, such as involvement with cheating, smoking, bullying, and drug abuse. Clique groups that are formed during elementary school can undermine the status of some students by causing them to become a target for teasing or social rejection. Many parents wish that peers had less influence on self-esteem. Another way to think about the growing influence of peers is to recognize their potential to support academic progress. Peers can be a powerful source of motivation for individuals to adopt healthy social norms. The purposes of this chapter are to (a) acknowledge that many students perform poorly on academic tests, indicating they need access to tutoring, (b) review how school models address distinctions in student ability and pace of learning, (c) examine strategies to remediate academic limitations of students, and (d) describe the parent responsibility to monitor literacy skills in early childhood. Generational Perspectives Activities present topics to discuss with family members and close friends about tutoring children for literacy and achievement at school.

Peer Teaching in the School

Benefits of Inter-Age Grouping

Advocates of peer tutoring believe this practice could become common if public schools were reorganized. The historic rationale for grouping students based on grade level was to make instruction less complex and to minimize differences in student achievement. On the other hand, grouping students by grade level also has the less desirable effect of rendering students less able to seek tutoring from more competent peers. The impression that students in the same grade are seen as similar in ability encourages competition among students. If, instead, the school purpose was to support tutoring of peers, then a broad range of class performance would be desirable so students could serve as teachers along with the adult teachers who supervise classrooms.

Consider an international comparison. The elementary schools in Great Britain are based on a different kind of organizational structure that deliberately favors student participation with inter-age tutoring (Owens & Valesky, 2021). Children aged 4–7 years are placed in what is called Infant Schools, where they attend the same classroom with a four-year spread in the age of their peers. Older students, aged 8–13 years, attend a Junior

DOI: 10.4324/9781003534655-14

School, where they are provided opportunities to collaborate, enabling them to achieve teamwork skills. Here are some benefits of inter-age grouping.

- Older children develop responsibility to provide assistance for their younger classmates.
- Younger children have access to more mature models that they can attempt to imitate.
- Younger proficient students can interact with older students of a similar mental age.
- Slower students do not feel that they are unfavorably compared with others in their class.
- Group activities are for all abilities and interests and not based upon grade expectations.

The U.S. public schools were initially established in the 1860s, and the basis for school organization has been grade level. Soon it became obvious that a slower rate of progress by some students would prevent them from meeting grade-level expectations in the same amount of time as higher-achieving classmates. Instead of focusing on adjustments to accommodate differences in individual rates of progress, the dominant practice was to fail slow students and require them to repeat the same grade in the following year. Since 2020, more than half of the nation's school districts have adopted a policy to retain students whose reading scores in third grade show they are struggling to meet the basic standards for literacy (Ozek & Mariano, 2023).

Proposals for Non-Graded Schools

During the 1960s, research on variability revealed that by the time students are nine years old, there is already a four-grade spread in their levels of achievement. Growth within persons is also variable because students do not progress at the same rate across all curriculum subjects. The outcomes of testing may show that a fifth-grade student scores at the sixth grade in spelling and reading but at the seventh grade in mathematics and science. Because this student is advanced in most curriculum subjects, what do you suppose would be the best grade placement?

In reply to this question, John Goodlad, former Dean of the College of Education at UCLA and President of the American Educational Research Association, proposed the introduction of non-graded elementary schools. This innovative school structure would facilitate continuous student progress, accept variation in individual pace of learning, arrange classes based on peer grouping similar to the British schools, and provide mental stimulation for slow learners, the gifted, and all other students in between (Goodlad & Anderson, 1959).

An example of an operational non-graded secondary school was described by B. Frank Brown (1963), Principal of Melbourne High School located near the Kennedy National Space Center at Cape Canaveral, Florida. All the students at Melbourne enrolled in six subjects with placement in each subject determined by the achievement test scores and faculty judgment. Each subject had multiple sections, ranging in difficulty reflected by five 'phases' for instruction. For example, students enrolled in phase 1 mathematics studied fundamentals they should have learned during elementary school. At the other end of the difficulty scale, students in phase 5 studied calculus, a difficulty level usually provided for students assigned to accelerated or gifted programs. A Melbourne student could be in phase 3 for English, phase 2 for science, and phase 1 in mathematics. Transferring to another phase up or down could take place any time during the school year based on performance-level changes. Principal Brown argued, "If public schools in America are ever to achieve the ideal of having individuals progress at their own rate, some form of non-grading must be instituted."

Despite the practical merit of non-graded schools to respect student differences in ability, allow individuals to move forward at their own pace, access tutoring help from more competent classmates, and evidence of success when this approach was put into operation, the non-graded organizational structure was rejected. School administrators resisted the idea because it was a departure from the organizational plan they had been oriented to and thought to be preferable. Parents also opposed non-graded schools because they wanted to know how their children were progressing in relation to grade placement. As a result, scores on tests and report cards reflecting grade-level achievement became the main criteria for teacher, parent, and student expectations.

Outcomes of Peer Teaching

Peer tutoring assumes that younger students will benefit from guidance provided by older students who are entrusted to act as teacher assistants. Tutoring is not always successful, but it does recognize that children are capable of not only learning but also teaching. What was not understood for a long time was that the tutors themselves experience important learning gains. During the 1960s, President John F. Kennedy challenged educators across the country to explore new methods to support potential dropouts that would enable them to stay in school and graduate. He identified significant forthcoming shifts in the labor market that were bound to occur because of emergent automation. Many of the unskilled jobs that had typically been filled by dropouts would in time be expected to disappear. In response to the president's appeal for innovation, many urban school districts set up experimental programs that were focused on peer tutoring (Riessman, 1965).

One project was Mobilization for Youth, a massive initiative meant to help elementary students from poor neighborhoods in New York City who had difficulty with reading. The volunteer tutors assigned to provide help were high school students. Psychologist Riessman (1965), a consultant for the project, observed that the younger children found tutoring sessions satisfying but did not seem to be learning much. In contrast, the high school tutors were enthused about being involved in a leadership role and reported significant improvement in self-esteem. Regardless of how effective they were, the untrained tutors expressed satisfaction because they were trying to help someone else learn. Other observable and significant outcomes were that the teenage tutors became more interested in the ways younger students learned and acquired new skills and attitudes they applied in their own high school classes. Some teenagers tutoring elementary arithmetic, for example, showed considerable improvement in their own mathematics classes. More benefits from learning by teaching were confirmed by testimony of the participants (Gartner et al., 1971).

Because anecdotal reports provided only subjective estimates of tutoring outcomes, a decision was made to have the Mobilization for Youth research staff conduct control studies. Cloward (1976) and his associates focused on changes in the student achievement test scores. Results showed that tutors made striking gains in achievement scores, much larger than the elementary students they were tutoring. Over five-months younger students with deficiencies grew an average of six months in reading while the students tutoring them gained 3.4 years on achievement tests (Strom et al., 2022).

Training Peers as Tutors

The unforeseen academic benefits experienced by peer tutors were welcome. However, some other strategy was needed to ensure that students being tutored would also make good progress. A team of social scientists led by Ron and Peggy Lippitt (1970) from the University of Michigan worked with colleagues in the public schools to develop a training program for volunteer high school tutors that would help them meet remedial academic needs of younger students, enrich opportunities for modeling, and increase motivation to learn. These experiments were conducted at elementary schools in the central city and suburban Detroit. The upper-grade students engaged in this cross-age helper program were provided an orientation to learn what younger students are like and what causes some to experience problems. Each tutor learned to cooperate with a younger child's classroom teacher and assist a particular student directly. As a rule, the self-impression of tutors as being an 'expert' was more easily sustained when s/he was at least two grade levels ahead of the student being tutored. Cross-age helpers were given weekly training sessions about motivation and teaching techniques led by a classroom teacher, counselor, or building principal.

The cross-age helper program was adopted by many large city school districts across the country as the most effective way to prepare peer tutors (Lippitt, 1975). This strategy remained popular until 1990 as the preferred method to equip tutors since the usual result for both parties was higher achievement and greater self-confidence. In addition, the students who were being tutored demonstrated improvement in attitudes toward learning, and they became more willing to request help. Tutors gained valuable practice in finding out the perceptions of younger students and recognized the importance of being able to collaborate with a child's classroom teacher.

Tutoring for Reading

Reading Deficiencies by Third Grade

The need for tutoring continues to be underestimated by most parents and grandparents. The Annie E. Casey Foundation (2010) published a ten-year longitudinal study of 4,000 students titled *Early Warning: Why Reading by the End of Third Grade Matters*. This benchmark report revealed approximately 40% of students could not read at grade level and initiated the motivation to launch a national campaign targeting reading at grade level as a goal for all students in the nation. The Kids Count Data Center of the Annie E. Casey Foundation (2024) provides a website for educators and parents to learn the status of student academic performance for the nation, state, and local school district: https://datacenter.aecf.org/

Third grade is a pivotal time when students are expected to shift from learning how to read to the more comprehensive goal of relying on reading as the main tool for learning about other subjects in the curriculum (Annie E. Casey Foundation, 2010, 2024). Unfortunately, each year more than 80% of students from low-income families cannot perform at grade-level proficiency. These students are also the most rapidly increasing segment of the school population. Since 2020, more than half of the nation's school districts have established a common policy to retain students whose reading scores at the end of third grade shows they struggle to meet basic standards of literacy (Ozek & Mariano, 2023; Nickow et al., 2020).

Over 40 years ago, Jean Chall (1983), a reading expert at Harvard University, predicted that a national emphasis on literacy would become necessary for students to be able to succeed in a technological society. She explained there would be a need to go beyond the customary focus on helping children learn how to read, called basic literacy, to also concentrate on the need for self-directed reading. By adding this new emphasis, students would be able to learn more on their own within a digital environment, allowing them to access unprecedented knowledge that goes beyond what can be provided by teachers in the classroom.

National Assessment of Educational Progress

National Assessment of Educational Progress (NAEP) is referred to as *The Nation's Report Card* (2024a, 2024b). This test is administered at two-year intervals to students in grades 4 and 8 and every four years in grade 12. Results present data on reading knowledge, skills, and performance change. In 2022, results for reading scores showed 33% of grade 4 students nationally were at or above the NAEP Proficient level. In mathematics, 36% of grade 4 students scored at or above the NAEP Proficient level.

When students with deficits are asked to tell what makes reading difficult, they most often blame the words. Vocabulary research has consistently determined that higher order thinking depends on having a sufficient understanding of word meanings. Experts express concern regarding the decline in literacy recorded on the Nation's Report Card (2024a, 2024b). The average scores of 12th graders have been in decline for over two decades. Teachers of every grade have observed many students seem to rebel against reading. Adolescents view texting, videos, graphics, podcasts, tweets, and Google searches as preferable ways to retrieve information than reading in-depth materials or listening carefully to direct teacher instruction (Toch & Cohen, 2024).

The consequences of poor verbal and numeracy skills are complicated by common social promotion practices that allow nearly all students to graduate from high school. The average high school graduation rate for most of the states has risen to over 80%, highest ever recorded. However, college placement test scores indicate that over half a million of the students entering higher education are required to enroll in remedial reading or remedial mathematics courses that do not include college credit. A further tragedy is that 40% of students at two-year colleges and 25% at four-year universities fail to finish these remedial classes. Estimates are that fewer than one in ten students who start college in remediation graduate from community colleges in three years, and only one-third complete bachelor's degrees in six years. Fortunately, because of broader thinking about college requirements for jobs, greater attention is being given by many students to other options such as apprenticeships and short-term tech schools that can build pathways to promising careers (Brickman, 2024).

The American College Test (ACT) (2024) is administered in high school to students interested in attending college. The test used by many college and university admissions departments is taken by 1.5 million high school students covering English, mathematics, reading, and scientific reasoning. Taking the test requires 3.5 hours. If students are not satisfied with their score, they are allowed to retake the exam. Analysis of results has consistently identified 'inability to grasp complex texts' as the main reason students are assigned to remediation courses. The practice of skim reading does not match the comprehension level that is gained by reading slowly, concentrating, and engaging in reflection. Being assigned to remedial education is the single greatest predictor that a student will quit college before graduating (Fisher & Frey, 2023; Fisher et al., 2022).

Looking toward the future, the Georgetown University Center on Education and the Workforce (2024) forecasts that, compared to 2021 when 68% of jobs required postsecondary education, the proportion is expected to rise to 72% by 2031 with 42% of the positions requiring at least a bachelor's degree. Only 28% of jobs will be filled by individuals whose background is limited to a high school diploma. The predicted job growth for all 50 states, from 2021 to 2031, can be reviewed at the Georgetown University site titled *After everything Projections of Jobs, Education, and Training Requirements through 2031.*

Smartphones and Student Performance

The use of smartphones in the classroom has become a topic of widespread debate as it relates to the poor academic performance of students. Some European nations such as France, Netherlands, Italy, Hungary, and Sweden have, for now, chosen to ban student use of smartphones during the school day (Chadwick, 2024). Some of the common reasons given are student distraction, erosion of concentration, and the loss of focus.

In the United States, Johnathan Haidt's (2024) book *The Anxious Generation* explains the shift from a play-based childhood to a phone-based process of growing up with implications for academic development. According to Haidt, the four foundational harms to children include: social deprivation, sleep deprivation, attention fragmentation, and addiction. Children are moving from play to being on the smartphone for excessively long periods. Similar concerns are expressed by Maggie Jackson's (2018) *Distracted: Reclaiming our Focus in a World of Lost Attention* and also *Attention Span* by Gloria Mark (2023). This international debate is in the early stages but urges educators, parents, and school administrators to determine whether and in what ways smartphones could be used at school.

Focus on Individual Learning

Mary was a retired elementary teacher. Her daughter told Mary that granddaughter Elizabeth in second grade was eight months behind in reading grade level. Mary said "let Elizabeth come visit me this summer and I think we will see some improvement." Following the summer visit with Mary, her granddaughter was retested and scored above grade level. Mary understood that tutoring is almost always more effective than group instruction. This situation underscores the significance of one-to-one instruction. Currently, access to free tutoring in public schools is generally restricted to students attending Title I schools, where 40% or more of the student population come from low-income families. Public schools should not be allowed to outsource their obligation for the tutoring instruction students need to meet academic proficiency standards (National Center for Education Statistics, 2024).

School in the Cloud

Adults usually underestimate the potential of students to tutor their peers. An exception was Sugata Mitra, Professor of Educational Technology from Newcastle University in England, who was a recipient of the annual Technology Entertainment Design (TED) award that included a cash prize of $1 million to invest in his dream of establishing a school in the clouds. Mitra was recognized for his many experiments that involved students from resource-scarce environments in India, Asia, and Africa. These studies confirmed elementary and middle-school age students can effectively tutor classmates about computer tasks. According to Mitra, "Education that does not include an understanding of the Internet and how to live with it, is deficient" (Mitra 2015, 2018, 2019, 2022; Modi, 2022).

Khan Academy – The American Nonprofit Educational Organization

Salman Khan (2012, 2024) is responsible for a tutoring revolution that benefits students across the globe. He was brought up by his immigrant single mother and completed graduate degrees in engineering and finance at MIT and Harvard before assuming an executive position in a hedge fund company. When relatives asked Salman to tutor Nadia, his nine-year-old cousin, in mathematics, he had to devise a strategy to overcome distance since she lived in New Orleans, and he was in Boston. He posted video lessons on YouTube for Nadia using his voice along with a virtual blackboard for tutoring. Before long he began to receive compliments from other students who discovered his lessons online and found them helpful. Then, in 2008, Salman founded the Khan Academy as a nonprofit venture supported by Google and Bill and Melinda Gates Foundation.

Khan's (2012) first book *The One World Schoolhouse: Education Reimagined,* reported that poor test score ranking of American students compared to other nations should concern leaders in education. This situation can improve for students attending the online Khan Academy who are able to access 4,000 free videos on his website. Help in being able to meet state standards for mathematics is the greatest need of students, but additional lessons are available in art history, chemistry, computer programming, computer science, economics, and health. Each of the video presentations are about ten minutes long. The Academy also provides teachers with real-time feedback about the progress of their students assigned to complete Khan lessons as homework. The premise is that students work at their own pace to reduce personalized learning gaps and master basic concepts (Khan, 2024). By pausing and repeating videos that show step-by-step processes for solving problems, student comprehension increases more than occurs following a one-time demonstration by the teacher. Peer teaching should be recognized by a commendation letter in the school file of a student.

Khan Academy Help Center (2024) in cooperation with the College Board devised the official SAT (Scholastic Aptitude Test). Practice to help high school students prepare for this examination is often used as criteria for admission to colleges. The approach includes test-taking tips and strategies and interactive practice questions. Students also receive eight full-length practice tests that have been prepared by the College Board design team. This strategy reinforces what students learn in school by focusing on knowledge and skills essential for college. The Khan Academy test preparation program has been translated into many languages; 100 million people across the globe use this platform each year. Research has found 20 hours of work on the Khan Academy SAT site was associated with an average score gain of 115 points for 4.3 million students who complete the SAT each year. Leading researchers cite considerable evidence that testing expands opportunity, accounting for the return to require testing of Harvard University student applicants as of 2025 (Hoekstra, 2024).

College Advising Corps

Another motivational source for low-income students is the College Advising Corps (2024) that supplements high school counseling services by pairing recent college graduates, many first in their family to earn a degree among students from low-income schools nationwide. These near-peer advisors are employed full time in high schools and provide personalized advice to over 200,000 students attending 691 high schools about being able to successfully navigate the path to college. A good place to learn more about this novel counseling program is at the Duke University online site at https://community.duke.edu/program/college-advising-corps/

Tutoring in Other Countries

Japanese Elementary Teacher Training

The United States could learn to improve elementary teacher preparation from practices in Japan. Unlike American elementary teachers, prospective elementary teachers in Japan are required to major in an academic subject such as science, mathematics, or history Tsujimoto and Yamasaki (2017). In practice, a Japanese teacher goes to the first-grade classroom and provides instruction only in mathematics for them. At the end of the class hour students remain to wait for a teacher from another subject while the mathematics teacher moves on to another room where s/he provides instruction in mathematics to second graders. The result is that students from kindergarten through grade 12 are continually exposed to specialists who provide instruction in mathematics and other subjects. Longer-range results in Japan are that many students complete calculus, whereas a comparatively small proportion of students in the United States get beyond beginning algebra (Okada & Bamkin, 2022; Tsuneyoshi, 2018).

Reliance on academic subject matter specialists works well for Japan as demonstrated by the fact that most students there perform well on academic tests. This makes it easier to recruit mathematics teachers since mathematics is a common asset among students, so some pursue it as a major in college. Whether it is Japan, Korea, Singapore, Taiwan, or China, the preparation of elementary teachers focuses on the development of academic strength in a single subject they will teach. Americans discuss school improvement but seem to overlook this basic difference that usually places our students well behind peers from competitor nations. Japanese students attend school six days a week, wear uniforms, and go beyond the customary subjects to also study computer programming, home economics, and moral education. Students have additional responsibilities at school such as cleaning up their classrooms (Tsujimoto & Yamasaki, 2017).

Tutoring in South Korea

Advocates of tutoring outside the classroom explain this strategy produces achievement for other nations. For example, 60 years ago most South Koreans were illiterate. In contrast, 15-year-olds from that nation now rank seventh in mathematics internationally on achievement tests. The shift that enabled South Korea to become an academic superpower can be attributed to after-school tutoring that is subscribed to by most families. Students attend free public school during the day and go to cram schools in the evening where tutoring is provided for a fee. Most Korean parents spend almost 20% of their annual income on tutoring (Yeon-woo, 2024). Text messages are sent to the parents each time students arrive for a tutoring session. Other messages with test result details are sent often regarding student progress. Twice a month tutorial teachers phone the parents with feedback and identify deficits in student scores.

When 6,600 students from 116 Korean high schools were surveyed, after-school tutoring teachers were rated much higher than public school teachers for being well prepared, devoted to individual learning needs, respecting student opinion, and treating everyone in class fairly. More American students could perform better if tutoring is emphasized instead of teachers presenting lessons that students can acquire on their own by reading. Tutoring focuses on helping to reduce deficiencies, but group instruction generally overlooks individual needs. *The Korean Times* has documented that tutoring expenses are now the largest burden on many household budgets as parents try to keep up with other families to provide the instruction children need Yeon-woo, L. (2024).

Tutoring in the United Kingdom

Fundamental changes appear needed in student attitudes about tutoring and achievement. Consider students who attend Oxford and Cambridge University in England. They represent the top achievers in the countries from which they have been drawn. All these students are required to attend weekly tutorials. The rationale for this long-standing practice is that everyone, no matter how intelligent, can learn more when their limitations are made known and remediated by support; tutoring increases scope of knowledge and level of competence, encourages a sense of humility, and establishes teamwork skills needed for success in most occupations (Carmody, 2024).

The Program for International Student Assessment

What kinds of outcomes can be expected when there is a national emphasis on tutoring? The Program for International Student Assessment (PISA) is a triennial survey meant to evaluate educational systems globally to recognize achievement and detect needs for curriculum improvement. In 2022, the 15-year-olds from 80 countries completed examinations in science, mathematics, and reading (National Center for Education Statistics, 2024). The six top-ranked nations in mathematics were all Asian including Singapore, Macau (China), Chinese Taipei, Hong Kong (China), Japan, and the Republic of Korea. More specifically, the United States scored thirty-fourth in mathematics, sixteenth in science, ninth in reading, and eighth in financial literacy.

It is noteworthy that the top six nations all support intensive tutoring because they believe in equality, are convinced all students are capable, can perform well if given individual help, and are willing to work hard. Several considerations can be drawn from the strategy applied by leading nations.

(1) Students should understand involvement in tutoring does not imply a person is stupid; instead, the goal is helping individuals of all performance levels to maximize achievement.
(2) Everyone should have access to free tutoring instead of restricting assistance to government financial support for the students from low-income families.

(3) Americans should bear in mind that elementary teachers in Japan, South Korea, China, Taiwan, Macau, and other countries whose students routinely outperform American students are all trained as specialists in a single academic subject. They teach only that subject to students of various ages. This means the teacher goals include detection of individual deficiencies and referral for added instruction needed for tutoring.

(4) American public schools should be expected to provide free tutoring, discontinue the inequitable practice of making middle-income families hire private tutors, and orient all students to a sensible attitude about tutoring as an integral aspect of instruction needed by everyone.

Tutoring in the United States

Most elementary-grade students are not getting the assistance they need. By some estimates just one in ten receives intensive tutoring. Scheduling is often cited as a reason. If tutoring occurs after school hours, this ensures a low rate of participation. Families who consent to after-hours tutoring need to figure out their child's transportation. Most research has shown that tutoring during school hours has roughly twice the impact as after-school tutoring, and so it should be part of the school day (Nickow et al., 2020; Wall, 2023).

Nickow et al. (2020) have prepared a report titled PreK Tutoring Programs and Student Learning Outcomes: A Systematic Review and Meta-Analysis of the Experimental Evidence. However, by far the greatest disadvantage to student progress are the empty schools during summer. Shutting down schools for three months a year is not driven by reason. Summer should be devoted to full-time individual tutoring for all students so they would commonly have the prospect of a brighter future (Strom et al., 2019).

Another obstacle is the recruitment of tutors. One natural resource to tap is the nation's 600,000 aspiring teachers. Before they start student teaching, educators in training often spend extensive time as observers in K-12 classrooms. Some teacher training programs have started to reassign that time for tutoring, enabling aspiring teachers to acquire real experience. A related concern with tutoring programs is evaluation of their effects.

Conclusion

Elementary school teachers struggle with providing individual tutorial help, allowing students of different achievement levels to advance at their own pace and balance the merits of competition and working together in cooperative teams. Peer tutoring usually contributes to the achievement of all these goals. For the tutored, additional gains include greater interest in education, better test scores, increased task persistence, and greater self-confidence. For tutors, the chance to act as a tutor offers an opportunity to gain influence, recognition, and status. Being a tutor fosters healthy attitudes and social skills that can be used throughout life for getting along with others. These benefits occur whether tutors are average, low achievers, or gifted.

Student tutors require training and supervision. When they lack training for their task, peer tutors can expect too much of students, do the work for them, rely on coercive strategies, or score papers improperly. Given parent support and practical orientation of volunteer peers for teaching, the outcomes can be more favorable. Training can help tutors understand younger students and know what causes some students to struggle in particular subjects. Student tutors learn to cooperate with a younger child's teacher and acquire techniques to assist the student directly. Americans should carefully consider adopting the view of Asian nations about the best focus to prepare elementary teachers; they would major in one subject instead of expecting them to teach all subjects in the curriculum.

There is much to be learned about how tutoring can be more prominent in the context of growing peer influence on student attitudes and concerns. When grade inflation is common, learning deficits go undetected, so the need for tutoring is often overlooked. Every school should have a schedule that provides opportunity for all students to get tutorial support and sometimes assume a tutoring role. Instead, most of our elementary schools are closed over the summer, so student deficits are not addressed. This is a serious national problem that should be considered by all school districts. There should also be increased support from communities where churches and synagogues recruit and train older adults to become additional tutors for primary-grade students.

Key Concepts

1. Students from other countries are expected to perform well and devote most of their time to study. This academic orientation should be more common for American students who, by comparison, have poor study habits reflected by excessive time communicating with friends and involvement with entertainment.
2. Helping individuals identify their learning deficiencies should be followed by involvement with tutoring. Students should assume responsibility for poor performance instead of blaming extrinsic factors over which they lack control.
3. Tutoring focuses on helping students become aware of personal cognitive limitations and overcoming them. In contrast, group instruction overlooks the wide range of differences in individual learning needs that must be met by some other means.
4. Grade inflation exists at all grade levels in each state and school district. This deception presents a serious risk because it overlooks detection of learning needs, condones mediocre performance, and causes students to acquire unjustified confidence in their abilities.
5. Private tutoring companies should not be expected to perform tasks that are part of the school mission with its resources intended to meet educational needs of all students. Tutoring should become an aspect of instruction students and families recognize is essential for everyone.
6. Teachers seen as particularly effective tutors and who enjoy this task should be given the option of a full-time assignment working one to one with students self-referred or by teachers in classrooms.
7. All students should have access to free tutoring and be encouraged to use this powerful tool to improve their achievement performance in all the curriculum subjects they enroll in.
8. One definition of friendship is to always look out for the best interests of someone we care about, share feelings and ideas with them, and provide advice that supports growth and maturity. This means a friend would always recommend tutoring to improve performance.
9. Teachers support comprehension by finding or making videos of unfamiliar or difficult lessons and placing these resources on the school website. Then students review a problem-solving process multiple times, pause as needed, eventually comprehend the lesson, and avoid peer embarrassment in class.
10. Parents can support or discourage student involvement with tutoring. Parents should teach children that everyone should acknowledge their academic limitations. The personal admission of need for tutoring is a condition that must be met before teachers can help individuals overcome their limitations.

Generational Perspectives Activities

10.1 Discussion
10.2 Conversations With Young Children
10.3 A Scenario: Reasoning and Problem-Solving
10.4 Chapter Review
10.5 Parent and Grandparent Self-Evaluation
10.6 Storytelling

10.1 Discussion

1. Tell your experiences of being tutored by someone who understood a subject better.
2. How are slow students in classes you have observed helped to overcome limitations?
3. What are the benefits students might gain from serving as a teacher's tutoring assistant?
4. Why should students be promoted or held back without meeting grade-level standards?
5. How do you feel about students with low test scores being given high report card grades?
6. How do you think we could provide free tutoring for students of all backgrounds?
7. How do you feel about parents having to pay private companies to tutor children?
8. How do student grades given today compare to your own grades in school?
9. What should be expected when a student has deficiencies in a school subject?
10. How do you feel about having older students tutor students who are younger?

10.2 Conversations With Young Children

1. If you needed tutoring, would you be embarrassed to ask for it?
2. What tutoring benefits have you gained from an adult? a peer?
3. Why doesn't your school offer tutoring over the summer months?
4. What do you know about how other countries provide tutoring?
5. What have relatives told you about their own tutoring experience?
6. What has your teacher told the class about the benefits of tutoring?

10.3 A Scenario: Reasoning and Problem-Solving

Nancy and John were just informed by daughter Jenny's third-grade teacher that she should attend a summer tutoring program at school. As a family friend, what are your suggestions?

a. Try to find out her test performance in reading and mathematics.
b. Can she be tutored by a college student chosen by the parents?
c. Find out who is going to provide the summer school tutoring.
d. What are the responsibilities to be expected of the parents?
e. Why weren't parents notified earlier Jenny had a problem?
f. Other

10.4 Chapter Review

1. What insights from the chapter will I try to apply in my relationships?
2. What is the most important key concept for me presented in this chapter?
3. Which elements of this chapter do I wish I had known about earlier?

10.5 Parent and Grandparent Self-Evaluation

1. If my child Jenny is not performing well in academics,
    a. should I blame myself for not monitoring better?
    b. should I take away privileges to punish Jenny?
    c. can I provide the tutoring Jenny needs at home?
    d. is Jenny being negatively influenced by peers?
    e. Other _____

2. The way I feel about peer tutoring at school is
    a. kids cannot substitute for competent teachers
    b. students should be trained to assume this task
    c. I like the idea of using student talents to tutor
    d. kids are more motivated to learn from peers
    e. Other _____

3. Self-directed reading on the Internet was
    a. never an expectation by my teachers
    b. something I frequently did on my own
    c. often expected of me by my parents
    d. Other _____

4. The Khan Academy
    a. seems like a wonderful resource for students
    b. I have not visited with my child
    c. has not been recommended to me by teachers
    d. I would like my child to try some assignments
    e. Other _____

5. My understanding of tutoring in Asian countries
    a. demonstrates they are way ahead of the United States
    b. suggests Americans need to reform teacher education
    c. shows parents expect better performance by children
    d. is that academics has higher priority than social media
    e. Other _____

6. I believe American parents should consider
    a. investing some of their income on tutoring for children
    b. having students devote more time to classroom learning
    c. revising the daily schedule to make the school day longer
    d. have students attend school six days a week
    e. Other _____

10.6 Storytelling

Historically, storytelling has been a dominant classic and progressive method of teaching around the world. The purposes of a storyteller are to present imaginary or real-life examples showing how some concept applies to a particular situation. People like stories, they pay attention to the procession of events, and usually remember aspects of a story for a long time. Your stories can reinforce the concepts in this chapter for family members and classmates. Please share your stories with them.

References

American College Test. (2024). *The ACT test.* https://www.act.org/content/act/en/products-and-services/the-act.html

Annie E. Casey Foundation (2010, January 1). *Early warning! Why reading by the end of third grade matters: A Kids Count Special Report on the importance of reading by 3rd grade.* https://www.aecf.org/resources/early-warning-why-reading-by-the-end-of-third-grade-matters

Annie E. Casey Foundation, Kids Count Data Center (2024). *Trusted well-being data on children and young people in the United States.* https://datacenter.aecf.org/

Brickman, M. (2024, February 21). *Breaking the college remediation cycle.* American Enterprise Institute. https://www.aei.org/education/breaking-the-college-remediation-cycle/

Brown, B. F. (1963). The non-graded high school. *The Phi Delta Kappan, 44*(5), 206–209. http://www.jstor.org/stable/20342905

Carmody, M. (2024). *Getting into Oxford and Cambridge 2025 entry* (27th ed.). Trotman.

Chadwick, L. (December 29, 2024). Which countries in Europe have banned or want to restrict smartphones in schools? *Europe News [euronews].* https://www.euronews.com/next/2024/12/29/which-countries-in-europe-have-banned-or-want-to-restrict-smartphones-in-schools

Chall, J. S. (1983). *Stages of reading development.* McGraw-Hill. https://www.learner.org/wp-content/uploads/2019/06/RWD.DLU1_.ChallsStages.pdf

Cloward, R. (1976). Teenagers as tutors of academically low-achieving children. In V. Allen (Ed.), *Children as teachers: Theory and research on tutoring.* Academic Press.

College Advising Corps. (2024). *Bright futures ahead: Annual report 2022–2023.* https://collegeadvisingcorps.org/

Fisher, D., & Frey, N. (2023). *The vocabulary playbook: Learning words that matter, K-12.* Corwin.

Fisher, D., Frey, N., & Lapp, D. (2022). *Teaching reading: A playbook for developing skilled readers through word recognition and language comprehension.* Corwin.

Gartner, A., Kohler, M., & Riessman, F. (1971). *Children teach children: Learning by teaching.* Harper & Row.

Georgetown University Center on Education and the Workforce. (2024). *After everything: Projections of jobs, education, and training requirements through 2031.* https://cew.georgetown.edu/cew-reports/projections2031/

Goodlad, J., & Anderson, R. (1959). *The non-graded elementary school.* Harcourt, Brace & World.

Haidt, J. (2024). *The anxious generation: How the great rewiring of childhood is causing an epidemic of mental illness.* Penguin.

Hoekstra, H. (2024, April 11). *Return to required testing.* Harvard University. https://www.fas.harvard.edu/2024/04/11/return-to-required-testing/

Jackson, M. (2018). *Distraction: Reclaiming our focus in a world of lost attention.* Prometheus Books.

Khan Academy Help Center. (2024). *Moving from official SAT practice to official digital SAT prep on Khan Academy.* https://support.khanacademy.org/hc/en-us/articles/17921365165581-Moving-from-Official-SAT-Practice-to-Official-Digital-SAT-Prep-on-Khan-Academy#:~:text=The%20new%20Official%20Digital%20SAT,Math%20and%20Reading%20and%20Writing

Khan, S. (2012). *The one world schoolhouse: Education reimagined.* Twelve.

Khan, S. (2024). *Brave new words: How AI will revolutionize education (and why that's a good thing).* Viking.

Lippitt, P. (1975). *Students teach students.* Phi Delta Kappa Educational Foundation.

Lippitt, P., & Lippitt, R. (1970). The peer culture as a learning environment. *Childhood Education, 47*(3), 135–138. https://doi.org/10.1080/00094056.1970.10727242

Mark, G. (2023). *Attention span: A groundbreaking way to restore balance, happiness and productivity.* Hanover Square Press.

Mitra, S. (2015). Minimally invasive education: Pedagogy for development in a connected world. In P. Rothermel (Ed.), *International perspectives on home education: Do we still need schools?* (2015th ed., pp. 254–277). Palgrave Macmillan.

Mitra, S. (2018). New systems for children's learning: Changes required in education. In K. Koutsopoulos, K. Doukas, & Y. Kotsanis (Eds.), *Handbook of research on educational design and cloud computing in modern classroom settings* (pp. 22–33). IGI Global.

Mitra, S. (2019). *The school in the cloud: The emerging future of learning.* Corwin.

Mitra, S. (2022). The internet as a subject in schools. *Prospects.* https://doi.org/10.1007/s11125-022-09620-x

Modi, P. (2022, December 2). *All you need to know about Sugata Mitra's hole in the wall experiment* [Video]. Education Next. https://www.educationnext.in/posts/is-self-learning-the-best-way-to-learn

National Center for Education Statistics. (2024). *Highlights of PISA 2022 U.S. results.* https://nces.ed.gov/surveys/pisa/pisa2022/index.asp

The Nation's Report Card. (2024a). *National achievement-level results.* National Assessment Education Progress: Reading. https://www.nationsreportcard.gov/reading/nation/achievement/?grade=4

The Nation's Report Card. (2024b). *National achievement-level results.* National Assessment Education Progress: Mathematics. https://www.nationsreportcard.gov/mathematics/nation/achievement/?grade=4

Nickow, A., Oreopoulos, P., & Quan, V. (2020, July). *The impressive effects of tutoring on Prek-12 learning: A systematic review and meta-analysis of the experimental evidence.* National Bureau of Economic Research. https://www.nber.org/system/files/working_papers/w27476/w27476.pdf

Okada, A., & Bamkin, S. (Eds.). (2022). *Japan's school curriculum for the 2020s: Politics, policy and pedagogy.* Springer.

Owens, R., & Valesky, T. (2021). *Organizational behavior in education: Leadership and school reform* (12th ed.). Pearson.

Ozek, U., & Mariano, L. T. (2023, October 11). *Think again: Is grade retention bad for kids?* The Thomas B. Fordham Institute. https://fordhaminstitute.org/national/research/think-again-grade-retention-bad

Riessman, F. (1965). The "helper" therapy principle. *Social Work, 10*(2), 27–32. http://www.jstor.org/stable/23708219

Strom, P. S., Hendon, K. L., Strom, R. D., & Wang, C.-H. (2019). How peers support and inhibit learning in the classroom: Assessment of high school students in collaborative groups. *School Community Journal, 29*(2), 183–202. http://www.schoolcommunitynetwork.org/SCJ.aspx

Strom, P. S., Strom, R. D., Sindel-Arrington, P., & Wang, C.-H. (2022). Tutoring support and student voice in middle school. *School Community Journal, 32*(1), 39–62. http://www.schoolcommunitynetwork.org/SCJ.aspx

Toch, T., & Cohen, L. (2024, July 9). *Could tutoring be the next big bipartisan school reform?* Future Ed. https://www.future-ed.org/could-tutoring-be-the-next-big-bipartisan-school-reform/#:~:text=The%20support%20prompts%20the%20question,it%20to%20help%20their%20kids

Tsujimoto, M., & Yamasaki, Y. (2017). *The history of education in Japan (1600–2000).* Routledge.

Tsuneyoshi, R. (Ed.). (2018). *Globalization and Japanese exceptionalism in education: Insider's views into a changing system.* Routledge.

Wall, P. (2023, March 22). *Tutoring isn't reaching most students. Here's how to vastly expand it.* https://www.chalkbeat.org/2023/3/22/23650920/tutoring-covid-learning-loss-expand-pandemic/

Yeon-Woo, L. (2024, July 13). Korean households spend more on tutoring than food, housing. *The Korea Times.* https://www.koreatimes.co.kr/www/biz/2024/07/602_353629.html#:~:text=Kim%20and%20Yoon's%20anxiety%20reflects,first%20quarter%20of%20this%20year

Chapter 11

Praise, Encouragement, and Motivation

Learning to appreciate the influence of praise, encouragement, and motivation contributes to mental health and positive thinking. The purposes of this chapter are to (a) examine the effects of praise and encouragement on child motivation and self-esteem, (b) explore new ideas and ways of seeing events and situations, (c) consider how parents can help children interpret failure, (d) describe how children perceive effort as a factor related to school achievement, (e) review the studies about praise and self-esteem as a way to improve child academic performance, (f) identify the dangers of narcissism for students and discourage school retention practices, (g) apply self-evaluation to determine child strengths and needs, and (h) enable students to admit their academic deficiencies. Generational Perspectives Activities present topics to discuss with family members and close friends about motivation, praising children, and encouraging them.

Differences Between Encouragement and Praise

The Importance of Optimism

Norman Vincent Peale (1898–1993) was a well-known clergyman serving the Marble Collegiate Church in New York City. Peale's (1952/2003) book called *The Power of Positive Thinking* received national acclaim and resulted in him receiving the Presidential Medal of Freedom, the highest civilian honor in the United States. Peale explained that the trouble with most of us is that we would rather be ruined by praise than saved by criticism. Learning to appreciate the influence of praise, encouragement, and motivation contributes to mental health and positive thinking.

Parents, grandparents, and teachers should recognize differences between encouragement and praise. Encouragement can support motivation that is needed to cope with difficult tasks while praise should be reserved as confirmation that a student has reached a particular goal or demonstrated a valued skill. Adults should provide encouragement when performance is mediocre and give praise when performance shows improvement.

Each of us stray from what we intuitively believe to be the right path to provide children positive reinforcement. Three-year-old Haley was helping me (her grandfather) wash dishes. Standing on a chair by the sink, while soaking herself and the floor, Haley handed me what she said was a clean glass. I could see the glass was coated with some mysterious substance. "Good job," I said before reevaluating the accuracy of my comment, and then added, "Thank you for helping me. Looks like you missed something so try to clean this glass again."

Praising Child Ability and Effort in School

Carol Dweck (2007), Professor of Education at Columbia University, conducted a study on the effects of praise and attitudes toward failure among 400 fifth graders in 20 New York City schools. Before her experiments, it was widely believed praising children for their intellectual abilities would boost their self-confidence. However, Dweck hypothesized that this strategy might backfire when students encountered failure. She administered nonverbal IQ tests with puzzles easy enough for everyone to succeed. After the test, students were informed of their scores and given a single line of praise. They were randomly divided into two groups; one group was praised for their intelligence with comments like, "You must be really smart at this," while the other group was praised for their effort with remarks such as, "You must have worked really hard."

In Dweck's subsequent round, students were given a choice between taking a more difficult test that promised greater learning and another easy test like the first. Among students praised for their effort, 90% chose the more difficult puzzles. In contrast, the majority of those praised for intelligence opted for the easier test. The 'smart kids' avoided challenges, likely due to a fear of making mistakes and appearing less intelligent. Next, having artificially induced a round of failure, all students were given a difficult test designed for students two years ahead of their grade level, ensuring failure for everyone. The two groups reacted differently to their failure. Those praised for effort believed they had not concentrated enough and engaged more with the puzzles, while those praised for intelligence felt their failure showed that they were not smart after all.

Following this contrived failure, a final easy test was administered. Students praised for effort improved their scores by 30%, while those praised for intelligence performed 20% worse than they did initially. Dweck (2014) concluded that concentrating on effort gave children a variable they could control, whereas concentrating on intelligence removed this sense of control, and provided no strategy for coping with failure. Students who believed intelligence is a fixed trait and a key to success tended to discount the influence of effort. They perceived effort as evidence of insufficient natural talent. Related research by Duckworth (2018) has confirmed the importance of perseverance on motivation across all income and age levels including preschoolers.

Carol Dweck (2007, 2014) encouraged a mindset where students believe that hard work and persistence are keys to overcoming failure. She maintained that praising talent is misguided whereas praising effort and progress is beneficial. The ability to respond to failure with increased effort rather than giving up has been studied by many researchers. Resilient individuals with persistence maintain motivation over long periods despite delayed gratification. Parents often mistakenly believe that their children cannot detect adults' true intentions. Just as adults recognize insincere apologies, children can perceive the hidden agendas behind praise, especially those older than 7.

Wulf-Uwe Meyer (1992), a psychologist in Germany, studied 500 students aged 8–19 who watched videos of students receiving praise. By age 12, children believed that teacher praise indicated a lack of ability and a need for encouragement. Students who lagged often received excessive praise, which the teenagers came to dismiss, instead viewing teacher criticism as a more genuine sign of belief in their potential. Excessive praise from parents and grandparents can lead to the opposite of its intended effect.

Parents Helping Children Interpret Failure

Ignoring student failure and focusing on positive behavior is not a universal practice. Dweck's studies at the University of Illinois and in Hong Kong were replicated by Ng et al. (2007). Instead of administering IQ tests at school, mothers brought children to campus in Champaign, Illinois, and the University of Hong Kong. While the mothers waited, half of the children were given a difficult test designed to induce a sense of failure. During a five-minute break before the second test, mothers, informed about their child's score and falsely told it was below average, were allowed to interact with their children, with hidden cameras recording these interactions. Most American mothers avoided negative comments, remaining upbeat and discussing topics unrelated to the test. In contrast, Chinese mothers focused on the test results, emphasizing the need for concentration. After the break, Chinese students improved their scores by 33%, more than twice the gain of their American counterparts. Despite stereotypes, Chinese mothers were as affectionate as American mothers and no more likely to show disapproval (Pomerantz et al., 2014).

Offering praise has become a common solution for the anxieties of American families. With parents away from their children for most of the day, they often feel the need to elevate their support when they return home. In the limited time they have together, parents want their children to feel supported, loved, and believed in.

Recognize Limitations of Encouragement

Offering encouragement instead of praise for ability or effort is an effective means to motivate achievement. This is because encouragement supports tutoring as the best path for students of all achievement levels to improve their performance. Telling students who get low test scores to work harder has been the usual mistake that teachers have made to increase achievement instead of recognizing a key to competence involves finding tutorial help to get on track. There are 7.3 million disabled students enrolled in special education programs, and everyone else who periodically encounters difficulty should always be encouraged to seek help (Schaeffer, 2023). Many schools are failing by not providing the free tutoring students need.

During the early 1990s, the student retention rate, holding an individual back to repeat the same grade again, rose dramatically because most school districts decided to adopt more strict standards for promotion because some students were graduating who were unable to read. Then, in 1995, New York City became the first big city to reverse its retention policy, followed by Chicago, Los Angeles, and other urban districts all reaching the same conclusion – that retention prevents progress, and students often perform more poorly the second time they repeat a grade. In fact, retaining a student in the primary grades (K-grade 3) reduces the odds of high school graduation by 60% (Andrew, 2014; Zinsser, 2023).

The solution to underachievement is not social promotion because academic deficits become cumulative as a child moves on to a higher grade but instead emphasizing help for correction. In view of the strong case against retention, one might suppose educators would seldom choose this risky practice. However, surveys have consistently shown that half to two-thirds of elementary teachers believe that retaining a poor-achieving student is good practice (Zinsser, 2023). The faulty reasoning is reflected by these comments of primary-grade teachers.

- My experience tells me that keeping a student back is necessary to maintain standards.
- Holding students back puts them on notice they are responsible or suffer consequences.
- Retention is the best method to motivate slackers that they must take studies seriously.

Teachers in the early grades do not get feedback about the negative outcomes of their retention decisions. Otherwise, they would recognize why researchers are agreed that the best response to failure in any subject is tutoring.

The Myth of Linking Praise and Self-Esteem

Self-Esteem as a National Goal

Nathaniel Branden wrote *The Psychology of Self-Esteem* (1969/2001) in which he claimed self-esteem is the single most important quality to influence success. Before long, this belief spread across the nation, that whatever efforts were necessary to elevate student self-esteem should be made by schools. In 1986, the California legislature created an official self-esteem task force that alleged improvement in self-esteem would result in many benefits, from lowering incidence of welfare dependence to decreasing rates of teen pregnancy and raising school achievement scores (California State Department of Education, 1990). These arguments propelled self-esteem to become a national goal, especially for children. Anything that could undermine self-esteem was suspect and had to be eliminated. Competition was discounted. Coaches stopped recognizing only outstanding teams and started to give trophies to all the participating teams. Teachers stopped using red pencils, criticism was generally replaced by undeserved praise, and the parents began to display bumper stickers or signs in front of their house boasting about the academic distinction of their children, such as "My child is an honor student at Brent Elementary School."

The contention that praise, self-esteem, and academic performance rise and fall together was challenged. Between 1970 and 2000, over 15,000 articles appeared on the relationship between self-esteem and many desirable goals. Most of the results were contradictory or inconclusive. Accordingly, the Association for Psychological Science invited Roy Baumeister, Professor of Psychology at Florida State University and a leading proponent of self-esteem to review the research literature. Baumeister et al. (2003) determined that most studies on self-esteem were flawed science. Generally, the 15,000 articles had invited people to rate their self-esteem and intelligence, career success, or relationship skills. Self-reports were found to be unreliable because people with high self-esteem had inflated perception of their abilities. Only 200 of the 15,000 studies applied credible design methods to correlate self-esteem with other factors.

After reviewing these 200 studies, Baumeister et al. (2003) concluded that high self-esteem did not improve performance or career achievement. Similarly, high self-esteem did not reduce the use of alcohol or violence. Extremely aggressive and violent people frequently think highly of themselves, debunking the theory that people are aggressive to compensate for their low self-esteem. Baumeister believed that the continued appeal of self-esteem is related to parental pride in child achievements which is so strong that when parents praise children, it is not far from praising themselves. At the same time, many parents place their children in pressure-oriented education settings so that later they can qualify to enter well-known universities. There is parent reliance on constant praise to soften the intensity of having to deal with pressure expectations of these conditions.

Fifteen years later, Baumeister and Vohs (2018) presented a follow-up study. The original research had found no sign that raising self-esteem would make children better students, more moral adults, or people with more satisfying and stable relationships. Before the rise of the national self-esteem movement, parents worried about children becoming conceited, so they often tried to teach the value of humility. Baumeister reported his own research focus had shifted from self-esteem to self-control. A resulting book titled *Willpower: Rediscovering the Greatest Human Strength* was written by Baumeister and Tierney (2012). This book makes known some secrets of self-control and how to master it.

Narcissism and Childhood Self-Impressions

Narcissus was a character in Greek mythology who fell in love when he viewed his own reflection in a pool of water (Rose & Spawforth, 2016). This is a tragic story because the self-fascination meant Narcissus was unable to establish a close relationship with anyone else. He became so self-absorbed that, eventually, he wasted away and died. As workers at the cemetery prepared for his funeral, they discovered that the body of Narcissus was gone. It had been transformed into a pale yellow and white flower that blooms in the spring called *narcissus* or better known as a daffodil. In psychology, the term *narcissism* refers to someone who feels superior, believing s/he is more entitled, and deserves the admiration of others. Individuals who show these characteristics are often regarded as egotistical, conceited, lacking in empathy, and having an exaggerated sense of self-importance.

Psychologists Jean Twenge and Keith Campbell (2010) found that narcissism levels are rising and can cause serious problems in social relationships, including domestic abuse. When narcissists feel a lack of the admiration they seek, the amount of attention they crave, or are exposed to failure or rejection, they blame others or resort to aggression. Twenge (2017, 2023) believes that the overemphasis on self-esteem in the past generation should be replaced by a healthier focus on the development of humility and empathy. The fixation on praise also has economic, labor, and social implications. Overpraised children later demonstrate narcissism at the workplace and in personal relationships. Narcissists working in teams do poorly in crediting others for achievements, a fact that makes for trouble with coworkers. Twenge and Campbell (2010) administered the Narcissistic Personality Inventory (Raskin & Terry, 1988) to 16,000 college students and found that narcissism scores were 30% higher than when the inventory was first given to adolescents and young adults 30 years earlier.

Longitudinal Evidence of How Narcissism Begins

During early childhood, narcissism and self-centeredness are normative behavior patterns. For example, when 5-year-olds are asked who, in their classroom, is good at arithmetic, most students identify themselves by raising their hand. It is not until about 8 years of age, in third grade, that students begin to compare themselves with performance of peers and recognize their abilities are not exceptional. The first longitudinal evidence on how narcissism originates was shown by collaborative research from the Netherlands, England, and the United States (Brummelman et al., 2016.) The sample in this international study was 565 children aged 7–12 years. They and their parents were interviewed at six-month intervals over a period of 18 months.

Students completed the Child Narcissism Scale (Thomaes et al., 2008) that includes items such as 'Kids like me deserve something extra,' and 'I am a great example for other children of my age to follow.' The Parent Overvaluation Scale was presented to the adults containing items such as 'My child deserves special treatment' and 'I would be disappointed if my child was just a regular child.' Children also completed a self-esteem measure while the adults took a parental warmth assessment. In addition, parents were asked how smart they thought their children were after which researchers measured actual intelligence. The findings were that parents who overestimated their child's ability were no smarter than others their age. Another assessment centered on fabrication of book titles and the names of nonexistent people. The parents were asked if they thought their children were aware of books such as *The Tale of Benson Bunny* and names of newsmakers such as *Queen Alberta*. Parents who overvalued reported that their children were indeed familiar with these books and people that they did not realize were fictitious.

The more parents overvalued their children, the more narcissistic child responses became six months later. Narcissistic children reported their parents placed them on a pedestal, praising them for almost everything they did and rarely giving criticism. When parents see their children as more special than their peers, the children internalize the perception they are superior and should be given special privileges, an outlook reflecting the core of narcissism. In contrast, when parents treat their children with affection and appreciation, the children know they are valued as individuals (Brummelman et al., 2016).

So is it a bad thing for children to be narcissistic? Most people see them as just annoying or arrogant, but there is evidence that this characteristic also produces aggression. According to McManus et al. (2022), since narcissistic children feel more entitled and want other people to admire them, narcissists do not like it when peers do not provide the desired amount of attention, compliments, and reject them. In turn, they tend to lash out aggressively that predicts provoked aggression.

Can we distinguish between narcissistic children and those with favorable self-esteem? Narcissism refers to feelings of being better than others, more entitled than peers, and therefore more deserving of admiration from others. In contrast, self-esteem is a more genuine feeling of being worthy. Brummelman et al. (2016) pointed out that parents who overvalue children can harm them and could be more helpful if the children feel warmth from them, as determined by child reports, not parent self-reports. Parents can show warmth and affection without telling children they are better than peers and without conveying they are more entitled than others.

Internal Source of Motivation

The Link of Self-Esteem and Self-Evaluation

Praise and encouragement are helpful external sources of motivation. In addition, internal motivation requires support. Critical self-evaluation enables students to know when to think well of themselves and when to change behavior based on conditions needed for improvement. In the middle grades, students first acquire a capacity to look at things from the viewpoint of others and apply self-examination to their feelings, thoughts, and motives. When self-esteem is accompanied by the ability to self-evaluate, the usual result is growth instead of egocentrism. However, few children get help from parents to learn how to judge themselves. What students become depends in part on feedback given about their behavior. When feedback is only positive, learning deficits are not detected, and students cannot accurately gauge personal progress.

Student Recognition of Learning Deficiency

Strom et al. (2022) conducted an online polling study about tutoring. The subjects were 190 seventh- and eighth-grade students (104 females, 86 males) from a middle school in the United States. The findings showed that students who were behind their peers in reading grade level denied they had a problem with the subject (41.1%), felt embarrassed and would not ask for help (55.3%), and blamed their difficulties on poor teachers (45.3%). Students reported they would ask classmates or friends for help if a subject is difficult to understand (71.1%), ask the teacher questions (61.1%), and seek no help even though it may mean failing (16.3%). Parents and schools should help students adopt a new social norm that favors tutoring. The goals of tutoring are to identify errors by observation and interaction, detect ways to correct mistakes, arrange for guided practice, and monitor performance for growth. A basic change is necessary to transform student attitudes about learning and self-confidence.

The international students who attend Oxford and Cambridge Universities in England represent the top 2% of achievers from their home country (Carmody, 2024). Nevertheless, they are required to attend weekly tutorials. The rationale is that everyone, no matter how intelligent, can learn more if their individual limitations are identified and corrected by remedial support. Involvement with tutoring increases knowledge and competence, urges a sense of humility, and establishes teamwork skills fundamental for success in most occupations.

Principles for Application by Parents

Parents should try to apply the following aspects to their teaching role in helping their children grow and adjust to the challenges facing them.

- Students need encouragement more than praise to motivate achievement. Helping children adopt rigorous standards while assuring them their parents and teachers believe they can reach these goals is a message that can lead to greater competence and self-confidence.
- A serious risk is pressure to rush learning, forego reflective thinking because it takes too long, and examine alternatives superficially before making decisions. Teachers can control the pace of lessons and should understand time and learning are linked. Practicing desired skills is the way to ensure they are learned and available for future reliance in problem-solving.
- Making mistakes should be a common expectation of students along with recognition that some degree of failure is necessary for learning. When students are led to believe failure should never happen or should be ignored when it occurs, they prevent the growth that comes from acknowledging and correcting deficiencies.
- Report card grades are rarely assigned for study skills or social skills, but most parents realize these skills are important factors that contribute to success. When teachers

report on good student behaviors the same day they are demonstrated by students at school, parents are able to reinforce commendable conduct in a timely manner and renew a commitment to encourage positive and corrective aspects of child development (Strom & Strom, 2014).

Conclusion

Most parents, grandparents, and teachers use praise more than encouragement to motivate student achievement. This is a risky orientation that leads students to overestimate their abilities, undervalue the need to work hard, ignore learning deficiencies, and deny their need for tutoring. Making mistakes should be a common student expectation along with realization that failure is an aspect of learning that can be overcome by support and effort. If students believe failure can be avoided or denied, they deprive themselves of challenges needed to face more complex tasks.

In the past American students did not need as demanding an education as today because our country dominated the global economy. However, in the emerging marketplace, American students must become motivated to adapt to the rigorous effort required of them and understand how they rank in terms of international competition. First, peers should assume leadership for revising time management habits. Spending six hours a day phoning and texting, engaging in social networks, and watching media is excessive and detracts from the time needed for study. Second, students can establish a peer norm that encourages classmates to realize their limitations and take advantage of support. Third, schools should become transparent in revealing student deficits, based on low test scores, instead of continuing the errant practice of inflating grades so parents and students are unable to recognize a need for help. Finally, students and parents should insist that schools provide free tutoring, available to everyone, and support the nation's aspirations to become a world leader in education (Strom et al., 2022).

The connection between self-evaluation and self-esteem should be understood. Parents regret that children are often vulnerable to misdirection because they depend so much on the approval of peers. Yet so little is done to help children balance the opinions of peers with the way they see themselves. When families avoid teaching children to self-evaluate, peers can insist that expectations of the group deserve the highest priority. Students should be taught to evaluate themselves by applying growth-oriented criteria and obtain feedback from mature sources, so they are able to follow their path to become responsible adults.

Key Concepts

1. Encouragement supports determination in managing difficult tasks while praise should be reserved to confirm that a child has achieved a particular goal or demonstrated a valued skill. Give encouragement when performance is mediocre and praise evidence of improvement.
2. Emphasizing effort gives students a variable they can control. This allows them to see themselves as in charge of their own success. Focusing on intelligence, how smart someone is, takes it out of a child's control and does not offer a recipe for responding in failure situations.
3. Students should adopt the belief that the way to bounce back from a failure is to ask for help, work hard, and continue trying. People with persistence rebound well and

sustain their motivation through lengthy delayed gratification that might be necessary to achieve their goal.
4. Excessive praise has become a common remedy for coping with anxieties and worries. When parents are with children, they want them to hear things loved ones cannot convey during the day, that we are on your side, we are here for you, believe in you, and want you to succeed.
5. The overemphasis on self-esteem should be replaced with a healthier emphasis on humility and empathy. Overpraised children demonstrate narcissism in relationships. Narcissists do poorly in crediting others for achievement and have difficult marriages and trouble relating to coworkers on the job.
6. Narcissistic children report that parents have placed them on a pedestal, praising them for everything they do and rarely criticizing them. When children are viewed by parents as more special than peers, children often believe they are superior, should be admired by others, and deserve to receive special privileges.
7. Many families and teachers orient children to believe they should not make mistakes. In contrast, creative children realize they may be wrong repeatedly before a solution to a problem is discovered. They do not become discouraged by mistakes but instead motivated by eliminating options that do not lead to solutions.
8. Continued effort after making mistakes fosters improved performance. The pleasure of success occurs when setbacks and previous defeats have been overcome. In addition, exposure to mistakes can generate development of valuable qualities like courage, resilience, and resolve.
9. When teachers arrange for the cost of academic mistakes to be low enough, students feel comfortable viewing problems and ideas in new ways. In such situations, students become willing to take a chance knowing the mistakes they are bound to make can be corrected, will ultimately lead to success, and not affect their grades.
10. Parents who deny failure of children as a method to protect their self-esteem unintentionally prevent experiences needed to grow up and cope with events when first tries are not enough, and quitting is a poor choice. Student success requires detection of mistakes, intention to correct them, renewed motivation to perform better, and assurance that the results will be positive. Parent-teacher collaboration always supports better student performance (Strom & Strom, 2014).

Generational Perspectives Activities

11.1 Discussion
11.2 Conversations With Young Children
11.3 A Scenario: Reasoning and Problem-Solving
11.4 Chapter Review
11.5 Parent and Grandparent Self-Evaluation
11.6 Storytelling

11.1 Discussion

1. What are situations where you rely on praise more than you rely on encouragement?
2. How has the self-esteem movement influenced how you think about child motivation?

3. How does praise and reward from teachers influence the self-impression of students?
4. In what situations would encouraging greater child effort be a poor solution?
5. What have children told you about the failures and setbacks they experience in school?
6. In your observation how do families usually interpret situations where children fail?
7. Why do you suppose many adults find it so difficult to provide constructive criticism?
8. What should be done to reduce the likelihood younger relatives will be narcissistic?
9. How do you help children understand that some failure is necessary for learning?
10. How do relatives react when they find out you have failed in achieving some goal?

11.2 Conversations With Young Children

1. Do you think some parents praise children more than is good for them?
2. What have parents and grandparents shared with you about their failures?
3. Do you see any benefit from children having to encounter failure situations
4. How do teachers at school help by sometimes being critical of your work?
5. What memories do you have of grandparents criticizing your behavior?
6. Who provides you with the right amount of praise and criticism?

11.3 A Scenario: Reasoning and Problem-Solving

Matthew's kindergarten teacher informed his parents that he is often a troublemaker in class. What advice would you give Matthew's parents?

a. Ask the teacher to let you visit the class as an observer.
b. Ask Matthew to explain what he does that bothers others.
c. Consider transferring Matthew to some other school.
d. Find out what the principal knows about the situation.
e. Other _____

11.4 Chapter Review

1. What insights from the chapter will I try to apply in my relationships?
2. What is the most important key concept for me presented in this chapter?
3. Which elements of this chapter do I wish I had known about earlier?

11.5 Parent and Grandparent Self-Evaluation

1. Criticizing the quality of my child's homework

   a. it is not my role but an obligation of the teacher
   b. I want my child to accept criticism from adults
   c. I will tutor my child if I know how to do the work
   d. I do not monitor the quality of my child's homework
   e. Other _____

2. I praise my child when

   a. performance scores on tests are at or above grade level
   b. progress is made on tasks being assigned by the teacher
   c. hard work and persistence are evident from observation

d. effort is recognized as the key to becoming successful
e. Other _____

3. I want my child to know the best way to handle failure is to

   a. ask for tutorial assistance
   b. persist in working hard
   c. seek encouragement from peers
   d. believe in yourself as capable
   e. Other _____

4. My reaction to child narcissism is

   a. disappointment with self-centeredness
   b. wondering if a child will ever grow up
   c. to be an example of humility and caring
   d. to encourage personality goals for children
   e. Other _____

5. Being able to admit limitations is

   a. a lesson I want to teach children
   b. difficult for most people I know
   c. a valuable lesson to learn
   d. a key to personality development
   e. Other _____

6. I would favor having more opportunities for child self-evaluation in school if

   a. this could help students practice making judgments
   b. this would diminish child narcissism
   c. this would enable students to judge their progress
   d. this would enlarge the scope of curriculum
   e. Other _____

11.6 Storytelling

Historically, storytelling has been a dominant classic and progressive method of teaching around the world. The purposes of a storyteller are to present imaginary or real-life examples showing how some concept applies to a particular situation. People like stories, they pay attention to the procession of events, and usually remember aspects of a story for a long time. Your stories can reinforce the concepts in this chapter for family members and classmates. Please share your stories with them.

References

Andrew, M. (2014). The scarring effects of primary-grade retention? A study of cumulative advantage in the educational career. *Social Forces*, 93(2), 653–685. https://doi.org/10.1093/sf/sou074

Baumeister, R. F., Campbell, J., Krueger, J., & Vohs, K. (2003). Does high self-esteem cause better performance, interpersonal success, happiness, or healthier lifestyles? *Psychological Science in the Public Interest*, 4(1), 1–44. https://doi.org/10.1111/1529-1006.01431

Baumeister, R. F., & Tierney, J. (2012). *Willpower: Rediscovering the greatest human strength*. Penguin Press.

Baumeister, R. F., & Vohs, K. D. (2018). Revisiting our reappraisal of the (surprisingly few) benefits of high self-esteem. *Perspectives on Psychological Science, 13*(2), 137–140. https://doi.org/10.1177/1745691617701185

Branden, N. (2001). *The psychology of self-esteem A revolutionary approach to self-understanding that launched a new era in modern psychology*. Jossey-Bass. https://dl.icdst.org/pdfs/files4/265c224996b4d2ea756fc71a0b144911.pdf (Original work published 1969)

Brummelman, E., Thomaes, S., & Sedikides, C. (2016, February). Separating narcissism from self-esteem. *Current Directions in Psychological Science, 25*(1), 8–13. https://doi.org/10.1177/0963721415619737

California State Department of Education. (1990). *Toward a state of esteem: The final report of the California task force to promote self-esteem and personal and social responsibility*. https://files.eric.ed.gov/fulltext/ED321170.pdf

Carmody, M. (2024). *Getting into Oxford and Cambridge 2025 entry* (27th ed.). Trotman.

Duckworth, A. (2018). *Grit: The power of passion and perseverance*. Scribner.

Dweck, C. (2007). *Mindset: The new psychology of success*. Ballantine Books.

Dweck, C. (2014). *The power of believing that you can improve*. TED Talk. https://www.ted.com/talks/carol_dweck_the_power_of_believing_that_you_can_improve

McManus, K. C., Pillow, D., & Coyle, T. (2022, December). Narcissism and academic performance: A case of suppression. *Personality and Individual Differences, 119*. https://doi.org/10.1016/j.paid.2022.111820

Meyer, W.-U. (1992). Paradoxical effects of praise and criticism on perceived ability. *European Review of Social Psychology, 3*(1), 259–283. https://doi.org/10.1080/14792779243000087

Ng, F., Pomerantz, E., & Lam, S. (2007). European American and Chinese parents' responses to children's success and failure: Implications for children's responses. *Developmental Psychology, 43*(5), 1239–1255. https://doi.org/10.1037/0012-1649.43.5.1239

Peale, N. V. (2003). *The power of positive thinking*. Touchstone. (Original work published 1952)

Pomerantz, E., Ng, F., Cheung, C., & Qu, Y. (2014). Raising happy children who succeed in school: Lessons from China and the United States. *Child Development Perspectives, 8*(2), 71–76. https://doi.org/10.1111/cdep.12063

Raskin, R., & Terry, H. (1988). A principal-components analysis of the narcissistic personality inventory and further evidence of its construct validity. *Journal of Personality and Social Psychology, 54*(5), 890–902. https://doi.org/10.1037/0022-3514.54.5.890

Rose, H. J., & Spawforth, A. (2016). Narcissus. In *Oxford classical dictionary*. Oxford Press. https://doi.org/10.1093/acrefore/9780199381135.013.4334

Schaeffer, K. (2023, July 24). *What federal education data shows about students with disabilities in the U.S.* Pew Research Center. https://www.pewresearch.org/short-reads/2023/07/24/what-federal-education-data-shows-about-students-with-disabilities-in-the-us/

Strom, P. S., & Strom, R. D. (2014). Personal digital assistants and pagers: A model for parent collaboration in school disciplines. *Journal of Family Studies, 8*(2), 226–238. https://doi.org/10.5172/jfs.8.2.226

Strom, P. S., Strom, R. D., Sindel-Arrington, T., & Wang, C.-H. (2022). Tutoring support and student voice in middle school. *School Community Journal, 32*(1), 39–62. http://www.schoolcommunitynetwork.org/SCJ.aspx

Thomaes, S., Stegge, H., Bushman, B. J., Olthof, T., & Denissen, J. (2008). Development and validation of the Childhood Narcissism Scale. *Journal of Personality Assessment, 90*(4), 382–391. https://doi.org/10.1080/00223890802108162

Twenge, J. M. (2017). *iGen: Why today's super-connected kids are growing up less rebellious, more tolerant, less happy – and completely unprepared for adulthood, and what that means for the rest of us*. Simon & Schuster.

Twenge, J. M. (2023). *The real differences between Gen Z, millennials, Gen X, boomers, and silents – and what they mean for America's future*. Atria.

Twenge, J. M., & Campbell, W. K. (2010). *The narcissism epidemic: Living in the age of entitlement*. Free Press.

Zinsser, K. M. (2023). *No longer welcome: The epidemic of expulsion from early childhood education*. Oxford University Press.

Chapter 12

Sometimes I Like to Play by Myself

Parents want young children to spend time with peers of their age and gender. Scheduling play dates, attending early childhood programs, and visiting parks all present opportunities to practice getting along with peers and offer chances to develop social skills that will be needed in kindergarten. Parents think of playing with friends as a benefit for their child but often wonder if there are advantages of a schedule allowing a child to spend some time alone. The purposes of this chapter are to (a) explain why all parents should arrange the schedule of their child so s/he will be guaranteed to spend some time doing things alone each day; (b) describe the importance of parent lifestyle as the most influential way to persuade children that everyone needs access to solitude, and (c) suggest conditions students should understand about the important relationships between solitude, creative thinking, and problem-solving. Generational Perspectives Activities present topics to discuss with family members and close friends about the capability of children to do things by themselves.

Parent Monitoring of Family Time

Teaching in an inner-city elementary school is a difficult position but one that can be potentially rewarding. A common observation among these teachers is that their students are mostly from low-income families with crowded living conditions, arrive at school restless, seem unable to sit still, or sustain attention in completing assignments. They act out impulses instead of reflecting about what is expected of them and how they are supposed to behave. Because these students generally lack the ability to concentrate, they tend to interrupt and distract classmates (Strom, 1965, 1966). This poor academic behavior causes teachers to devote considerable time and effort to establish conditions that are needed to support learning. Educators report that many of their students have not developed the inner resources essential for sustained inquiry. The forecast is not much better for students from middle-income homes who often complain "There's nothing to do if computers, mobile devices or television are unavailable" (Haidt, 2024; Hixenbaugh, 2024; Mark, 2023).

Schedule Quiet Time for Children

Fortunately, when adults encourage solitary play, boredom and inattention can be less common. Making this transition will be difficult because most adults do not believe that children need to have privacy (Véliz, 2024). In fact, children are often led to suppose that being alone, even when adults supervise from a distance, is a kind of punishment or type of solitary confinement. Parents might resent intrusion by their children when they are trying to pay attention to something. But adults generally underestimate the seriousness of children when they are involved with play. Moreover, the frustration effects of interrupted solitary play include a reduction of persistence for tasks and lowering of ability to concentrate. The younger a child is, the more vulnerable s/he is to being disturbed at play. This comes as no surprise to day care and preschool staff members who express disappointment about their always being unable to grant requests of children for periodic privacy (Frost et al., 2021).

Competition for Ways to Spend Time

Learning to get along with peers is a socialization skill children will get help with during the elementary grades. At the same time, learning to value solitude will likely begin at home or not begin at all (Cain, 2012; Cain et al., 2017). The number of children in a school classroom and frequency of interruptions combine to make most solitary activities a low priority and practically impossible. Then too, once children are enrolled in elementary school grades, after-school organized group activities (such as little league football, soccer, boys and girls clubs, and after-school programs) become available with common appeal to be with peers. Certainly, extracurricular experiences are beneficial for everyone. However, parents should not ignore their responsibility to ensure the schedule of their child includes time for choosing to do things alone. Achieving this goal is not to be underestimated. It can be especially difficult, especially for parents who admit they are unable to schedule uninterrupted time for their own leisure interests. Learning to provide and protect quiet periods of a child should be seen as an important achievement of parents.

Think about what happens in many homes. Mom and Dad have been away at work all day, so, after dinner, they participate in some activity with their child. Then, to obtain privacy for themselves, the parents may direct the child to get ready for bed, even though the time to do so is earlier than appropriate. A healthier strategy is for parents to plan and arrange for private time by telling their child about what they will do during quiet time:

> It is quiet time now to be by yourself, to do what you enjoy like coloring, drawing, looking at books, playing with action figures or other toys that interest you. TV and cell phones will be off. Mom and Dad are going to have quiet time too. The light in your bedroom will be left on while you do whatever you like by yourself. In 30 minutes, we will come to your room to tuck you in, turn the light off and kiss you good night so you can get to sleep.

This approach helps a child understand that everyone in our family needs quiet time which is enjoyable and offers benefits that cannot be found when preoccupied by the presence of others.

Mothers as Examples of Finding Time

Strom et al. (2004, 2008) determined that a powerful lesson for parents to teach children is that they value solitude by arranging solitary time for themselves. The significance of this conclusion was identified by a study to examine the self-impressions of 1,545 Black, Hispanic, and White mothers and their 10–14-year-old adolescents. Specifically, 739 mothers were White (n = 385), Black (n = 269), and Hispanic (n = 85). The 806 adolescents were White (n = 346),

Black (n = 290), and Hispanic (n = 170). The goal of this study was to determine what each generation separately observed to be the assets and limitations of the parents.

Both generations completed the *Parent Success Indicator* (PSI), an instrument that rates maternal performance on 60 items, equally divided into these six subscales (Strom, 1985):

Communication Scale – skills of advising children and learning from them,
Use of Time Scale – making decisions about the ways in which time is used,
Teaching Scale – the scope of guidance and instruction expected of parents,
Frustration Scale – attitudes and behaviors of children that bother parents,
Satisfaction Scale – aspects of the parent role that bring satisfaction, and
Information Needs Scale – things parents need to know about their child.

A factor validation of the instrument was conducted by Collinsworth et al. (1996). A weighted method corresponding to the ethnic proportions of the population was applied to construct a national standard that could be used as a comparative reference. In general, both generations saw mother's performance as favorable. Teaching got the highest rating followed by Satisfaction. Mothers felt that Information Needs were their greatest limitation while adolescents reported observing their mothers were prone to Frustration. The amount of time mothers and adolescents spent together was identified as the most significant independent variable to influence perceptions of parent performance. Other variables such as family income and marital status had limited impact.

Mothers reported that arranging time for personal leisure was their most difficult task, ranking it sixtieth out of 60 possible situations. Adolescent children also identified maternal inability to arrange time for personal leisure time by ranking it fifty-seventh out of 60 items (Strom et al., 2008). This limitation should be considered in a broader context than just as an example of maternal sacrifice. Children, even in early childhood, need their mothers to be examples of how to manage personal stress. Mothers should set aside the time needed for relief and show how they can achieve the sense of balance and control needed for a healthy life. There is abundant evidence that most employed mothers suffer from considerable stress because they have multiple responsibilities that usually include care of children, obligations to a husband, support for aging parents, satisfying the demands of an employer, and managing the household. Together these pressures motivate many mothers to overschedule their children, depriving them of the free time to allow a sense of control and opportunity to decide the things they want to do alone.

Fathers as Examples of Finding Time

Similar results with the PSI were determined in a study by Beckert et al. (2006) of 517 middle-class Black and White fathers and their adolescent daughters and sons. Specifically, 102 fathers were Black, and 126 fathers were White. The 289 adolescents, ages 10–14, consisted of 104 Blacks and 185 Whites. It was clear that not all fathers encounter the same parenting obstacles experienced by low-income fathers in their ethnic group. These fathers were similar to the sample of mothers described earlier in reporting their greatest difficulty was being able to schedule time for personal leisure. This inability to model time management, to plan and arrange discretionary time, has an influence on most contexts that implicate parental guidance. If parents are stressed or fatigued, the time they spend with children usually includes more nonproductive conflict and less mutual satisfaction.

Most fathers have less responsibility than mothers for childcare and child supervision. As a result, it seems improbable that a father would be able to teach his children to cope with multiple demands on their time when he cannot arrange moments for personal relief and renewal (Strom et al., 2014). Many children likely conclude that their parents have yet to learn how to deal with daily pressures that cause feelings of being hurried and helpless about lack of control over their allocation of time. Consequently, some adolescents decide to seek sources outside of the family for advice and examples of how to cope with stress (Strom et al., 2008).

The Value of Solitude

Learning to Play Without Peers

Sherry Turkle is a professor at Massachusetts Institute of Technology. Turkle's (2017) book titled *Alone Together: Why We Expect More From Technology and Less From Each Other* examines how thinking is different in a digital society. She contended that learning to value solitude and arrange to spend time in privacy remains the overlooked bedrock for early child development. Home-schooled children can more easily be scheduled so they can have time by themselves (Jacobs & Jack, 2024). Parents should provide children this valuable gift so they can explore on their own. Children should be able to use their imagination, reflect about situations and events, and process ideas and feelings without the ever-present distraction of devices. When parents fail to teach children to enjoy solitude, the children will equate solitude with loneliness and perceive it as punishment instead of a wonderful resource (Hertz, 2021).

Turkle (2016) describes her research illustrating the discomfort that many people feel when they are left alone for even a few minutes. College students in one of Turkle's experiments were asked to remain silent for 15 minutes without using their cell phone. Before the clock was set to begin the task, participants were asked if they wanted to consider administering a mild electroshock to themselves if they were to become bored. Everyone said no and ignored the mild shock meter the experimenter demonstrated and placed beside each of them. Yet, after only six minutes, many of the students felt bored and attempted to try the fake shock meter.

These results are disappointing but should not be surprising. Many adults while waiting at a stop light or standing in line at a store report they feel bored and reach for their cell phone. People are so accustomed to being constantly connected that being alone seems to be a problem technology ought to solve for them. Whenever people are reluctant to be alone, they struggle to pay attention to themselves. Individuals who feel secure in being by themselves are more able to listen carefully to what others have to say. This familiar result occurred for students attending a five-day summer camp where all electronic devices were banned. The usual observation of campers was that it was peaceful when you have nothing to do except think quietly and talk directly to friends without distraction (Turkle, 2016, 2021).

The Imaginary Companions

When children are involved with solitary play, they fantasize more than when they play with friends or parents. Nevertheless, although parents acknowledge that solitude seems to be the best condition to practice fantasy and exercise imagination, some of them worry about their child when s/he expresses a desire to participate in solitary play. This apprehension is related to the high priority society assigns to extroversion and sociability. In contrast, studies described by Allen (2017), Cain (2012), and Cain et al. (2017) have shown that two-thirds of highly creative people at all ages are introverts.

Some parents have reservations about whether solitary play is healthy for young children. One father reported, "Playing by oneself could be fine in some cases. But my four-year-old son appears to be the victim of hallucinations. He sometimes mentions having conversations with Roy, his fantasy companion." If this father had listened carefully, he would recognize that during solitary play, it is the child who controls the imaginary friend. In fact, total control over any fictitious companions is a source of pleasure for children but not parents. Instead, some parents might suppose the power that comes with being a boss is not good for children because it could cause them to be less cooperative. However, cooperation implies being able to share power. Children who feel powerless cannot cooperate; they can only comply. When children spend time without peers, they can set priorities for what they will do and gain experience in planning which will guide them to achievement (Behr & Rydzewski, 2023).

If imaginary companions appear at all, they are created by children between ages 3 and 6, and these products of fiction are no longer present after age 10. Children who have imaginary companions are not lonely, timid, or socially maladjusted. They are normal, live in families of all sizes, constellations, social status, and races. It is estimated that from 20% to 50% of children experience fictitious companions. Studies by Taylor (2013) have found highly creative children are far more likely than less creative peers to interact with imaginary companions. These findings were corroborated by retrospective studies of highly creative adults who share similar memories about enjoying their play with imaginary companions.

Parents should accept the content of children's fantasy play. It is unreasonable to interpret child play as though it reflects adult motives. The main concern of parents should be to preserve imagination that can promote adjustment at every age throughout life. A poem by Robert Louis Stevenson (1885/2020) titled *The Land of Counterpane* presents an example of a child's solitary play and encourages parents to consider their point of view about how play stimulates early imagination and creativity.

> When I was sick and lay a-bed,
> I had two pillows at my head,
> And all my toys beside me lay,
> To keep me happy all the day.
>
> And sometimes for an hour or so
> I watched my leaden soldiers go,
> With different uniforms and drills,
> Among the bed-clothes, through the hills.
>
> And sometimes sent my ships in fleets
> All up and down among the sheets,
> Or brought my trees and houses out,
> And planted cities all about.
>
> I was the giant great and still
> That sits upon the pillow-hill,

And sees before him, dale and plain,
The pleasant land of counterpane.

The Positive Power of Solitary Play

Children govern the behavior of everyone involved in their stories during solitary play. This expression of imagination is normal in early childhood. But there may be times when some children report conversations with imaginary companions that parents consider disturbing. For example, 4-year-old Derek told his mom that he did not have to pick up the toys in his room as directed by her because Danny, his fictitious friend, told him he did not have to do it today. Some parents respond with punishment or a reminder that lying is an unacceptable behavior, and they want their children to stop making up stories. This reaction is meant to reinforce a distinction between right and wrong and intended to foster moral development. However, Derek's mother wisely saw this situation differently as demonstrated by her reaction. She said, "Tell Danny that your mother is the person who decides how our house is taken care of and the chores that are expected of everyone including Derek." The mother did not refer to Derek as a liar nor discourage his relationship with an imaginary friend. Instead, she called attention to the fact that Derek can make up stories, but she will not approve excuses for not doing the chores assigned to him.

Parent Encouragement of Reflection

Children observe the importance their parents assign to reflective thinking. Preschoolers typically ask many questions daily. Parents who listen to this continual expression of curiosity cause their children to recognize that asking questions is an important way to learn. Similarly, waiting for a child to answer questions underscores the priority parents give reflective thinking. Some parents misinterpret the silence that comes after a question they ask a child. Adults may suppose that the silence indicates a lack of understanding. Some teachers behave the same way by assuming that waiting for an answer takes too long or the other students will be unwilling to wait for classmates to reflect before responding. Adults who judge the thinking of children in this way usually revise the questions they have just asked or resort to giving clues about the expected answer. This common practice of rushing children supports a premature response and ignores individual pace of decision-making called cognitive tempo. The term cognitive tempo refers to the speed at which an individual processes information, reaches judgments, and solves problems.

Psychologist Jerome Kagan published the Matching Familiar Figures Test (MFFT) for children ages 6–12 that measures constructs of reflection and impulsivity (Kagan et al., 1964). In this test, children are asked to select from six pictures that appear similar to the one picture that is identical to the model. Children who show *impulsive tempo* act on first impressions without pausing to evaluate the quality of their replies. So they react quickly and make many errors. By comparison, children who have a *reflective tempo* take more time as they carefully examine each of the pictures. Because they think before responding, reflective children are more accurate, and they make fewer mistakes. *Cognitive tempo* is evident by age 2 and becomes stable by age 4. Researchers have found that cognitive tempo seems related to early patterns of interaction between children and parents.

Children want to please their parents and can tell when adults are impatient and unwilling to wait for them to think before answering a question. Parents should show patience or risk imposing a disadvantaged response on children. Waiting long enough for answers is a valuable skill in posing questions and encouraging reflective thinking. The only way children can be reflective is when they are allowed sufficient time to think by themselves. By insisting that child answers are given quickly, without delay, parents unintentionally encourage impulsive behavior. School success requires the ability to reflect, and the need for this ability increases as a child advances through the grades.

Solitude and Development of Expertise

The power of parent environment influence was reinforced by Ericcson and Pool (2017) and Ericcson et al. (2007). Fifty years ago, two parents from Hungary, László and Klara Polgár, decided they would challenge the popular assumption that women don't succeed in areas that require spatial thinking, such as chess. They wanted to underscore the power of education. The Polgárs homeschooled their three daughters, and as part of their education the girls started playing chess with their parents at a very young age. Their systematic training and daily practice paid off. By 2000, all three daughters were ranked in the top ten female players in the world. The youngest, Judit, born in 1976, had become a chess grandmaster at age 15, breaking the previous record for the youngest person to earn that title. Today, Judit is regarded as the strongest female chess player of all time.

What Do Experts Have in Common?

Ericcson and Pool (2017) sought to discover the factors that enable extraordinary performers to become more proficient than their competition. He compared three groups of violinists who all attended the same elite music academy in Berlin, Germany. First, professors from the academy were asked to estimate the competence of each student by ranking them in three groups: (a) the best violinists, likely to become international performers (b) the good violinists likely to play concerts with other musicians, and (c) those likely to become violin teachers. All the musicians were then interviewed and asked to keep diaries for a designated period that detailed the way they used their time.

Significant differences were found by Ericcson and Pool (2017). All three groups spent about 50 hours each week engaged in music activity. However, the two best-performing groups spent most of their time practicing in solitude, 24 hours a week for the best performers compared with nine hours for the lowest group. The best violinists rated practicing alone as their most important activity. Elite musicians, even those who perform regularly in groups, identify practice with colleagues as 'leisure' compared to solo practice where the work really gets done. They found similar views about the importance of solitude when he interviewed experts from other fields. Time spent in 'serious study alone' was the strongest predictor of skill for tournament chess players. A grandmaster spends 5,000 hours, five times as long as intermediate level players, studying the game by themselves.

Amount and Quality of Practice

Why would being alone have such significance for the development of expertise? Ericcson and Pool (2017) explained that when a person is alone, s/he can engage in deliberate practice, without distraction, which is a key factor in exceptional achievement. As individuals practice deliberately, they identify tasks or knowledge beyond their reach, strive to upgrade their performance, monitor personal progress, and make revisions as needed.

Practice sessions that fall short of this standard are less useful and can even be counterproductive because they reinforce existing cognitive mechanisms instead of improving them. Deliberate practice can be done best by oneself because this requires intense concentration, and the presence of other people can be distracting. But most important is the deliberate practice involves working on a task that is the most challenging. Only when people are concentrating alone can they go to that part of a task that represents the greatest challenge. To improve, we must as individuals be the one who initiates the move, whereas when working with others, individuals are allowed to generate the nature of activity for improvement only a small proportion of the time.

It's not just assumptions regarding gender differences in expertise that have crumbled. Benjamin Bloom (1985), Professor of Psychology at the University of Chicago and author of *Developing Talent in Young People*, examined the childhood experiences of 120 elite performers who had received international awards for exceptional contributions to their field. Bloom found no correlation between IQ and superior performance across a broad range of contexts, including chess, piano, tennis, swimming, sculpture, mathematics, and neuroscience. Bloom concluded that amount and quality of practice seemed the most important factor in gaining outstanding status.

Assessment of Growth-Oriented Risks

By encouraging children to spend time in reflection and helping them to recognize the rewards of growth-oriented risks, students become more likely to take such risks. People who stop taking risks become more narrow-minded and less able to adjust to change. They show more rigid behavior and less flexibility in thinking. It seems ironic that the pattern of behavior they rely on to prevent danger causes them to take an ominous risk, to stop learning. This is a great mistake because people who quit changing can no longer adapt and, as a result, their trajectory for development ends.

A better response to the over-choice environment encountered by most people is to seek solitude to reflect on possible courses of action and accurately assess the risk of involvement with each choice. Then they can count on relatives, friends, and coworkers to also monitor this delicate ability that appears essential for survival and to ensure personal improvement. When these conditions are in place, taking risks can support quality of life now and in the future (MacRae et al., 2018).

Overcoming Boredom

A powerful but little understood obstacle to productive thinking is boredom. Being bored causes irritability because of exposure to something that seems uninteresting or finding oneself in a situation where there is nothing to do. Many adults express boredom with their daily affairs. When people say, "Thank goodness it's Friday," what do they mean? Do they mean that their job provides so much pleasure and stimulation that the sheer excitement of it cannot be sustained more than five days at a time? Perhaps they mean the obligations of work fail to meet their need for a sense of purpose and cause them to look forward to more interesting activities on the weekends or vacations. Maybe they mean that it would be nice to stop working. Winning the lottery and having enough money to quit the job is a common dream. Another way to view the prevailing impression is that it confirms alienation from employment is widespread. And, as adult boredom increases, younger people also have difficulty finding stimulation at school (Kellerman & Seligman, 2023).

Boredom as a Common Experience

Historically, high-achieving students have complained of boredom about having to wait while teachers helped slower students catch up with a lesson. Today, however, even average and below average students complain they are bored, some as early as the primary grades 1–3. The complaints offered by a growing proportion of students are seen as ominous signs of discontent with the existing education system (Raccanello et al., 2022).

"I'm bored" is often heard from students in schools worldwide. Boredom is a topic that teachers rarely discuss with students but warrants attention to minimize the negative effects it has on students in schools. For example, in Germany, Feuchter and Preckel (2022) investigated 1,861 students at five schools regarding (a) intensity of boredom, (b) boredom due to under-challenge, and (c) boredom due to over-challenge. Results determined that for the classes of mathematics and German language all three types of boredom increased during the 3.5-year longitudinal study. However, ability grouping significantly reduced the intensity of boredom for gifted students in special classes.

Problems of Excessive Boredom

Studies have determined that boredom diminishes attention, interferes with concentration, and is generally cited by dropouts as a reason for quitting school (Hari, 2022; Mark, 2023). Many adolescents consider their schooling to be a disappointing experience. They believe that school is boring, lessons are uninteresting, assignments have little practical application, and there is a lack of community and sense of belonging in the classroom.

Assor et al. (2002) discovered in a survey of 800 middle school students that teachers were able to enhance three types of autonomy recognized as being highly valued by students: (a) ensuring that tasks are perceived as relevant for them; (b) allowing criticism of the classroom environment without suffering a penalty; and (c) providing choice that contributes to autonomy. Collaboration between teachers and students seems an effective path to increase mental stimulation and diminish negative outcomes of boredom.

Era of Global Perspectives

The emergence of global perspectives is transforming the way nations view themselves and how they are seen by other countries. International comparisons are increasingly being used to judge the relative pace of social progress and identify priorities to apply for domestic reforms. Media disseminates information about accomplishments of nations, as in the case of Japan for its low crime rate, Australia for welcoming immigrants, Singapore for arranging low-income housing, and the United States for trying to ensure civil rights (Light, 2000).

Coincident with this awareness, the United Nations adopted international education comparisons as the best way to determine baseline goals, measure progress, detect national deficits, and identify high-achieving countries as help agents. Some quality-of-life criteria are currently pursued on a global scale. One example is implementing early childhood education as a right for all children. Related efforts involve ranking nations according to their proportion of students who go on to attend secondary education. The Programme for International Student Assessment (PISA) (National Center for Education Statistics, 2024) represents the Organization for Economic Co-operation and Development in 80 nations. PISA monitors educational systems by measuring student performance in mathematics, science, reading, financial literacy, and creative problem-solving and recommending school improvement.

Students require greater guidance and emotional support than can be offered by schools. The care, instruction, and supervision by parents have a powerful influence on personal success in the classroom and throughout life. Because the United States aspires to leadership in being able to raise healthy, well-adjusted, and successful children, one way to enhance this potential is by defining higher expectations for parents and grandparents, developing standards that identify assets and learning needs, and allocating economic resources based on variance from an accepted standard. Our nation has some distance to go to achieve our goals for education, but the future is bright when families and schools combine their efforts to ensure mental health and well-being of all children.

Conclusion

The same language that created the word *loneliness* to describe the disappointment that is associated with being alone also created the word *solitude* to express the pleasure of privacy (Hertz, 2021). The productive use of privacy is a lesson that can easily be learned at home but not acquired in any early childhood group environment. Young children are not allowed to decide to withdraw from the presence of others in day care. Parents manage how children spend time and can arrange a schedule that includes daily opportunities for children to spend time doing things by themselves. However, this practice contradicts the lifestyles of adults who acknowledge that arranging time for themselves is their most difficult task. Parents want to have privacy for themselves but often do not recognize children need privacy too. Reflective thinking requires conditions that are without distraction and enables thoughtful decision-making. American inventor Thomas Edison (1847–1931) stated, "The best thinking has been done in solitude. The worst has been done in turmoil" (Daum, 2016).

If the increasing expression of boredom can be seen as a wake-up call for society, it will encourage greater focus on the preservation of imagination and capacity for internal stimulation that is supported by an appreciation for solitude. Creativity is most prominent when curiosity becomes a norm, opportunities exist to practice reflective thinking, and access to imagination becomes a common asset.

Because children require greater guidance and emotional support than can be offered by schools, the care, instruction, and supervision by parents have a powerful influence on personal success in the classroom and throughout life. The United States aspires to a leadership role in being able to raise healthy, well-adjusted, and successful children. One way to enhance this potential is by defining higher expectations for parents and grandparents, developing standards that identify assets and learning needs, and allocating economic resources based on variance from an accepted standard. Our nation has a considerable distance to go to achieve our goals for education, but the future is bright when families and schools combine their best efforts to ensure the mental health and well-being of all children.

Key Concepts

1. Having time to appreciate solitude is often overlooked as an essential aspect of creative development in early childhood. Children should be encouraged to engage in imagination, reflect on situations, and process ideas and feelings without the ever-present distractions of technology devices and other distractions. Unless parents teach the enjoyment of spending time doing things by oneself, children will likely equate solitude with being lonely and being punished.

2. Encourage children to reflect on information they find when searching the Internet. Young children become accustomed to fast communication and feedback online when playing video games. This expectation for immediate feedback should not carry over to the complicated tasks of information processing. Reflective thinking necessitates solitude and supports better judgment. Remind the child that to act on information in a hasty way without reflection is often the cause of poor decisions that can be harmful.
3. Most people are unaware that two-thirds of highly creative people are introverts who enjoy spending time by themselves as well as getting along with others. They use the time alone to reflect, consider the pros and cons of decisions they want to make, and enjoy the company of their imagination. Solitary play helps to develop powers of concentration, persistence, and completion.
4. During solitary play, children govern the actions of every party in the stories they devise. This expression of imagination is normal during early childhood and allows for expressing feelings of dominance that are often denied when adults take over most of their activities.
5. Analyzing out loud what to do before a course of action is taken illustrates reflective thinking. Alternatives should be weighed as part of the process to determine the most suitable response. Reflective thought produces better decisions than impulsive thinking. Helping a child transition from reliance on impulsivity to reflective thought is an important lesson. Reinforce that reflection takes more time but provides greater benefit.
6. Reflective children think before they act, so they are more often accurate and make fewer mistakes than do impulsive children who react quickly and make many errors. Cognitive tempo is evident by age 2, seems stable by age 4, and relates to interaction between mother and child (or the principal caregiver and the child).
7. Consider using the five-second waiting rule when presenting questions for a child to consider. By encouraging children to use time to process information, adults discourage hasty and impulsive responses. When children have time to concentrate and deliberate, they learn to value creative thinking.
8. Becoming a creative person may sometimes require a willingness to oppose conformist thinking of the peer group. This attitude requires courage, which families can nurture by helping children realize that their worth does not depend on always seeing things as others do.
9. Parents and children should talk about how situations and events may be seen by others. By talking about the 'mental state' of characters seen on television, in books and stories, and during website visits and daily interaction children have with peers, parents support social understanding and empathy that is needed to respond in a way that is socially beneficial.
10. Parents and caregivers evaluate children daily but rarely provide them opportunities to practice self-assessment. Self-control can be more common when children acquire healthy self-evaluation practices instead of relying only on adults or the peer group to determine how well they are doing.

Generational Perspectives Activities

12.1 Discussion
12.2 Conversations With Young Children
12.3 A Scenario: Reasoning and Problem-Solving

12.4 Chapter Review
12.5 Parent and Grandparent Self-Evaluation
12.6 Storytelling

12.1 Discussion

1. What are some reasons why you sometimes feel the need to be by yourself?
2. How do you feel when a child prefers to play alone instead of with friends?
3. What do you suppose are the benefits children gain from their solitary play?
4. How can solitary play be arranged for children living in crowded apartments?
5. How do you feel about the solitude parents arrange for your grandchildren?
6. What difference does it make if children gain a desire to experience solitude?
7. How do your relatives differ in their extent of reliance on having solitude?
8. What are some obstacles that discourage children from valuing solitude?
9. How important is solitude for learning to participate in creative thinking?
10. How often do you think that children should have solitary time for play?

12.2 Conversations With Young Children

1. What are some things that you like to do alone, all by yourself?
2. What are some things that Mom or Dad like to do by themselves?
3. What do you think about when you have time to spend by yourself?
4. How often do you daydream or imagine things you want to happen?
5. How do teachers set aside time for you to think about things alone?
6. Why do you sometimes want to play alone instead of with friends?
7. How would you feel if you were not allowed to spend time alone?
8. What do you suppose people learn when they spend time alone?

12.3 A Scenario: Reasoning and Problem-Solving

Problem-solving scenarios present an opportunity to look at situations that might happen for a family and think about possible solutions. Your task is to look at the pros and cons of choices that are stated, think of additional options, identify relevant information that might be missing, find out how teammates view the alternatives, and defend your reasoning about the advice that you consider best.

Many children spend considerable time in group care where solitary play and reflective thinking cannot be arranged. Given the relationship between creative thinking and solitude, it seems innovations are needed to ensure early experience includes solitude. What do you think?

a. Early childhood educators should tell parents to arrange time for child solitude.
b. More children should be home-schooled so caregivers can have a solitude schedule.
c. Adults cannot arrange solitary time for themselves, so children may not need it either.
d. Parent education should include lessons on how they can support creative thinking.
e. Be careful about overscheduling extracurricular activities for your child.
f. Other _____

12.4 Chapter Review

1. What insights from the chapter will I try to apply in my relationships?
2. What is the most important key concept for me presented in this chapter?
3. Which elements of this chapter do I wish I had known about earlier?

12.5 Parent and Grandparent Self-Evaluation

For each question, place a check beside statements that describe your feelings. You may want to give several answers on some items. If your feelings are not on the choices list, write them on the line marked 'Other.' If a lesson persuaded you to change your mind, make it known by underlining any statements showing these answers reflect a change in feelings.

1. I arrange a schedule for myself that includes solitude and reflective thinking
    a. because it helps to clarify my ideas and make more informed decisions
    b. since I have found this kind of retreat allows me to evaluate my behavior
    c. when there are too many things going on and I need to sort things out
    d. but can seldom make it happen because my pace of life is so rapid
    e. Other _____

2. The way I try to communicate the importance of solitude to my grandchildren is to
    a. help them understand that arranging solitude and reflection is important in my life
    b. enable them to avoid placing too much time and attention on social media
    c. ask them to tell me about their priorities for the way they spend time
    d. remind them that creative thinking requires time for reflection
    e. Other _____

3. My observation has been that the parents of my grandchildren
    a. make sure the child's schedule is not overloaded so s/he can spend time alone
    b. do not believe it is important to arrange daily solitude in the child's schedule
    c. provide a good example by regularly setting aside solitary time for themselves
    d. maintain a hectic schedule themselves so they ignore child need for solitude
    e. Other _____

4. My grandchildren may not recognize their need to have solitude because
    a. they are so dependent on spending as much time as possible with peers
    b. they are not aware of the connection between solitude and creative thinking
    c. they suppose being alone is a form of punishment instead of an opportunity
    d. they are growing up in an environment where they never spend time alone
    e. Other _____

5. If my grandchild told a teacher that s/he was bored, I would hope that the teacher would
    a. ask for suggestions that can reduce the amount of boredom
    b. remind him/her to pay more attention to the lesson
    c. tell the parents that s/he is too distracted during class

d. blame the boredom on her and ask her to think about it
   e. Other _____

6. The reason my grandchild is sometimes bored at school is because

   a. some of the courses are not considered interesting or relevant
   b. the content of lessons in class are too difficult to comprehend
   c. the subject matter is too easy and targets the slow students
   d. Other _____

7. One way teachers might help students better appreciate solitude is to

   a. allow time for reflection without talking as a part of some activities
   b. discourage students from quickly raising hands when questioned
   c. orient them to understand that highly creative people value solitude
   d. make some assignments that involve time that is spent in solitude
   e. Other _____

8. My grandchildren get to observe their parents use solitary time

   a. when they read the newspaper, books, or are on the Internet
   b. during the time they watch TV alone
   c. when they relax and ignore distractions
   d. doing physical exercise for health
   e. Other _____

9. I think all the adults in my family should try to

   a. wait longer for children to answer questions
   b. encourage involvement with solitary activity
   c. discourage reliance on impulsive thinking
   d. present themselves as valuing reflection
   e. Other _____

10. Creative people in all age groups experience boredom

    a. less than others because they always have goals
    b. when others do not provide them enough stimulation
    c. rarely since they rely more on their own imagination
    d. only when they lack access to their mobile devices
    e. when class assignments do not allow for creativity
    f. Other _____

12.6 Storytelling

Historically, storytelling has been a dominant classic and progressive method of teaching around the world. The purposes of a storyteller are to present imaginary or real-life examples showing how some concept applies to a particular situation. People like stories, they pay attention to the procession of events, and usually remember aspects of a story for a long time. Your stories can reinforce the concepts in this chapter for family members and classmates. Please share your stories with them.

References

Allen, D. C. (2017). *Introverts: How to use your hidden strengths to succeed in an extrovert world.* CreateSpace Independent Publishing.

Assor, A., Kaplan, H., & Roth, G. (2002). Choice is good, but relevance is excellent: Autonomy-enhancing and suppressing teacher behaviours predicting students' engagement in schoolwork. *British Journal of Educational Psychology, 72*(2), 261–278. https://doi.org/10.1348/000709902158883

Beckert, T., Strom, R., & Strom, P. (2006). Black and White fathers of early adolescents: A cross-cultural approach to curriculum development for parent education. *North American Journal of Psychology, 8*(3), 455–469.

Behr, G., & Rydzewski, R. (2023). *When you wonder, you're learning: Mister Rogers' enduring lessons for raising creative, curious, caring kids.* Hachette.

Bloom, B. (Ed.). (1985). *Developing talent in young people.* Ballantine.

Cain, S. (2012). *Quiet: The power of introverts in a world that can't stop talking.* Crown.

Cain, S., Mone, G., & Moroz, E. (2017). *Quiet power: The secret strengths of introverted kids.* Rocky Pond.

Collinsworth, P., Strom, R., & Strom, S. (1996). *Parent Success Indicator:* Development and factorial validation. *Educational and Psychological Measurement, 56*(3), 504–513. https://doi.org/10.1177/0013164496056003012

Daum, K. (2016). *37 Quotes from Thomas Edison that will inspire success.* https://www.inc.com/kevin-daum/37-quotes-from-thomas-edison-that-will-bring-out-your-best.html

Ericcson, A., & Pool, R. (2017). *Peak: Secrets from the new science of expertise.* HarperOne.

Ericcson, A., Prietula, M., & Cokely, E. (2007, July–August). The making of an expert. *The Harvard Business Review, 85*(7), 114–121.

Feuchter, M. D., & Preckel, F. (2022). Reducing boredom in gifted education – evaluating the effects of full-time ability grouping. *Journal of Educational Psychology, 114*(8), 1477–1493. https://doi.org/10.1037/edu0000694

Frost, J., Wortham, S., & Reifel, S. (2021). *Play and child development* (4th ed.). Pearson.

Haidt, J. (2024). *The anxious generation: How the great rewiring of childhood is causing an epidemic of mental illness.* Penguin Press.

Hari, J. (2022). *Stolen focus: Why you can't pay attention – and how to think deeply again.* Crown.

Hertz, N. (2021). *The lonely century: How to restore human connection in a world that's pulling apart.* Crown Currency.

Hixenbaugh, M. (2024). *They came for the schools: One town's fight over race and identity, and the new war for America's classrooms.* Mariner Books.

Jacobs, E., & Jack, A. (2024, October 14). The boom in home schooling. *The Financial Times.* https://on.ft.com/4fcesyZ

Kagan, J., Rosman, B. L., Day, D., Albert, J., & Phillips, W. (1964). Information processing in the child: Significance of analytic and reflective attitudes. *Psychological Monographs: General and Applied, 78,* 1–37. https://doi.org/10.1037/h0093830

Kellerman, G. R., & Seligman, M. (2023). *Tomorrowmind: Thriving at work with resilience, creativity, and connection – now and in an uncertain future.* Atria.

Light, P. C. (2000, December). *Government's greatest achievements of the past half century.* Brookings.

MacRae, I., Furnham, A., & Reed, M. (2018). *High potential. How to spot, manage, and develop talented people at work* (2nd ed.). Bloomsbury Business.

Mark, G. (2023). *Attention span: A groundbreaking way to restore balance, happiness and productivity.* Hanover Square Press.

National Center for Education Statistics. (2024). *Program for international student assessment (PISA).* Organization for Economic Cooperation and Development (OECD), U.S. Department of Education. https://nces.ed.gov/surveys/pisa/

Raccanello, D., Florit, E., Brondino, M., Roda, A., & Mason, L. (2022). Control and value appraisals and online multiple-text comprehension in primary school: The mediating role of boredom and the moderating role of word-reading fluency. *British Journal of Educational Psychology, 92*(1), 258–279. https://doi.org/10.1111/bjep.12448

Stevenson, R. L. (2020). *A child's garden of verses*. Independently Published. (Original work published 1885)
Strom, R. D. (1965). *Teaching in the slum school*. Charles E. Merrill Books.
Strom, R. D. (1966). *The inner-city classroom: Teacher behaviors*. Charles E. Merrill Books.
Strom, R. D. (1985). Developing a curriculum for parent education. *Family Relations, 34*(2), 161–167. https://doi.org/10.2307/583887
Strom, R. D., Strom, P. S., Strom, S., Shen, Y., & Beckert, T. (2004, Winter). Black, Hispanic, and White American mothers of adolescents: Construction of a national standard. *Adolescence, 39*(156), 669–686. PMID: 15727406
Strom, R. D., Strom, P. S., & Beckert, T. E. (2008). Comparing Black, Hispanic, and White mothers with a national standard of parenting. *Adolescence, 43*(171), 525–545. PMID: 19086668
Strom, R. D., Amukamara, H., Strom, P., Beckert, T., Strom, S., & Griswold, D. (2014). Strengths and learning needs of African American fathers. *Journal of Family Studies, 7*(1), 40–55. https://doi.org/10.5172/jfs.7.1.40 (Original work published 2001)
Taylor, M. (Ed.). (2013). *The Oxford handbook of the development of imagination*. Oxford Press.
Turkle, S. (2016). *Reclaiming conversation: The power of talk in a digital age*. Penguin.
Turkle, S. (2017). *Alone together: Why we expect more from technology and less from each other*. Basic Books.
Turkle, S. (2021). *The empathy diaries: A memoir*. Penguin.
Véliz, C. (2024). *The ethics of privacy and surveillance*. Oxford University Press.

Part IV

Mental Health and Development

Chapter 13

Conflicts and Learning to Get Along

Many young children spend considerable time in group care where they are influenced by immature peers. This familiar situation calls for adult awareness of how children contribute to and interfere with early socialization of peers. Parents should know how to teach peaceful ways to resolve conflicts. Parents should also recognize cognitive limitations of children and how this implicates the management of their fears about war, death, and injury. The purposes of this chapter are to (a) examine the social dynamics associated with dominion play, (b) explain why it is important to make sure that young children are aware of mutual rights, (c) demonstrate effective methods for children to resolve some conflicts instead of expecting adult caregivers to always act as judges, (d) reflect on why children around the world rely on fantasy to manage fears and worries, (e) recognize the ways children perceive death at different ages, and (f) prevent adult misinterpretation of child motives when they engage in pretend play. Generational Perspectives Activities present topics to discuss with family members and close friends about child conflicts and learning to get along with others.

Civil Behavior and Territoriality

Young children are more age-segregated than during previous generations. Their day care and preschool experiences can be beneficial but present caregivers with the challenge of teaching civil behavior to the age group that is least mature. This circumstance encourages reflection about how socialization attitudes and skills should be taught to children in group care settings.

First, consider some common conditions of child relationships with peers. The adults who supervise 2–6-year-olds are typically disappointed by their daily observation of selfishness and possessiveness. The usual caregiver response is to encourage sharing and cooperation instead of what appears to be continuous conflict. This advice ignores a phenomenon that Ardrey (2014) and de Waal (2017) have described as territoriality, the inclination of creatures to declare a particular space as their own. Territorial behavior is observed throughout the animal kingdom. Coyotes and wolves mark their territory by leaving a scent outlining boundaries of their space. Fish attack larger fish that try to invade their space. Cats behave in the same way if another cat ventures into their yard (de Waal, 2022).

A similar intention to identify and protect territory is pervasive among human beings. One way people identify differences in social status is by the amount of space someone commands. As a rule, wealthy people own large properties surrounded by high fences with signs that read 'No trespassing.' Less affluent families also try to establish their territory by erecting lower fences and aspiring to own a larger home with more extensive property. When we enter a place of business, the lower-ranked employees can be seen working in cubicles that allow minimal privacy and sense of control. Elsewhere are the offices of executives, the largest of which belongs to the manager, president, or chief economic officer (Cohen et al., 2024; Mattan et al., 2017).

Dynamics of Dominion Play

When children claim a play space or insist they own a specific toy, this is an example of dominion play. According to Harris (2024), this type of play is normal among young boys and girls 2–6-years-old. However, dominion play can sometimes interfere with group functioning, so adults must have a conversation with children about the need for mutual rights. Children face territorial situations in preschool, day care, kindergarten, at home, or elsewhere on a play date.

Think about Pam and John. Both these 4-year-olds attend the same preschool. Pam, in tears, approaches the teacher to report that John refused to let her play with him. The teacher gestures she understands Pam's feelings and suggests they talk with John. After John explains that he is trying to build a zoo and does not want helpers, the teacher turns to Pam, who insists she wants to be John's partner anyway. Because John is not infringing on anyone else's territory, the teacher defends John's right to privacy by telling Pam that she should find someone else to play with or play alone. Forcing John to let Pam into the zoo area against his will would violate his right to privacy and could cause poor relationships between the two children. In similar circumstances, the teacher would defend Pam's right to privacy. When children cannot count on the teachers to defend their privacy, they develop feelings of helplessness instead of confidence.

Sometimes, dominion play can interfere with rights of other children. In these situations, limitations must be set not to deny anyone space but to restrict space so others can satisfy their needs (Cohen et al., 2024). For example, four-year-old Marshall visited a roundhouse at the railroad yard over the weekend. As soon as he arrived at the preschool on Monday morning, Marshall decided he would build a replica using blocks. Unfortunately, he chose to situate his project right beside the block shelves, thereby preventing other children from accessing play materials for themselves.

After observing unsuccessful efforts by peers to get Marshall to move his roundhouse, the teacher said, "Marshall, the reason everyone wants you to move the roundhouse is because where you have it keeps them from being able to get to the shelves where the blocks are stored." Marshall said, "They better not touch it, or the roundhouse could fall down." Another suggestion was made by the teacher, "Marshall, can you see any place to move the roundhouse so that other children can play with blocks too?" Marshall is definite about not moving his structure. Then the teacher suggested, "I know that you do not want to move it, but we have to find another spot." Undaunted, Marshall announced, "The roundhouse is already built so it cannot be moved." Another possible location by the window was recommended. In response, Marshall said, "No way." The teacher made another proposal, "I could help you move the roundhouse close to the window or you could move it by yourself." Marshall replied, "Nope." Without further comment, the teacher dismantled the roundhouse and moved it close to the window, so everyone in class could access the block shelves. Marshall immediately resumed play with the roundhouse as if nothing had happened.

Most children will more readily accept adult suggestions than Marshall, but even if they do not, providing face-saving options is a more powerful and effective method to teach than resorting to punishment, embarrassment, sarcastic comments, or making specific commands (Abraham, 2018). Children can learn to work alongside private space of others in a classroom. This accommodation of mutual rights is essential to support the origins of social competence. As a rule, when a child's right to privacy is respected, s/he becomes less defensive and will welcome play with the same children who were recently rejected.

A basic lesson many parents fail to teach is helping children realize that mutual rights is the best way to support early development of social competence. When children know they can depend on supervising adults to defend their privacy, they acquire confidence and do not need to withdraw from situations that could otherwise be overwhelming. Young children model behavior of adults they observe. A usual overlooked aspect of decision-making is that gaining the ability to think of multiple ways to solve problems is better than biting, taking the belongings of others, or responding in verbally vindictive ways. Generating face-saving alternatives can be modeled by grownups as the best method to solve conflicts (Harris, 2024).

In time, children generally decide that it is alright to play with one companion, but no one else is welcome. By excluding all others, the pair communicates their view that "two is company and three is a crowd." Adults generally disapprove of this kind of exclusionary conduct and suggest the children should like everyone. Grownups are rarely able to meet such an expectation themselves. A better response is to accept that, in most situations, children should be permitted to select friends. Because friendship requires some amount of privacy to develop, it is appropriate to respect child preferences for playing together at some distance from currently unwanted peers (Haidt, 2024).

Dominion Play Guidelines

Strom and Strom (2024) recommend that parents, grandparents, babysitters, day care staff, and kindergarten teachers apply these guidelines to support the social development of children younger than 7 years. Child need for control of spaces and ownership should be respected.

- Establish limits for mutual rights. Encourage children to respect privacy of peers.
- Permit decisions of children about who they choose to have as their play partner.
- Observe conflicts before considering whether an intervention seems appropriate.
- Provide face-saving alternatives as a method to restore mutual rights of children.
- Thinking of options calls for creative thinking that can be provided by most adults.
- Recognize socialization requires direct experience in resolving disputes with peers.
- Avoid imposing guilt as a reaction to conflict in favor of seeking a peaceful solution.
- Children should be asked to think about possible solutions for their disagreements.
- Ability to think of options is a lifelong asset for managing personal stress.

Amount of Time in Group Care

National Study of Child Group Care

What happens when caregivers lack understanding about the common need for dominion play, overlook the importance of mutual rights, deny privacy, force sharing, resolve conflicts by using coercive methods, and insist on forcing apologies by some of the players? Socialization is adversely affected. Most parents and grandparents should be informed about the most expensive study ever conducted by Belsky et al. (2007, 2020) regarding the experience of day care. This ten-year investigation involved 1,360 children living in ten cities in the United States. The study was financed by a U.S. government grant of more than $100 million. The purpose was to evaluate the effects of non-maternal care on infants and preschoolers in group care arrangements.

The national representative sample of children in day care before their first birthday was compared with other children taken care of at home by older relatives or nannies. Follow-up data was gathered at 6 months of age, 15 months, 24 months, 54 months, and finally in kindergarten. The conclusions of the national assessment were based on child ratings by mothers, caregivers, and kindergarten teachers. The results reported by Belsky et al. (2007) showed the impact of group care was the same regardless of quality, child gender, or household income. Time was identified as the single most important factor. The more hours children spent away from parents, the more behavior problems they demonstrated. Specifically, children in group care for 30 hours a week were observed by mothers, caregivers, and kindergarten teachers to act in more aggressive ways toward others than those attending group care for less than ten hours a week.

Differences between the most aggressive children and peers were not a matter of standing up for personal rights but instead their inclination to verbally or physically attack classmates and to make continual demands for extra attention from the teacher. Children who attended day care from infancy were the most easily frustrated, the least cooperative, most egocentric, least task-oriented, and most distractible. These children lacked self-control and were prepared to fight to get their way (Belsky et al., 2020). Currently, there are 22.1 million children in the United States below age 6 who are enrolled in group care (Center for American Progress, 2023).

Importance of Social Competence

A universal problem among children attending group care is failing to learn mutual rights. Children who spend many hours each week in day care settings are less able to demonstrate competence in socialization skills than peers who spend fewer hours a week in group care. According to Zinsser (2023), in the elementary school grades, the consequences of social incompetence included invading the space of other students, going up and down the aisles and bothering peers, distracting others from being able to study, taking belongings of classmates, and acting in ways that prevent the conditions that are conducive for students to study.

Memorizing the alphabet and citing numbers in sequence have been the customary ways parents prepare children for preschool. This exclusive focus ignores the social skills that are needed to get along with immature peers. Williams and Lerner (2019) and Zinsser (2023) suggested that most parents need guidance because they generally overemphasize the importance of academic readiness while failing to provide enough attention to social development. Mothers, fathers, and grandparents, whose focus is on verbal communication, encourage ability to follow directions and engage successfully in group activities that can help children get the most from their time in preschool and reduce misbehavior.

Milestones for 5-Year-Olds

Each child has a unique timing for learning skills and various accomplishments. At age 5, children are constantly learning how to control emotions. At the same time, they are starting kindergarten and having to make new friends. Normally, they are crossing milestones of child development which will lead them to acceptable social behavior and cognitive growth. These milestones include (Tapp, 2024; Wisner, 2024):

- choosing friends on their own,
- following directions,
- testing boundaries,
- losing baby teeth,
- using the bathroom solo,
- dressing themselves,
- becoming a fluent talker,
- treating others fairly,
- knowing what is real and what is fiction, and
- beginning to understand money and numbers.

Parents should be aware of some milestones of emotional and social development to identify normal versus abnormal behavior of a 5-year-old child. The following signs of concern warrant consultation with a pediatrician: (a) the child cannot say their first and last name, (b) does not play with a variety of toys or play different games, (c) does not respond to others, (d) has extreme emotions such as shyness or is overly fearful, (e) is unable to wash their hands, (f) cannot draw a picture, (g) or lose skills s/he once possessed. There are many deviations that can be dealt with in remediation with successful outcomes, such as speech therapy, vision correction, and hearing accuracy. Conversations with a pediatrician are encouraged to keep parents informed about child normative behavior at different ages (Wisner, 2024).

Grandparents as Child Caregivers

Most millennial parents (born between 1980 and 1997 – the oldest are 45 and youngest are 28) cannot afford the current costs of sending a child to group care (Strom & Strom, 2024). Only 23% of mothers and 3% of dads reported that they can afford to stay home with young children. The United States Department of Health and Human Services standard recommended for affordable federal benchmark care is 7% of family income (Center for American Progress, 2023). But in over half of the states, parents must pay 25% or more of family income on childcare (Calderón, 2023). You can check the conditions in your state by going to the reference for Lurye (2022). In addition, grandparents are often implicated. Evidence has consistently shown that about 75% of older relatives live within 30 miles of at least one adult child (Choi et al., 2020).

The typical motivation for proximity to relatives is because parents want to be nearby so they can provide needed care for their aging parents. In return, the reason many grandparents move closer to daughters and sons is so they can help care for young grandchildren while the parent(s) are at work (Hurst, 2022). Grandparents and other relatives can be a valuable resource and currently provide about the same amount of care as children receive when they are in group care arrangements.

Because many millennials (born between 1981 and 1996) have decided they want to delay having children, this means Generation X (born 1965–1980) and baby boomers (born 1946–1964) have become the oldest grandparents in history. Some of these grandparents plan to enjoy their golden years by eating out at restaurants more often and traveling to distant places they have dreamed about instead of being expected by their children to serve as caregivers for young grandchildren. This lack of support for parents has caused some millennials to feel as though they have been abandoned (Parks, 2023; Strom & Strom, 2021).

The Little Soldier

A common risk taken by parents and other caregivers is to misinterpret the motives of children at play. Children are curious and often frightened by news reports, particularly scenes of war and death in the Middle East and terrorist attacks in other places. The American Academy of Child and Adolescent Psychiatry (AACAP) (2023) summarizes guidelines for parents about how to talk to children about terrorism and war. Further, the AACAP reported that parents are often asked by children many of these questions about terrorism: Who will take care of children if our parents must go to war? Will my dad have to become a soldier? What if the terrorists attack our school, buses, subways, and houses? What should I do if someone comes into the school with a gun? Parents recognize they are not fully prepared to adequately react to these kinds of questions from their young children.

Young children everywhere who ask such questions rely on fantasy as a powerful tool to help them reduce their fears, anxieties, and worries (Garvey, 2023). Parents and grandparents should be aware of stages of mental development that govern the way children interpret meaning of death and why many find engaging in conflict-oriented play appealing (Harris, 2024). Accurate interpretation of child motives enables adults to permit children a more reasonable choice of toys and themes to guide play (Haidt, 2024).

Child Stages in Comprehension of Death

Parents wonder how watching evening news on television containing reports about war in the Middle East and flow of refugee immigrants on the southern border of the United States might have an influence on their child. Some feel uncertain about whether to allow children to play with toy weapons or military electronic games (Pevzner, 2014). Barbara is a 35-year-old mother of two preschoolers. Even before the growth in fear of domestic terrorism became common, she and her husband believed violent toys could motivate lawless behavior. She said:

> We knew that our decision to deny weapon toys would be difficult for our young sons to understand. It would be easy to conform to the majority opinion, but that would mean a lowering of our standards of integrity. After overhearing my child tell his cowboy companions that he was going to shoot and kill him, I felt inclined to say, 'Donnie, you don't mean that.' I reconsidered and thought maybe I should sit down with him and explain that when you kill someone, they are dead and can never breathe again. We wanted him to learn that guns don't solve problems but make more problems. Finally, not knowing what to do or say, I ignored him and went on feeling guilty.

Barbara's dilemma is familiar and reflects the concerns many parents have about gun control. Perhaps the problem can be diminished by examining what children mean when they talk about killing and dying. The meaning of death presents misconceptions of young children. They see death as a reversible process. Whether at play with hide-and-go-seek or cowboys, all the people killed are expected to recover quickly and live again. The conventional cartoon on television reinforces this notion when the rabbit falls off a cliff and hits the ground with a thud. Then, in keeping with the reversible concept of death, the rabbit is brought back to life. The same thing happens when children see an actor on a television show die and a few days later appear as a guest on a talk show.

Consider this conversation between a father and his 5-year-old son while playing together (Strom, 1978):

Son: Dad, I'm going to dress up like an army man.
Father: You look like a soldier. I was a soldier once.
Son: Why?
Father: The country needed me. We were having a war.
Son: Dad, did you die?
Father: No, I was lucky.

The realization that death is permanent happens in stages. Between 3 and 5 years of age, there is curiosity and questioning about death. Unfortunately, many adults try to suppress this curiosity and believe it is impolite for their child to ask an elderly neighbor, Mrs. Thompson, when she is going to die. In contrast, several generations ago, most children witnessed at least one deathbed event, typically death of a grandparent. Yet the young child believes that death is not final; it is like being less alive. Just as sleeping people can wake up, and people on a trip can return, so too a dead person can come back to life. The coffin limits movement, but dead people must continue to eat and breathe. People buried at the cemetery must be aware about what is happening, they are sad for themselves and feel it when someone thinks about them. Dying disturbs the young child because life in the grave is seen as boring and unpleasant. But, most of all, it bothers the child because death separates people from one another. And, at this young age, a child's greatest fear is separation from parents.

Young children are self-centered and preoccupied by current events, so they are unable to recognize how a death in the family can impose future demands, including the permanent loss of someone's presence, their comfort, love, encouragement, and perhaps financial support. Because these understandings do not emerge until a later age, small children might not express their grief immediately or even cry like their adult relatives or friends. In fact, it is common to mistakenly conclude that a child is coping well with the loss of a loved one. But bear in mind little children are unable to fully comprehend the situation and can tolerate only short periods of sadness. Because it is easy for them to be distracted, they may appear finished with grief and mourning earlier than is the case (Cohen et al., 2017; Nemours KidsHealth, 2020, 2021).

Even young children recognize words are an insufficient form of support for someone experiencing grief and that what matters most is just being there to console them. For example, 4-year-old Amanda did not come in from the backyard when first called by her mother. Later, when her mother asked Amanda to explain why she was late, the little girl replied, "I was helping Judy." The mother wanted more information. "What were you doing?" Amanda said, "Well, her doll's head got crushed." The mother wondered aloud, "How could you help to fix that?" Amanda had a good answer and said, "I was helping her cry."

Children between 5 and 9 years of age personify death, view it as an angelic character who makes rounds in the night to start life for some individuals and end it for others. The big shift in the child's thinking from the first stage to this stage is that death is recognized as possibly being final. It is no longer perceived as just a reduced form of life. This perspective of death emerges with increased personal experiences that suggest certain separations will be permanent. When a pet goldfish dies, her mother buys a new one because, she says, the old one is gone forever. Claude Cattaert's (1963) classic story of *Where do Goldfish Go?* illustrates how children are upset by adults whose insensitive reaction to the death of pets is that they can be replaced by purchasing a new dog, cat, or bird. When Valerie's goldfish unexpectedly dies, no one appears bothered except her; yet the whole family is overcome with sorrow when grandfather dies, even though his death had been anticipated for years by everyone. When a pet dies, helping children cope with the loss should be an important family conversation (Nemours KidsHealth, 2020).

It is not just families who should become more aware and sensitive to child feelings about death. In conversations with college students preparing to become kindergarten or first-grade teachers, we asked them: What would you do if some morning you arrived at school and the class goldfish was found dead? The range of responses included these comments: "I would deliver a eulogy; say we will declare a day of mourning; conduct a formal burial; discuss the virtues of the deceased; consider the afterlife of fish; invite friends to share testimonials; talk about human death and what it means; or – flush the fish and say, 'Take your books out. It is time for oral reading.'"

Parents realize that it is impossible to guarantee a long life for pets we love but believe they can reduce the exposure children have with death that appears on television. The outcome of this decision to protect youngsters is a refusal to allow them to observe programs that feature involvement of the police, censoring aggressive cartoons, and ambivalence about local news reporting of violence or death in the community.

The typical 5–9-year-old child believes the cause of death is external and personifies death as being an outside agent. Because they conceive of death as a person, children feel it is possible to avoid death if protective measures are taken. Thus, one child might claim that his grandfather will not die because the family is taking such good care of him. Children of single parents admit that they worry most about "What will happen to me if my mother dies?" It can be reassuring to know plans are made so they will be taken care of in case of an unexpected death.

Finally, around ages 9 to 10, most children realize death is not only final but inevitable. It will happen to them too no matter how clever they are or how well they take care of themselves. Instead of imagining death as controlled by an external agent, they realize internal, biological forces are involved. As children accept universality and certainty of death, changes in attitudes and outlook can be observed. They begin to show concern about the meaning of life, their purpose for being on earth, and ways to achieve personal goals. This means values become an important influence in shaping their behavior (Levine, 2020).

Children across the globe are increasingly exposed to television scenes showing death and destruction. Others see death on television with such regularity war is a common fear and worry. Children look to parents for answers about death, but our attitude is the most relevant response. Parents should explain their religious beliefs about what happens to people after they die. Bear in mind that young children love mystery and will adopt adult uncertainty if we acknowledge some things are unknown to us as well as share our faith beliefs.

Comparative Influence of Toys and Players

Safety should always be the first concern when parents buy toys for children. However, it is unwise to overemphasize the effects of toys but not emphasize that the adults who play with children are a significant influence. Otherwise, the impact of playthings is exaggerated while the impact of players is underestimated. The function of parents cannot be fulfilled by buying only the right toys and forbidding wrong ones. Creativity does not reside in toys but the interaction between people who play with them. Research on creative behavior and modeling shows that parents should play with children, become involved instead of limiting themselves to judging the value of playthings. The assumption that certain toys can have a disabling effect on personality of children is unwarranted, but the view that adults can have a favorable influence through play has been demonstrated.

Parents should stop the practice of censoring the content of child fantasy play, except in cases of bodily danger. Once the direction of children's pretending becomes the sole choice of adults, children are no longer decision-makers. And, in fantasy play, making choices is essential for participation. Adults can share in determining the agenda if they are willing to accept the role of being a play partner. It is unfair to interpret the content of child play as though it represents adult motives. When an actor portrays a killer in a movie or stage play, an audience may judge the performance to be convincing and deserving of recognition. However, when a child chooses to pretend the same type of role, the reasons for deciding to become that character may receive greater attention from adults than the child's performance. Such interpretations of child play cause attribution of motives that children do not possess. Child motives to kill one another temporarily with toy weapons are unrelated to adult motivation for violent activity.

Most parents want children to learn nonviolent ways to settle personal disputes. One way to achieve this goal is by sustaining a long-term emphasis on conflict resolution. It is important that relatives accept stages of normal development in understanding the finality of death. When the war play of children is construed as a personality defect or prelude to adult violence the motives of children are unfairly judged. Pretending helps kids confront common fears of war, death, and injury and provides them with a vicarious sense of control over such events. Abbott and Burkitt (2023) recommend that parents and other caregivers avoid censoring the focus that children choose for their pretending and instead urge understanding of how to solve disputes by enacting their own values during parent-child play.

Principles for Application

1. Learning to respect mutual rights is the basis of social competence. When children know that supervising adults will defend their privacy, they develop a sense of self-confidence instead of feeling helpless and wanting to withdraw from situations that would otherwise be seen as overwhelming.
2. Young children model the behavior of adults they observe. An overlooked but vital aspect of decision-making is ability to generate alternative solutions for conflicts instead of hitting, biting, taking things from others, or reacting in verbally vindictive ways. The ability to think of face-saving options is modeled by adults who demonstrate they can think of options when there are child conflicts.
3. Respect the motives of young children whose fantasy behavior is governed by imagination. Young children consider death a temporary condition, so they delight in shooting and killing one another in war play. Adults aware of the limited comprehension children

have of death are less inclined to misinterpret their motives in favor of approving a broad range for child pretending.
4. Encourage children to pretend as a method to process fears and anxieties. Children can reduce fears by repeatedly confronting them during play settings they are able to control. Parents who recognize the benefits of this strategy refrain from judging the focus of child pretending. They also show support by willingness to repeat fearful scenarios and themes children choose during family play. Greater awareness of consequences of war becomes possible when adults focus on the functions of military hospitals, permanent disabilities some people suffer, coping with the loss of friends and loved ones, and negotiations for peaceful relationships between enemies.
5. Institutional reforms are justified in teacher education. There is a sufficient knowledge base about early cognitive development to warrant a college degree focused on early childhood. Graduates of such programs could join public schools at the same pay scale as elementary-grade teachers. The word *preschool* should be replaced with *early childhood education*.

Conclusion

Parents and caregivers should understand the psychological and physical aspects of early child development. With training, caregivers become more able to accept social limitations of children, respect their need for dominion play, preserve mutual rights, and show ways to solve conflicts. This combination of strategies along with avoiding excessive time children spend in group care is essential to help them acquire socialization skills for getting along with others.

Key Concepts

1. Play is an activity where children often express the desire to be in control. When they claim a play space or insist on their ownership of a certain toy, this dominion-type play is normal among children from age 2 to age 6.
2. Adults should establish mutual rights for children as a basis for socialization in groups. When children are unable to look to adults to defend their privacy, they are likely to develop feelings of helplessness instead of self-confidence.
3. Because friendship requires a certain amount of privacy to develop, it is appropriate to respect the preference of two children to play by themselves, somewhat at a distance from unwanted peers.
4. When adult intervention is needed during play conflicts, provide children a range of face-saving alternatives to restore mutual rights. This is difficult at first because this approach requires identifying options and creative behavior by the adults.
5. Children need to make decisions. An often overlooked but important aspect of decision-making is to reflect about the possible solutions for problems. Ability to generate options is an asset for managing stress throughout life.
6. The more hours a week infants and preschoolers are in group care, the more probable it is they will exhibit behavior problems. Those in group care for more than 30 hours a week are far more aggressive than their peers in group care less than ten hours a week. Grandparents who live nearby could provide individual care sometimes that would diminish child time in group care.

7. Children who attend day care from infancy until kindergarten are more easily frustrated, less cooperative, more egocentric, less task-oriented, and more distracted. These children have not developed self-control, so they are inclined to fight to get their own way.
8. Preschool teachers believe that parents overemphasize child preparation for academic skills while giving insufficient attention to the social skills boys and girls need to be able to get along with peers.
9. It is unfair to interpret the content of child play as if it reflected adult motives. Pretending to be a bad character does not mean a child is on the path to becoming a delinquent.
10. Pretending helps children to confront their fears of war, death, and injury and provides a vicarious sense of power or control over such events. Playing fearful events over and over enables children to reduce the effects these powerful and frightening issues have on them.

Generational Perspectives Activities

13.1 Discussion
13.2 Conversations With Young Children
13.3 A Scenario: Reasoning and Problem-Solving
13.4 Chapter Review
13.5 Parent and Grandparent Self-Evaluation
13.6 Storytelling

13.1 Discussion

1. What strategies have you relied on to improve the way that children treat playmates?
2. How is a child's speech influenced by attending a day care center or a preschool?
3. Share your observation of child selfishness or lack of concern for views of others.
4. Why do you suppose young children talk to themselves while they are pretending?
5. How do you speak differently to preschoolers than to the children who attend school?
6. How do you feel about allowing young children to watch shows that include death?
7. How do you suppose children attempt to reduce the extent of their fears and worries?
8. What steps have you taken in talking to children about the death of their pet animal?
9. How do you feel when you observe young children shoot each other as they play war?
10. In what ways do adults misinterpret child motives when they engage in pretend play?

13.2 Conversations With Young Children

1. What do you suppose happens to people when they are dead?
2. How do you solve conflicts with other children in your class?
3. What would you like to change about the group care center?
4. Would you like to spend more time in group care or less time?
5. What is your favorite part of playing with your toy soldiers?
6. How do you manage fears and worries when they happen to you?

13.3 A Scenario: Reasoning and Problem-Solving

Parents are concerned about affordable childcare. What solutions do you recommend?

1. Invite grandparents to provide free supervision for young children
2. Lobby the government to increase financial support for childcare
3. Have communities recruit high school volunteers to be caregivers
4. Ask churches to identify older adults who would be willing to help
5. Other _____

13.4 Chapter Review

1. What insights from the chapter will I try to apply in my relationships?
2. What is the most important key concept for me presented in this chapter?
3. Which elements of this chapter do I wish I had known about earlier?

13.5 Parent and Grandparent Self-Evaluation

1. I would favor universities providing four-year education degrees in early childhood
    a. with graduates being put on the same pay scale as later elementary-grade teachers
    b. so these professionals would know how to meet education needs of young children
    c. because child brain development is the most rapid for this age group
    d. the community should care about having a relevant curriculum for preschoolers
    e. Other _____

2. If children in my care wanted to play warfare by using their toy soldiers, I would
    a. be glad to join in and focus on the hospital role to help any of the victims
    b. recommend they play something else that does not result in death or injury
    c. suggest the warring parties attempt to negotiate to enable a lasting peace
    d. urge them to consider the hidden price of war in terms of death or injury
    e. Other _____

3. Child understanding about the finality of death means that I should
    a. not try to interpret their motives when they participate in pretend play
    b. ignore assertions they make about the benefits of eliminating their enemy
    c. talk to them and explain that no one really understands about death
    d. gradually teach them my religious beliefs about death and the future
    e. Other _____

4. I would like day care centers to limit service to children for
    a. ten hours or less every week
    b. however long parents need it
    c. no more than 30 hours a week
    d. until it produces misbehavior
    e. Other _____

5. Grandparents who do not want to take care of grandchildren should
    a. be able to make that choice without having to feel guilty

b. consider how this decision can affect their family status
c. be allowed to pursue some of their long-standing dreams
d. leave the main responsibility for raising children to parents
e. Other _____

6. How often do you see children who have not learned mutual rights?

a. most of the families that I observe on a regular basis
b. children generally are not taught to care about others
c. narcissism is a major problem in our neighborhood
d. parents don't teach concern for well-being of others
e. Other _____

7. How well are children learning to make decisions about conflicts?

a. generating options does not seem to be a common practice
b. bullying to decide who is right appears to be more common
c. I think they too often look to adults to act as judges
d. they are not learning, and this will disadvantage them
e. Other _____

13.6 Storytelling

Historically, storytelling has been a dominant classic and progressive method of teaching around the world. The purposes of a storyteller are to present imaginary or real-life examples showing how some concept applies to a particular situation. People like stories, they pay attention to the procession of events, and usually remember aspects of a story for a long time. Your stories can reinforce the concepts in this chapter for family members and classmates. Please share your stories with them.

References

Abbott, R., & Burkitt, E. (2023). *Child development and the brain: From embryo to adolescence* (2nd ed.). Policy Press.

Abraham, A. (2018). *The neuroscience of creativity.* Cambridge University Press.

American Academy of Child & Adolescent Psychiatry. (2023, September). *Terrorism and war: How to talk to children [No. 87].* https://www.aacap.org/AACAP/Families_and_Youth/Facts_for_Families/FFF-Guide/Talking-To-Children-About-Terrorism-And-War-087.aspx

Ardrey, R. (2014). *The territorial imperative: A personal inquiry into the animal origins of property and nations.* StoryDesign.

Belsky, J., Caspi, A., Moffitt, T., & Poulton, R. (2020). *The origins of you: How childhood shapes later life.* Harvard University Press.

Belsky, J., Vandell, D., Burchinal, M., Clarke-Stewart, K., McCartney, K., Owen, M., & The NICHD Early Child Care Research Network. (2007, March). Are there long-term effects of early childhood care? *Child Development, 78*(2), 681–701. https://doi.org/10.1111/j.1467-8624.2007.01021.x

Calderón, M. (2023, August 10). *Why child care is essential for a healthy start and how we're standing up for babies. Every child thrives.* W. K. Kellogg Foundation. https://everychildthrives.com/why-child-care-access-is-essential-for-a-healthy-start-and-how-were-standing-up-for-babies/?gad_source=1&gclid=EAIaIQobChMIpeXqnqamhQMV_HJ_AB3lPgwqEAAYASAAEgJoWfD_BwE

Cattaert, C. (1963). *Where do goldfish go?* Crown.

Center for American Progress. (2023, December). *Data dashboard: An overview of child care and early learning in the United States.* https://www.americanprogress.org/article/data-dashboard-an-overview-of-child-care-and-early-learning-in-the-united-states/

Choi, H., Schoeni, R., Wiemers, E., Hotz, V. J., & Seltzer, J. (2020, April). Spatial distance between parents and adult children in the United States. *Journal of Marriage and the Family, 82*(2), 822–840. https://doi.org/10.1111/jomf.12606

Cohen, D. H., Stern, V., Balaban, N., Gropper, N., & Andris, J. (2024). *Observing and recording the behavior of young children* (7th ed.). Teachers College Press.

Cohen, J. A., Mannarino, A. P., & Deblinger, E. (2017). *Treating trauma and traumatic grief in children and adolescents* (2nd ed.). Guilford Press.

de Waal, F. (2017). *Are we smart enough to know how smart animals are?* W. W. Norton.

de Waal, F. (2022). *Different: Gender through the eyes of a primatologist*. W. W. Norton.

Garvey, D. (2023). *Little brains matter: A practical guide to brain development and neuroscience in early childhood*. Routledge.

Haidt, J. (2024). *The anxious generation: How the great rewiring of childhood is causing an epidemic of mental illness*. Penguin.

Harris, N. (2024, September 20). Types of play and why they're important for child development. *Parents*. https://www.parents.com/types-of-play-6835400

Hurst, K. (2022, May 18). *More than half of Americans live within an hour of extended family*. Pew Research Center. https://www.pewresearch.org/short-reads/2022/05/18/more-than-half-of-americans-live-within-an-hour-of-extended-family/

Levine, M. (2020). *Ready or not: Preparing our kids to thrive in an uncertain and rapidly changing world*. Harper.

Lurye, S. (2022, March 31). The states with the most and least affordable child care. *U.S. New & World Report*. https://www.usnews.com/news/best-states/articles/2022-03-31/states-with-highest-and-lowest-cost-of-daycare

Mattan, B. D., Kubota, J., & Cloutier, J. (2017, May 25). How social status shapes person perception and evaluation: A social neuroscience perspective. *Perspectives on Psychological Science, 12*(3), 468–507. https://doi.org/10.1177/1745691616677828 PMID: 28544863

Nemours KidsHealth. (2020). *When a pet dies: Helping kids cope*. https://kidshealth.org/en/parents/pet-death.html

Nemours KidsHealth. (2021). *When a loved one dies: How to help your child*. https://kidshealth.org/en/parents/death.html

Parks, K. (2023, December 3). Millennials feel 'abandoned' by parents not available to help raise grandkids: 'Too busy'. *New York Post*. https://nypost.com/2023/12/03/lifestyle/millennials-feel-abandoned-by-parents-not-available-to-help-raise-grandkids/

Pevzner, H. (2014, April 4). Is war play bad for kids? *Scholastic*. https://www.scholastic.com/parents/family-life/parent-child/war-play-bad-kids.html

Strom, R. D. (1978). *Growing together. Parent and child development*. Brooks/Cole.

Strom, R. D., & Strom, P. S. (2021). Learning throughout life about the needs of all generations: Recognizing and counteracting generational isolation. In M. London (Ed.), *The Oxford handbook of lifelong learning* (2nd ed., pp. 183–206). Oxford University Press.

Strom, P. S., & Strom, R. D. (2024). *Mental health and relationships from early adulthood through old age*. Routledge.

Tapp, F. (2024, August 12). 8 ways to prepare your kid for the first day of kindergarten. *Parents*. https://www.parents.com/kids/education/kindergarten/first-day-of-kindergarten-ways-to-prepare/

Williams, P. G., & Lerner, M. (2019, July 22). School readiness. *The American Academy of Pediatrics, 144*(2), e20191766. https://doi.org/10.1542/peds.2019-1766; https://publications.aap.org/pediatrics/article/144/2/e20191766/38558/School-Readiness

Wisner, W. (2024, June 25). 5-year-old child development milestones. *Parents*. https://www.parents.com/5-year-old-developmental-milestones-620713

Zinsser, K. (2023). *No longer welcome: The epidemic of expulsion from early childhood education*. Oxford University Press.

Chapter 14

Relationships With Parents and Peers

Parents, grandparents, and teachers are recognized for being sources of child guidance. However, the favorable ways children contribute to the social learning of peers are less well understood and appreciated. Children want to learn from classmates about many experiences. Teachers are aware peer influence is a powerful asset, but it is the most difficult resource for them to manage. Peers are a major force because more time is spent with them than adults, and peer attitudes and actions can support or interfere with healthy socialization. Adults should be aware of social contexts where peers can have a significant influence on growth and student learning (White & Berns, 2022). The purposes of this chapter are to (a) identify socialization lessons that are best taught by peers, (b) describe student belonging and rejection experiences, (c) provide reasons for teaching children to accept group and individual differences, (d) explain school inclusion practices and ways federal education policy contributes to child equity, (e) present ways parents and teachers can provide peer pressure protectors for students, and (f) discuss how peers and adults can shape healthy group norms of behavior during childhood. Generational Perspectives Activities present topics to discuss with family members and close friends about child relationships with parents and peers.

Unique Lessons From Peers

The potential of friends to influence socialization is shown by lessons children learn mainly from peers in their age group. The relevance of such lessons is they can support or prevent necessary emotional adjustments across a broad range of interpersonal situations.

Peers Provide the First Experiences With Equality

Children want to be with companions and enjoy their attention. The peer age group is in the best position to satisfy these needs. When members behave according to a group social norm, the rewards include attention, acceptance, and emotional support (Bukowski et al., 2019).

Different Standards Expected by Peers

The basic conditions of managing a home (food, shelter, health, safety, money) make it difficult for young children to declare complete autonomy from parents. Nevertheless, young peers usually demonstrate willingness to listen to friends about dilemmas they face and encourage each other to express their differences in the presence of parents (Ali & Chin, 2023).

Peer standards are more easily attainable and provide a rationale for collective child opposition to directives given by adults.

Parents and Teachers Often Overlook the Positive Influence of Peers

Peers present many experiences that are essential for social and emotional growth. For example, children must rely on others in their age group as the most reasonable standard for self-comparison, chances to express themselves without experiencing guilt, fear of punishment, and opportunities to share leadership. They encourage peers to strive for independence and sense of interdependence, belonging to another important group besides the family or school (Strom et al., 2019).

Children Learn Friendship From Peers

Becoming part of a group requires acquiring skills that are motivated by peers. These skills typically include cooperation, sharing ideas, striving for independence, showing discontent and anger, and reconciliation following arguments. Such lessons can be learned more easily from peers than from parents. Students discover what friends will tolerate, and they become aware of conduct the group will not condone. Most students gain a feeling of belonging in their peer group and believe they are accepted. Students find they must learn from peers the constructive ways to resolve conflicts although aggressive and dysfunctional strategies can still be prominent (DeAngelis, 2023; White & Berns, 2022).

Experiences of Belonging and Rejection

Beginnings of Social Prejudice

Helping students view themselves as successful is necessary to support mental health. Students also grow by learning to see others in positive ways. The most prominent scholar on the subject of prejudice was Gordon Allport (1954/1979) of Harvard University. He determined that before age 10, children less often participated in social rejection. Most activities of young children are noncompetitive, so their self-concepts are rarely threatened. Students whose academic performance is greater than others in the early grades seldom announce superiority and those who score below average do not yet report feelings of inferiority because intellectual norms have yet to be established. In childhood, the status of parents is the main source of child self-esteem. Children accept as their own the value they believe their parents have attained.

The environment changes dramatically as children enter middle school and junior high. Then individuals can no longer depend on what parents have achieved as the basis for self-pride. Another important shift is that, instead of meeting the expectations of just one teacher, students are expected to satisfy the demands of multiple teachers, each of whom provide instruction in different subjects. From this time forward, students must earn their personal social standing. In classes they begin to encounter greater competition and failure along with critical and unfriendly remarks from classmates. Peers are quick to detect weaknesses of individuals and identify them by expressing insults or statements intended to be hurtful. Consequently, students in middle grades experience a sharpening sense of self and overall decline in self-esteem. Teachers should plan experiences that can enable everyone to view themselves favorably without having to find fault with peers (Sobel & Alston, 2021).

As peers replace parents in supplying the group norms, roles, and models with whom to identify, students gravitate to classmates for acceptance, information, and emotional support. Belonging to a peer group becomes so important that methods of the group are rarely challenged. Instead, most students are eager to conform. Group members are less anxious if they behave the same way as peers without quite understanding why. This inclination to adopt group values and attitudes without really knowing the reasons can sometimes lead to acceptance of misconduct that students would otherwise recognize as wrong.

Becoming part of a group must be somewhat exclusive for a group to become significant. Around age 10 students form cliques where classmates from similar backgrounds and standards prefer to hang out together and sometimes refuse to accept others who are different. Although this can be a reasonable way to find and develop friendships, there are also negative outcomes (Bukowski et al., 2019). Allen and Cowdery (2022) explained that level of rejection sometimes escalates to the overt expression of verbal intolerance and prejudice. Allport (1954/1979) indicated that social prejudice is more common among 10-year-olds than among students in high school.

It is gratifying to realize negative social prejudice (i.e., rejection) declines as the level of education rises. However, researchers Baumeister and Bushman (2021) and Schwartz et al. (2021) have shown that the results of early peer rejection can last for a lifetime. Individuals who become targets of racial, religious, ethnic, and other prejudices must divert some energy from healthy forms of interaction to strategies that can provide self-protection. Acceptance, rejection, and self-concept are inseparable. To suggest minority students who experience prejudice the most should ignore the low estimates the dominant group has of them is to presume children are able to avoid being influenced by impressions of classmates. On the contrary, the way that others feel about us impacts the way we are treated by them and how we see ourselves as well.

Acceptance of Group Differences

In addition to establishing anti-bully policies, boards of education can amend how history is presented to students. Students in the elementary school are more accepting of differences when they are made aware of how groups sometimes targeted for rejection have contributed to our nation (Allen & Cowdery, 2022). During the 1960s, schools began to acquaint students with certain of the notable African Americans who previously were denied recognition even though their initiatives improved the quality of life for Americans. In the 1970s, Latinos were first portrayed in a way that acknowledged the contributions of leaders from this subpopulation. Current efforts center on the recognition of people who have been outstanding advocates for the rights of disabled persons, those who have been abused by their peers, racial justice organizations, and others who have shaped history and should be included in a curriculum that chronicles evolution of society. These practices were implemented initially by the California Fair, Accurate, Inclusive, and Respectful Education Act (FAIR) (2011) that ensures contributions and roles of underrepresented racial, ethnic, and cultural populations are included in school grades 1–12 U.S. and California history lessons, classes, and curricular materials.

Present concerns center on antisemitic behaviors reflected by student at high schools and universities. A nationwide poll commissioned by the U.S. News & World Report

(Camera, 2024) reported that two-thirds of students in higher education regard antisemitism as a problem on their campuses. Gordon Allport (1954/1979) wrote *The Nature of Prejudice*, the seminal reference for this issue in social relationships. Over 50 years later, Dovidio et al. (2005) led 44 collaborators to comment about aspects of Allport's leadership. Learning lessons about acceptance of others remains difficult to learn for all age groups (Fitzgerald et al., 2019).

Students should be taught to recognize that fear can be a valuable emotion if it motivates cautious behavior that protects us from harm. People are wise to be guided by the fear of taking illegal drugs, chatting with online predators, or riding as the passenger of a drunk driver. These kinds of dangers warrant consideration because they have potential to threaten self-preservation. On the other hand, the fear of groups whose behavior is a departure from social norms does not serve a survival purpose, compromise safety, place general welfare at risk, or diminish individual freedom to pursue a lifestyle of personal choosing. Fear of group differences in school can be sustained only by dissemination of information that is used to justify the abuse of selected groups. Three school superintendents in Illinois – Michael Lubelfeld et al. (2018) – collaborated in their book *Student Voice: From Invisible to Invaluable* to illustrate the benefits of student polling as a method to diminish peer abuse in schools.

Consequences of Name Calling

A popular statement that has traditionally been recited by children was "Sticks and stones can break my bones, but names will never hurt me." Scholars have since determined this statement to be false because research has shown that being called disappointing names can hurt with extent of harm depending in part on the age of the victim. Before adolescence, students are unable to access the defense mechanism known as rationalization. Therefore, they are inclined to believe negative comments that others make about them. Parents struggle to convince children that such insults are false and should be dismissed. Consider 8-year-old John who, in tears, tells his mother that Roger has been calling him a 'retard,' John's mother points out, "John, you are in the highest reading group in your class and Roger is in the lowest reading group. This means that for Roger to call you a retard is silly." However, John is not old enough to rationalize, an ability that does not emerge until about 10 years of age. So John remains convinced he must be whatever Roger calls him. Strom et al. (2012) point out there are many sad stories of peer mistreatment like these that implicate the need for educating students to avoid name-calling in favor of treating one another with respect and kindness. Peer mistreatment can have lifelong consequences for self-esteem and undermine the confidence individuals have of their capacity for success (Ali & Chin, 2023; Schwartz et al., 2021).

School Inclusion Practices

In the elementary school, students engage in clique groups with classmates who share some of their interests (Allen & Cowdery, 2022). This practice can be beneficial but also lead to the exclusion of others, most often peers with disabilities. The treatment of students with disabilities has varied throughout history. At times they were considered enemies and disliked, imprisoned, or even killed. Before the 1960s, the most common response was segregation of disabled students from nondisabled students. Since then, there have been improvements in the public recognition that individuals with disabilities are neither helpless nor hopeless, but they require assistance to develop their talents. This perspective is reinforced by federal government policies regarding employment, access to buildings, education opportunities, and the positive psychology movement applied to preparation of professionals. The expectation that disabled students can become productive members of society is shared by teachers, parents, employers, and the disabled. Transforming potential to become achievement is facilitated when regular teachers and special education teachers partner with parents, emotional support is provided by classmates, suitable standards of conduct are applied, and instruction strategies are implemented that enable disabled students to be integrated with nondisabled peers (Allen & Cowdery, 2022).

Stimulus for educational reform was a revelation in the 1970s that more than one million students were being excluded from public schools and denied education services. Mainstreaming refers to providing school for special education students in regular classes, a practice that began after Congress passed the Education for All Handicapped Children Act (1975). The common practice of establishing a timeline for school-related laws was permanently waived. Instead, this reform is intended to govern national education policies permanently. In the past generation, the law has been altered to reflect shifting considerations. The latest revision in 2023, Individuals with Disabilities Education Act (IDEA) (2004, 2023) requires inclusion of special education students from early childhood in all aspects of life at school including extracurricular activities. In addition to school assessments, Zubler et al. (2022) suggested all parents should be kept informed by the school about evidence-based milestones to assure awareness regarding the developmental status of their child.

Types of Student Disabilities

There are numerous categories that describe student disabilities and relate to the services covered by the Individuals with Disabilities Education Act (2023). The number of students enrolled in special education is estimated at 7.5 million and accounts for 15% of all public school students. Most attend inclusion classrooms for much of the day with peers not in special education. Table 14.1 shows the percentage distribution of students with disabilities (ages 3–21) by type for the 2022–2023 school year (National Center on Education Statistics, 2024).

Table 14.1 Children and Youth Types of Disabilities

Disability Type	Percent
Specific learning disability	32
Speech or language impairment	19
Other health impairment	15
Autism	13
Developmental delay	7
Intellectual disability	6
Emotional disturbance	4
Multiple disabilities	2
Hearing impairment	1

Source: National Center for Education Statistics. (2024, May). *Students with disabilities. Condition of education*. U.S. Department of Education, Institute of Education Sciences. https://nces.ed.gov/programs/coe/indicator/cgg

Conditions for public schools that serve the 7.5 million students in special education include the following:

- Free public education for disabled persons between ages 3 and 21.
- Access to education in a regular classroom guaranteed unless a person's handicap is such that services cannot be properly offered there.
- School placement and other education decisions are made only after consultation with a child's parents. Continuation in a program requires a reevaluation once every three years based on testing at no cost to the parents.
- Parents can examine and challenge all school records that bear on identification of their child as disabled and the kind of education environment set for student placement. The expense of this independent educational evaluation is borne by the school (Sobel & Alston, 2021).

Cooperative Learning and Inclusion

Research has identified cooperative learning as an effective way to implement inclusion (Johnson & Johnson, 2022; McLeskey et al., 2017). More than other approaches, this strategy ensures that students with disabilities have opportunities to interact with nondisabled students. Furthermore, meta-analyses have found that cooperative learning favorably impacts classroom management when special education students are present. Teachers report that special education students in cooperative groups have greater self-esteem, feel less frustrated, and learn to listen (Johnson et al., 2014). Encouragement from peers can help to overcome obstacles that might prevent student progress if they were required to work alone.

Teacher observation is the basis for estimating progress of special education students in acquiring teamwork skills during the primary grades. When educators can detect student learning needs, an Individualized Education Plan (IEP) is prepared that includes appropriate intervention involving teachers and parents. Strom et al. (2013) examined the peer assessment of 297 middle-grade students including 39 who were classified as special education students. All the students were administered the Teamwork Skills Inventory after four weeks of working together in cooperative inclusive teams. The peer and self-evaluation ratings of general education students and special education students were compared to assess teamwork skills and deficits in both groups. Results showed special education students assigned themselves higher scores than given from general education teammates on 24 of the 25 items. Both groups rated general education students as showing the most teamwork skills. Considerations for improving teamwork skills were recommended to general education teachers, special education teachers, middle-grade students, and their parents.

Research about grandparents who take care of disabled children is a neglected aspect of empirical studies. More than 80 international resources were reviewed and analyzed, focused on the expectations and activities that might be appropriate for a grandparent–grandchild dyad (Venkatesan, 2024). To illustrate, joint responsibility tasks with children aged 3–5 could include setting the table, emptying wastebaskets, putting the toys away, and sweeping and mopping. Between ages 5 and 7, children could help to make beds, sort and fold clothes, water plants, and care for pets. From ages 7 to 10, grandchildren can join grandparents in making lunches, washing dishes, preparing salads and desserts, loading the washing machine, and vacuuming. Working together can be mutually satisfying and teaches children how to assume their share of responsibility. Grandparents of disabled children were found to encounter unique challenges like emotional stress, isolation, lack of peer support, the demanding nature of caregiving, and concern about the future of their grandchildren with disabilities. Financial burdens for medical expenses, therapies, and provision of special education services were additional areas of consideration.

Peer Pressure Protectors

Teacher Peer Pressure Protectors

One cost of building a strong sense of belonging to any group is social conformity. This has benefit when a group expects someone to demonstrate healthy behavior. When this is not the case, individuals must be capable of withstanding pressure from their peers because caving in to group demands could jeopardize mental and physical health, integrity, safety, and personal goals (Zubler et al., 2022). Teachers and others working with youth can prepare them to cope with peer pressures to adopt dysfunctional behavior as the price for them to avoid group rejection. All children should have access to peer pressure protectors. Teachers can help shape constructive peer norms in the following ways and enable students to withstand negative peer pressure.

- Families rely on educators to take initiatives because school is the place where peers are most often together. Encouraging extracurricular activities and after-school programs is a way to support healthy interaction with others who have similar interests and goals that might not become known in a classroom. The benefit for students can be attained when teachers are willing to be advisors for participants in after-school activities and clubs.
- Teachers can set peer influence on a healthy course by arranging cooperative learning teams where peers provide mutual support to think critically and creatively (Strom et al., 2024).
- By showing acceptance of imagination, teachers can alter peer judgment. For example, John is a creative sixth grader. During the past when John proposed original ideas, his classmates would usually laugh, and the teachers felt it was their role to protect John by insisting the laughter stop. However, this year the teacher listens to John's ideas and, when his peers begin to jeer, she says, "Let's pursue John's idea." She writes the idea on the board and challenges the students to explore beyond their already expressed surface reaction. She points out that we want to consider whether John's idea has value and what implications could be for us. In this way the teacher obligated the class to think about John's idea instead of dismissing it without reflection. During the ensuing conversation students came to the following conclusions: (a) sometimes good ideas are not recognized when first expressed, (b) judging a concept before understanding it is a form of ideational prejudice, and (c) John's ideas are good. These conclusions contributed more to the welfare of John and the class than trying to protect John from classmates who choose to laugh when they do not understand.
- Teachers encourage self-reliance and individuality by rewarding questions in the face of peer pressure to prevent questions, beginning during middle school and junior high. The emerging unwillingness to be seen by peers as curious inhibits growth and suggests a false impression that students can become self-directed without motivation to explore their questions. Instead, if we want students to continue learning after they complete

school, asking questions must become part of the attitude and skill set they develop. Support for questioning does more to improve learning than any other teacher response in school and at home (Levine, 2021; Strom et al., 2019).

- One reason for urging students to ask questions is so they will challenge the thinking of their peer group instead of supposing all norms are sensible, fair, and deserve support.
- Students should have opportunities to discuss the nature of clique groups, how they affect others, and what can be done to prevent inappropriate rejection. If someone is behaving in unacceptable ways toward others, peer rejection is the natural response.
- When teachers help students establish friendships, students become less vulnerable to rejection from cliques. Two can stand apart easier than one. While all students should have opportunities to make friends at school, some classes appear more conducive to friendships. These relationships are more apt to flourish if teachers make assignments where students work together as pairs or in threes instead of alone or in large groups.
- Most students are achievement-oriented and adopt actions leading to recognition. Extra credit is sometimes given for competition. Caring about other people is observable and could be seen by students as a form of accomplishment that deserves consideration in status and leadership (e.g., tutoring, volunteering in a hospital or nursing home, peer counseling). Similarly, when teachers see how newcomers are treated without directing students to welcome them, recognition can be given to those whose initiative enabled newcomers to feel they belong.
- Teachers can counter peer dependence by making themselves available for conversation outside class. This allows students somewhere else to turn with their problems rather than to one another. To fulfill this role, teachers must be seen as approachable and trustworthy. Students believe some teachers are too difficult to talk to, leaving them without a potentially valuable source of adult assistance.

Parent Peer Pressure Protectors

Parents should also be involved in providing peer pressure protectors for daughters and sons.

- The best way to minimize peer pressures at home is to encourage individuality. Parents do this by avoiding comparisons of achievement or limitations among their children. When one child is used as a standard of behavior for a sibling, the result can be sustained rivalry and jealousy instead of lifelong reciprocal support and pride (Ladd & Parke, 2021).
- Encourage children to value solitude as a time to reflect, self-evaluate, and look at things anew. Solitude allows the individuality and creativity students need so that being around age mates for long periods of time does not lead to excessive dependence.
- Parents need to make themselves available to listen, especially about the difficulties of maintaining friendships. This task requires high priority, takes time, and is inconvenient. Do it anyway. From grade 5, around age 10, problems involving classmates and friends are likely to become continuous and, depending on how parents respond, they may be asked for advice often or not at all. Help children learn how to get along without threatening their withdrawal to force concession by others. Share your mistakes – this requires self-disclosure (Levine, 2021).
- Allow privacy. Let students confide in you when they will, without insisting that you be told everything happening in their lives. Trust is essential for being able to build

intimate relationships, and parents play the most prominent role in helping adolescents acquire this attribute.
- Recognize that the status of a daughter or son no longer depends exclusively on the pecking order at school. For example, students with low social status can satisfy their need for acceptance and belonging as well as enjoy interaction after school when they go online to communicate with cyber friends. The opportunity to build friendships in a broader context has expanded with the Internet, and there may be more conversation with cyber friends online than face-to-face communication at school. Parents should encourage cyber friendships with peers who live in other communities.

The Power of Peer Influence

Judith Rich Harris was a good student. After earning her degree from Brandeis University, she entered the doctoral program in psychology at Harvard University. A year later, in 1960, she was dismissed with the explanation that the "originality and independence of her work were not up to Harvard standards." Then Judith joined a publishing company to become an editor responsible for developmental psychology manuscripts. The materials she read seemed to reflect common beliefs more than scientific evidence, a retention of views that celebrated the unmatched power of family influence.

In 1994, Judith developed a new theory of child development that challenged the traditional belief that parents are the greatest influence on socialization and personality of children. Harris (1998/2009) provided evidence for her assertion that peers had the greatest prominence. In her book *The Nurture Assumption: Why Children Turn Out the Way They Do*, she presented the view that peers who usually spend most of their time together have become far more influential than in the past. In the preface Harris wrote, "This book has two purposes: first, to dissuade you of the notion that a child's personality-what used to be called 'character'-is shaped or modified by the child's parents; and second, to give you an alternative view of how the child's personality is shaped." The assertions about the power of peers were difficult for many people to accept. Harris provided results from investigations that corroborated her hypothesis and compared empirical studies of parents and peers as sources of nurture. Harris's recommendation was that parents should carefully monitor their child's choice of friends.

The initial reaction of specialists in child development was to ignore the evidence and attack Harris as trying to undermine authority of parents and the education they give to children. However, in 1995, Harris's theory received the American Psychological Association George Miller Award for the outstanding contribution to developmental psychology. Ironically, George Miller was Chair of Psychology at Harvard University 35 years earlier when Harris was dismissed from the doctoral program. Harris's book is regarded as a research classic. Developmental psychologists are generally agreed that by the time children reach middle school, peer influence becomes the most powerful influence on student socialization (Harris, 2009).

Principles for Adult Application

1. Inclusion is the federal government policy of ensuring students in special education are not considered helpless or hopeless but as needing assistance to develop their talents. One

aspect of this policy is to participate with non-special education peers throughout the day in regular classrooms as well as during extracurricular opportunities after school hours.
2. Encouraging involvement in extracurricular activities supports healthy interaction with peers who have similar interests and goals that might not become known during a class. The benefits for students are enriched when older adults volunteer to serve as advisors for after-school clubs and other types of activities where their talents can be a resource.
3. Parents can minimize peer pressure by encouraging individuality. This can be done by avoiding comparisons of achievement or shortcomings of siblings. When one child is used as a standard of behavior to judge a sibling, an unintended result can be sustained rivalry and jealousy instead of lifelong reciprocal support and mutual pride.
4. The status of a daughter or son no longer depends exclusively on the pecking order at school. This means students with low social status in the classroom can satisfy their need for acceptance and belonging and enjoy conversation by going online to talk with cyber friends. The Internet has expanded the context for building friendships.

Conclusion

Peers have a powerful influence on the social development of one another. They provide the first substantial experience with equality and present standards that are more attainable than ones generally imposed by grownups. Children consider peer group norms to be the appropriate criteria to apply for self-evaluation. They find out about friendships mostly from peers who also encourage the acquisition of cooperation, empathy, compromise, and pursuit of independence. These lessons are more often gained from classmates than from adults. Boys and girls discover what friends will tolerate and identify the conduct they will not accept. Most middle school students join a clique that allows them to feel that they are accepted and belong. However, some students experience racial, religious, or ethnic discrimination. Prejudice is a more common attitude and behavior during middle school than high school, and people targeted suffer more than commonly supposed. The way others feel about us motivates how we are treated and, therefore, impacts the way we see ourselves. Teachers should give assignments that help middle school students view themselves favorably without finding fault with peers.

Key Concepts

1. Peers provide the first experience with equality. Everyone wants companionship and enjoys attention others give them. The peer group is in the best position to satisfy these needs. When members behave in an approved way according to the social norm, their group rewards them with attention, acceptance, and emotional support.
2. The peer group presents a separate set of standards for behavior than what is expected by the adults. Peer standards are more attainable and provide justification for opposition to directives from adults. Classmates are willing to listen to their common dilemmas and encourage one another to express differences in the presence of grownups.
3. Children use members of their age group as the most reasonable basis for self-comparison, chances to express themselves without fear of punishment, and opportunities to share leadership. They motivate one another to strive for independence and provide a needed sense of belonging to another important group besides the family and the school.

4. Peers learn friendship mainly from classmates and how to get along with people of the same status. Becoming part of a group requires exhibiting skills that are expected by peers such as cooperation, sharing feelings, striving for independence, and reconciling following arguments. Such lessons are more easily learned from peers than from parents.
5. Students below the age of 10 show less social rejection of peers. Activities for young children are noncompetitive, so self-concepts are not threatened by strengths of others. Better performers in the early grades rarely announce superiority, and those below average do not report feelings of inferiority since performance norms have yet to be established.
6. From the middle grades onwards, students can no longer depend on what their parents have accomplished as the basis for self-pride. They must earn their own social standing. In classes they face more competition and failure along with unfriendly remarks of others. Peers detect limitations, and some of them express their negative views as insults or hurtful statements.
7. Group members feel less anxious when they behave in the same way as others without quite knowing why. This inclination to adopt the values and attitudes of peers without understanding the reasons can sometimes promote the acceptance of behavior that students would otherwise recognize as being wrong and inappropriate.
8. Negative social prejudice expressed by personal rejection is likely to decline as the level of education rises. However, evidence shows that the consequences of children being rejected can last for a lifetime. Individuals who are a target of racial, religious, ethnic, or other prejudice must divert energy from healthy personal development to self-protection.
9. Fear is valuable when it motivates caution to protect us from harm. However, fear of groups whose behavior departs from norms does not threaten safety, place, or undermine freedom to pursue a lifestyle of our choosing. Fear of differences can be sustained only by misinformation used as a basis to justify the abuse of selected groups.
10. Before adolescence students lack access to rationalization, a powerful mechanism of defense. This means younger students are inclined to believe negative comments others say about them. Mistreatment can have lifelong effects for negative self-impression as well as undermine the confidence individuals have about their capacity for success.
11. Inclusion is the policy of ensuring students in special education are seen as requiring help to developing their talents. One aspect of this policy is for them to participate with non-special education peers in regular classes and extracurricular activities after school.

Generational Perspectives Activities

14.1 Discussion
14.2 Conversations With Young Children
14.3 A Scenario: Reasoning and Problem-Solving
14.4 Chapter Review
14.5 Parent and Grandparent Self-Evaluation
14.6 Storytelling

14.1 Discussion

1. How is peer pressure different now from when you were growing up?
2. What do you recall about why some kids were excluded from peer groups?
3. How do prejudices taught to you compare with those taught to grandchildren?
4. How were disabled children treated by students when you were in school?
5. How was your relationship with parents different than for your grandchildren?
6. What have grandchildren told you about special education students at their school?
7. Compare peer dependence of grandchildren with your dependence at their age.
8. What did you and your friends like to do together after the school day was over?
9. What events can you recall where you felt that the peer group mistreated you?
10. What are some norms you would like established for children at school?

14.2 Conversations With Young Children

1. What have teachers told you about why there is school inclusion?
2. How do classmates pressure you about the way to behave at school?
3. What behaviors have you adopted from classmates at your school?
4. Which of your friends in class are involved with special education?
5. How much of a problem is name-calling by students at your school?

14.3 A Scenario: Reasoning and Problem-Solving

Leslie is telling a neighbor about James, her third-grade son. Last year, his inclusion class had one special education student, but this year there are four of them. Leslie worries the teacher will have to spend more time helping disabled classmates. What do you recommend?

a. Remove James from the public school and enroll him in a private school.
b. Talk with teachers to find out how they think the situation will affect James.
c. Arrange for a private tutor to help James with any academic deficiencies.
d. Visit the school principal to find out how she sees this academic situation.
e. Other _____

14.4 Chapter Review

1. What insights from the chapter will I try to apply in my relationships?
2. What is the most important key concept for me presented in this chapter?
3. Which elements of this chapter do I wish I had known about earlier?

14.5 Parent and Grandparent Self-Evaluation

1. My feelings about school inclusion practices

   a. I feel it is a fair way to help both groups of students
   b. my school never oriented me to understand inclusion
   c. I would like to know how students see this concern
   d. the school should offer evidence that it is successful
   e. Other _____

2. In my view, the teaching students get from their peers

   a. adds to the benefit they receive from adult teachers
   b. is greater in the social context than adult teachers
   c. helps them to adopt healthy group social norms
   d. can enable them to acquire a needed sense of empathy
   e. Other _____

3. What do you want to better understand about school inclusion?

   a. the reasoning for implementing this national policy
   b. how schools orient parents of nondisabled students?
   c. how progress of special education students is evaluated?
   d. Can students ever get out of a special education program?
   e. Other _____

4. As a student, how did you react when some kids were called names?

   a. I went to report this kind of harassment to the teacher
   b. I didn't like it but did nothing to stop the name-callers
   c. I told my parents and hoped they would tell the school
   d. I tried to comfort the individual being called names
   e. Other _____

5. I have observed harassment and bullying at my workplace

   a. especially targeting the women
   b. by those with higher positions
   c. and we can report it to our supervisor
   d. was not much of a problem for us
   e. Other _____

6. I did not have special education friends

   a. were a source of satisfaction for me
   b. I did not have special education friends
   c. were discouraged by my other friends
   d. were never a topic of discussion with my parents
   e. Other _____

7. Narcissism is so common among primary students

   a. I would like cooperative learning to be introduced earlier
   b. parent workshops should focus on children getting along
   c. grandparents should be a source of caring about others
   d. their social development appears to be slighted at school
   e. Other _____

8. When it comes to dominion play among children,

   a. I find it difficult to generate good options
   b. I would welcome training in this context
   c. the options that I provide seem pretty good
   d. my performance is poor
   e. Other _____

14.6 Storytelling

Historically, storytelling has been a dominant classic and progressive method of teaching around the world. The purposes of a storyteller are to present imaginary or real-life examples showing how some concept applies to a particular situation. People like stories, they pay attention to the procession of events, and usually remember aspects of a story for a long time. Your stories can reinforce the concepts in this chapter for family members and classmates. Please share your stories with them.

References

Ali, S., & Chin, M. (2023). *The peer effect: How your peers shape who you are and who you will become.* New York University Press.

Allen, E. K., & Cowdery, G. E. (2022). *The exceptional child: Inclusion in early childhood education* (9th ed.). Cengage Learning.

Allport, G. (1979). *The nature of prejudice.* Basic Books. (Original work published 1954)

Baumeister, R., & Bushman, B. (2021). *Social psychology and human nature* (5th ed.). Cengage Learning.

Bukowski, W., Laursen, B., & Rubin, K. (Eds.). (2019). *Handbook of peer interactions, relationships, and groups* (2nd ed.). Guilford Press.

California Fair, Accurate, Inclusive, and Respectful Education Act (FAIR). (2011). *FAIR Education Act.* Wikipedia. https://en.wikipedia.org/wiki/FAIR_Education_Act

Camera, L. (2024, May 13). Students at top universities call antisemitism a problem, poll finds. *U. S. News & World Report.* https://www.usnews.com/news/national-news/articles/2024-05-13/poll-students-at-top-universities-call-antisemitism-a-problem

DeAngelis, T. (2023, January 13). *How to help kids navigate friendships and peer relationships.* American Psychological Association. https://www.apa.org/topics/parenting/navigating-friendships

Dovidio, J. F., Glick, P., & Rudman, L. A. (Eds.). (2005). *On the nature of prejudice: Fifty years after Allport.* Blackwell.

Education for All Handicapped Children Act. (1975). Pub. L. No. 94-142, 89 Stat. 773. https://www.govinfo.gov/content/pkg/STATUTE-89/pdf/STATUTE-89-Pg773.pdf

Fitzgerald, H., Johnson, D., Qin, D., Villarruel, F., & Norder, J. (Eds.). (2019). *Handbook of children and prejudice: Integrating research, practice, and policy.* Springer.

Harris, J. (2009). *The nurture assumption: Why children turn out the way they do* (2nd ed.). Free Press. (Original work published 1998)

Individuals with Disabilities Education Act. (2023, November 29). *Two updated documents emphasize need for early childhood inclusion, transition for children with disabilities.* https://sites.ed.gov/idea/early-childhood-inclusion-transition-for-children-with-disabilities/

Individuals with Disabilities Education Act. (2004). Pub. L. No. 108-446, 118 Stat. 2647. (2004). https://www.govinfo.gov/content/pkg/PLAW-108publ446/pdf/PLAW-108publ446.pdf

Johnson, D. W., & Johnson, R. T. (2022). Learning together and alone: The history of our involvement in cooperative learning. In N. Davidson (Ed.), *Pioneering perspectives in cooperative learning: Theory, research, and classroom practice for diverse approaches to cooperative learning* (pp. 44–62). Routledge.

Johnson, D. W., Johnson, R. T., Roseth, C., & Shin, T. (2014). The relationship between motivation and achievement in interdependent situations. *Journal of Applied Social Psychology, 44*(9), 622–633. https://doi.org/10.1111/jasp.12280

Ladd, G. W., & Parke, R. D. (2021). Themes and theories revisited: Perspectives on processes in family-peer relationships. *Children, 8*(6), 507. https://doi.org/10.3390/children8060507

Levine, M. (2021). *Ready or not: Preparing our kids to thrive in an uncertain and rapidly changing world.* HarperCollins.

Lubelfeld, M., Polyak, N., & Caposey, P. J. (2018). *Student voice: From invisible to invaluable.* Rowman & Littlefield.

McLeskey, J. L., Rosenberg, M., & Westling, D. (2017). *Inclusion: Effective practices for all students* (3rd ed.). Pearson.

National Center for Education Statistics. (2024). *Students with disabilities. Condition of education.* U.S. Department of Education, Institute of Education Sciences. https://nces.ed.gov/programs/coe/indicator/cgg

Schwartz, D., Ryjova, Y., Kelleghan, A., & Fritz, H. (2021, May–June). The refugee crisis and peer relationships during childhood and adolescence. *Journal of Applied Developmental Psychology, 74.* https://doi.org/10.1016/j.appdev.2021.101263

Sobel, D., & Alston, S. (2021). *The inclusive classroom: A new approach to differentiation.* Bloomsbury Education.

Strom, P. S., Strom, R. D., Wingate, J., Kraska, M., & Beckert, T. (2012). Cyberbully: Assessment of student experience for continuous improvement planning. *National Association of Secondary School Administrators Bulletin, 96*(2), 137–153. https://doi.org/10.1177/0192636512443281

Strom, P. S., Thompson, M., & Strom, R. (2013). Teamwork evaluation by middle grade students in inclusion classrooms. *Middle Grades Research Journal, 8*(3), 83–97. https://eric.ed.gov/?id=EJ1146281

Strom, P. S., Hendon, K. L., Strom, R. D., & Wang, C.-H. (2019). How peers support and inhibit learning in the classroom: Assessment of high school students in collaborative groups. *School Community Journal, 29*(2), 183–202. http://www.schoolcommunitynetwork.org/SCJ.aspx

Strom, P. S., Strom, R. D., & Wang, C.-H. (2024). Peer and self-assessment of teamwork skills in high school: Using a multi-rater evaluation method for cooperative learning groups. *International Journal of Educational Reform, 33*(1), 81–100. https://doi.org/10.1177/10567879221082969

Venkatesan, S. (2024). Grandparenting children with disabilities: An introductory review with focus on theories and measurements. *World Journal of Advanced Research and Reviews, 21*(3), 1997–2008. https://doi.org/10.30574/wjarr.2024.21.3.0968

White, S., & Berns, R. (2022). *Child, family, school, community: Socialization and support* (11th ed.). Cengage.

Zubler, J., Wiggins, L., Macias, M., Whitaker, T., Shaw, J., Squires, J., Pajek, J., Wolf, R., Slaughter, K., Broughton, A., Gerndt, K., Mlodoch, B., & Lipkin, P. (2022, March). Evidence-informed milestones for developmental surveillance tools. *Pediatrics, 149*(3), e2021052138. https://doi.org/10.1542/peds.2021-052138

Chapter 15

Fears of Parents and Children

Fears and worries are more prevalent in early childhood. The reason is because boys and girls have active imaginations and are less able to distinguish the truth from fiction. Growing up in the current environment includes additional worries because media sources cause children to become aware of potential dangers and present parents with reminders that it is their responsibility to prevent risky situations. These factors encourage parents to reflect about teaching children how to react to fears and worries in a manner that can help them sustain mental health. The purposes of this chapter are to (a) describe how children can learn to evaluate possible danger, (b) explain the balance of caution and trust children should rely on, (c) establish family rules that children should always apply as a method to prevent them from taking unreasonable risks, (d) consider ways to help children realize fear is a universal experience throughout life, (e) encourage continuous sharing of fears and worries in the family, (f) identify prominent worries of students as they progress in elementary school, and (g) acknowledge parental fears about the well-being of their children. Generational Perspectives Activities present topics to discuss with family members and close friends about the fears of parents and children.

Parents and Child Safety Concerns

Risk Assessment and Help Sources

Parents and grandparents whose own fears lead them to suppose most people cannot be trusted are unable to teach children that there is a need to trust others. It is essential that children have an overall impression their environment is a safe and friendly place instead of a place populated by unfriendly and dangerous people. Nevertheless, motivated by personal anxieties and worries, some parents decide to discourage children from talking to any adult they do not know. This decision creates a reciprocal dilemma because if children are directed not to speak to strangers, then strangers should not talk to children even when they might be a valuable source of help (Kearney, 2023).

The accuracy of this perception is confirmed by surveys of kindergarten through third-grade students. When children of these ages are asked to describe their greatest fears, strangers are the source that is mentioned most often. Children acknowledge their parents have taught them this fear. But how accurate is this common lesson taught about strangers? The National Center for Missing and Exploited Children (2024a) identifies each reported case of a missing child to be an abduction by an unknown individual, kidnapping by a noncustodial parent, or a runaway who chooses to be somewhere else than home.

However, the belief that missing children are a homogenous group has caused unnecessary confusion and unwarranted fears. Consequently, when parents lack information, they tend to suppose that strangers are the common cause of missing children.

But is this conclusion accurate? Every day 2,300 children under age 18 in the United States are declared missing, a total of 460,000 a year. The single largest subgroup is composed of juveniles who decide to run away from home. Of the children kidnapped, about 99% are abducted by their father who does not have custody. Less than 1% of the children kidnapped are abducted by strangers. Michelle DeLaune, Director of the National Center for Missing and Exploited Children, explained that an unwarranted public fear about strangers has become firmly established over the past few years. She pointed out, "We have found that generally children do not have the same level of understanding about strangers as adults. Therefore, this is a difficult concept for youngsters to grasp." The 'stranger danger' message has been ineffective. Based on what is known about individuals who harm children, the danger to children is far greater from someone they or their family knows than from a stranger (DeLaune, 2024). Greater benefit for children is to build needed confidence and self-esteem to be as safe as possible in a potentially dangerous situation instead of teaching them to look out for a particular kind of person (Kearney, 2023).

Awareness of Sex Offenders

Parents are upset when they are informed by local government officials that a registered child molester has been allowed by the court to move into their neighborhood. An example of the types of information regarding local sex offenders can be found online by state; for example, see the websites for the Alabama Law Enforcement Agency (2024) and Probation Information Network (2022). Parents are similarly bothered by reports about children being exploited by pedophiles on the Internet. Sometimes it can seem as though there is no end to the dangers implicating children. Parents should go on the Internet to their state Law Enforcement Agency and provide their zip code to find out if there are sex offenders living nearby, nature of their criminal conviction, distance from your house and their address, and details about the individuals with photos so you will be able to recognize them on sight. The government practice is to send a flyer to all residents who live within 2,000 feet of a sex offender moving into a neighborhood. The sex offenders are not allowed to live near school zones or day care centers.

The mission of the National Center for Missing and Exploited Children (2024b) is to help find missing children, reduce child sexual exploitation, and prevent child victimization. They work with families, victims, private industry, law enforcement, and the public to assist with preventing child abductions, recovering missing children, and providing services to deter and combat child sexual exploitation (Office of Public Affairs, U. S. Department of Justice, 2024).

In response to what parents see as an unfriendly environment, some conclude that it is necessary to discourage children from having contact with anyone who is a stranger. These protective practices reinforce the need for parents and grandparents to reflect about whether their methods are protecting children or scaring them. How can adults place concerns into perspective so that safety instead of fear dominates their behavior? The growth of awareness about the potential for child harm is bound to become a source of worry for families. Still, parents need to carefully examine personal fears in relation to evidence before it is possible to help their frightened children confront situations that might be unsafe for them.

The goals should always be to achieve a balance for concerns about safety, fear, and trust. This is a crucial balance because how parents manage their own fears determines how they will prepare children to live in a world where unsafe situations often exist. One way to start is by teaching children how to assess risk, an ability that governs the extent of fear for people of any age (Strom & Strom, 2021). In the Dunedin, New Zealand, longitudinal study by Guiney et al. (2024), 937 individuals were followed from birth to age 45. This study examined the association between child sexual abuse (as retrospectively reported at age 26) and risk for adverse mental health outcomes across adulthood. Those who were child sexually abused survivors were more likely than their peers to experience thought disorders, suicide attempts, health risk behaviors, systematic inflammation, poor oral health, sexually transmitted diseases, high-conflict relationships, financial difficulties, antisocial behavior, and cumulative problems across multiple domains in adulthood. The higher risk for most specific problems was small to moderate, but the cumulative long-term effects across multiple domains reflected considerable individual and societal burdens.

Critical Thinking About Crime

The national rate of serious crime has been declining for five years. In contrast, the media coverage of crime stories has increased during the same time (Gramlich, 2024). Some families decide they will avoid watching the local news because so much content relates to scary events while so little news focuses on stories of good things happening in a community. The American Academy of Child and Adolescent Psychiatry (2023) provides parents with guidelines for how to talk to children about terrorism, crime, war, and violence. The fact that negative reports get more attention on television, the Internet, and in the newspapers is a poor reason to ignore objective evidence. Because most cases of kidnapping, child abuse, and missing children implicate family members, the rational conclusion is for communities to devote greater support and effort to improving healthy family life (DeLaune, 2024; Kearney, 2023).

Parent Separation and Child Custody

About 700,000 divorces and annulments take place across the United States annually while approximately two million marriages are recorded. Thus, far more people get married every year than get divorced. Long-standing assertions that half of all marriages will end in divorce are exaggerations. When it comes to first marriages, about 43% are dissolved. The second and third marriages fail at a higher rate with 60% of second marriages and 73% of third marriage ending in divorce. Childless couples (66%) are more likely to get a divorce while 40% of divorces involve couples who have children together (Bieber, 2024).

Separated and divorced parents with child custody should avoid conversations with their children about strangers being a major threat. The courts assign custody to mothers in over 90% of cases, so the most likely individual to kidnap children is their noncustodial fathers (Kearney, 2023). This means mothers should evaluate their situation before deciding what should be said to daughters and sons about missing children. It might not be in a child's best interest to be told that parents without custody are the most probable kidnappers.

If a mother decides she is not in a high-risk group since there has been no custody battle and no threats have been made by their former spouse, then the parent should assess and decide if conversations with children about mistreatment by others should focus on possible dangerous situations and constructive ways of responding to them. On the other hand, if an ex-spouse appears to be a potential problem, certified copies of court-ordered child custody document should be placed in the child's file in the school office. And, if a noncustodial parent threatens to take the child, the principal and teachers should be alerted so that they do not allow any child to leave the school premises with an unauthorized adult (Bieber, 2024).

Parents from single and intact families should stop warning children about all strangers. The fact is strangers are not the common cause of danger. In many cases involving crimes against children, the child knows the perpetrator. This person could be a relative, older friend, brother of a playmate, or a man in the neighborhood. Children can be taught to run away from strangers, but teaching them to say "No," or "I want to go home," as a way to avoid adults they are familiar with, and their parents have trusted, is a more different challenge.

School Shootings and Bully Behavior

Gun violence in the United States is a public health crisis and the leading cause of death among students under 19 years of age. The United States records 57 times as many shootings at schools as all other major industrialized nations combined. The purpose of a national study led by Rapa et al. (2024) was to determine the frequency of school-related violence across a quarter century (1998–2022). During this time there were 1,453 school shootings. The most recent five years have reflected a substantially higher number of shootings than any of the prior 20 years.

Peter Langman (2009, 2017, 2021) is a psychologist and researcher with the National Threat Assessment Center of the U.S. Secret Service who serves as a consultant regarding cases of school shootings across the globe. Langman's book *Warning Signs: Identifying School Shooters Before They Strike* presents practical, research-based guidance on anticipating and preventing mass attacks and is intended for use by the school community (administrators, educators, and students from elementary school to college age), mental health professionals, law enforcement officers, and parents. Many parents fear the possibility that a mentally unstable person will go to their child's school and harm students. Awareness of our inability to assure complete protection of students has motivated policies that increase the number of armed guards at schools, always have local police on the premises, and allow selected faculty to carry a concealed weapon so they could respond to anyone threatening student security.

Ridicule as Bullying

When someone makes fun of classmates by teasing them, teasers often explain that their motivation was just for fun, not to cause the feelings of other individuals to be hurt. Generally, students who bully one another in this manner trivialize their actions and do not understand the consequences for victims of teasing. Schools and parents should unite their efforts to establish norms of decency for how students treat one another and consider this to be an essential focus of social development (Kraizer, 2005a, 2005b). To illustrate, government reports on the relationship of teasing and school violence have been overlooked by most of the public. Name-calling and ridiculing are rarely referred to as bullying even though such behavior undermines the mental health of victims (Langman, 2009, 2021).

When some victims finally respond to mistreatment by using violence, motivations they describe usually implicates teasing more than physical bullying. Reports from adolescent murderers who could no longer put up with being called nasty names have commonly identified ridicule as the main reason for taking desperate actions.

Most bullying takes place at school. In an investigation by Kloo et al. (2024), survey data of 1,830 elementary school students in Sweden showed that teachers who revealed high levels of warmth, caring, and supportiveness together with strong teaching levels of structure, control, and demandingness were more likely to have students who reported less bullying victimization. This data also demonstrated that the association between authoritative teaching in the classroom and bullying victimization remained statistically significant, although there was a slight decrease over the course of the two-year study. The study showed that the influence from the school reinforces the prospect that good teachers are able to reduce the mistreatment of children.

Child Sense of Hope

Many school districts and civic organizations, such as Kiwanis (2024), have established anti-bully programs with parents, teachers, students, and administrators as participants across the nation. One promising example meant to deal with the emotional cost of teasing and bullying has been established by Florida Department of Education. This option known as the Hope Scholarship gives students who claim harassment of any kind to have an opportunity to transfer to another public school or an eligible private school to obtain a free scholarship. School districts throughout Florida are responsible to notify families about the Hope Scholarship program financed by the state sales taxes for motor vehicles. All schools reporting student requests for Hope Scholarships are monitored for faculty behavior by the Florida Department of Education (2024).

People who exploit children typically use methods that would be ineffective with adults. They use intimidation, most effective with children who have not been taught to ever challenge adult authority. Elementary students trusted by parents to use their judgment when a situation seems to present danger are less likely to do as they are told by a coercive adult. Inner strength is needed to countermand directives children believe could jeopardize their own safety. When children in the primary grades acquire confidence, learn family rules about asking for help, and feel that it is the right thing to do, they can become more resilient and prepared to evaluate danger, manage scary situations, and still regard their world as a safe place (Goldstein & Brooks, 2023; Marino, 2024).

Responses to Child Fears

Denial and Belittling Fears

Some children face denial from parents that their fearful experiences are unique. Each of us has heard someone tell us, "I know just how you feel." The fact is none of us know how another person feels. But this common limitation of empathy, ability to participate in another person's experience, becomes less disturbing when we recognize this confirms our assumptions about individuality. For parents and grandparents, it means the fears and worries of children should be respected whether we have had a history of similar experiences or not (Krznaric, 2014). YouTube (2024) illustrates some of the first fears shown by babies as they experience seeing their shadow, looking in a mirror, tasting a lemon, viewing fireworks, going through a car wash, and drinking from a hose. Parents often react with laughter to child's expression of fears.

Besides denial and empathy, ridicule is a familiar response to fear. However, laughing at another person's fears does not decrease their fear. Instead, the effect is to lower the individual's confidence. Statements such as, "There is nothing to be afraid of in the dark," or "It's just a dream and not real," might be well-intended, but they still inspire shame for having fears grownups declare as unwarranted. To laugh at someone's fears or call them a wimp, a sissy, or a chicken, undermines the relationship. Children and adults whose feelings are ridiculed soon stop sharing their experiences. The tragedy for parents is this reduces the chance to know their children well and teach them about how to manage fears and worries.

Overcoming Fears

The first step in overcoming fear is to acknowledge it. Because young children identify closely with parents, a sound way to reduce harmful consequences of fears is for parents to admit their own fears and worries. A child who is afraid of the dark, being alone, or starting school should be assured that fear is a natural reaction, and telling someone about fears does not make someone a coward. Courage is not the absence of fear but the mastery of fear. When people lose touch with the possibilities of danger, they lose a healthy sense of caution that serves to protect them (Jackson, 2023; Levine, 2012, 2021).

A certain degree of fear is essential for an individual to exercise good judgment. Plato, the Greek philosopher, observed that "Courage is knowing what to fear." Although parents may insist there is no danger in the dark, a child observes that mom does not go out alone at night, and doors to the house are double locked when the family goes to bed. Children should not be made to feel ashamed of expressing their feelings of fear. After all, adults are afraid of getting old, being alone, getting fat, losing employment, developing cancer, falling, becoming a burden, not having money for retirement, and social rejection. However, adults have some idea about what fear is, whereas children worry long before they can comprehend the concept of fear (Chansky, 2014).

A child whose fears are unshared carries the additional burden of loneliness. No other aspect of experience is more deserving of compassionate attention than someone's fears. Also, no aspect is more baffling to a child or those wanting to provide help (Hertz, 2021). Certainly, children should have someone they can go to who will listen to their worries without judging them. They can have this experience when their parents accept them unconditionally. No child should have to repress fear or pretend bravery to gain the esteem of loved ones. When worries family members have in common and those unique to each person are identified, they are more able to help one another.

Formation of Family Safety Rules

Sherryll Kraizer is Executive Director of the Coalition for Children, founded in 1983. This coalition focuses on the prevention of child abuse and interpersonal violence and is committed to developing and providing positive programs for schools and families. As part of the Take a Stand Program, she has written two useful practical handbooks, specifically, one for families and the other for schools (freely accessible online) to help children be better communicators and ask for help when they need it (Kraizer, 2005a, 2005b). She reported that the characteristics of children who are more likely to be victimized by bullying are often picked on, tend to have low self-esteem, insecure, lack social skills, often called names and excluded, cry easily, cannot defend themselves, appear different from mental and physical norms, and do not have support from family or friends. All forms of bullying are abusive and provide opportunities for families and schools to teach children how to get along, be considerate, and become part of a community or group.

Parents should establish family safety rules to protect children from known and unknown dangers. Boys and girls should be told that their family rules must always be followed. "Never go anywhere without telling your mom, Dad, Grandma or the babysitter" is a good rule because this can prevent situations parents would not condone. Encouraging children to trust their intuition and gut feelings about situations is also important because parents will not always be around when there is a need for assessment of danger. Children should know that "Any person who tries to get you to break a family rule is a bad person. That person should get in trouble so tell your parents, Grandma, your teacher, the principal – right away when someone is bad." This rule defines bad people in terms of behavior instead of their appearance. Children should apply the bad person rule to people they do not know as well as familiar faces without emphasizing danger from either source.

The Department of Homeland Security recommends families discuss safety and become aware of ways they can reduce danger (Marino, 2024). Children should know our government tries to protect us by issuing media warnings such as amber alerts, screens travelers at airports to ensure flying security, and armed marshals are assigned to some airplanes. Parents should let children know how to contact some designated individual if family members get separated. Boys and girls should know a phone number to reach a close friend or relative and understand where to go if they ever find themselves alone, how to dial 9-1-1 if anything seems wrong, how to answer a phone without letting callers know they are alone, and what to do to report a dangerous situation such as a fire. A young child should be taught how to tell a policeman their name, full names of their parents, home address, phone number, where parent(s) work, and what to do if they believe someone is bothering them. When a child can answer correctly such questions in the presence of relatives and friends, the adults can make it known that they are pleased with how the children are able to demonstrate what they have learned about safety. These simple but important lessons are not learned quickly, so patience and practice are essential.

Opportunities to Be an Example

We were just finishing breakfast at Denny's, seated in a booth nearby the cashier. There were six soldiers dressed in national guard uniforms preparing to pay their bill. Then, a woman from the booth next to ours stepped forward to thank each of the men and women for their service to the country and shook their hands. Her young son, perhaps 4 years old, stood behind his mother and observed her behavior. A couple minutes later the waiter provided our bill, so we got up to pay, waiting behind a single soldier at the cashier. Suddenly, the little boy we saw earlier emerged from the booth where his mom remained seated. He approached the soldiers and said, "Thank you for your service," and extended his arm for a handshake. The soldier said, "Thank you. Are you eating here today?" "Yes," said the boy. "What will you have for breakfast?" The boy said, "Chocolate pancakes" and ran back to his mother. He then said, "I told you; I'm not afraid anymore." The example of his mother was an important lesson. Don't become so fearful and cautious that you overlook opportunities to meet strangers who could become friends.

Fears of School-Age Children

The Beginnings of "Don't Worry"

The advice that children give friends is "Don't worry." Excessive worry can block critical thinking and preoccupies people so they cannot pay attention to the demands of daily affairs. On the other hand, worry can have a positive side. Worries act as a rehearsal for danger by causing us to concentrate on specific problems that we might otherwise ignore and motivates us to seek solutions in advance. Some people appear more able to benefit from focused attention that worries present because they can switch the process off and turn away from worries when it is time to attend to other obligations. Those who are unable to snap out of it and remain fixed on their worries do so at considerable cost to their performance at school, home, and work (Carbonnell & Winston, 2016).

Young children (ages 3–6) are often introduced to worrisome messages about their safety. However, even though some degree of worry is normal, being anxious and feeling depressed can increase with perceived number of worries. Studies to improve understanding of how worry impacts mental and physical health have focused mainly on the experience of adults and their relationships at work and in the home (Kellerman & Seligman, 2023). This narrow scope of inquiry is being enlarged because adult patients suffering from excessive worry usually associate the origin of their disorder with events that occurred when they attended elementary school (Bortfeld & Bunge, 2024; Strom & Strom, 2021).

When adults respond quickly and consistently to bullying behavior, they send the message that it is unacceptable behavior. Schools can best help students by talking about bullying in the classroom, providing a safe academic environment as well as extracurricular activities, and developing a citywide bullying prevention program (Stopbullying.gov, 2024).

New Considerations for Families

Parents should be aware of some common student fears that are upcoming as their child grows older and spends more time at school. Parents and children should regularly discuss the fears and worries they have for one another and amend them if it seems necessary. Teaching personality goals should always be a priority for helping children find their way in an uncertain world. To share dreams of the future, a good book for parents and children to read together is *The Wonderful Things You Will Be* (for ages 3–7), by Emily Winfield Martin (2015).

1. A big worry for parents and children in elementary school is coping with uncertainty about performance in the classroom, especially doing well on required tests and preparing for a career. Parents should be pleased that students assign high priority to their studies, and most students want their parents to be proud of them. However, many children report that parents expect them to do better than classmates on tests and grades, even when they lack superior abilities. Pressures to achieve unreasonable expectations can cause unnecessary stress (Jackson, 2023; Levine, 2012, 2021; Strom & Strom, 2021, 2024).

A study of 3,900 students in grades 8–10 in Portugal found that more of them ranked school as a greater worry (61%) than family matters (14%) (Matos et al., 2016). However, instead of talking to parents about fears, students were more likely to talk to peers (18%) than family members (6%). The largest proportion, 45%, responded to worries by seeking ways to distract themselves from problems, a troublesome but common escapist strategy. A new context for the expression of fear was also noted, economic and financial concerns about their own future.

2. Another common worry is physical appearance. Most students going through puberty are preoccupied by how peers see them. This is one reason teenagers are so quick to adopt the new clothing styles of their peers. Parents sometimes trivialize clothing fads claiming they are expensive, encourage conformity, and do not matter in the long run. A more sensible response is to realize that external conformity of dress style does not mean that a student lacks individuality or can be pressured to conform in other aspects of behavior (Webb et al., 2017).
3. Boys and girls worry about being popular and having a boyfriend or girlfriend, a goal that peaks at about ages 12–14. It is wise to accept a student's desire to be popular instead of belittling an interest in being well thought of by others. The desire for peer approval does not replace the influence of parents. The duration of parent influence is as long or short as parent willingness to encourage personal development of their child. Adolescents also need to realize (a) their age group tends to focus more on benefits than the costs of risky behavior, and (b) they tend to make more high-risk decisions when doing things with peer groups than alone. Consequently, there may be times when popularity should be set aside in favor of discouraging the group intentions or walking away (Abbott & Burkitt, 2023; Haidt, 2024).
4. "I worry my parents might get a divorce or could die." Students seldom express these worries to parents (Kearney, 2023). However, parents should anticipate these kinds of fears and describe preparations they have made in the event of their untimely death. "If Dad and I died, Aunt Joyce has agreed to be your guardian. We know that she would raise you in the way we feel is best. Each year we put money into an insurance policy to pay for your college tuition." Part of a teen's concerns deals with how his or her future would be in jeopardy. Talking is reassuring and letting them know the favorable status of your marriage.
5. Students also worry about how friends treat them. This concern reaches a peak in eighth grade and is greater among gay youth (Strom et al., 2012). The meaning of friendship and how to maintain good relationships without compromising personal values is a topic many students wish would be discussed in their family. Romantic relationships can be a major worry for students who may break up or are mistreated by dating partner. Parents willing to talk about these concerns are respected because it shows they realize complications that must be considered.
6. Elementary students are often afraid of bullies. Feelings of resignation that nothing can be done to stop peer abuse or expecting adults to deal with every incident should be replaced with a collective resolve by students to assume their unique responsibility related to misbehavior by classmates. When teachers present a structured agenda allowing students to make known their feelings of peer abuse, constructive norms of response to prevent it can emerge (Kraizer, 2005a, 2005b). In a similar way, teachers should not assume students who show cruelty and lack self-control are incapable of personality improvement, so it is not justified to give up on them (Kennedy & Brausch, 2024).

Discussion can support the motivation students need to take on their important role to ensure safety of classmates. These conversations also improve perspective taking by the adults. Studies have found that compared with students, teachers and administrators underestimate the scope of bullying, consider school to be a safer place, and judge incidents of bully behavior as being less serious (Strom et al., 2012). A suitable agenda invites student opinions in inclusive classrooms to express their feelings about peer mistreatment. Teachers can reinforce accurate student impressions by having classroom discussions about peer mistreatment and describing summaries of research about bully behavior (Forber-Pratt et al., 2024).

The expectation that class time should be used efficiently means teachers have choices to make about balancing instruction and paying attention to student concerns. Some educators and parents wonder whether discussions of peer relationships are appropriate when the main purpose of curriculum is to prepare students for a career. This is a shortsighted perspective. Over the past decade, substantial evidence has been discovered that students who are unable to get along with peers have far higher rates of absenteeism, dropout, truancy, incarceration, suicide, and murder. Devoting class time to dialogue on issues that bother students is justified (Kennedy & Brausch, 2024; Langman, 2009, 2017, 2021).

Mental Health Worries

There is concern among parents about the mental health and well-being of children. Schumacher et al. (2024) conducted a poll for the Kaiser Family Foundation. The nationally representative sample of 6,292 U.S. parents of school-age children included Whites (n = 1,725), Blacks (n = 1,991), Hispanics (n = 1,775), Asians (n = 693), and American Indian/Alaskans (n = 267). Parents were asked whether their children had been called names or racial slurs, treated unfairly by a teacher, hurt, threatened, harassed, had a teacher or some other adult assumed something bad about them had ever taken place in their family. Half of parents said their school-aged children had such negative experiences. In addition, Black parents (40%), Asians parents (26%), and Hispanic parents (23%) agreed that race or ethnicity was a major or minor reason for the treatment compared to a smaller share of White parents (16%). Asian (71%), Black (64%), and Hispanic (60%) parents reported being more confident that life overall for the next generation is going to be better than for their generation compared to 34% of White parents who say the same.

Child Worries About Uncertainty

Fears of uncertainty are reported by school children in many countries. For example, researchers Stiehl et al. (2023) in Austria conducted 52 workshops with 896 students to determine the fears of transitioning from primary to secondary grades. Scenarios of fearful and uncertain situations were presented to students to evaluate their intended coping strategies for application in the transition. Small group discussions were formed where students proposed strategies to help cope with these fears. Major thematic clusters were distinguished between mainly four types of fears:

- *Fear of peer victimization* was mentioned in all of the workshops and most often referred to being excluded, 'not being wanted.' The word *bullying* was used as an umbrella term to describe prejudice, being ridiculed, made fun of, and laughed at by the

classmates in the new setting. Students said the main reason for peer victimization was judging people based on their physical appearance, being perceived as ugly or different and therefore unacceptable.
- *Fear of being alone* in the new environment was talked about in most of the workshops. This meant uncertainty about expectations, how things would be at the new school, too demanding or difficult. What will be expected of students created the stress of uncertainty and not having friends to turn to for support.
- *Fear of victimization by authority figures*, being treated unfairly, such as being ridiculed or severely disciplined in front of peers.
- *Fear of academic failure* can be reduced by teachers. Every school should have policies to support tutoring and counseling to help students plan their individual path, encourage progress and evaluate improvement.

Students reported that they appreciated receiving a letter from their new teachers welcoming them to the new school year. Starting the first day with a group assignment encouraged getting to know everyone and was described by students as 'very nice.' The flexible classroom seating arrangements were described as helpful because it gave students chances to get to know others. The final results also showed that students had more social fears compared to academic fears.

Conclusion

Television and the Internet remind parents of many situations that could harm their children. In turn, parents convey these fears to children. Mothers and fathers should make sure they teach children to assess risk instead of believing exceptional situations represent a norm. It is important to support a balance between children's need for caution and their need for trust. Instead of viewing trust as a naive orientation to contemporary life, recognize that trust is the basis for intimate relationships, mental health, and have a sense of community. By establishing family rules for responding to potential danger, guidance can be given without also creating excessive worry. Teachers can lead discussions about bully behavior and inform students of their obligation to report peer abuse whenever it is observed.

As children get older, they become more able to describe their fears and worries. Parents and grandparents should be willing to listen to these concerns and share some of their own past and present concerns. Identifying the common worries of students as they transition from the primary grades to middle grades is relevant to support preservation of mental health.

Key Concepts

1. Parents whose fears cause them to suppose most people cannot be trusted are incapable of teaching children to trust others, a necessary outlook for becoming able to establish close and durable relationships. It is essential for children to have an overall impression that their world is mostly safe and friendly.
2. Strangers are not a common danger. In most crimes against children, they know the perpetrator who might be a relative, brother of a playmate, or a man living nearby. Parents should establish family safety rules to protect children from dangers that are known and unknown.

3. Elementary students trusted by parents to use their own judgment when a situation appears to present danger are less likely to do what they are told by a coercive adult. Inner strength is needed to countermand directives children believe could jeopardize their safety.
4. The first step in overcoming fear is to acknowledge it. Because young children identify closely with parents, an effective way to reduce the harmful consequences of children's fears is for parents to admit some of their own fears and how things worked out for them.
5. Children should have someone they can go to who will listen to fears without judging them. They can have this experience when parents and grandparents are ready to accept them unconditionally. No child should have to repress fear or pretend bravery to gain the esteem of loved ones.
6. One way to reduce child anxiety is to read books in which a character faces similar situations to those experienced by young listeners. Talking about how character may feel and that these feelings bother children too helps recognize that telling our fears is a way to manage them better.
7. When teachers present a structured discussion agenda that encourages students to make known their impressions of peer abuse, constructive norms of response to prevent abuse can emerge. In a similar way, teachers should avoid assuming students who lack self-control and show cruelty are incapable of improvement, so it is justified to give up on them.
8. A certain degree of fear seems necessary to exercise good judgment. Children should not be made to feel ashamed of expressing fear. The child whose fears and worries are unsuspected or unshared bears the added burden of being alone with fears and worries.
9. Studies have shown that students who choose parents as listeners to their concerns are much less inclined to worry about being liked by classmates, failure at school, uncertainty about career, and relationships with friends than students who choose nonfamily listeners like peers, teachers, or sources on the Internet.
10. Talking is an effective way to relieve stress because it enables us to feel that we are not alone and helps us to better organize our thoughts. On the other hand, talking to oneself often increases stress.

Generational Perspectives Activities

15.1 Discussion
15.2 Conversations With Young Children
15.3 A Scenario: Reasoning and Problem-Solving
15.4 Chapter Review
15.5 Parent and Grandparent Self-Evaluation
15.6 Storytelling

15.1 Discussion

1. What do you suppose are sources of worry for your grandchildren?
2. What things worry you the most about your daughters and sons?
3. What do you believe your daughters and sons worry about the most?
4. What are the main worries that you have about your grandchildren?
5. How can you help other relatives when they are fearful or worried?

6. What methods seem the best for you to deal with fears and worries?
7. How could family members help you with your worries and fears?
8. What are some of your worries that are related to physical health?
9. What habits do grandchildren have that are worrisome for you?

15.2 Conversations With Young Children

1. What do your friends tell you they fear the most?
2. What are the biggest fears and worries for you?
3. How do you try to cope with fears and worries?
4. How could schools help students with their fears?
5. What do friends do to help you cope with fears?
6. How have your fears changed as you get older?
7. What do your parents seem to worry about most?
8. What fears bother your grandparents the most?
9. How do you help others who are worried?

15.3 A Scenario: Reasoning and Problem-Solving

Some elementary students are reluctant to share fears and worries with grownups, so they lack a mature source of feedback that is needed to cope with personal struggles. Cynthia's parents have observed that sometimes she cries about things that bother her, yet she chooses not to confide in them. What course of action would you recommend for Cynthia's parents?

a. Tell her that everyone has fears and worries and describe some of your own.
b. Let her know that you want to help but cannot without knowing information.
c. Ask the school counselor whether it is wise to visit a clinical psychologist.
d. Talk to Cynthia's teacher to learn if she has insights about peer problems.
e. Other

15.4 Chapter Review

1. What insights from the chapter will I try to apply in my relationships?
2. What is the most important key concept for me presented in this chapter?
3. Which elements of this chapter do I wish I had known about earlier?

15.5 Parent and Grandparent Self-Evaluation

Directions: For each question, place a check beside statements that describe your feelings. You may want to give several answers on some items. If your feelings are not on the choices list, write them on the line marked 'Other.' If a lesson persuaded you to change your mind, make it known by underlining any statements showing these answers reflect a change in feelings.

1. My greatest fears relate to
    a. physical health problems
    b. managing financial affairs

c. loss of my independence
d. loss of spouse or partner
e. Other _____

2. Fears I am reluctant to share with my children

   a. relate to my health problems
   b. concern my financial affairs
   c. involve loss of independence
   d. are about living alone
   e. Other _____

3. My greatest worries about my daughter or son are

   a. separation and divorce
   b. taking on too much debt
   c. lack of religious faith
   d. lack of time with spouse
   e. Other _____

4. As I get older, my inclination to worry is

   a. more than when I was younger
   b. less than when I was younger
   c. about the same as it has been
   d. involving more family relatives
   e. Other _____

5. I worry about my grandchildren

   a. being hurt in some accident
   b. experimenting with drugs
   c. remaining too self-centered
   d. not getting a job
   e. not getting enough education
   f. Other _____

6. In conversation with my children and grandchildren,

   a. I have told them about my fears
   b. I avoid the mention of my fears
   c. I urge everyone to be cautious
   d. I identify dangers to consider
   e. Other _____

7. The methods I rely on for dealing with worries are to

   a. spend time with prayer
   b. get physical exercise
   c. tell concerns to a friend
   d. engage in meditation
   e. Other _____

8. My knowledge about the fears of grandchildren

   a. is based on reports from their parents
   b. comes from what they have told me
   c. is meager because I never ask them
   d. is drawn from memories at that age
   e. Other _____

9. Because fear is a prominent emotion at every age,

   a. this should be a topic of conversation with grandchildren
   b. children can learn from relatives how we manage fear
   c. we make a mistake by avoiding conversations about it
   d. sharing fears with the family can lead to more support
   e. Other _____

10. Talking with grandchildren about bullies at their school is

    a. a topic that I have not brought up
    b. could increase my understanding
    c. not a pleasant issue so I avoid it
    d. an obligation of parents, not me
    e. Other _____

15.6 Storytelling

Historically, storytelling has been a dominant classic and progressive method of teaching around the world. The purposes of a storyteller are to present imaginary or real-life examples showing how some concept applies to a particular situation. People like stories, they pay attention to the procession of events, and usually remember aspects of a story for a long time. Your stories can reinforce the concepts in this chapter for family members and classmates. Please share your stories with them.

References

Abbott, R., & Burkitt, E. (2023). *Child development and the brain: From embryo to adolescence* (2nd ed.). Policy Press.

Alabama Law Enforcement Agency. (2024). *Criminal justice information services, sex offender registry.* https://www.alea.gov/node/270

American Academy of Child & Adolescent Psychiatry. (2023, September). *Terrorism and war: How to talk to children.* https://www.aacap.org/AACAP/Families_and_Youth/Facts_for_Families/FFF-Guide/Talking-To-Children-About-Terrorism-And-War-087.aspx

Bieber, C. (2024, May 30). Revealing divorce statistics in 2024. *Forbes Advisor.* https://www.forbes.com/advisor/legal/divorce/divorce-statistics/

Bortfeld, H., & Bunge, S. A. (2024). *Fundamentals of developmental cognitive neuroscience.* Cambridge University Press.

Carbonnell, D., & Winston, S. A. (2016). *The worry trick: How your brain tricks you into expecting the worst and what you can do about it.* New Harbinger.

Chansky, T. E. (2014). *Freeing your child from anxiety, revised and updated edition: Practical strategies to overcome fears, worries, and phobias and be prepared for life – from toddlers to teens.* Harmony.

DeLaune, M. (2024, February 6). *Testimony of Michelle C. DeLaune,* National Center for Missing and Exploited Children for the United States, House Education and the Workforce, 118th Congress. https://www.congress.gov/event/118th-congress/house-event/LC72987/text

Florida Department of Education. (2024). *K-12 Scholarship programs: The Hope Scholarship.* https://www.fldoe.org/schools/school-choice/k-12-scholarship-programs/hope/

Forber-Pratt, A. J., Espelage, D. L., Rose, C. A., Hanebutt, R. A., Woolweaver, A. B., Robinson, L. E., Ingram, K. M., & El Sheikh, A. J. (2024, September). Elementary school staff perspectives on bullying involvement among students with disabilities. *International Journal of Disability and Social Justice.* https://www.scienceopen.com/hosted-document?doi=10.13169/intljofdissocjus.4.2.0071

Goldstein, S., & Brooks, R. (Eds.). (2023). *Handbook of resilience in children* (3rd ed.). Springer.

Gramlich, J. (2024, April 24). *What the data says about crime in the United States.* Pew Research Center. https://www.pewresearch.org/short-reads/2024/04/24/what-the-data-says-about-crime-in-the-us/

Guiney, H., Caspi, A., Ambler, A., Belsky, J., Kokaua, J., Broadbent, J., Cheyne, K., Dickson, N., Hancox, R., Harrington, H., Hogan, S., Ramrakha, S., Righarts, A., Thomson, W. M., Moffitt, T. E., & Poulton, R. (2024, February). Childhood sexual abuse and pervasive problems across multiple life domains: Findings from a five-decade study. *Development and Psychopathology, 36*(1), 219–235. https://doi.org/10.1017/S0954579422001146

Haidt, J. (2024). *The anxious generation: How the great rewiring of childhood is causing an epidemic of mental illness.* Penguin Press.

Hertz, N. (2021). *The lonely century: How to restore human connection in a world that's pulling apart.* Crown Currency.

Jackson, M. (2023). *Uncertain: The wisdom and wonder of being unsure.* Prometheus.

Kearney, M. S. (2023). *The two-parent privilege: How Americans stopped getting married and started falling behind.* The University of Chicago Press.

Kellerman, G. R., & Seligman, M. (2023). *Tomorrowmind: Thriving at work with resilience, creativity and connection – now and in an uncertain future.* Atria.

Kennedy, A., & Brausch, A. M. (2024). Emotion dysregulation, bullying, and suicide behaviors in adolescents. *Journal of Affective Disorders Reports, 15.* https://doi.org/10.1016/j.jadr.2023.100715

Kiwanis. (2024). *Join the fight to end bullying.* https://www.kiwanis.org/who-we-are/youth-protection/bullying-prevention/

Kloo, M., Thornberg, R., Wänström, L., & Espelage, D. L. (2024). Longitudinal links of authoritative teaching and bullying victimization in upper elementary school. *Educational Psychology, 44*(2), 171–188. https://doi.org/10.1080/01443410.2024.2325594

Kraizer, S. (2005a). *Take a stand: Preventing bullying, interpersonal conflict & violence, family handbook.* Coalition for Children. https://safechild.org/wp-content/uploads/2023/07/Take-A-Stand-Parent-Handbook.pdf

Kraizer, S. (2005b). *Take a stand: Preventing bullying, interpersonal conflict & violence, teacher handbook.* Coalition for Children. https://safechild.org/wp-content/uploads/2023/07/Take-A-Stand-Teacher-Guide.pdf

Krznaric, R. (2014). *Empathy: Why it matters, and how to get it.* Penguin.

Langman, P. (2009). *Why kids kill: Inside the minds of school shooters.* Palgrave Macmillan.

Langman, P. (2017). *School shooters: Understanding high school, college, and adult perpetrators.* Rowan & Littlefield.

Langman, P. (2021). *Warning signs: Identifying school shooters before they strike.* Langman Psychological Associates.

Levine, M. (2012). *Teach your children well: Why values and coping skills matter more than grades, trophies, or "Fat envelopes".* HarperCollins.

Levine, M. (2021). *Ready or not: Preparing our kids to thrive in an uncertain and rapidly changing world.* Harper Perennial.

Marino, C. (2024). *Terrorists on the border and in our country.* Humanix.

Martin, E. W. (2015). *The wonderful things you will be.* Random House.

Matos, M. G. de, Camacho, I., Reis, M., Costa, D., Galvão, D., & Team Aventura Social. (2016). Worries, coping strategies, and well-being in adolescence: Highlights from HBSC study in Portugal. *Vulnerable Children and Youth Studies, 11*(3), 274–280. https://doi.org/10.1080/17450128.2016.1220655

National Center for Missing and Exploited Children. (2024a). *About us.* https://www.missingkids.org/footer/about

National Center for Missing and Exploited Children. (2024b). *Is your child missing?* https://www.missingkids.org/gethelpnow/isyourchildmissing

Office of Public Affairs, U. S. Department of Justice. (2024, July 1). *U.S. Marshals find 200 missing children across the nation during operation we will find you 2.* https://www.justice.gov/opa/pr/us-marshals-find-200-missing-children-across-nation-during-operation-we-will-find-you-2

Probation Information Network. (2022, April 25). *Sex offender registry requirements across the United States.* https://www.probationinfo.org/sex-offender-registry/

Rapa, L. J., Katsiyannis, A., Scott, S., & Durham, O. (2024, April). School shooting in the United States: 1997–2022. *Pediatrics, 153*(4), e2023064311. https://doi.org/10.1542/peds.2023-064311

Schumacher, S., Hamel, L., Artiga, S., & Pillai, D. (2024, August 1). *Well-being of children and parents: Highlights from the KFF survey on racism, discrimination, and health.* https://www.kff.org/racial-equity-and-health-policy/poll-finding/well-being-of-children-and-parents-highlights-from-the-kff-survey-on-racism-discrimination-and-health/

Stiehl, K. A. M., Krammer, I., Schrank, B., Pollock, I., Silani, G., & Woodcock, K. A. (2023). Children's perspective on fears connected to school transition and intended coping strategies. *Social Psychology of Education: An International Journal, 26*(3), 603–637. https://doi.org/10.1007/s11218-023-09759-1

StopBullying.gov. (2024). *Effects of bullying.* https://www.stopbullying.gov/bullying/effects

Strom, P. S., Strom, R. D., Wingate, J. J., Kraska, M. F., & Beckert, T. E. (2012). Cyberbullying: Assessment of student experience for continuous improvement planning. *NASSP Bulletin, 96*(2), 137–153. https://doi.org/10.1177/0192636512443281

Strom, R. D., & Strom, P. S. (2021). Learning throughout life about the needs of all generations: Recognizing and counteracting generational isolation. In M. London (Ed.), *The Oxford handbook of lifelong learning* (2nd ed., pp. 183–206). Oxford University Press.

Strom, P. S., & Strom, R. D. (2024). *Mental health and relationships from early adulthood through old age.* Routledge.

Webb, H. J., Zimmer-Gembeck, M., Waters, A., Farrell, L., Nesdale, D., & Downey, G. (2017, December). "Pretty pressure" from peers, parents, and the media: A longitudinal study of appearance-based rejection sensitivity. *Journal of Research on Adolescence, 27*(4), 718–735. https://doi.org/10.1111/jora.12310

YouTube. (2024). 10 Babies experiencing things for the first time. *BabiezTV.* https://www.youtube.com/watch?v=ObJgJizBFh8

Chapter 16

Self-Control, Resilience, and Patience

Parents and grandparents know they should teach children skills related to self-control, resilience, and patience. These valuable assets are among the qualities collectively defined as emotional intelligence. The evaluation of child progress in learning such difficult lessons can be observed by how they get along with peers, extent to which they show concern about feelings of others, and their willingness to delay gratification, being able to wait for the things they want. The purposes of this chapter are to (a) explore the response of adults to misbehavior of young children in group care settings, (b) explain reasons why patience is essential to achieve emotional balance and mental health, (c) consider executive brain function and relationship to self-control, goal setting, and planning, (d) examine some of the risks associated with overscheduling children, (e) discuss student willingness to wait and develop patience, and (f) reveal why willpower and self-control are seen as predictors of achievement. Generational Perspectives Activities present topics to discuss with family members and close friends about child self-control, resilience, and patience.

Misbehavior in School

Teachers in a workshop were asked these two questions: (a) What changes would you like to see in how students treat their teachers? and (b) What changes would you like to see in the way parents treat the teachers of their children? Educators of all grade levels described an increase in number of students whose lack of self-control is demonstrated in unhealthy ways as they respond to challenges. Some of the common signs of dysfunction are outbursts of anger, cursing to express frustration, threatening peers and teachers, and withdrawing from group activities. Greene (2021) reported many parents show similar responses when they are informed about the misbehavior of their child. Becoming upset and making threats happens more now than during the past according to observations of teachers with lengthy years of experience in the classroom.

Troubling Reactions of Parents

Teachers reported the most troubling reaction of parents is denial, refusing to accept any negative feedback about the misbehavior of children. Such adults frequently take their child's side rather than accept responsibility for correction of misbehavior. This response causes trouble because students then believe parents condone their misconduct. What seems to happen is that, with the gradual erosion of authority in the family, some parents have adopted a new definition of their role, to act as a buffer for children against outside

DOI: 10.4324/9781003534655-21

authority figures, including teachers at school. Parents spend less time with their children than they prefer and want to make sure the time together is mutually satisfying. So, rather than imposing punishment when it is appropriate, parents ignore discipline and instead issue warnings or threats. They suppose this response will endear them to children. However, the common outcome is that it undermines the scope of child civil behavior and social maturity (Hoskyn et al., 2017).

Teachers point out that parents are the only people with their unique role for guidance of social and emotional adjustment. Accordingly, educators attempt to motivate parents to become involved by providing the education their children need. The success of students depends on teachers and parents each making their separate contributions. When child deficiencies involve academic subjects, parents may not possess the knowledge that is needed for tutoring, so schools assume this task. However, when student deficiencies involve social misconduct, parents are implicated. They are the teachers who are the most responsible for important lessons about growing up.

Suspensions for Misbehavior

Preschool suspension or expulsion rates are shocking across the United States (Zinsser, 2023, Zinsser et al., 2022). In response to this problem, the state of Connecticut began an Infant and Early Childhood Mental Health Consultation (ECMHC) that has been operating successfully for two decades. This project has expanded to become prevalent in all 50 states. The approach includes social workers who collaborate with parents and childhood care providers. The social worker observes students during preschool and at home before bringing parents and teacher together to talk about setting mutual expectations and implementing a united action plan. When teachers have access to consultants and parents are cooperative, the risk of child suspension declines (Newland et al., 2024; Silver et al., 2023).

Self-Control as a Predictor of Health and Wealth

The Dunedin Longitudinal Study

Some people might suppose that the large-scale suspensions of preschoolers reflect a lack of training among early childhood caregivers. However, student lack of self-control must not be overlooked. Self-control in early childhood has been confirmed to be a predictor of health and wealth in adult life. This conclusion is based on results of the Dunedin Study, a longitudinal investigation in New Zealand, which began in 1973 by Richie Poulton et al. (2015). Indicators of self-control for the 1,037 three-year-old participants were evaluated by their teachers, parents, and observers. The criteria for preschooler observation included whether a child showed behaviors such as low frustration tolerance, lack of persistence, difficulty finishing tasks, impulsive actions without reflective thinking, trouble waiting for their turn, and acting restless.

When the children were 32 years old, data was gathered to assess indicators of health and wealth. The impulsivity of children demonstrating low self-control and consequent failure to participate in long-term planning led to additional problems in adulthood. In terms of health and well-being, they were far more likely to drop out of high school, have an unplanned pregnancy, become single parents, have a criminal conviction, and become dependent on alcohol, tobacco, or illegal drugs (Poulton et al., 2015).

Financial status was also implicated. By age 32, there was evidence that those having poor self-control as children were less likely to save money, have a retirement account, or own homes than peers who exhibited greater self-control. The group with the lowest self-control reported the greatest financial problems. Lack of self-control was more predictive of money problems than social class or IQ scores of the children (Poulton et al., 2015).

One alternative to support child self-control about money management is a unique television program called *The Centsables* (2024). This 30-minute Saturday morning presentation targets 5–11-year-olds on the Fox Business Network. Six animated superheroes provide weekly lessons that conclude with multiple choice questions to assess money comprehension. Teaching children about fiscal responsibility at a young age is important. And what better way to have them recall what they learned than having animated superheroes teach them the lessons? That's where *The Centsables* come into play, a group of friendly bankers by day and superheroes by night who dispatch villains and rescue people from financial traps. Members of this elite group include investment counselor Hamilton, bank tellers Franklin and Penny, bank greeter Suzy B, and security guards Grant and Jackson. When transformed into their alter egos, the group acquires superpowers that include superspeed, ability to control water, becoming a giant, and ability to command the wind. The series is based upon comic books that first featured the characters.

Unstructured Activity and Self-Direction

Parenting articles give opinions about bringing up children. Some observers suggest a rigid 'tiger mom' strategy is best while others recommend greater flexibility. A contrast in views is provided by Barker et al. (2014), who asked 70 parents of 6–7-year-olds to keep track of their child's daily schedule for a week and estimate aspects of the typical schedule of their children for a year. Researchers categorized each activity as more structured or less structured. Structured activities were soccer, dance, music lessons, and gymnastics; less-structured activities were library visits, solitary play, pretending, and watching television. Children were evaluated for self-directed executive function by using a verbal task in which they generated elements of a category and could decide on their own when to switch from one subcategory to another. The more time children spent with less-structured activities, the better their self-directed executive function. These findings represent the first evidence that time spent with a broad range of less-structured activities outside formal schooling predicts goal-directed behaviors that are not explicitly specified by an adult, and more time spent in structured activities predicts poorer goal-directed behavior (Barker et al., 2014).

Organized or Unorganized Child Play

The thinking processes of children are influenced by how their time is spent. Historically, it was common for children to improvise activities on their own, to regulate dialogue with peers, and devise rules to guide behavior of every person who participated in group play. This tradition of self-governance during play has largely vanished in the past generation. The shift is related mostly to parent fears about child safety, adult criminals, and security. According to the National Council of Youth Sports (2024), about 60 million American children currently are sports participants. The players are supervised by six million adult coaches in games with rules such as little league soft ball, basketball, baseball, soccer, golf, and football. There is increasing concern about the consequences of this vast adult takeover of children's play. In past generations when the children directed their own activities, play occurred in a context of just 'having fun.' Because rules were vague and often in dispute and no adults were present to make the decisions or enforce the rules, children had to recognize a need for some sort of rules and bargain about what was seen as 'fair.' Everyone was involved and learned to enforce fairness, an exercise in consent and cooperation.

Adult-organized sports provide guidance, but the cost is denying children an opportunity to practice policing themselves because they do not have to rely on self-regulation. Instead, adults decide when a game will be scheduled, where the game will be played, who will occupy each position, whether pitches are balls or strikes, if a hit is a fair or a foul ball and keep score. Holman (2024) stated that opportunities for children to self-control their own unorganized play and manage conflict should be encouraged, so self-regulation decisions become a larger aspect of child development.

In competitive sports, winning is the main goal. When winning becomes the exclusive emphasis, mistakes are no longer allowed, and play is no longer just for fun. The education of coaches for children at play is more important than commonly supposed. One reason for this assertion is because 70% of soccer and softball players quit organized games before puberty. Weinberg and Gould (2023) reported the reasons children give for quitting teams are (a) loss of interest, (b) not fun, (c) takes too much time, (d) coaches play favorites, (e) the coach is a poor teacher, (f) tired of playing, (g) too much emphasis on winning, (h) want to do other things, (i) need more time for study, and (j) too much pressure from the coach and parent spectators.

This difference between child-directed play and adult-directed play warrants consideration. The greater amount of time children used to spend at play governed entirely by themselves allowed lots of decision-making practice to develop a group of cognitive skills referred to as *executive function*.

Zelazo and Carlson (2020, 2021) explained that *executive functioning* is defined as factors involved with self-regulation. Good executive functioning is associated with any of the following:

- Better predictor of academic success than intelligence test scores
- Ability to shut out distractions while paying attention to the teacher
- Reflective thinking instead of being directed by impulsive thinking
- Avoiding misconduct at school and the interruption of thinking by peers
- Being more able to focus on a task and concentrate on finding a solution

Poor executive functioning is associated with any of the following:

- High rates of dropout from school before graduation
- Participation with illegal drugs and substance abuse
- Criminal activity involvement and school misbehavior
- More frequent diagnosis as attention-deficit disorder

The child's ability to have self-control during play is the main purpose of executive function. Scientists have found that thinking processes governing judgments are mediated by executive function. Children with good self-regulation can pay attention to their teacher despite multiple distractions, follow directions, have greater control of their emotions, avoid misconduct, interpret communication cues and views of others, rely on reflective thinking instead of being impulsive, and demonstrate self-discipline (Holman, 2024; Hoskyn et al., 2017; Meltzer, 2018; Weir, 2023).

Teaching Self-Control Skills

Games With Focus on Attention

Kindergarten teachers identify child self-regulation skills as their top concerns. Teachers cannot teach when children are unable to pay attention, overcome distractions, or help each other remain regulated. Research by McClelland (2019) has found that a good approach during preschool is to encourage active games such as Simon Says and Freeze Tag, both requiring high levels of executive function that test a child's ability to focus attention, working memory to remember a set of rules, and exhibit self-control, qualities that are predictors of academic success. The game of Simon Says involves three or more players. One child takes the role of Simon and gives directions that the others must follow only when prefaced by the phrase, Simon Says. For example, Simon says, 'Kneel down,' or Simon says, 'Touch your feet with your hands.' Players are eliminated if they follow directions that are not immediately preceded by the trigger phrase, 'Simon says.' The ability to pay attention and distinguish between valid and invalid commands, instead of physical ability, is the key to success in the game.

Megan McClelland (2019), Professor of Early Childhood at Oregon State University, gauges self-regulation behavior of preschoolers by using the Head-to-Toes game. Children are told to imitate movements of the teacher as she touches her head or toes. Later, they are told to do the opposite of the teacher, touching their toes when she touches her head. This would seem a simple exercise, but it is one that requires a high level of executive function with an emphasis on paying attention, concentrating, reliance on short-term memory to follow rules that may change, mental flexibility (to do the opposite of what one was told earlier), and self-control.

McClelland and Tominey (2018) conducted a study for the National Institute of Child Health and Human Development. The goal was to track 430 boys and girls from the time they were age 4 until they reached age 25 and identify factors with the most influence on completing a college degree. During early childhood parents were asked to rate their child on items such as 'plays with a single toy for a long period' or 'gives up easily when faced with difficulties.' Reading and mathematics skills were evaluated at age 7 using standardized tests and again at age 21.

Unexpectedly, scores on reading and mathematics did not significantly predict whether students would eventually finish college. Instead, students rated one standard deviation higher, that is 34% higher, on attention span-persistence observed by parents at age 4 had nearly 50% greater odds of completing a bachelor's degree by age 25. The salient point is that attention and persistence skills can and should be taught to children in the current era of near-constant distraction. Scheduling time in class for all students to take part in active games such as Simon Says, Freeze Tag, and Red Light/Green Light are effective tools to boost self-regulation and improve academic skills (McClelland & Tominey, 2018).

Goal-Directed Problem-Solving

Phillip Zelazo and Stephanie Carlson (2021) devised a test called the *Minnesota Executive Function Scale* that evaluates how well children apply executive function to goal-directed problem-solving. The Scale is an app tablet game for 2–7-year-olds that takes less than five minutes to complete. Children are directed to sort a stack of picture cards according to color, placing a picture of a red rabbit in one pile and a picture of a blue boat in another. Midway through the test, the evaluator makes a change in the task and tells the child to now sort the pictures by shape instead of by color. The typical three-year-old has difficulty in switching thinking and consequently keeps sorting according to the original rule. The four- and five-year-olds usually can adjust and follow the new rules. Zelazo and Carlson believe this improvement is related to a developmental leap in self-reflection that emerges around age 4. This leap help children recognize they know two different ways to sort cards, that, in turn, enables them to decide which rules to follow.

Zelazo and Carlson's work (2020) also involves training children regarding the use of reflection and rules. After training, they measure performance and record neural activity to determine if children improve on tasks for which they were not trained. Results suggested that it is possible to facilitate the development of executive functioning. Maybe during this age stage, as executive functioning and relevant brain regions undergo rapid change, there is a chance for intervention.

Resilience and Age

Being able to quickly recover after experiencing predictable or unforeseen setbacks requires resilience. People of every age need resilience because adverse events are bound to happen throughout life. For example, some adults encounter mental health obstacles in marital relationships, suffer disappointing situations at work, cope with issues related to caregiving of older relatives, and become concerned about future health and finances during retirement. Adults less often reflect on the resilience in children, even though many boys and girls must manage challenges about their academic progress, getting along with classmates who mistreat them, and a need to amend personal goals that seem unattainable (Ginsburg & Jablow, 2020; Goldstein & Brooks, 2023).

Levels of Resilience

Stuart Lustig (2022) is the National Medical Executive for Behavioral Health at Cigna Healthcare. He has conducted surveys to determine levels of resilience for various age groups. These surveys have discovered that resilience is most prevalent among 5–10-year-olds (45% of them). A less prevalence rate of 34% has been found for 11–13-year-olds. Resilience continues to erode to 35% for students aged 14–17 and falls to the lowest level of 22% among 18–23-year-olds. The good news is that, after age 23, when people become parents, the rates of prevalence for resilience rise again to 42%.

Relationships and Resilience

Goldstein and Brooks (2023) explained that relationships are the foundation of a child's resilience. Spending time with loved ones, listening to child concerns, and expressing encouragement should be common family practice. Strong relationships with caregivers can enable a child to feel loved, safe, and secure. In turn, this feeling of safety promotes a sense of confidence and willingness to explore or to recover from setbacks. Resilient children usually perform well when they try to solve problems and are good at learning new skills. This is because they are more willing to try again when things do not go the way they want the first time.

Private Speech and Attention

Make-believe play that is driven by imagination supports self-discipline because children engage in private speech while they pretend. They talk to themselves regarding what they intend to do and ways they will carry out their plans. Observations comparing how preschoolers behave across a broad range of activities have determined that the amount of private speech in relation to self-regulation is greatest during imaginative play (Whedom et al., 2021). Also, the use of self-regulating language is predictive of better executive functioning. In contrast, the more structured play becomes, especially when adults take over and dominate the activity, the less children have opportunities to participate in private speech. Private speech helps children to verbally guide behavior and attention by helping to detach themselves from distractions in their environment. As private speech is important for children to engage in from ages 3 to 7, this speech should not be interrupted or limited by parent or teacher control (Day & Smith, 2013).

Preschool and kindergarten teachers must decide the amount of child self-talk they will allow. There is evidence that students who mutter to themselves perform better because language is a stimulant that guides self-speakers through their thought processes. During this time children may talk out loud to themselves while involved in various activities. In a study of 5-year-old children (29 behaviorally at-risk students and 43 controls), results showed that 78% of children performed motor tasks better when they talked to themselves than when they were quiet. Both groups found tasks more difficult when self-speech was stifled by being told not to talk out loud (Winsler et al., 2009).

Guo and Dobkins (2023) studied the relationship between private speech use and cognitive performance in young adults (mean age 20.21 years). Results of the investigation showed that young adults often rely on private speech, especially when trying to pay attention where specific details are involved, such as in cooking, and progressive steps are needed to do some tasks. They performed better on trials for which they produced a greater amount of private speech. In addition, they benefited from talking to themselves in times of stress and anxiety because it heightened the focus necessary to solve problems. Similar to young children, young adults with a higher use of private speech are hindered if asked to keep quiet.

Children and Patience

Tolerance for Frustration

Frustration is a frequent experience for individuals who feel they should not have to wait for things. Instead of recognizing that frustration increases their impatience, they are inclined to blame others for causing them to become upset. For example, the customers who are standing in a grocery store checkout line may be heard to complain about the store management. More cash registers should be open, so no one ever must be inconvenienced with waiting. When drivers are behind a car that does not move as soon as a traffic light turns green, the need for more patience seldom comes to mind. Instead, the other driver is likely portrayed as someone who should not be behind the wheel. When this process is used for the interpretation of other events that take place daily, all frustrations are considered justified because they identify the failure of others to behave properly. Some children who observe parents and teachers believe frustration and impatience are suitable responses when it is more appropriate to wait (Gazzaley & Rosen, 2016).

Many children endure the frustration that comes with being rushed. Hari (2022) contends that when teachers are in a hurry, they deny students the time needed to process new information or strategies to consider for solving problems. Consequently, hasty information-processing methods are adopted. Instead of withholding judgment until all possible aspects of some problem have been explored, hurried students who cannot wait are inclined to end an Internet search too soon and draw premature conclusions based on partial information. These are high prices to pay for trying to speed up the pace of learning. Teacher efforts to rush the pace of lessons or abbreviate the time needed to practice newly introduced skills cause some students to fall behind and others to perform below their ability. Strom and Strom (2021) stated that time and learning are always linked; children learn what they spend time doing and from those who participate with them.

Jackson (2018, 2023) and Mark (2023) explained some of the reasons why being able to tolerate frustrations is necessary. Patience enables adults to accommodate immaturity of children, accept limitations of colleagues, make allowances for personal shortcomings, and cause people to treat others in respectful ways. It would be a mistake to abandon these attributes as common goals everyone should strive to attain. Parents should understand the only people who qualify as examples of maturity for children are those who consistently demonstrate patience and show tolerance for frustration.

Patience and Delay of Gratification

There is concern that self-control behavior such as willingness to delay gratification and ability to show patience are in decline. A failure of willpower is seen as the root of problems such as consumer debt, obesity, addictions, relationship issues, and violent behavior. If people believe their wants should be met immediately, they abandon the goal of learning how to manage frustrating events that require impulse control. Over 50 years ago, Walter Mischel, Professor of Psychology at Stanford University, explored self-control in young children at the University Lab School. Between 1968 and 1974, Mischel (2014) and colleagues posed this challenge to 500 four-year-olds: "If you wait until I (the experimenter) go to the school office and come back, you will be given two marshmallows to eat. If you cannot wait until I get back, come to the front of the room and take one marshmallow from the teacher's desk."

Mischel's task presented a lure of enjoying an immediate reward of one marshmallow or choosing to demonstrate self-restraint to get the greater reward of two marshmallows later. The experimenter left the room for 15 minutes. This probably seemed a long time for two-thirds of the children who resorted to covering their eyes so they could not look at the marshmallows, making up fantasy games to distract themselves, singing songs, or staring at the trees outside. In contrast, one-third of the children could not wait until the experimenter came back, so they went forward within a minute to claim one marshmallow.

The significance of emotional differences among these children was not evident until a follow-up study was conducted 14 years later (Mischel et al., 1989). Dramatic distinctions were reported between students who years earlier had resisted temptation and classmates who showed no inclination to be patient, wait, or demonstrate self-restraint. Those who received two marshmallows for their delay of gratification had grown up to be more socially competent, self-assertive, and capable of handling the frustrations of daily life. They were less prone than more impulsive peers to become upset when faced with unanticipated problems and did not show disorganization when pressured by peers. Teachers observed them as more self-reliant, confident, trustworthy, counted on to assume initiative in uncertain situations, less distractable when trying to concentrate, and remain able to delay gratification in pursuit of their goals.

In contrast, these attributes were less often observed in adolescents who earlier settled for one marshmallow. This group was more often described by teachers as stubborn and indecisive, easily upset, likely to regress or withdraw when presented with stress. They were inclined to jealousy, ever ready to complain they were treated unfairly, inclined to begin conflicts, and show a quick temper. Even by late adolescence they had not acquired self-control. The ability to postpone satisfaction and instead persevere to gain long-term goals is recognized as necessary for success in many situations throughout life, ranging from staying on a weight control diet to completing requirements for a high school diploma (Mischel, 2014).

Besides being more able to manage demands related to daily living, those who waited patiently at age 4 differed in other ways as adolescents that contribute to achievement. In the estimate of their parents, they were more able to put their ideas and feelings into words, listen to the logic of other people, apply reasoning, concentrate, plan goals, evaluate personal progress, and display zest for learning. Further, they performed better on the Scholastic Aptitude Test (SAT), a standard measure often required for admission to college. The children who came forward to get one marshmallow at age 4 had an average verbal score of 524 and 528 on their quantitative (mathematics) score. In comparison, the two-thirds of students who waited longest earned scores of 610 and 652, a total difference of 210 points (Mischel, 2014; Mischel & Ayduk, 2017).

Marshmallow results for child delay of gratification at age 4 were twice as powerful a predictor of SAT scores in late adolescence as IQ scores at age 4. This means self-imposed ability to deny impulses and wait for gratification by remaining perseverant in gaining a longer-term, self-chosen goal significantly impacted academic achievement. Conversely, a lack of self-control in childhood also predicts delinquent behavior in adolescence (Siegel & Welsh, 2016).

Forty years after the Marshmallow experiments, 59 members of the original sample were located and invited to complete willpower tests that can assess self-control in adults. The earlier results were reinforced. In addition, Casey et al. (2011) examined brain activity using functional magnetic imagery with 26 adult members from the original sample. When presented tempting stimuli, the adults who originally demonstrated low self-control revealed different brain patterns from peers with high self-control. Researchers concluded that the prefrontal cortex brain region that controls executive function such as making choices was more active in those with higher self-control.

Opportunities to Practice Waiting

There is considerable evidence that a hurried and rush-oriented environment undermines development of patience and willingness to delay gratification. These conditions increase the need to arrange situations where children have opportunities to practice patience and learn how to wait (Haidt, 2024; Whitbourne, 2021). For each of the following situations, the explanation told to a child should focus on what it means to wait, why sometimes all of us must wait, and how important it is for us to avoid becoming frustrated while waiting. Telling a child how much longer some activity may take can add to comprehension about the concept of time. In certain situations, however, it is better to explain that waiting may take longer than expected and so remaining calm is the way to react to unforeseen delays. These experiences can offer practice in learning to wait.

1. *Grocery Store.* Choose a check-out line where you can tell that you will have to wait. Explain to the child, "We are standing in this line with others buying things they need, just like us. Sometimes we must wait to get things we want." This shows patience instead of frustration by expressing complaints. While waiting, the child can be asked to transfer grocery items onto the conveyer belt or counter.
2. *Taking Turns.* When someone is talking, interrupting them suggests that his or her views are unimportant. Many television shows feature experts who routinely interrupt colleagues. Waiting to talk is a courtesy, reflects patience, and can maximize the opportunity to learn. Children wanting to express their views can be told to wait until a teacher calls on them or their mother finishes what she has to say.
3. *Meal Time.* The principle of anticipation, waiting for something we want, is practiced when a child helps set the table or prepare a meal. Parents should explain that dinner must be made, and everyone has some responsibility. People should show patience by staying seated and waiting until everyone has finished their meal.
4. *Reading.* Children learn patience when parents and grandparents read books to them that require more than a single visit. Unlike storybooks, the chapters in books do not always have conclusions but build to a climax and an ending. This experience requires waiting for the next night to move ahead with the story. Anticipation of serial type movies and progressive television programs are motivators to sustain interest.
5. *Advance Scheduling.* An example of conveying the principle of anticipation is to tell a child, "We are going to the zoo Saturday, which is five days from now." Letting the child know ahead of time provides experience in looking forward to some event while also having to delay gratification. You can ask the child to keep track and count the days until the time arrives for going to the zoo.
6. *Saving Money.* A child wants a bicycle that could cost many weeks of allowance. Learning to save money by putting some in a bank is evidence of patience and willingness to delay gratification. The child can be kept informed about the current balance and remainder sum that is needed. When the total for the big purchase is reached, the child and parent can go to the store and buy it.

Willpower and Self-Control

Roy Baumeister, a social psychologist at Florida State University, maintained that self-control could be the most valuable of human virtues and should be given high priority in the education of adults as well as children. Experiments by Baumeister and Tierney (2012) have revealed how behavior is governed by willpower. Most problems that plague people, such as addiction, overeating, crime, domestic violence, racial prejudice, unwanted pregnancy, sexually transmitted diseases, education failure, financial debt, and lack of exercise, implicate some degree of self-regulation as a central factor. Psychology has found that two main characteristics, intelligence and self-control, are responsible for many benefits. But, despite years of research, O'Bryan et al. (2021) pointed out scholars have yet to find out how to produce lasting increases in intelligence. However, studies have found Baumeister and Tierney self-control orientation using willpower can be strengthened by practice and become a powerful difference in the lives of ordinary people. A person's willpower can influence most aspects of life from managing time to saving for retirement, getting exercise, following a diet, and resisting temptation.

Conclusion

Parents have the unique function of educating their children to acquire attitudes and skills needed for the development of self-control and self-discipline. Many parents fail to fulfill this basic aspect of teaching and are unaware of the mental health consequences. Problems of misbehavior begin in early childhood groups and can implicate relationships in adulthood. Patience and willpower are additional characteristics parents need to teach. Decision-making for young children can be encouraged by involvement in active games, such as Simon Says, that call for careful attention, following rules, and listening to directions. Adult-organized sports for children offer guidance about aspects of popular games but often at the child's cost of being denied practice they need in learning how to make critical decisions.

Key Concepts

1. Do not require children to express inauthentic apologies. This practice denies them the benefit of reflection. Wanting to redress a hurt we caused is a valuable quality that can emerge only when we think about our behavior and then decide to make amends.
2. Unstructured make-believe and imagination play supports self-discipline because children engage in private speech while they pretend. They talk to themselves about what they intend to do and the ways they will carry out their plans.
3. Failure to teach children self-control has damaging results. Some indicators of child self-control observed by parents, teachers, and others at 3 years of age have been found to be good predictors of health and financial status at age 32.
4. Active games like Simon Says and Freeze Tag require high levels of executive function that test a child's ability to focus attention, working memory to recall a set of rules, and demonstration of self-control, qualities that are excellent predictors of academic success.
5. Students rated high on attention-span persistence by parents at age 4 had nearly 50% greater odds of earning a bachelor's degree by age 25. Greater emphasis is needed on teaching attention and persistence skills instead of giving up because of distractions.
6. When teachers hurry to cover materials for testing, they deny students sufficient time to process information or examine strategies to consider in solving problems. As a result, hasty methods of information processing are adopted that jeopardize judgment.
7. Some reasons to tolerate frustration are that patience enables adults to accept immaturity of children, accommodate the limitations of coworkers, make allowances for personal shortcomings, and cause people to treat others with respect.
8. Lack of willpower is considered the root of such problems as consumer debt, obesity, addictions, relationship issues, and violent behavior. When people believe their wants must be met immediately, they abandon the goal of learning to manage frustrating events that require impulse control.
9. Resilience is most prevalent among 5–10-year-olds (45%). Rates of resilience then decline among higher age groups, showing the lowest levels among young adults (22%). Prevalence rates rise again among grownups age 23 and older (42%).

10. A hurried lifestyle undermines patience and willingness to delay self-gratification. It is important for adults to arrange conditions that encourage children to practice patience and learn to wait.

Generational Perspectives Activities

16.1 Discussion
16.2 Conversations With Young Children
16.3 A Scenario: Reasoning and Problem-Solving
16.4 Chapter Review
16.5 Parent and Grandparent Self-Evaluation
16.6 Storytelling

16.1 Discussion

1. What conditions do you suppose contribute to a decline in self-control and patience?
2. What have you observed about the self-control that parents exhibit for children?
3. What has your grandchild been taught about the ways s/he should express anger?
4. What situations have you observed that appear to be frustrating to young children?
5. What are the benefits and shortcomings of having adults govern children's sports?
6. Why is the lack of child attention in class such a problem reported by teachers?
7. How do families and schools contribute to frustration and impatience of children?
8. What can be done to help children delay gratification, be willing to wait for things?
9. How can patience be acquired in a society that emphasizes doing things quickly?
10. Who was the most patient person you have known and how did s/he show it?

16.2 Conversations With Young Children

1. Do you like games children organize themselves or games organized by adults?
2. Who is the most patient adult you know, and what has s/he taught you about patience?
3. Why do you talk to yourself while you are involved with pretend play?
4. How well do you pay attention when teachers are talking to students in class?
5. During class do teachers allow enough time to learn, or do you feel rushed?

16.3 A Scenario: Reasoning and Problem-Solving

Four-year-old Adam who lives down the street tells children who pass by that he owns his house, front yard, sidewalk, and everything else that is connected to his residence. Sometimes he yells and hits my grandson Lewis and other children. What should be done about Adam?

a. Tell Lewis it is ok for him to hit Adam back.
b. Talk with Adam and try to reason with him.
c. Tell Adam's parents about his misbehavior.
d. Forbid your grandchild to go by Adam's house.
e. Other _____

16.4 Chapter Review

1. What insights from the chapter will I try to apply in my relationships?
2. What is the most important key concept for me presented in this chapter?
3. What elements of this chapter do I wish I had known about earlier?

16.5 Parent and Grandparent Self-Evaluation

1. The patience I show toward others is

   a. declining as the pace of social change increases
   b. is growing because getting older brings patience
   c. influenced by technology expectations for speed
   d. poor and should improve to become more helpful
   e. Other _____

2. Situations where my self-control is lacking are

   a. having eating habits that are unhealthy
   b. becoming angry about political matters
   c. responding to drivers who do not show courtesy
   d. buying things that are beyond my budget
   e. Other _____

3. My observation is that, compared to the past, children now

   a. demonstrate less self-control
   b. demonstrate more self-control
   c. seem to be more self-centered
   d. show less concern about others
   e. Other _____

4. The frustrations of my grandchild's parents center on

   a. having to bargain with children for discipline
   b. getting children to complete assigned chores
   c. motivating a commitment to study for school
   d. interrupting the constant contact with friends
   e. Other _____

5. Self-control and patience are

   a. behaviors that I am still striving to attain
   b. qualities I have not possessed for a while
   c. unlikely achievements even at my age
   d. important goals for me to reflect on more
   e. Other _____

6. My grandchild's parents

   a. are able to accept and process negative feedback about their child
   b. take their child's side when a teacher criticizes the child's behavior
   c. deny that behavior of their child ever deserves criticism by others

d. correct child's behavior when misconduct is brought to their attention
e. Other _____

7. I believe the shift from child-directed play to adult-directed play

   a. is alright because it usually results in learning good sportsmanship
   b. ensures that kids get to play in an environment that is more safe
   c. eliminates chances for children to be decision-makers and negotiate
   d. is unreasonable since it ignores a child's need to develop self-regulation
   e. Other _____

8. I believe the more time children spend in less-structured activities

   a. the more self-directed and self-regulated they become
   b. they more often identify their goals and get to pursue them
   c. there is more boredom since adults do not tell them what to do
   d. self-control is increased because more decision-making is possible
   e. Other _____

9. I have observed that my grandchildren

   a. are learning to wait and demonstrate patience
   b. express frustration when they must wait
   c. reach premature decisions instead of reflecting
   d. get upset when they must delay gratification
   e. Other _____

10. I consider myself to be a family example of resilience

    a. always
    b. often
    c. seldom
    d. never

16.6 Storytelling

Historically, storytelling has been a dominant classic and progressive method of teaching around the world. The purposes of a storyteller are to present imaginary or real-life examples showing how some concept applies to a particular situation. People like stories, they pay attention to the procession of events, and usually remember aspects of a story for a long time. Your stories can reinforce the concepts in this chapter for family members and classmates. Please share your stories with them.

References

Barker, J. E., Semenov, A., Michaelson, L., Provan, L., Snyder, H., & Munakata, Y. (2014, June 17). Less-structured time in children's daily lives predicts self-directed executive functioning. *Frontiers in Psychology, 5*(593). https://doi.org/10.3389/fpsyg.2014.00593

Baumeister, R., & Tierney, J. (2012). *Willpower: Rediscovering the greatest human strength*. Penguin.

Casey, B. J., Somerville, L. H., Gotlib, I. H., Ayduk, O., Franklin, N. T., Askren, M. K., Jonides, J., Berman, M. G., Wilson, N. L., Teslovich, T., Glover, G., Zayas, V., Mischel, W., & Shoda, Y. (2011). Behavioral and neural correlates of delay of gratification 40 years later. *Proceedings of the*

National Academy of Sciences of the United States of America, 108(36), 14998–15003. https://doi.org/10.1073/pnas.1108561108

The Centsables. (2024). Be Centsable. *smart.com.* https://www.centables.com

Day, K. L., & Smith, C. L. (2013, 2nd Quarter). Understanding the role of private speech in children's emotion regulation. *Early Childhood Research Quarterly, 28*(2), 405–414. https://doi.org/10.1016/j.ecresq.2012.10.003

Gazzaley, A., & Rosen, L. D. (2016). *The distracted mind: Ancient brains in a high-tech world.* MIT Press.

Ginsburg, K. R., & Jablow, M. (2020). *Building resilience in children and teens: Giving kids roots and wings* (4th ed.). American Academy of Pediatrics.

Goldstein, S., & Brooks, R. (Eds.). (2023). *Handbook of resilience in children* (3rd ed.). Springer.

Greene, R. (2021). *The explosive child: A new approach for understanding and parenting easily frustrated, chronically inflexible children* (6th ed.). Harper.

Guo, X., & Dobkins, K. (2023, November). Private speech improves cognitive performance in young adults. *Consciousness and Cognition, 116.* https://doi.org/10.1016/j.concog.2023.103585

Haidt, J. (2024). *The anxious generation: How the great rewiring of childhood is causing an epidemic of mental illness.* Penguin Press.

Hari, J. (2022). *Stolen focus: Why you can't pay attention – and how to think deeply again.* Crown.

Holman, C. (2024). *The serious work that free play can do.* Bloomberg. https://www.bloomberg.com/news/articles/2024-08-20/kids-need-room-for-risky-play-enter-the-adventure-playground

Hoskyn, M., Iarocci, G., & Young, A. (Eds.). (2017). *Executive functions in children's everyday lives: A handbook for professionals in applied psychology.* Oxford University Press.

Jackson, M. (2018). *Distracted: Reclaiming our focus in a world of lost attention.* Prometheus.

Jackson, M. (2023). *Uncertain: The wisdom and wonder of being unsure.* Prometheus.

Lustig, S. (2022, May 19). *Managing stress and building resilience.* National Medical Executive Behavioral Health, Cigna. https://www.cigna.com/static/www-cigna-com/docs/may-children-and-families-handout-2022.pdf

Mark, G. (2023). *Attention span: A groundbreaking way to restore balance, happiness and productivity.* Hanover Square Press.

McClelland, M. (2019, April 29). The skills & tools of self-regulation. *Early Learning Nation.* https://earlylearningnation.com/2019/04/megan-mcclelland-the-skills-tools-of-self-regulation

McClelland, M., & Tominey, S. (Eds.). (2018). *Self-regulation and early school success.* Routledge.

Meltzer, L. (Ed.). (2018). *Executive function in education: From theory to practice* (2nd ed.). Guilford Press.

Mischel, W. (2014). *The marshmallow test: Mastering self-control.* Little, Brown & Company.

Mischel, W., & Ayduk, O. (2017). Willpower in a cognitive domain-affective processing system: The dynamics of delay of gratification. In K. Vohs & R. Baumeister (Eds.), *Handbook of self-regulation: Research, theory and application* (3rd ed.). Guilford Press.

Mischel, W., Shoda, Y., & Rodriguez, M. (1989, May 26). Delay of gratification in children. *Science, 244*(4907), 933–938. https://doi.org/10.1126/science.2658056

National Council of Youth Sports. (2024). *Every young person has a right to play sports in safety.* https://ncys.org/about-us/

Newland, R., Silver, R., Herman, R., Hartz, K., Coyne, A., & Seifer, R. (2024). Child-focused infant and early childhood mental health consultation: Shifting adult attributions to reduce the risk for preschool expulsion. *Infant Mental Health Journal, 45*(3), 249–262. https://doi.org/10.1002/imhj.22104

O'Bryan, E. M., Beadel, J. R., McLeish, A. C., & Teachman, B. A. (2021, December). Assessment of intolerance of uncertainty: Validation of a modified anagram task. *Journal of Behavior Therapy and Experimental Psychiatry, 73.* https://doi.org/10.1016/j.jbtep.2021.101671

Poulton, R., Moffitt, T., & Silva, P. (2015). The Dunedin multidisciplinary health and development study: Overview of the first 40, years with an eye to the future. *Social Psychiatry and Psychiatric Epidemiology, 50*(5), 679–693. https://doi.org/10.1007/s00127-015-1048-8

Siegel, L., & Welsh, B. (2016). *Juvenile delinquency: The core* (6th ed.). Cengage Learning.

Silver, H. C., Schoch, A. E., Loomis, A., Park, C., & Zinsser, K. (2023, January). Updating the evidence: A systematic review of a decade of infant and early childhood mental health consultation

(IECMHC) research. *Infant Mental Health Journal, 44*(1), 5–26. https://doi.org/10.1002/imhj.22033

Strom, R. D., & Strom, P. S. (2021). Recognizing and counteracting generational isolation. In M. London (Ed.), *The Oxford handbook of lifelong learning* (2nd ed., pp. 183–206). Oxford University Press.

Weinberg, R. S., & Gould, D. S. (2023). *Foundations of sport and exercise psychology* (8th ed.). Human Kinetics.

Weir, K. (2023, April 21). *How to help kids understand and manage their emotions.* American Psychological Association. https://www.apa.org/topics/parenting/emotion-regulation

Whedom, M., Perry, N., Curtis, E., & Bell, M. (2021). Private speech and the development of self-regulation: The importance of temperamental anger. *Early Childhood Research Quarterly, 56,* 213–224. https://doi.org/10.1016/j.ecresq.2021.03.013

Whitbourne, S. K. (2021, October 2). 3 ways to teach yourself to wait: There are a few tricks impatient people can learn to relax. *Psychology Today.* https://www.psychologytoday.com/us/blog/fulfillment-at-any-age/202110/3-ways-to-teach-yourself-to-wait

Winsler, A., Fernyhough, C., & Montero, I. (Eds.). (2009). *Private speech, executive function, and the development of verbal self-regulation.* Cambridge University Press.

Zelazo, P., & Carlson, S. (2020). The neurodevelopment of executive function skills: Implications for academic achievement gaps. *Psychology & Neuroscience, 13*(3), 273–298. https://doi.org/10.1037/pne0000208

Zelazo, P., & Carlson, S. (2021, March). *Minnesota Executive Function Scale, technical report.* Reflection Sciences.

Zinsser, K. M. (2023). *No longer welcome: The epidemic of expulsion from early childhood education.* Oxford University Press.

Zinsser, K. M., Silver, H. C., Shenberger, E., & Jackson, V. (2022). A systematic review of early childhood exclusionary discipline. *Review of Educational Research.* https://doi.org/10.3102/00346543211070047

Part V

The Value of Grandparents

Chapter 17

Grandparent Goals and Expectations

Some people have been identified as the "world's greatest grandmother" or the "world's greatest grandfather." Their recognition can be seen on t-shirts, hats, coffee cups, greeting cards, and car bumper stickers. Grandparents are grateful for this show of affection from their relatives. But what the elders want most is to be seen by relatives as a favorable influence. In some ways, this ambition has become easier to attain because of the extended lifespan, improved health care, more lengthy retirement, and additional opportunities for mental stimulation. New challenges have also emerged that require a new mindset for grandparents. The purposes of this chapter are to (a) describe ten goals with rationale grandparents can use as criteria to guide behavior and gauge personal effectiveness, (b) examine grandparent rights and responsibilities for family consideration, and (c) identify nontraditional practices grandparents can choose to pass on as their legacy. Generational Perspectives Activities present topics to discuss with family members and close friends about grandparent goals and expectations.

Traditions and Needs for New Goals

Worldwide Grandparent Populations

The United States Census Bureau estimates that the number of grandparents in the United States is 70 million (Anderson et al., 2024). This is a larger population than the total number of students who attend preschool through colleges and universities. *The Economist* (2023a) reported the age of the grandparent has arrived across the globe. The ratio of grandparents to children is higher than ever in history, a fact with big consequences. Alburetz Gutierrez of the Max Planch Institute for Demographic Research estimated for *the Economist* that there are 1.5 billion grandparents, a figure that will rise to 2.1 billion by the year 2050. Interestingly, the number of grandparents varies by nation with high numbers of grandparents in countries with lower fertility rates and longer life expectancies. For example, grandparents make up 29% of the population in Bulgaria with a fertility rate of 1.75 and life expectancy rate of 75.80 years. In contrast, grandparents are only 10% of the population in Burundi, a country in East Africa with a fertility rate of 4.79 and life expectancy rate of 63.82 years (Worldometers, 2024).

Reliance on Social Security

In 1935, the United States Congress enacted legislation to establish Social Security (Social Security Administration, 2024). This historic document was signed by President Theodore

Roosevelt. At that time the average American lifespan was 55 years. So most retirees collected benefits for only a short time. In contrast, people now, on average, can expect to live two decades longer than they did in 1960 (*The Economist*, 2023b). In 2024, life expectancy for the United States was 79.46 years (Worldometers, 2024). People are generally thankful for this gift of additional years, but they realize the benefit also means it is necessary to decide how to use the increased time and depend on income from Social Security. Most women initially become grandparents when they are 50 years old. This means they have greater opportunities than previous generations to provide affection, care, and guidance to grandchildren, from birth until the years of young adulthood. Many grandparents will live long enough to know great grandchildren (Westrick-Payne, 2023a, 2023b).

Goal 1. Reinforce Goals of Parents for Their Children

The erosion of traditions has resulted in an ambiguous role for most grandparents. They want to think well of themselves but find it difficult because this requires pursuit of a poorly defined function. Establishing a role means setting goals, pursuing a course of direction, and periodically evaluating progress. Unless grandparents try to fulfill responsibilities, they cannot claim to succeed in attaining them. So this is the dilemma of modern grandparents – they want to succeed but lack a set of rights and responsibilities to use as criteria for self-evaluation (Strom & Strom, 2021).

When Margaret was invited by Amy to attend a weekly class for grandparents, she said, "Why should I take a class on how to be a grandparent because it just comes naturally to me. I raised three children who all became successful, so I must have known something." Margaret is right. Raising three children to be responsible adults is a significant accomplishment. However, being a good parent does not ensure a person will later become a good grandparent. One reason is because other relatives should be involved in defining the expectations of grandparents. The goals parents have for raising children should be the most important ones to guide the behavior of grandparents. When grandparents understand parent goals, they can reinforce lessons the parents want taught. This information is not revealed by intuition; it does not come naturally (Strom & Strom, 1991b, 2018a, 2018b).

On the contrary, what seems to come naturally is enthusiasm for a relationship with the grandchildren that focuses mostly on entertainment, with less attention given to being a partner with parents. Doing what comes naturally often means not paying attention to responsibilities. Grandparents who believe their purpose in the family is to fulfill the wishes of grandchildren may unintentionally support selfishness, egocentrism, narcissism, and self-absorption. Being able to help children take necessary steps toward growing up by considering the needs of others is an important contribution to personality development. Grandparents can support parent plans only when they are informed of their intentions. Some grandparents say, "I don't want to interfere in my children's lives; they should be allowed to raise their daughters and sons the same way I did." Yet grandparents are bound to interfere when they misunderstand or ignore the goals of their grandchild's parents. The grandparent role must be first and foremost based on establishing a supportive partnership with parents (Strom & Strom, 1997, 2018a, 2018b).

Grandparents sometimes disagree with some of the current parenting practices, especially those that appear to contradict the ones they followed while bringing up their children. It should be recognized that, as the process of growing up evolves in response to changing conditions, some corresponding shifts are necessary in the way parents fulfill their guidance role. When grandparents know how the middle generation sees its responsibilities, they are more informed, less critical, and better prepared to help.

Grandparents often underestimate the contribution they could make to the socialization of grandchildren. When they are asked whether being a grandparent is easier or more difficult than anticipated, their usual response is that being a grandparent is easier and less demanding because parents have all the responsibility. In contrast, we have not found mothers or fathers who reported that being a parent is easy. One observation is the responsibility for raising children has become disproportionate, with many grandparents deciding to remove themselves from any obligations. Certainly, there are exceptions when grandparents carry a heavy load and become the main source of supervision and instruction to raise their grandchildren alone. About 6.7 million grandparents live with a grandchild, and one-third of those are responsible for childcare (Buck et al., 2024). Still, there is a significant difference between being mainly responsible for grandchildren and the more common practice of non-involvement. Sharing obligations for nurturing grandchildren seems most appropriate.

Goal 2. Families Should Define the Grandparent Role Together

Many people go through life without finding out what their relatives expect of them. The grandparent role can become clearer when it is defined with other family members. Realize that grandparents are only one of the parties who are involved in determining their relationship with relatives. Rights and responsibilities that are identified in cooperation with relatives can become a guide for grandparents to evaluate their success. Use Tables 17.1 and 17.2 to identify your own rights and responsibilities and include the opinions of your sons, daughters, and/or in-laws (Strom & Strom, 1991a).

(1) Look at Table 17.1 and Table 17.2.
(2) Use a pencil to circle the G (for Grandparent responses) beside the Rights in Table 17.1 and the Responsibilities in Table 17.2 you feel are acceptable.
(3) Ask your son, daughter, and/or in-laws to share their opinions by circling the P (for Parent responses) beside those items in the Rights and Responsibilities Tables 17.1 and 17.2 they think are appropriate for you.
(4) Discuss the Rights and Responsibilities items that clarify family agreements and those where there may be disagreements. Through this process of sharing, you and your relatives can identify reasonable expectations and make known the mutually acceptable aspects of your role.

Table 17.1 Rights of Grandparents

As a grandparent, I would like the right to		
1. Hear from my grandchildren on a regular basis	GP	P
2. Spend some time alone with my grandchildren	GP	P
3. Pursue my own personal interest and hobbies	GP	P
4. Say 'no' when requests are made for babysitting	GP	P
5. Participate in special events of grandchildren	GP	P
6. Give advice to my sons and daughters	GP	P
7. Give advice to my grandchildren	GP	P

(*Continued*)

Table 17.1 (Continued)

As a grandparent, I would like the right to		
8. Be informed of grandchild's problems and successes	GP	P
9. Know the school progress of my grandchildren	GP	P
10. Maintain rules of my home during family visits	GP	P
11. See grandchildren if there is a divorce	GP	P
12. Express my religious and moral point of view	GP	P
13. Discuss financial needs of family members	GP	P
14. Talk about things that are right and wrong	GP	P
15. Choose a lifestyle of my own preference	GP	P
16. Expect reasonable assistance from my family	GP	P
17. Know the parenting goals of my sons/daughters	GP	P
18. Encourage grandchildren to spend their time wisely	GP	P
19. Help care for grandchildren when there is a crisis	GP	P
20. Get acquainted with the parents of my grandchild's peers	GP	P

Source: Adapted from *Becoming a Better Grandparent: A Guidebook for Strengthening the Family*, by R. D. Strom and S. K. Strom (1991a), Sage, p. 24. Copyright © 1991 by R. D. Strom & S. K. Strom.

Goal 3. Express Your Feelings, Opinions, and Concerns

We asked grandparents and their grandchildren about the closeness of their relationship. Generally, older adults portrayed the bond as much closer than was reported by grandchildren. This difference occurs in part because children are more willing to share opinions and feelings. As people age, many of them find it difficult to talk about their emotions, or they refuse to communicate personal feelings. When grandparents fail to make their views known, they forfeit the give-and-take dialogue with grandchildren that could help them see things in new ways and change their minds about ideas, events, and situations (Jackson, 2023).

Table 17.2 Responsibilities of Grandparents

As a grandparent, I would like the responsibility to		
1. Acquaint grandchildren with their parents' childhood	GP	P
2. Share family history and traditions	GP	P
3. Give advice to sons/daughters	GP	P
4. Give advice to grandchildren	GP	P
5. Provide an example of religious faith	GP	P
6. Cooperate with my grandchildren's other grandparents	GP	P
7. Keep learning for personal improvement	GP	P
8. Find out my grandchildren's views and feelings	GP	P
9. Care for grandchildren if their parents cannot do so	GP	P
10. Use leisure time in constructive ways	GP	P
11. Set rules for my family when they visit	GP	P
12. Share financial resources with grandchildren	GP	P
13. Communicate regularly with my grandchildren	GP	P
14. Be an example of personal resilience	GP	P
15. Support good time management	GP	P
16. Be honest about my feelings and needs	GP	P
17. Reinforce the parenting goals of my sons/daughters	GP	P
18. Encourage grandchildren to value creativity	GP	P
19. Understand goals of individual grandchildren	GP	P
20. Encourage grandchildren to always tell the truth	GP	P

Source: Adapted from *Becoming a Better Grandparent: A Guidebook for Strengthening the Family*, by R. D. Strom and S. K. Strom (1991a), Sage, p. 25. Copyright © 1991 by R. D. Strom & S. K. Strom.

Ralph is a grandfather who wants to start a new tradition because he could see that some customs are changing for the better. He said:

> I cannot recall my grandfather ever saying, 'I love you, Ralph.' Instead, he was stern, serious, and avoided showing any signs of affection. On the other hand, my 14-year-old grandson Darin often tells me when we are together, on the phone, using email or text, 'I love you Grandpa.' I am grateful to Darin for teaching me this valuable lesson.

Relationships also suffer when grandparents establish a reputation for intolerance of how other people feel or interpret things. Eleanor learned this the hard way. After spending a week with her son's family, Eleanor woke up early and saw 4-year-old Joyce playing in the backyard sandbox. As they talked, Joyce mentioned, "Grandma, I have to be good for only two more days." Eleanor asked, "Why is that?" Joyce said, "Because that's when you go home." Some families do not behave in a normal manner when grandparents visit. There is a concerted effort to put on a performance because it is assumed grandparents are unable to accept family behavior that has become typical. Parents explain that a temporary suspension of their routine is easier than for grandparents to accommodate a different lifestyle than their own. The result of this charade is that grandparents are misled, not expected to adjust, and learning does not occur (Strom & Strom, 2020).

Goal 4. Get to Know Each Grandchild as an Individual

There is general agreement that individuality is an attribute that adults should encourage. Nevertheless, there are many households in which siblings are expected to behave alike, express the same interests, and achieve the same level of competence at school. When adults hold up the performance of an older sibling as the standard to judge success of younger ones, children can develop resentment toward brothers and sisters they are supposed to resemble. "Your brother excelled in mathematics and science, so why do you experience difficulty with these subjects." This remark can jeopardize self-esteem and prevent the friendship, mutual pride, and encouragement brothers and sisters should enjoy throughout life. It is satisfying to observe homes where siblings feel no pressure to compete with each other, and every brother and sister knows that s/he is accepted as an individual.

Sometimes this comment can be heard – "She is one of a kind." This suggests someone is recognized as unique and possesses attributes that distinguish her from others. Every grandchild should be seen in this way. However, some grandparents deny individuality by saying, "I want to be fair and not play favorites, so I treat all my grandchildren the same way." Instead, if the goal is to demonstrate equality, then it becomes wise to identify, accept, and encourage differences in talent, interest, and motivation of grandchildren. When grandchildren are seen as individuals, they can have a greater impact on grandparents and motivate greater efforts to remain in touch (Strom & Strom, 2019).

One of the joys grandparents experience is building a relationship with each grandchild. This goal can become more difficult as grandchildren increase in number. There is no merit in counting them as if they were status symbols by announcing, "I have 4 grandchildren; another person says I have 6, or 10 or 12 grandchildren." What matters is that an individual grandchild is well known and so it becomes possible to support that child's self-esteem, distinctiveness, personal goals, and provide feedback about progress in growing up (Samuel, 2017).

Goal 5. Consider Grandchildren as Sources of Learning

Social change enables new traditions to support better relationships between generations. Grandparents admit that getting to know grandchildren can be difficult for them. This lack of knowledge can be costly because young people tend to seek advice and guidance from adults they believe understand their struggles, goals, doubts, and concerns. It is poor reasoning to identify grandparents as the most mature relatives but nullify their potential by failing to keep them informed about experiences of younger relatives. If grandchildren believe the meager information grandparents have about them is sufficient, it means that older relatives are no longer considered valued sources of advice. This conclusion further supports role ambiguity by assigning grandparents an honorific status without a sense of purpose, function, or meaning (Schulte, 2014, 2019).

There is a related obstacle for consideration. Mary described this common problem (Strom & Strom, 1991b, p. 53).

> I don't like it when my daughter and son-in-law act as reporters about my grandchildren. They tell me all the good things that are happening, achievements at school, victories on sports teams, and other ways my grandchildren perform well. Disappointing child events or failures are never mentioned even though my grandchildren certainly must have such experiences too. The difficult side of life is never communicated to me because parents suppose I need to be proud and avoid worries. However, it is more important to me that I be accurately informed. I want to encourage my grandchildren when they face hard times; that is when I am needed most but cannot respond if all I get is favorable news. I cannot become a listener or source of guidance when every report is 'Just fine grandma'. My grandchildren must wonder sometimes if I even care to console them.

Partial or biased reporting can prevent grandparents from knowing what is happening and denies the opportunity to support the resilience children need when it is time to overcome failure (Goldstein & Brooks, 2024). Parents' reports that exclude the difficulties of grandchildren cause some grandparents to suppose that growing up at the present time must be relatively easy and free of worries or stress. This situation reflects how the grandparent role is defined in some families. Grandparents may want to question why relatives do not take them into their confidence. Even friends share more with each other than reports of their good times. Grandparents should tell relatives they want to hear directly from grandchildren. Grandchildren are expected to speak for themselves by phone, email, texting, or visiting – without parents being family messengers or interpreters.

Parents should tell their children grandparents want to be helpful but are unable to offer worthwhile advice unless they are well-informed. Grandchildren who share experiences acquaint older relatives with complexities of growing up and stimulate involvement in family problem-solving. Individual grandchildren will decide the extent to which they share feelings, but willingness almost always is increased when grandparents show a similar readiness to share the highs they find satisfying and the lows they struggle to overcome (Anderson et al., 2024).

Goal 6. Expect to Be Included in the Grandchild Schedule

We asked members of a grandparent class this question: What responsibilities do you expect of your grandchildren? Alice, one of the grandparents said:

> I don't feel my grandchildren should have any obligations toward me. Then Alice was asked, "How can your grandchildren become responsible if you deny them a sense of obligation to their family? When grandchildren are expected to show concern for loved ones, they are more likely to grow up with caring attitudes." Linda expressed her point of view, "When I think about obligations of my grandchildren, I would like them to show compassion to me when I am sick or don't feel well." The lady next to Linda asked, "How do the grandchildren who live far away know the times when you don't feel well?" Linda admitted they probably could not know because she does not tell them, supposing it might cause them to worry.

But, just as grandparents want to know when grandchildren are discouraged and need emotional support, younger relatives should be aware when grandparents are depressed and need some cheering up. Mutual self-disclosure and being able to count on one another is the basis for a close relationship (Strom & Strom, 2018a, 2018b).

Many children are as busy as their parents, trying to juggle time schedules packed with activities including after-school programs, soft ball practice, tutoring, and drama (Schulte, 2014, 2019). The scope of overscheduling is reflected by two little girls standing at the bus stop, each clutching their personal planner. One girl said: "Okay, I will move my ballet practice back an hour, reschedule gymnastics, and cancel piano while you shift your violin lessons to Thursday and skip soccer practice – that will give us from 3:15 to 4:15 on Wednesday the 16th to just play together." Finding time for relatives often depends on the availability of grandchild schedules.

Parents can tell their children they have a responsibility to stay in touch with grandparents and keep them informed about what is going on in their lives. If this connection is not in place, grandparents should ask daughters and sons about flexibility of a grandchild's schedule and question why they are left out of the schedule. Taking this action eliminates the otherwise likely prospect of being assigned the role of a cheerleader whose only expectation is to be present to observe grandchildren when they participate in competitive situations (Strom & Strom, 2020).

Goal 7. Share Optimism and Resilience for Mental Health

The optimism and resilience of children often reminds us that we should demonstrate the same attitudes (Goldstein & Brooks, 2024; Lustig, 2022). Hernandez et al. (2015) studied 5,134 adults aged 52 to 84. Those in the highest quartile of optimism were more likely to have intermediate and ideal cardiovascular health when compared to the least optimistic group. Individual cardiovascular health metrics of diet, physical activity, body mass index, smoking, blood sugar, and total cholesterol were found to contribute to the overall association.

An example of optimism between the generations is shown by Betty and her grandson Justin. Betty stopped by the apartment of her recently divorced son who was awarded custody of Justin, his 7-year-old boy. Betty came early to pick up Justin knowing it might require some effort to get him ready for church the following morning. Betty explained:

> My plan was to buy him some new shoes and get a haircut. I felt confident that whatever else he might need would be in the large sack of dirty laundry I took from his room and brought home to wash. Then a discovery – there was no underwear in the pile I was going to wash, not even one pair." "There were no undershorts in the laundry, Justin," I said while heading to the bathroom. "I'll wash those you have on while you take a shower and get ready for bed." "But I don't have undershorts on, Grandma," he explained. There haven't been any undershorts in my drawer all week, so I just didn't wear any." "You mean you went to school all week without underwear?" I asked while scrambling to think of stores that might be open at 9:30 on Saturday night. "Don't worry grandma," Justin said, "My pants are real thick, and tomorrow no one is going to know I don't have underwear on except you and me." So we went to church with no one knowing but us.

Betty's willingness to share Justin's sense of possibility, to make the best of an undesirable situation, was a good way to handle it. She later took steps to make certain more underwear would be available, and this was done without undermining the boy's respect for his father (Strom & Strom, 1991b).

Attitudes qualify or disqualify the people children choose as sources of emotional support. Whether grandparents are optimistic or pessimistic, these attitudes are a significant aspect of their legacy. More is involved than just a difference in point of view. Think about optimism and pessimism as explanatory styles people rely on to interpret troublesome situations. Kellerman and Seligman (2023) have determined that optimists do better in the classroom and at the workplace because they cheerfully persist when faced with setbacks while pessimists with equal ability choose to withdraw or give up. From middle age on (age 40), pessimists have weaker immune systems, higher incidence of infectious diseases, greater health issues, are more likely to feel depressed, and less able to generate resilience that is needed to recover from times of trouble. Pessimists are also uncomfortable to be around. These findings urge grandparents to adopt optimism as a basic attitude toward life, relationships, and daily affairs challenges.

If the grandparent role, especially in middle class White families, continues to decline in importance, many children will lose a potentially valuable resource while grandparents become more vulnerable to the outlook that life lacks purpose, meaning, and opportunity for influence. The aging process leads to physical and psychological limitations that commonly motivate negative self-impressions. An important insight is to realize that if grandchildren are continually exposed to pessimism, they can lose the creative capacity to see possibilities, including their own happiness. Being able to observe optimistic grandparents gives a favorable outlook children need to shape their future (Goldstein & Brooks, 2024).

Goal 8. Demonstrate Your Values as a Sign of Maturity

Generativity is defined as being a reduction of self-concern in favor of caring also about the well-being and satisfaction of others, providing help when it seems needed. This commitment was illustrated by Julia. After her children moved to Auburn, Alabama, they asked her to leave Dallas, Texas, and join them. Now she has an 8-, 6-, and 4-year-old to pick up from school and to supervise every day. Her children are pleased and grateful. Some people do not see the benefits of such maturity. One man attending the Strom grandparent class said:

> I can't figure out what's up with these empty nesters? Our children live in Florida, so we visit often. My wife is there now, taking care of two preschoolers while their parents are at work. Some of her friends do the same thing. I told her this is not the retirement lifestyle I planned. Do you understand the empty nesters?"

As leaders of the grandparent class, we replied that grandchildren are preschoolers for only a short time. They and their parents are fortunate to have a grandmother willing to assign high priority to their needs. Providing some reprieve for a relative from their daily tasks can be a valued gift, remembered by the parents and children as well.

The financial cost of group care for young children is higher than older adults suppose and presents a challenge for families. There are 11 million American children younger than 5 enrolled in some form of day care. In many states the annual price of group care is greater than a full year's tuition at a four-year college (Child Care Aware® of America, 2024). Recognize older adults (age 50+) have the AARP organization as an advocate that continually looks out for their welfare. Parents of young children are wondering if they should organize themselves since other age groups seem unconcerned about their obligation of raising the United States's youngest children.

Goal 9. Encourage Gender Equity Among Relatives

People are grateful for microwave ovens and dishwashers. However, there is still a need for grandmothers and grandfathers, mothers, and fathers, whether employed or retired, to more often share domestic chores. It seems clear that such a shift does not come easily for many older men who continue to be comfortable having grandmothers do all the housework. In these families, women take care of the home with little help from husbands. Grandfathers should engage in household tasks because it helps their wives and allows younger relatives to observe them as a constructive influence. In contrast, if grandfathers maintain traditional expectations for division of labor, their grandchildren are likely to dismiss them as sources of advice regarding gender relationships. Children are oriented to becoming a more equitable model of how families should cooperate. The lesson media, schools, classmates, and parents teach is there should be gender equality for girls and boys. Accordingly, children do not like to see grandma do all the cooking, shopping, washing, ironing, and housecleaning herself without help from grandfather. They interpret this as gender inequity and are reluctant to view grandfather in the way he wishes to be seen (Amigoni & McMullan, 2019).

More is involved than husbands who resist change. Attitudes of wives are implicated too. When husbands first try to do household tasks, the initial performance is unlikely to approach the standard held by their wives. Instead of expressing the judgment "you're hopeless in the kitchen," or "it's easier to do the job myself," wives should try to use responses that are more motivating. By demonstrating several times how to do a task, providing constructive feedback, encouraging another try after making a mistake, and offering favorable comments when there is a positive outcome, grandmothers help grandfathers share the load and act as a good example of mutual support in married life. Fairness is a value that has high priority among young people. Franz de Waal (2017) at Emory University shows what happens when monkeys experience a lack of fairness. [See www.TED.com – Moral behavior in animals]

Goal 10. Continue Learning to Ensure Self-Improvement

Grandparents who attend our classes are sometimes asked to describe their motivation for participation. Esther said:

> When my daughter and 9-year-old granddaughter heard I was going to take a grandparent education class, they told me, 'Grandma, you don't need to enroll in a course. We love you just the way you are.' These comments were meant to be a compliment, so Esther replied, 'I'm glad you feel I am successful but realize too that learning remains necessary at my age. I have to understand changes that are taking place and what these shifts mean for me so that I can adjust along with the rest of the family. Education is a key to my adjustment. So, encourage me to grow; I will appreciate it more than being told I do not need to learn.'

Esther took the initiative to establish appropriate expectations for personal development. She resembles others who have been told by peers who are unmotivated to learn or relatives who say, "Your behavior is acceptable to us, so you don't have to enroll in a grandparent course." Despite good intentions that are a basis for such remarks, they reveal other people do not recognize that by learning, a grandparent can become more successful. In effect, they underestimate the potential for self-improvement. The challenge for this generation is to establish an innovative and higher standard for learning than was the case in previous generations (Strom & Strom, 2020).

Conclusion

When younger relatives encourage grandparents to pursue further education, older adults should interpret this response as expression of confidence in their ability to learn. Grandparents can understand that loved ones want them to be an example for all family members showing that continued learning is essential for adjustment. Parents and children should let grandparents know they expect them to show a commitment to personal development, devote time to family, offer guidance to younger relatives, and demonstrate concern for the community. When grandparents are expected to be involved, they feel a sense of purpose and are more likely to continue helping the family and society.

The grandparent role presents some people with an unexpected loss of purpose, lack of direction, and need for guidance to figure out how to be a favorable influence in their family. The possibility of being seen as an informed family advisor increases by knowing about current challenges, concepts, and joys associated with bringing up children. Attending classes on child development, reading self-help books for parents, joining discussion groups, and volunteering in schools can improve understanding about growing up. These sources provide general knowledge.

Each grandparent should have conversations with their adult children to find out the specific goals they are trying to achieve in raising daughters and sons. The challenge to stay in touch with grandchildren is essential because these interactions are the best context for discovering the goals, worries, and satisfactions of individual grandchildren. The bond between grandparents and grandchildren is stronger when reciprocal learning is a goal since it motivates adults to listen and become willing to self-disclose so they can be better known. Many families are fragile and find it difficult to endure the levels of stress they encounter. Resilience is needed to manage the growing range of pressures that can jeopardize mental health. Each generation has an obligation to collaborate in attaining this goal. The grandparent role can be defined using ten goals to guide expectations of them so they can become a more favorable influence in the family.

Key Concepts

1. Maintain an optimistic attitude. The way grandparents see others and interpret situations is an important aspect of current influence and future legacy. By focusing on possibilities of people and events more than on limitations, you can exemplify a positive perspective that supports mental health and builds resilience when there are setbacks to be overcome.
2. Couples should adjust to social change. Women and men who accept social change are viewed as living in the present and considered as sources of advice. More grandparents should consider how changes in gender role expectations implicate their own behavior. By sharing household tasks, grandfathers reduce the workload of grandmothers, grow as individuals, and qualify themselves as an example of adjustment for younger people.
3. Broaden your goals for self-improvement. Physical exercise, travel, playing games, and having hobbies are worthwhile activities. Some time should also be devoted to education about your family role. By balancing what you want to learn with things you need to know, you can become a more favorable influence in the family.
4. Raise your expectations of peers. Grandparents should establish high standards for their peer group. These expected norms should include commitment to personal development and concern for welfare of others demonstrated by volunteering and taking an active part in community affairs to support a better future for everyone.
5. Goal setting is essential for success. Defining the grandparent role in cooperation with my relatives clarifies expectations, offers a sense of direction, and determines my priorities. Grandparents can judge personal progress better *when self-evaluation is focused on* how well goals set previously are met. Children and grandchildren should be asked for feedback.
6. Treat grandchildren as individuals. When grandchildren are treated as individuals, they can have a greater impact on you, cause you to understand them better, and stimulate you to keep in touch with them. Resolve to experience joys and difficulties of getting to know each grandchild as a separate person and make sure that you self-disclose so they can know you better as well.
7. The grandparent role should be based on reinforcing goals that guide a grandchild's parents. Having a partnership with parents is more likely when their education plans for children are understood and accepted by grandparents.
8. Communicate directly with grandchildren. Personal relationships are closer when they do not depend on third party involvement. In the presence of the entire family, indicate you want to hear from grandchildren directly instead of being given second-hand reports by their parents.

9. Accept your share of responsibility. Grandparents have less obligation to raise grandchildren. Recognizing this difference does not mean grandparents should underestimate their task. When grandparents define their role as being easy, it is usually because they have not accepted enough responsibility.
10. Grandchildren should feel responsible to keep grandparents informed about what is going on in their lives including pleasant and disappointing events. If grandchildren do not keep in touch, grandparents will not know when their emotional support is needed and are less likely to be seen as a source of advice, encouragement, and comfort.

Generational Perspectives Activities

17.1 Discussion
17.2 Conversations With Young Children
17.3 A Scenario: Reasoning and Problem-Solving
17.4 Chapter Review
17.5 Parent and Grandparent Self-Evaluation
17.6 Storytelling

17.1 Discussion

1. How are the obligations of parents different from what they were in the past?
2. What are some behaviors of parents that you have observed and admire?
3. What methods of raising children do relatives apply that disappoint you?
4. What is most satisfying about the adult-child relationships in your family?
5. What should parents teach children to expect from their grandparents?
6. What feedback do you give parents that they perform well in their role?
7. In what ways are parents more successful now than people in the past?
8. What should grandchildren be taught about obligations to grandparents?
9. What changes do you foresee in what families will expect of grandparents?
10. How is being a grandparent easier or more difficult than in previous times?

17.2 Conversations With Young Children

1. What do you talk about with your grandparents?
2. What things do your grandparents like most about you?
3. What things do you like to do with your grandparents?
4. How often do you get to visit with your grandparents?

17.3 Scenario for Problem-Solving

Jim is a grandparent who wants grandparent education for his community.

a. Encourage him to make his case to the city council.
b. Ask school principals to see if faculty would volunteer.
c. Ask the ecumenical conference of ministers to look into it.
d. Identify a couple of retired volunteers willing to help.
e. Other _____

17.4 Chapter Review

1. What insights from the chapter will I try to apply in my relationships?
2. What is the most important key concept for me presented in this chapter?
3. What elements of this chapter do I wish I had known about earlier?

17.5 Parent and Grandparent Self-Evaluation

1. My personal example for relatives

    a. should always be to demonstrate optimism
    b. can reflect social norms of my same-age peers
    c. should reflect concerns for the well-being of others
    d. can illustrate my goal of self-improvement
    e. Other _____

2. Defining my goals as a grandparent

    a. should include input from other relatives
    b. is for me alone to decide
    c. depends on our family traditions
    d. should alter based on social trends
    e. Other _____

3. I feel an obligation to keep grandchildren continuously informed

    a. about the conditions of my mental and physical health
    b. regarding my will and what will be left to each relative
    c. only about matters they ask me for an explanation
    d. regarding my expectations for each of them
    e. Other _____

4. I want grandchildren to understand how I feel about

    a. gender equity in performing household tasks
    b. equality in how our entire family defines itself
    c. equal educational opportunities for females
    d. the unfairness of relationships in our family
    e. Other _____

5. As more grandparents live longer,

    a. it seems fair that more be expected of them
    b. they should establish constructive norms
    c. they should be given community service options
    d. their Social Security should be tied to their wealth
    e. Other _____

6. Education for grandparents

    a. should be mandatory as education is for children
    b. should require family performance evaluation
    c. should be led by local higher education officials

    d. should acknowledge their individual needs
    e. Other _____

7. Grandchildren should participate in grandparent education by

    a. sharing information about the norms of their peer group
    b. asking questions about grandparent lifestyle
    c. providing reactions to grandparent ambitions
    d. offering recommendations to grandparents
    e. Other _____

17.6 Storytelling

Historically, storytelling has been a dominant classic and progressive method of teaching around the world. The purposes of a storyteller are to present imaginary or real-life examples showing how some concept applies to a particular situation. People like stories, they pay attention to the procession of events, and usually remember aspects of a story for a long time. Your stories can reinforce the concepts in this chapter for family members and classmates. Please share your stories with them.

References

Amigoni, D., & McMullan, G. (Eds.). (2019). *Creativity in later life: Beyond late style*. Routledge.

Anderson, L. R., Buck, C., & Hayward, G. M. (2024, February). *Grandparents and their coresident grandchildren: 2021*. United States Census Bureau. https://www2.census.gov/library/publications/2024/demo/p20-588.pdf

Buck, C., Hayward, G. M., & Anderson, L. R. (2024, March 19). *Grandparents living with grandchildren*. United States Census Bureau. https://www.census.gov/library/stories/2024/03/grandparents-living-with-grandchildren.html

Child Care Aware® of America. (2024, May 15). *New findings: Child care prices continue to rise as supply remains stagnant*. https://info.childcareaware.org/media/new-findings-child-care-prices-continue-to-rise-as-supply-remains-stagnant

de Waal, F. (2017). *Are we smart enough to know how smart animals are?* W. W. Norton.

The Economist. (2023a, January 12). *The age of the grandparent has arrived*. https://www.economist.com/international/2023/01/12/the-age-of-the-grandparent-has-arrived

The Economist. (2023b, January 16). *The glory of grandparents: Why the soaring number of grandmas and grandpas is a good thing*. https://www.economist.com/leaders/2023/01/16/the-glory-of-grandparents

Goldstein, S., & Brooks, R. B. (Eds.). (2024). *Handbook of resilience in children* (3rd ed.). Springer.

Hernandez, R., Kershaw, K., Siddique, J., Boehm, J. K., Kubzansky, L., Diez-Roux, A., Ning, H., & Lloyd-Jones, D. (2015, January). Optimism and cardiovascular health: Multi-ethnic study of atherosclerosis (MESA). *Human Behavior and Policy Review, 2*(1), 62–73. https://doi.org/10.14485/HBPR.2.1.6

Jackson, M. (2023). *Uncertain: The wisdom and wonder of being unsure*. Prometheus.

Kellerman, G., & Seligman, M. (2023). *Tomorrowmind: Thriving at work with resilience, creativity, and connection – now and in an uncertain future*. Simon & Schuster.

Lustig, S. (2022, May 19). *Managing stress and building resilience*. Cigna. https://www.cigna.com/static/www-cigna-com/docs/may-children-and-families-handout-2022.pdf

Samuel, L. (2017). *Aging in America: A cultural history*. University of Pennsylvania Press.

Schulte, B. (2014). *Overwhelmed work, love, and play when no one has the time*. Farrar, Straus and Giroux.

Schulte, B. (2019, July 21). A woman's greatest enemy? A lack of time to herself. *The Guardian*. https://www.theguardian.com/commentisfree/2019/jul/21/woman-greatest-enemy-lack-of-time-themselves

Social Security Administration. (2024). *Social Security history: Text of the 1935 Social Security Act.* https://www.ssa.gov/history/index.html

Strom, R. D., & Strom, S. K. (1991a). *Becoming a better grandparent: A guidebook for strengthening the family.* Sage.

Strom, R. D., & Strom, S. K. (1991b). *Becoming a better grandparent: Viewpoints on strengthening the family.* Sage.

Strom, R. D., & Strom, S. K. (1997). Building a theory of grandparent development. *International Journal of Aging and Human Development, 45*(4), 255–286. https://doi.org/10.2190/HAVE-HWKU-6BCG-9EY5

Strom, R. D., & Strom, P. S. (2018a). Education for grandparents in longevity societies. *Journal of Adult and Continuing Education, 24*(2), 208–228. https://doi.org/10.1177/1477971418810652

Strom, R. D., & Strom, S. K. (2018b). Raising expectations for grandparents: A three generational study. In J. Hendricks (Ed.), *The ties of later life* (pp. 133–139). Routledge.

Strom, P. S., & Strom, R. D. (2019). Grandparent education: Curriculum, instruction, and evaluation. In B. Hayslip & C. A. Fruhauf (Eds.), *Grandparent: Influence on the dynamics of family relationships* (pp. 331–346). Springer.

Strom, R. D., & Strom, P. S. (2020). Productive aging: Peer influence and retirement. *Educational Gerontology, 46*(11), 678–687. https://doi.org/10.1080/03601277.2020.1807085

Strom, R. D., & Strom, P. S. (2021). Learning throughout life about the needs of all generations: Recognizing and counteracting generational isolation. In M. London (Ed.), *The Oxford handbook of lifelong learning* (2nd ed., pp. 183–206). https://doi.org/10.1093/oxfordhb/9780197506707.013.9

Westrick-Payne, K. K. (2023a). *Prevalence of grandparenthood in the U.S., 2021. Family profile, FP-23-02.* National Center for Family & Marriage Research. https://doi.org/10.25035/ncfmr/fp-23-01

Westrick-Payne, K. K. (2023b). *Grandparents' characteristics by age. Family profile, FP-18-04.* National Center for Family & Marriage Research. https://www.bgsu.edu/ncfmr/resources/data/family-profiles/westrick-payne-grandparents-characteristics-age-fp-23-02.html

Worldometers. (2024, November 6). *Current world population.* https://www.worldometers.info/world-population/#google_vignette

Chapter 18

Grandparents Raising Their Grandchildren

The mission of the U.S. Department of Health and Human Services is to identify, promote, coordinate, and disseminate information about resources and best practices to help relative caregivers meet health, education, nutrition, and other child needs as well as pay attention to their own physical and emotional well-being (Goyer, 2021). The United States Congress passed the Support Grandparents Raising Grandchildren Act (2018) which established a federal advisory council to support grandparents and other non-parent relatives who raise children.

The purposes of this chapter are to (a) examine goals shared by successful grandparent surrogates, (b) explain why the goals of many grandparent caregivers must expand to become more relevant, (c) identify ways growing up has changed since grandparents raised their own sons and daughters, (d) suggest methods to cooperate with a parent who is expected to share some responsibility for childcare, (e) learn about community social services that are available, (f) explain the benefits, limitations, and procedures for operating grandparent support groups, and (g) emphasize the need for periodic relief of grandparents from their demanding caregiver role. Generational Perspectives Activities present topics to discuss with family members and close friends about grandparents raising their grandchildren.

Scope of the Challenge

Grandparent Commitment

Grandparents have always assumed responsibility for raising their grandchildren in cases of family tragedy such as death of a parent, divorce, separation, or abandonment of a child. Other conditions motivating full-time care of grandchildren in the United States are helping unmarried adolescent mothers, parent loss of employment, or a need to have free childcare and supervision. Many parents are suffering from addiction to drugs (Baime, 2024). Jones et al. (2024) estimated that, in the past decade, 321,566 American children lost a parent to drug overdose. Other parents abuse their sons and daughters, some are deployed overseas by the military, put in jail because of crimes, or show evidence of mental illness. In addition, some single parents are unable to provide all the care that their children need (Tracy et al., 2021).

In the United States in 2021, 2.74 million children were being raised by grandparents (Anderson et al., 2024; United States Department of Labor, 2024). The number of grandparents raising grandchildren was 2.07 million. Grandfamilies & Kinship Support Network (2022), a research and advocacy group, reports 45% of grandparent caregivers are over the age of 60, and 26% have a disability. Estimates are that childcare collectively provided by American grandparents saves taxpayers $4 billion a year. Tracy et al. (2021) pointed out grandparents typically do not apply for legal custody since this means having to take their adult children to court. Few grandparents become licensed foster care parents or legal guardians. This makes them ineligible for certain services and economic support states provide for licensed foster parents.

Most grandparents who raise grandchildren believe their responsibility for grandchild care is going to be permanent. In 2021, 84.7% of the grandparents have been caregiving for at least a year, and almost half (48.8%) have been doing so for five years or more (United States Department of Labor, 2024). People in every ethnic and income group experience unexpected demands, but the incidence is far higher among minorities. Anderson et al. (2024) indicated a greater percentage of Blacks (12%) and Hispanics (6%) than Whites (4%) reside with their grandparents. Regardless of why young relatives live with them, these grandparents share a common resolve to do what is needed to give grandchildren a stable and supportive environment.

Perspectives of Grandparents

Many grandparents believe that being responsible for the care of a grandchild requires giving up their freedom. They waited a long time for their own children to become adults, supposing it would then become possible to pursue personal ambitions. Maybe they planned to travel, begin hobbies, and participate in leisure activities with a spouse or friends. They may have imagined visiting grandchildren, doing occasional babysitting, and indulging younger relatives. However, these dreams never materialized because a daughter or son was unable to manage personal affairs. Even the future seems uncertain when grandparents are unable to predict how long they may have to raise someone else's child. Extraordinary demands on their time, energy, and finances combine to produce sustained stress (Ghertner, 2022; Strom & Strom, 2020).

Sometimes, grandparents are angry for being placed in a position of having many things they have no choice but to do. There are feelings of resentment toward relatives who created the situation, remorse, guilt about things they might have done wrong as parents, and doubts about their ability to manage the complex and daunting responsibilities of their new role. Grandma Rose shared her feelings of ambivalence with a grandparent class:

> I don't know whether God thought I did a poor job and wanted to give me a second chance or He thought that I did well enough to be given the job one more time. My daughter said she could not handle her children anymore and maybe I won't be able to handle them either.

Grandparents experience mixed emotions. They are sad for grandchildren and their own isolation from friends who do not understand their new mission. Some become depressed about having to give up previous aspirations to become free from continual responsibilities of caring for others. Despite these misgivings, surrogate grandparents generally affirm that they would follow the same path again to rescue grandchildren. They show resilience inspired by the love of family and caring for grandchildren changed their lives in positive ways (Martin et al., 2021).

Goals to Guide Family Obligations

Grandparents who raise grandchildren should adopt new goals consistent with their new guidance obligations. Otherwise, they remain locked in a state of regret and disappointment over being denied the attainment of their earlier dreams that are no longer sensible. A related danger is that grandchildren could feel unwanted and can see themselves as an obstacle to the happiness of grandparents. Such youngsters might be better off living with someone else who enables them to feel wanted and provide a sense of belonging. Foster care is a healthier option than being the recipients of care that is grudgingly being given by grandparents (McGowen et al., 2006; Strom & Strom, 2021).

Hope is difficult to find in households where the primary attitude is pessimism. This is because hope dies when people cease to have suitable dreams. People who are hopeful do not have more knowledge than others about the future. But they appear able to view possibilities based on the same evidence others rely on to support their despair. This favorable outlook has an important influence on family mental health. To prepare children for their future, it is essential to help them acquire hope. Hopeful people of every age are those who show resilience and apply constructive solutions for their problems (Kellerman & Seligman, 2023).

Research has determined optimists do better academically, in athletics, and on the job because they can cheerfully persist when confronted with setbacks, whereas pessimists of equal ability give up or choose to characterize themselves as being victims. Martin Seligman (2012), Professor of Psychology at the University of Pennsylvania and former President of the American Psychological Association, examined corporate productivity for Met Life Insurance Company. He found that optimistic sales employees outsold pessimistic colleagues by more than a third, and optimism was identified as a better predictor of employee value to the company than other standard measures. Because optimism has this favorable impact on work productivity, there is reason to suppose such an attitude could also be a positive factor for the task of bringing up grandchildren.

Grandchildren exposed to continual pessimism are at higher risk of depression and loss of their creative capacity to see possibilities, including their own personal happiness. A sense of optimism is an essential quality to motivate personality development and should be continually reinforced by grandparents who illustrate this fundamental attitude toward life and daily affairs. Grandchildren should be told on a regular basis that helping them grow up is a priority goal for grandparents, and they are the main sources of grandparent satisfaction (Henig, 2018).

Grandparents who underestimate what it takes to be seen as a valued source of guidance are bound to disadvantage grandchildren. The suggestion to join a grandparent class at a church, senior center, or public school should not be met with defensiveness or thinking the suggestion is an insult. It is better to accept the compliment others intend when they recognize the ability to grow and desire to succeed in a complicated role. As conditions of growing up change, parent practices must shift too. Education for grandparents that offers knowledge of childhood can significantly improve grandparent behavior in the estimate of three generations (Strom & Strom, 2020).

Grandparent and Parent Goal Agreement

Reports about grandparents raising grandchildren can be misleading when they imply that most grandparents lack resources. In two-thirds of the families where grandparents are primary caregivers, one of the child's parents lives in the same household. This situation commonly occurs when unwed teenagers have a baby. The teen pregnancy rate has been declining since 1991 (Centers for Disease Control and Prevention, 2024). About 70% of adolescent girls decide to keep their babies instead of giving them up for adoption. Maternal grandmothers typically assume responsibility for childcare while the young mother continues attending school or going to work. This situation sometimes includes considerable conflict between the women as each of them tries to build a close relationship with the child.

Examples of Mother-Daughter Conflict

An illustration of mother-daughter conflict is Carmen, who got pregnant at age 16. Her mother, Esther, agreed to take care of Juan, Carmen's son, so she could study to earn a general education certificate, GED. Five years later, Carmen still lives at home. Grandma Esther and grandson Juan spend most of their day together and get along well. When Carmen comes home after work, she is often tired, routinely denies Juan's request to play, and sometimes yells at him for behaving in ways she does not approve. This reaction leads Juan to seek the comfort of Grandma Esther. Carmen admits this behavior makes her jealous and guilty for being impatient. Sometimes, Carmen tries to regain Juan's favor by suspending Esther's rule about no snacks after dinner.

Carmen's behavior resembles noncustodial grandparents who spend too little time with grandchildren. Noncustodial grandparents seldom have obligations to teach or apply discipline; therefore, they spoil children instead of encouraging them to grow by reinforcing the rules of caregivers for good behavior. In this family, the roles have been reversed. Esther, Juan's grandparent, is the one who is distraught by the permissive behavior of her daughter Carmen. Esther believes that since she is the one who takes care of Juan most of the time, Carmen should support rules she has set for the boy instead of contradicting them.

Both Carmen and Esther need to agree about some well-defined responsibilities. Such complimentary roles are essential so that Juan can benefit from a stable environment, knowing both women love him and have the same expectations of him. One way to increase continuity is by establishing support groups for young parents living in households where grandparents act as main caregivers. Efforts to unite the adult generations are uncommon but have the potential to bring benefit for everyone rather than suppose grandparents are the only ones who require attendance at a support group.

Changes in Child Outlook on Relationships

The evolving child attitudes with age combined with a mature adult relationship is shown in the example expressed by Grandmother Mary.

> My daughter Lisa lives with us. Her 5-year-old son, Bobby, is a good boy who I take care of while Lisa attends college. Bobby's father has not paid support he was ordered to by the court. Still, he comes by when it is a birthday or holiday to give Bobby a piñata or other gifts. Lisa gets angry because Bobby likes his Dad and she wants to tell him, 'Your Dad is a jerk.' When Lisa brought this up again last week, my advice was, 'I realize that you feel bad about Bobby being favorably impressed by his Dad even though he is irresponsible. In time Bobby will consider who does the laundry, feeds him, provides care, and is

available when needed – his mother and grandmother. Try not to be overly disappointed with Bobby's early conclusions. The time that Bobby's father invests in him compared to your own will be evaluated more fairly by Bobby as he grows older. Remember too, Bobby can use all the affection he can get right now. Both of us should not say anything hurtful about his Dad. Some day Bobby will make up his own mind about the support base he has and realize who can be counted on.

Grandparent Views on Raising Grandchildren

An online survey by McGowen et al. (2006) targeted three groups of grandmothers. One group were custodial grandmothers with legal custody of their grandchildren; another group were co-resident grandmothers living with grandchildren and one of the parents; the third group were nonresident grandmothers who provided day care while parents were at work. The 124 primarily White participants were recruited by posting requests for volunteers on national and regional websites including the American Association of Retired Persons (AARP) and Grandparent Information Center at www.aarp.org/online-community.

Differences in Raising Children and Grandchildren

Two questions in the survey were as follows: How is raising grandchildren the same and different from bringing up your own children? Have there been changes in the way you behave as a parent now than you did with your own children? Only 24% of grandparents reported that having been a parent adequately prepared them for what they needed to understand about raising grandchildren because growing up and being a parent had changed so much in just one generation (McGowen et al., 2006).

Most reported they were more patient and relaxed with grandchildren than when raising their own children. They felt less anger and frustration and more concern about the needs of the child. A majority spent more time with grandchildren and participating in their activities. While bringing up their own children, different priorities were in place. At that time, they did not do as many things together or listen as much to the children. Now, grandparents agreed, housework can wait because being with children has greater priority.

To understand more about the motivation of grandmothers assuming their new role, they were asked: What happened in your child's family that caused you to become the main caretaker of grandchildren? The women gave 11 reasons for having to be a substitute parent: substance abuse, abandonment/neglect, working parents, immaturity, mental health, domestic violence, divorce, incarceration, financial problems, death, and military service. When neither parent was capable or willing to fulfill their role, grandmothers took over. Substance abuse was the most frequent reason followed by abandonment and neglect as a motivation for those who had to become custodial caretakers. Working parents were the major reason for co-resident and nonresident surrogates to provide daily assistance.

Quality of Life for Grandparents Raising Grandchildren

Another survey item in the McGowen et al. (2006) study asked: How has parenting grandchild affected the quality of life for you? Nonresident grandmothers (62%), custodial grandmothers (49%), and co-resident grandmothers (29%) felt that caring for their grandchildren had enriched their lives, and they were happier because of fulfilling their obligations. They had a renewed sense of purpose, more joy in their lives, and grandchildren helped them remain more active and feeling as though they were younger. In contrast, grandmothers at both levels of care disliked the fact they had less private time, had lost some freedom, and were obliged to sacrifice opportunities to do preferred activities with a spouse or friends. Many had been looking forward to an empty nest and had retirement dreams that had to be set aside. There was a common sense of disappointment about isolation, from being able to do things with their friends because of role demands.

Protection of Children From Family Abuse

Parent Problems Related to Drug Abuse

There are times when it may become necessary to protect grandchildren from their parents. Children have historically suffered at the hands of addicted fathers and mothers. Currently, there are many types of drugs that endanger families. In fact, drug and alcohol abuse along with related problems that implicate child abuse and neglect are the two most common reasons why grandparents must bring up grandchildren. Drug addicts lose their capacity to provide care for children and ability to take care of themselves. Bredehoft (2021) explained that the size of the parent population consuming illegal drugs is unknown, but related dangers for children are bound to continue in the future.

Ghertner (2022) reported the shocking fact that an estimated 21.6 million children in the United States (25% of total subpopulation) live in households where there is parental substance abuse. The enduring effects regarding parental use of drugs, alcohol, and tobacco on child well-being have been documented by Kuppens et al. (2020). This longitudinal observational meta-analysis included 56 studies, conducted in North America, Europe, Australasia, Asia, and South America, including outcomes for children aged 0–18. Results showed statistically significant differences that were more pronounced for parental drug use compared with tobacco use and alcohol use disorder. The affected children experience long-term detrimental effects.

Consider an example of dangerous outcomes for families. When Denise became addicted to cocaine, she left her 8-year-old son Jason with Edith, his grandmother. At the time Edith took charge of Jason she believed it would just be temporary until Denise completed a rehabilitation program. Three years went by without a phone call or letter. Then, one day Denise unexpectedly showed up at the front door and requested money so she could pursue job training. At first Edith said no because her intuition was the money would be used for drugs. However, after Denise threatened to take Jason with her, Edith relented and withdrew $800 from the bank. Ever since Edith has worried that someday Denise will return to threaten her again or abduct Jason. It seems the only way to protect Jason's safety and security is to petition the court for legal custody. This will be the most emotionally difficult thing Edith has ever done because she will have to prove to a judge that Denise is an unfit parent. If Edith wins custody, she can also lose any possibility of ever restoring a favorable relationship with her daughter. A battle in court will be expensive too and is likely to deplete funds Edith has been trying to set aside for retirement.

Grandparents Need to Manage Time Wisely

Grandparents often feel exhausted by the tasks they must perform. Sometimes, instead of pacing themselves wisely and accepting that certain chores may have to wait, people overlook their health and psychological needs. They fail to realize mental fitness and physical stamina must be preserved to remain a source of support for grandchildren. It is essential to schedule rest, pursue hobbies, and opportunities to learn. Regular exercise is never sufficient to counteract depression and build a positive outlook. Learning to deal with continuous stress and feeling a sense of control prevents giving up or becoming abusive (Blackburn & Epel, 2017).

Spending time alone while having other trusted adults supervise grandchildren can allow reprieve to recover perspective and renew motivation. These goals to gain relief are modest, so a person can do errands, attend religious service, go grocery shopping, and interact with friends. Nevertheless, some grandparents feel they must forego these forms of relief because there are no relatives to help or those willing to act as caregivers are unreliable and cannot be trusted. Free respite care is a service more religious institutions should provide to meet grandparent needs.

Become Aware of Social Service Resources

Grandparents do not anticipate having to pay to raise grandchildren. But this can be the situation grandparents encounter when parents do not fulfill their obligations. Typically, such parents have low incomes, so they are unable to provide any financial help. Then too, economic support may be unavailable from aunts, uncles, cousins, and other relatives who have a difficult time just supporting themselves. These difficulties reflect reports that the average annual income among grandparents raising grandchildren is about half the amount of income for nuclear families with children (Mutchler & Roldan, 2023). Grandparents of these children have the least economic resources and need the most public assistance. As the cost of support for older adults increases, social change will be necessary to prevent the growing inequity that occurs within the child cohort.

Grandparents should be well-informed about social services they are entitled to and how to access them. Grandparent-headed families can usually receive some financial aid from state agencies. Goyer (2021) recommended that social workers become key allies in these matters. There are possibilities to get a monthly federal grant, and students from low-income families are entitled to free meals when they attend a Title I school. The federal government designation of Title I is assigned when 40% or more students at a school are from poverty homes. Caregiver grandparents are typically eligible for child welfare, several hundred dollars a month. Because this is still insufficient, some grandparents have challenged why they do not get the higher amount that states provide foster care parents.

A Child Welfare Information Gateway (2020) study reported certain states have kinship care arrangements that can increase the stipend for caregiver relatives. However, getting state benefits requires grandparents to relinquish control of some decisions and follow the rules that have been established by the state. Social workers must approve certain decisions involving schooling, medical care, and permission to transport a child out of state. These constraints are unacceptable to some grandparents who believe the government should not have a voice in how they bring up grandchildren. However, if grandparents seek greater income assistance, they must be willing to forego being completely independent. One way that government ensures this extra money is used for child welfare is to monitor the spending of individual grandparents.

Some grandparents encumber unnecessary cost if local schools expect them to pay tuition unless one of the grandchild's parents lives in the district or can show evidence of court-assigned guardianship. One practical way to resolve this situation is submit a letter of explanation to the local district school board. This initiative usually results in being granted an exception to the rule. Unfortunately, insurance policies that include medical and dental coverage of minor-age children sometimes exclude grandchildren unless they can prove legal custody that courts are generally reluctant to grant.

Goals for Grandparent Support Groups

Learning With Peers

Grandparents who raise grandchildren are encouraged to join a support group. Group psychotherapy has been accepted as a helpful method to process feelings and emotions (Levine, 2023; Pappas, 2023; Rosendahl et al., 2021; Taku & Shackelford, 2024). Thousands of support groups that meet across the nation are named Grandparents as Parents, Grandmothers as Mothers Again, Second Time Around Parents, and Raising Our Children's Kids. Most groups include 5–20 members who believe that spending time with peers who face similar challenges will help them to reduce their feelings of isolation, offer mutual comfort, and reveal solutions to shared problems. Sometimes, purposes include informing lawmakers about family injustice or suggesting reforms about custody and visitation. These efforts have improved grandparent awareness and policies of courts and family agencies.

The learning grandparents gain from support groups is poorly documented. A notable exception is the series of practical guidelines offered by Dianne Bales (2024) at the University of Georgia Extension Division. Generally, members of a support group lead meetings themselves. No external funds are involved, and so there are no accountability demands to evaluate group progress or report results. However, national leaders of grandparent networks have expressed disappointing experiences at annual conferences that are convened by Generations United (2024), a coalition of 100 organizations that provide resources applicable to grandparent-headed households. Most of the difficulties support group leaders identify can be reduced by applying the following suggestions.

- Encourage optimistic attitudes and constructive behavior as a focus of the group experience
- Establish expectations for growth of every member
- Acquire and practice group process skills
- Emphasize better communication skills
- Recruit and train professional volunteers for leadership of support groups

Every community has some professional people whose job is to help families. Some of these people also devote some of their non-employment time to volunteering. When the leadership in support groups is shared with professional volunteers, grandparents make more progress than when leadership is limited to only members (Pappas, 2023; Rosendahl et al., 2021; Strom & Strom, 2011).

Optimism and Constructive Behavior

Support groups that meet face to face or online are often ineffective because of a format that allows participants to express complaints and gain sympathy or advice but does not arrange opportunities for individual growth (Drebing, 2016). Members often believe it is therapeutic for them to express disappointments to peers in similar circumstances, so they avoid being judged. Support group leaders recognize the dangers of this negative behavior (Goyer, 2021; Strom & Strom, 2021). The following statements reveal some of the strong emotions felt by the leaders.

> I come home after a meeting emotionally drained by listening to everyone . . . I disapprove of the inclination members have to pool their hostility . . . I have to limit the amount of time given to sharing feelings to one in every three meetings or group attendance drops off . . . People can't take it more often than that . . . I am uncertain about what to do with people who seem more interested in expressing endless discontent than making suitable adjustments in their lives. . . . Those who attain success commonly stop attending our meetings, so we never get to talk about what it took for them to be successful (Slorah, 2003).

These observations by support group leaders illustrate why their reform is necessary for group procedures. It is essential to replace an outlook that encourages people to see themselves as victims who benefit by taking turns presenting their sorrows, listening to the disappointment of others, and reassuring one another that somehow their troubles will end. Instead, the attitude that should characterize a support group calls on every member to contribute hope by sharing their small victories, identifying short-term goals, recounting humorous things that happen, and reminding one another of the good experiences they have in their lives.

When a favorable group outlook prevails, successful people continue coming to support meetings to share their strength and help others build confidence about prospects. The choice of attitude matters because, more than any other factor, attitude governs expectations and behaviors that a group can produce. Mental health depends on replacing corrosive emotions such as anger, hatred, and bitterness as soon as possible with a hopeful and healthy outlook to guide change.

Support for Self-Disclosure, Self-Evaluation, and Healthy Adjustment

When newcomers enter a support group, they should be provided a written statement that explains the developmental sequence that is expected of everyone. This helps individuals realize they must set personal goals to guide constructive engagement in the group. The progressive format we recommend includes three stages of support and development: (1) self-disclosure, (2) constructive self-evaluation, and (3) healthy adjustment.

During the first stage, self-disclosure, grandparents describe some of the difficulties they experience and are expected to listen carefully to others who tell about progress they are making in overcoming problems. At the outset most participants are inclined to make known their anger, disappointment, hopelessness, blame, and self-pity. The tendency to portray oneself as a victim is normal. Three or four sessions can be devoted to stage one for newcomers and adjustment to the group.

During stage two, constructive self-evaluation, members are expected to broaden their focus, to go beyond detailing unpleasant events and disappointment to begin involvement with constructive self-evaluation. Individuals are expected to reflect out loud and identify factors they have the power to alter. The reason for this shift is because it motivates people to turn away from the impression that their situation cannot be changed toward recognition that some things are subject to self-control. Stage two people are expected to identify ways they are trying to cope with their difficulties rather than perpetually continue to describe problems.

By the time most people have attended six to eight support group sessions, they are ready to enter stage three. Here the emphasis is on clarifying personal goals, sharing evidence about progress, describing periodic setbacks, and formulating ways to alter unsuccessful efforts. Stage three people are prepared to accept the full range of responsibilities as surrogate caregivers of grandchildren and demonstrate healthy adjustment to challenges. They are no longer hindered by earlier concentrations on feelings of bitterness or regret. Stage three people provide proof of resilience that adversity can be overcome if given access to encouragement, creative alternatives, and perseverance. Some participants stop coming to the support group, but others stay to act as mentors for those who struggle to make progress beyond stages one and two.

At stage three, healthy adjustment, other members of the group do more than just listen. They help to identify options that broaden the basis of personal choice. Additional functions of the group are to monitor the logic of everyone about possible outcomes of their choices, present alternative ways of seeking solutions, and remind one another about the productive use of energy. The duration of participant involvement at this stage is three or four sessions.

Some grandparents do not achieve the gains that are expected of everyone. Getting stalled often implicates depression. When people become depressed, they lose their capacity to consider alternatives for action. In such cases, it is important for leaders to recognize that a support group is not serving as a sufficient source to guide improvement. Accordingly, contacting a therapist and scheduling individual sessions is appropriate. Universities commonly maintain a counseling clinic that is open to all members of the community without cost or a minimal payment. Some grandparents are reluctant to consider counseling because they grew up with misconceptions about this form of treatment. Accordingly, part of the support group orientation should be providing awareness about the nature and benefits of clinical help. In addition, support group leaders require training to better identify the members failing to make expected progress.

Support groups should include some members who are at all three stages. Otherwise, some may become locked into stage one and rendered incapable of moving forward because they have inappropriate expectations and cannot observe members in stages beyond their own. When support groups are basically seen as a forum to express negative feelings, the constructive role of peers is minimized. This focus on self-pity is the reason people who make breakthroughs give for their decision to stop attending a support group. Most report they found it necessary to walk away to preserve their newfound mental health.

Apply Group Communication Skills

Leaders of support groups describe problems of coping with members who monopolize conversations, rationing time so that everyone has a chance to express themselves, intervening when anyone is cruel or mean toward others, keeping the group focused on main issues, and ending arguments between factions seeking to impose their agenda on the group. Leaders wish participants would take greater responsibility to make the group more productive and satisfying. However, the interviews we have conducted with participants reveal the dominant errant belief is that resolving problems as they come up is the responsibility of the group leader. This unreasonable expectation exempts members from having a share of the obligation to monitor group processes and grow from this experience. The orientation newcomers to a support group receive should make known that everyone in the group is responsible to foster healthy adjustment.

Many grandparents are convinced that support group peers are more able to understand them than anyone else. This belief can lead to limiting the discussion of important issues to support group members. An unintended effect is this practice further isolates members, causing them to interact less than they should with relatives. Counting on peers as the only audience to listen to concerns is a mistake. However, grandparents must try to make themselves most understood by relatives, particularly their children and grandchildren. Grandparents should have conversations with relatives whose points of view are sometimes similar but often different from their own. This is the only way to learn more about them and make oneself better understood. Grandparents who decide to reveal their feelings only within the support group deprive themselves of the intergenerational perspective needed to perform their role (Strom & Strom, 2021).

Limitations of support groups led by nonprofessionals are not documented in the mental health literature. When people experiencing similar problems are seen as the only ones able to understand, efforts are seldom made to speak to outsiders who might be more helpful because they can generate more creative responses. The danger of isolation is increased when outsiders themselves accept the false premises of support groups, thus causing them to avoid trying to understand someone whose problems they do not experience. An increasingly common reaction to people facing such ordeals is for others not just to listen but also suggest a support group to provide the comfort and companionship they are uniquely equipped to offer. The fact is everyone needs friends and relatives who listen, want to find out how they feel, and respond in helpful ways. This outlook that calls for caring, assistance, and maturity is more likely to prevail when support groups focus on communication skills and encourage increased dialogue within the family.

Principles to Guide Grandparent Behavior

1. Goal amendment is essential when grandparents become full-time caregivers. The revision is needed so the more comprehensive responsibilities of being a main source of child guidance can be met. Holding on to goals that are no longer reasonable can prevent the motivation and learning necessary to be successful.
2. Grandparents responsible for bringing up grandchildren should avoid the incorrect view that the only people able to understand and help them are others facing similar conditions. Instead, outsiders who are not burdened with extraordinary demands sometimes are able to recognize better options for dealing with complicated tasks.
3. Professionals (social workers, teachers, and clinical psychologists) whose purpose is to help families usually contribute time to volunteering. This group should be invited to facilitate grandparent support groups. Grandparents make more progress when professionals are involved in leading support group.
4. Churches and synagogues should volunteer facilities for grandparent support group meetings. They should also arrange for care of young children while the grandparents attend support meetings. This contribution often determines whether grandparents can arrange to attend and benefit from the influence of peers.

5. Schools should recruit local professionals or faculty who wish to volunteer to help guide grandparents about child development and leading grandparent support groups. Meetings can focus on aspects of child development, expectations for student achievement, common discipline problems, ways to support academic progress, and how to collaborate with teachers.

Conclusion

More grandparents are raising grandchildren than ever before. Their success depends on optimism and willingness to adopt new goals that are more appropriate and attainable. They should learn how the guidance expectations of being a parent have changed, become a listener to find out grandchild feelings, encourage creativity for problem-solving and reflective thinking, emphasize self-evaluation of children, understand what teachers expect of educators at home, recognize how to arrange assistance if a child falls behind at school, cooperate with the parent who shares childcare responsibilities, know about available community services to access, and get periodic relief from stress.

Full-time caregivers often rely on support groups for advice and comfort if the emphasis is on linking optimism and constructive behavior and when members are expected to progress through the essential stages of growth. There is a common need for better communication skills and lessons on the methods of raising grandchildren. Some family observers contend that until parent education is a regular resource, the education of grandparents can wait. However, this is not a matter of doing one thing before another. Both tasks should proceed at the same time because child development and family harmony require adjustment of all generations.

Key Concepts

1. Grandparents who bring up grandchildren should have goals that fit their obligations. Otherwise, they could remain locked in a state of regret and disappointment about being denied the chance to attain dreams chosen earlier in life that are no longer appropriate.
2. Hopeful people do not have more knowledge than others about the future. However, they can envision positive possibilities based on the same evidence others rely upon to support discontent. This outlook contributes to the resilience needed to manage setbacks.
3. The income of grandparents who raise grandchildren is approximately half the amount of annual income for nuclear families with children. Grandparents of these children often have the least of resources and are most in need of family services as well as support from community volunteers.
4. Some school districts expect grandparents who are temporarily or permanently caring for grandchildren to pay tuition unless one of the grandchild's parents live in the district, or they can provide evidence of court-assigned guardianship. A letter of explanation to the school board is usually honored to obtain a tuition waiver.
5. There are times when it is necessary to protect grandchildren from their parents. The misuse of drugs or alcohol along with consequent problems of child mistreatment and neglect are the two most common reasons grandparents must become main caregivers for grandchildren.

6. Instead of pacing themselves and accepting that certain household chores should be delayed, some grandparents ignore their health and psychological status. They do not recognize a need to give priority to physical stamina so they can remain a source of support for the children.
7. Spending time alone to do errands, go to church, visit the hairdresser or friends while other trusted adults supervise grandchildren allows reprieve for grandparents so they can recover perspective and renew motivation. Churches should identify these grandparents and provide free respite care.
8. Invite mental health professionals to volunteer their leadership in forming and monitoring grandparents raising grandchildren support groups. Also, they can evaluate the progress of individual participants and recommend further intervention.
9. Studies of grandparents raising grandchildren have found that, despite the demands, most of them believe grandchildren have enriched their lives, given them a renewed sense of purpose and meaning, provided more joy, and kept them more active and feeling younger.
10. Support groups for grandparents should be led by volunteer professionals who help members go through progressive stages of self-disclosure, constructive self-evaluation, and healthy adjustment instead of continually expressing discontent and portraying themselves as victims.

Generational Perspectives Activities

18.1 Discussion
18.2 Conversations With Young Children
18.3 A Scenario: Reasoning and Problem-Solving
18.4 Chapter Review
18.5 Parent and Grandparent Self-Evaluation
18.6 Storytelling

18.1 Discussion

1. What do you suppose are the greatest challenges for those who raise grandchildren?
2. How can public schools help grandparents fulfill the difficult role expected of them?
3. What social services do you believe should be made available to help grandparents?
4. How could churches become more supportive of families headed by grandparents?
5. What benefits could grandparents gain from being involved with a support group?
6. What personality attributes are needed by women raising their children's children?
7. What could communities do to support the mental health of full-time grandparents?
8. What help should caregiver grandparents expect from other relatives in their family?
9. How do you feel about grandparents bringing up their grandchildren when necessary?
10. How could some grandparents provide better care for children than their parents can?

18.2 Conversations With Young Children

1. What do you like most about living with your grandparents?
2. What are the most fun things you like to do with grandparents?

3. How well do you get along with classmates at your school?
4. How often do other members of the family come to visit you?

18.3 A Scenario: Reasoning and Problem-Solving

Mavis is raising her first-grade grandson. Her friends ask about the secret of her success.

a. Maintain optimism regarding the child, self, and the future.
b. Time management is the key to pacing obligations wisely.
c. Arrange for periodic respite from her many responsibilities.
d. Share observations with the child's teachers at school.
e. Other _____

18.4 Chapter Review

1. What insights from the chapter will I try to apply in my relationships?
2. What is the most important key concept for me presented in this chapter?
3. What elements of this chapter do I wish I had known about earlier?

18.5 Parent and Grandparent Self-Evaluation

1. If my children were to become unable to raise their children,
   a. I would try to take over childcare tasks for them
   b. I would hope a government agency assumes responsibility
   c. I would call a meeting of relatives to consider our options
   d. I would invite an adoption agency to meet with the family
   e. Other _____

2. I believe the most difficult grandparent task of raising grandchildren
   a. is adopting a new set of personal goals that fit their situation
   b. would be the economic demands of raising children again
   c. can be adjusting to all the stresses associated with the task
   d. is giving up dreams about how to spend time in retirement
   e. Other _____

3. I believe accepting the main caregiver role would mean
   a. pacing myself and setting priorities for all there is to do
   b. making sure that I get periodic relief to maintain health
   c. inviting relatives to help financially as best they can
   d. joining a local support group for grandparent caregivers
   e. Other _____

4. The success of grandparent support groups depends on
   a. having professionals volunteer to lead the group meetings
   b. making sure individual growth and health are the main goals
   c. sharing small gains in coping with emotional problems
   d. encouraging an attitude of optimism among all members
   e. Other _____

5. I think the greatest challenges for me would involve

   a. overcoming feeling of regret and blaming my children
   b. avoiding having my grandchildren to blame themselves
   c. revising my goals that were set before the new obligation
   d. maintaining friendships with people I will see less often
   e. Other _____

6. My assessment about the mental health of my adult children is

   a. they cope well with their challenges of parenthood
   b. they are not burdened by any addiction to drugs
   c. they treat children well and support their growth
   d. they experience normal stress and show resilience
   e. Other _____

7. I understand that grandparents who take over as child caregivers

   a. need to adopt some new goals that will enable adjustment
   b. should avoid becoming a complainer about their situation
   c. should join a support group and focus on personal progress
   d. should tell grandchildren they are a source of satisfaction
   e. Other _____

18.6 Storytelling

Historically, storytelling has been a dominant classic and progressive method of teaching around the world. The purposes of a storyteller are to present imaginary or real-life examples showing how some concept applies to a particular situation. People like stories, they pay attention to the procession of events, and usually remember aspects of a story for a long time. Your stories can reinforce the concepts in this chapter for family members and classmates. Please share your stories with them.

References

Anderson, L., Buck, C., & Hayward, G. (2024, February). *Grandparents and their coresident grandchildren: 2021*. United States Census Bureau. https://www2.census.gov/library/publications/2024/demo/p20-588.pdf

Baime, A. J. (2024, June 20). *When grandparents are called to parent – again*. American Association of Retired Persons. https://www.aarp.org/home-family/friends-family/info-2023/grandparents-become-parents-again.html

Bales, D. (2024). *Grandparents raising grandchildren*. University of Georgia Cooperative Extension. https://extension.uga.edu/publications/series/detail.html/89/grandparents-raising-grandchildren.html

Blackburn, E., & Epel, E. (2017). *The telomere effect: A revolutionary approach to living younger, healthier, longer*. Grand Central Publishing.

Bredehoft, D. (2021, August 5). How parental substance abuse affects children: A number of addicted parents overindulge or abuse their children. *Psychology Today*. https://www.psychologytoday.com/us/blog/the-age-of-overindulgence/202108/how-parental-substance-abuse-affects-children

Centers for Disease Control and Prevention. (2024, May 15). *About teen pregnancy*. Division of Reproductive Health. https://www.cdc.gov/reproductive-health/teen-pregnancy/index.html

Child Welfare Information Gateway. (2020). *How child welfare professionals access, use, and share information: Results from the National Child Welfare Information Study*. Children's Bureau,

Administration for Children and Families, U.S. Department of Health and Human Services. https://www.acf.hhs.gov/sites/default/files/documents/cb/information-study-executive-summary.pdf

Drebing, C. (2016). *Leading peer support and self-help groups: A pocket resource for peer specialists and support group facilitators*. Lulu.

Generations United. (2024). *Generations United improves the lives of children, youth, and older adults*. https://www.gu.org/who-we-are/

Ghertner, R. (2022). *National and state estimates of children living with parents using substances, 2015–2019*. U.S. Department of Health and Human Services, Office of the Assistant Secretary for Planning and Evaluation. https://aspe.hhs.gov/sites/default/files/documents/f34eb24c1aff-645bed0a6e978c0b4d16/children-at-risk-of-sud.pdf

Goyer, A. (2021). *Raising grandchildren: Support. If you're a grandparent caring for a child, here's how to find the help you need*. American Association of Retired Persons. https://www.aarp.org/relationships/friends-family/info-08-2011/grandfamilies-guide-support.html

Grandfamilies & Kinship Support Network. (2022, December). *Kinship/grandfamilies: Strengths and challenges* [Fact Sheet]. https://www.gu.org/app/uploads/2024/08/Network-General-Grandfamilies-Fact-Sheet-2022-FINAL-UPDATE.pdf

Henig, R. M. (2018, June 1). The age of grandparents is made of many tragedies. *The Atlantic*. https://www.theatlantic.com/family/archive/2018/06/this-is-the-age-of-grandparents/561527/

Jones, C. M., Zhang, K., & Han, B. (2024, May 8). Estimated number of children who lost a parent to drug overdose in the US from 2011 to 2021. *JAMA Psychiatry, 81*(8), 789–796. https://doi.org/10.1001/jamapsychiatry.2024.0810

Kellerman, G., & Seligman, M. (2023). *Tomorrowmind*. Atria Books.

Kuppens, S., Moore, S., Gross, V., Lowthian, E., & Siddaway, A. (2020). The enduring effects of parental alcohol, tobacco, and drug use on child well-being: A multilevel meta-analysis. *Developmental and Psychopathology, 32*(2), 765–778. https://doi.org/10.1017/S0954579419000749

Levine, A. (2023, September 7). The value of support groups: An overlooked way to increase mental health and emotional well-being. *Psychology Today*. https://www.psychologytoday.com/us/blog/things-to-consider/202309/the-value-of-support-groups

Martin, A., Albrechtsons, D., MacDonald, N., Aumeerally, N., & Wong, T. (2021, July). Becoming parents again: Challenges affecting grandparent primary caregivers raising their grandchildren. *Pediatrics & Child Health*, e166–e171. https://doi.org/10.1093/pch/pxaa052

McGowen, M. R., Ladd, L., & Strom, R. D. (2006). On-line assessment of grandmother experience in raising grandchildren. *Educational Gerontology, 32*(8), 669–684. https://doi.org/10.1080/03601270500494048

Mutchler, J., & Roldan, N. (2023). Economic resources shaping grandparent responsibility within three-generation households. *Journal of Family and Economic Issues, 44*(2), 461–472. https://doi.org/10.1007/s10834-022-09842-3

Pappas, S. (2023, March 1). Group therapy is as effective as individual therapy, and more efficient. Here's how to do it successfully. *Monitor on Psychology, American Psychological Associations, 54*(2). https://www.apa.org/monitor/2023/03/continuing-education-group-therapy

Rosendahl, J., Alldredge, C., Burlingame, G., & Strauss, B. (2021, March 22). Recent developments in group psychotherapy research. *The American Journal of Psychotherapy, 74*(2). https://doi.org/10.1176/appi.psychotherapy.20200031

Seligman, M. (2012). *Flourish: A visionary new understanding of happiness and well-being*. Atria Books.

Slorah, P. P. (2003). *Grandparents' rights: What every grandparent needs to know*. AuthorHouse.

Strom, P. S., & Strom, R. D. (2011). Grandparent education: Raising grandchildren. *Educational Gerontology, 37*(10), 910–923. https://doi.org/10.1080/03601277.2011.595345

Strom, R. D., & Strom, P. S. (2020). Productive aging: Peer influence and retirement. *Educational Gerontology, 46*(11), 678–687. https://doi.org/10.1080/03601277.2020.1807085

Strom, R. D., & Strom, P. S. (2021). Learning throughout life about the needs of all generations: Recognizing and counteracting generational isolation. In M. London (Ed.), *The Oxford handbook of lifelong learning* (2nd ed., pp. 183–207). Oxford University Press.

Support Grandparents Raising Grandchildren Act (2018). Pub. L. No. 115-196, 132 Stat. 1511. (2018, July 7). https://www.congress.gov/bill/115th-congress/senate-bill/1091/text

Taku, K., & Shackelford, T. K. (Eds.). (2024). *The Routledge international handbook of changes in human perceptions and behaviors.* Routledge.

Tracy, E. M., Braxton, R., Henrich, C., Jeanblanc, A., Wallace, M., Burant, C., & Musil, C. (2021). Grandmothers raising grandchildren: Managing, balancing and maintaining family relationships. *Journal of Women & Aging, 34*(6), 757–772. https://doi.org/10.1080/08952841.2021.1951114

United States Department of Labor. (2024). *Grandchildren being raised by grandparents.* Women's Bureau. https://www.dol.gov/agencies/wb/topics/grandparents-raising-grandkids

Chapter 19

Grandparents Giving and Seeking Family Advice

Grandparents in many families are not expected to give or seek advice from young relatives. In such cases, grandparents are deprived of feeling their experience matters, their insights remain relevant, and their advice continues to have value. Learning from younger generations should be a common practice for grandparents to improve their perspective, judgment, and relationships. The purposes of this chapter are to (a) explain how the norms of giving and seeking family advice have been transformed, (b) describe the benefits that usually come from giving and seeking family advice, (c) identify contexts where every generation should continue to give and seek advice, (d) confirm peer advice can be valuable throughout life, and (e) review effective methods for offering advice to loved ones. Generational Perspectives Activities present topics to discuss with family members and close friends about grandparents giving and seeking family advice.

Parents have many sources of advice on how to bring up their children. Self-help authors explain strategies they recommend, counseling psychologists appear on television or the Internet to answer questions about ways to manage misbehavior, and educators arrange classes to support greater collaboration between the teachers at schools and teachers at home (Goldstein & Brooks, 2024). There are so many professionals who claim they know how to raise children that parents are sometimes confused about whose advice to follow. Parents appreciate having many sources of guidance and are grateful they can consider a broad range of alternatives. Children also benefit when parents decide to explore the advice of individuals who are recognized as competent advisors. However, in many families, grandparents are not among the sources parents turn to for advice. In such cases, grandparents are deprived of feeling their experience matters, their insights remain relevant, and their advice continue to have value.

Givers of Advice Should Tell the Truth

Relatives cannot teach young children the importance of honesty if observations adults report are flawed. Some grandparents believe that always telling the truth is no longer sensible because they feel pressure to say whatever relatives want to hear. Sometimes, this means failing to draw attention to the differences between what is right and wrong. People who doubt there is a need to consistently convey truth assume that lying might be necessary sometimes to preserve a family relationship. However, this strategy does not preserve a relationship; instead, it reinforces a social arrangement. The reason is authentic relationships are always based upon self-disclosure, the only way to really be known by another person (Tan, 2022). Here is a story about how Nancy discovered this insight when visiting her daughter and family.

> Nancy had bought a yellow sweater for her 7-year-old grandson Todd and thought it would look great on him. After Todd opened his gift and looked at the sweater, he commented, 'Grandma, thank you but I don't like it.' Nancy's feelings were hurt, so she sought comfort from her daughter. Todd's mother listened and then said, 'Mom, I'm sorry Todd is not excited about the sweater, but we encourage him to always express his feelings. This means there are times when he says things we would prefer not to hear, but Todd's feelings will be known and that is important to us.'

When a grandparent class was asked to react to Todd's story, their responses showed how a single event can be interpreted in a variety of ways. Wanda expressed her concern about how Todd dealt with his grandmother's sweater choice. She said, "I like that Todd was honest but wish that he could have figured out some way to avoid hurting his grandmother's feelings." Claire emphasized the need for adjusting to the grandmother's choice. "My grandson was given a pink shirt from a relative but didn't want to wear it because he saw pink as a color for girls. Then a neighbor got the same kind of shirt, but it was purple, so they traded. Apparently, Todd thought purple was ok for boys of his age." Leona's interpretation was to enlarge grandmother's choice, and she said, "The grandmother should have talked to Todd before she bought the sweater. Todd, what are your favorite colors for clothes? Grandparents should try to determine grandchild preferences instead of supposing that they will be pleased with anything they are given."

Optimistic people do not fear the cost of telling the truth, being honest in how their feelings are expressed (Goldstein & Brooks, 2024; Sukel, 2016). This is because they can see worthwhile qualities in most people, the world, and their own situation. In this respect, they resemble young children whose choice to view in an intuitive way provides optimism and trust, attitudes that support their mental health. Grandparents should try to recover the optimism and trust they lost somewhere along the way before younger relatives are willing to value them as advisors (Kellerman & Seligman, 2023).

Giving Advice and Family Respect

There is benefit in understanding how the concept of respect in families has changed. Some older relatives are disappointed when they observe that grandchildren are not obedient to their parents. However, it is a mistake to suppose disagreement between daughters, sons, and their parents indicates child disrespect. The same dispute grandparents regard as a breakdown in family authority may be interpreted by parents and children as an essential exchange of opinions. In the past generation, the goals of parents have shifted from expecting obedience to encouraging children to think for themselves and make known their views (Strom & Strom, 2024).

When children are encouraged to assert themselves, there is bound to be a corresponding increase in family conflict. Accordingly, accepting and expressing differences becomes necessary for development of maturity in a diverse society, and learning this lesson should not be left to chance. This is why elementary school teachers expect students to be responsible for resolving some of their own disputes. In the past, for reasons of efficiency and time, teachers often denied children involvement in resolving their disagreements. When students were caught fighting on the playground, a teacher would usually step in and insist that one of the parties apologize or risk punishment. This meant a still angry child could be heard to mumble "I'm sorry" to an adversary, even though s/he did not have feelings of remorse. For years these situations caused children to conclude that to be seen by grownups as polite was more important than to be seen by them as honest. In effect, children learned to say what the supervising adults wanted to hear rather than expressing their actual feelings, recognizing that otherwise punishment was the predictable outcome (Strom & Strom, 2021).

Grandparents can be frustrated by how grandchildren seem to disrespect their parents. After observing an incident where generational differences were expressed, one grandmother reminded her daughter, "When you were growing up, you never talked back to me like that." Grandma's memory is probably correct. In the past, respect was reserved for fewer people. There was less concern about equality of minorities, women, the disabled, and children. Students now are taught that the views of everyone are important. Adults are expected to consider child self-assertion as a healthy way to behave. Unlike coercion, that is imposing our will on others, self-assertion is stating how situations are seen and making clear the principles for which we stand (Divecha, 2020).

Self-Disclosure as a Necessary Risk

Becoming an advisor requires expressing observations and opinions. Many grandparents are unwilling to provide suggestions or make comments for fear it could produce conflict. Other elders prefer to keep their opinions private unless a relative specifically asks for their advice. Consider Judy's story.

> My three-year-old grandson, Randy, had just told me "No" in response to a suggestion that I made about moving his toys away from the door to prevent anyone tripping over them. My son-in-law scolded him "I don't ever want you to say 'No' to your grandma. In fact, I don't want you to say 'No' to any adult. After Randy went back outside to play, I said to his dad, "You know, it could be dangerous to teach children they must never say 'No' to an adult. There are awful people in the world. What if an adult were to tell Randy, 'Come here boy, I will give you candy,' or 'Let's play a game but you must not tell Mom or Dad.' Immediately my son-in-law called Randy back into the room. "Son I'm sorry but Daddy told you something wrong. There will be times when your mother and I would want you to say 'No' to suggestions made by other adults."

> Sometimes, advice should be offered without it having to be requested, especially when a grandparent sees a possible danger or potential for trouble that may not be recognized by parents or grandchildren. When some people need advice the most, they may be the least inclined to seek help. Keep in mind that when anyone gets upset, s/he is temporarily unable to access creative thinking, the ability to generate practical solutions for problems. During these times, caring advisors are needed to propose reasonable options for consideration. Suggesting courses of action is important but often overlooked as a function of being an advisor. Showing willingness to listen to someone describe their troubles is not enough. Individuals experiencing difficulties need options to take into account before they can reach personal decisions (Divecha, 2020).

Parents should view grandparents as being a valuable source of advice. However, some grandparents excuse themselves from obligation by stating, "My children have more schooling than I do so my advice would not be worth much." Albert Einstein was considered a genius and saw things differently. His observation was "Wisdom is not the product of schooling but the lifelong effort to acquire it" (Graydon, 2023). Exaggerating how much formal education equips people to solve problems can be costly when it excludes observations of those with less formal education who might possess greater insight, better judgment, and ability to make more rational decisions. When the impressions of grandparents are reflected on, a broader range of possibilities can emerge. Still, when younger relatives decide to take a different path than recommended by grandparents, this should not be seen as an insult. No one should expect the advice they give will always be followed by loved ones. All relatives should be encouraged to reflect before they make independent decisions.

There is evidence that people can change their mind at any age. Grandparents deny this possibility if they withhold advice and thereby prevent relatives from deciding for themselves whether recommendations made to them are relevant and deserve to alter behavior. Harris (2023) reported we can learn from the world's leading risk takers. There is always some risk in giving advice because this exposes our perspective. Moreover, risk taking typically declines with age. Taking risks is essential for growth and to remain influential. When grandparents avoid giving advice to younger relatives, they lose the chance to present insights that could improve decision-making and forfeit an opportunity to be seen as helpful. Relatives cannot benefit from grandparent views unless elders are willing to make them known. Experience must be shared to continue having value for younger generations (Strom & Strom, 2020).

The interpretation of family disagreements has also been transformed (Tan, 2022). One implication is grandparents should be expected to assert themselves in a similar way as younger relatives. Relatives should encourage grandparents to give advice, bearing in mind that parents and grandchildren will consider the advice as part of their individual examination and decision-making. Even teenagers generally provide advice to parents. In the best of relationships, giving advice is reciprocal. Each person can accept or reject advice of others. Yet, when people do not share ideas, concerns, feelings, and worries, their impressions about the best courses of action remain unknown to those who might benefit from considering them (Strom & Strom, 2011).

Observing grandparents participate in family disagreements enables the grandchildren to recognize older relatives are willing to expose their thinking to scrutiny. There will always be disagreements that need to be processed to attain mutual understanding. Disagreements can be solved in a negative way or take a positive path – and children learn from observing adult relatives express and accept differences. Grandparents who decide against offering advice that relatives can critically examine prevent a benefit the rest of us enjoy – external monitoring of our thinking processes that sustains mental viability. Being retired typically means getting less critical feedback about reasoning and thinking than was the case during the years of employment.

Give and Seek Advice Between Generations

Another new custom for grandparents is to seek advice from their younger relatives. The problem is that many older adults are embarrassed about admitting ignorance when they must make decisions, even though they urge other relatives to seek advice when they feel it is needed. For example, this question was presented to members of a grandparent class: How do you suppose your grandchildren could help manage the anxieties, worries, and concerns that you experience? Emma replied, "My grandchildren tell me about the troubles of their brothers and sisters, so I am aware of when they need me." Lisa thought her family could help most by making a strong effort to behave properly. In this way, she would not have to worry about them. Sam admitted, "It is difficult for me to think of how my grandchildren could help me with worries because they really don't understand my situation." Not one grandparent acknowledged the potential of young relatives to help by listening to the adult worries and making suggestions for grandparent consideration.

Telling another person about worries means revealing doubts, concerns, uncertainties, confusion, and indecision. This is especially difficult for older people who believe that seeking advice is an admission of weakness, evidence that someone lacks independence. This view is outdated, no longer sensible or wise, and should be a behavior people should leave behind.

Grandparents should avoid conveying the false impression they are totally independent and able to solve all their own problems without the social media resources that younger relatives rely on (Davis, 2023; Strom & Strom, 2020). When grandchildren observe this independent behavior in older relatives, they are likely to believe grandparents are living in the past. Telling confidential problems to listeners from a different age group (known as reciprocal learning) helps individuals of any age better organize their thinking (Strom & Strom, 2011). Families should revise their time management priorities so that they can spend enough time together. Hughes (2023) reported the typical family spends only about six hours together each week.

Some Advice is Only Nonverbal Shown by Example

People think that giving advice is only verbal. However, advice takes a different form when the observation of someone's behavior is implicated. Cho and Xiang (2023) considered the association between formal volunteering and loneliness among older adults. Their sample was made up of 5,000 persons, aged 60 and older, who did not report experiencing loneliness at the beginning of the 12-year study. Self-reported engagement in volunteering was classified by three levels: (0, no volunteering; 1, less than 100 hours a year; and 2, more than 100 hours a year). Volunteering over 100 hours a year was associated with a lower risk of loneliness as compared to non-volunteers ($p = .008$). This protective effect was not observed for the people who volunteered less than 100 hours a year ($p = .246$). Researchers concluded engagement in moderate to high levels of volunteering can protect older adults from loneliness. Additional opportunities for formal volunteering should be offered to reduce loneliness in later life while also conveying the benefits of helping others to the observing younger relatives in the family (Hertz, 2021).

Reliance on Prayer for Guidance

Everyone can benefit from prayer, but, because older adults are generally more religious, they rely upon prayer more often to figure out solution to their problems than younger people (Pew Research Center, 2020). The prayer content of older adults could include requests for ways to communicate more effectively, learning to show more trust in relatives who love them and want to help, and willingness to consider changes in personal behavior that may be necessary (Peale, 2003). Guidance can come from conversations with relatives and friends, followed by reflective thinking and prayer to assess the worthwhileness of their advice. God is known to work in mysterious ways but, as the author of logic, He also works in practical ways. Solutions usually require changes in more than one person, including the individual praying for others.

Some grandparents are critical of younger relatives because they do not rely on prayer as often to deal with their personal problems. This difference sometimes relates to greater maturity of grandparents and their willingness to be governed by faith. On the other hand, young people are more inclined to make use of talents God has given them, to consider themselves as capable of overcoming most problems. They may pray but also consult with an expert or friend in their social network to make recommendations. God wants us to seek direction by prayer, but He is also the source of talent expressed by others who can make suggestions and acquaint us with unrecognized resources that may be needed to support solutions (Pew Research Center, 2020).

Advice From Peers Is Needed Throughout Life

Children are growing up in an era that only slightly resembles conditions encountered by parents and grandparents. As more experiences of youth diverge significantly from adults, the inclination is to seek guidance from peers. Most mothers have jobs, so their young children spend a lot of time in day care or preschool, where conversations are mostly with immature companions (Garvey, 2023). In elementary school, students often participate in after-school programs with peers to occupy them until their parents return home from work. These extensive periods of age segregation guarantee that the opinions of peers become powerful in shaping the feelings and thoughts of children (Borda, 2016; Harris, 2009).

Seeking peer advice can offer advantages throughout life. Many adults believe the only people who understand them are those who are confronted by similar challenges. This view has motivated formation of support groups where people with similar concerns meet on a regular basis to share impression about managing challenges of their situation. Extraordinary benefits are claimed for spending time with people whose comparable situation enables them to comprehend what it is like to contend with problems like caring for an aging relative, being a single parent, bringing up a handicapped child, or living with an Alzheimer's disease victim (Levine, 2023).

Because members of support groups are expected to offer nonjudgmental support, it is natural for these groups to become a preferred source of advice. Support groups can have a valuable purpose because participants gain comfort knowing they are not alone in managing problems and that it is possible to improve their situation. Nevertheless, it is a mistake to regard peers as the single audience to listen to our concerns even when talking to them may be easiest. Each of us should continue interacting with groups whose experiences are different from our own, so we learn about them while making ourselves better known (Strom & Strom, 2021).

Cultural continuity is undermined when peers are allowed to become the main source of advice because this divides the population by ages into special-interest populations. Then too, because a rapidly changing society assigns greater importance to the present than the past, older people are no longer seen as models for behavior. Instead, each generation identifies with well-known persons of their own or next higher age group. In technological nations such as the United States and Germany, the present and future are given higher priority than the past. As a result, the elevated status that was once assigned to older people suffers a decline. They are no longer considered to be experts, except on matters related to aging and cultural traditions of the past (Strom & Strom, 2018).

Present Advice in a Careful Manner

According to Divecha (2020), family conflict is normal; it's the repair that matters. The way advice is offered sometimes matters as much as the content of advice. Participants in a grandparent class were discussing their relationships with in-laws. The in-laws are sons-in-law, daughters-in-law, and their parents. The class generally agreed in-law relationships should not be limited to seeing each other only on occasions like weddings, funerals, and graduations. Both sides of a family should collaborate to support a healthy relationship for the adult children instead of presenting them with frustration and disappointment over who provides the most lavish gifts, insists on having priority for holiday visits, and is identified as interfering the most. In-laws should communicate as friends on a regular basis. Consider insights by three grandmothers – Sally, Maria, and Katherine.

> Sally, who had recently returned from a civilian assignment for two years at an air force base in Japan, wanted to describe some of the problems younger Japanese women commonly experience with their domineering mothers-in-law. She pointed out that the mother-son bond supersedes the husband-wife relationship in Japan, and this can often be the cause of bitterness, conflict, and jealousy between the older and younger women.

Maria, a Mexican American grandmother said:

> I would like to share an experience about trying to deal with potential jealousy of two women who could compete for attention, affection, and time of someone they both love. I am a widow and have one son named Eddie. Shortly after Eddie got married, he and his wife Salina came over for dinner. Eddie had just washed his hair, so it was shiny and nice. I ran my finger through his hair as I so often had done during the years he was growing up. Then, when I went to the kitchen, I overheard Salina say, 'When are you ever going to cut loose from your mother's apron strings? I did not say anything. Instead, I waited until we had enjoyed our meal. At that time, Maria spoke, "Salina, I heard what you told Eddie. Let me ask, do you love your mother?" "Of course," Salina said. Maria replied, "Well, there are two great loves in the life of most men – love they have for their wife and their love for a mother. They are very different kinds of love. I hope Eddie's love for both of us doesn't cause jealousy between you and I." Salina started to cry and said, "I'm sorry Mom – I love you." Maria added that I get along well with Salina and are willing to offer each other advice, knowing that both of us want to be successful in our complementary roles." Maria's story drew applause from her classmates.

Katherine wanted to talk about one of her in-laws. She said:

> There may be times people have to go beyond giving advice and implement it for the well-being of a loved one who cannot evaluate the benefits it could provide them. A big problem I experienced was wondering how to help my mother-in-law who seemed to be slowly killing herself drinking alcohol. She would not admit to having a problem and

her son, my husband, denied it too saying, "Mom is not that bad and doesn't hurt anyone. Yet, one time when she was babysitting for our two-year-old Luke she passed out at the mall; we had to pick up Luke at the police station. I decided to take control in this situation. My father, a psychologist, scheduled an appointment for my mother-in-law with a physician specializing in alcohol abuse. On the day of the appointment, we were uncertain how to handle possible resistance. As it turned out we had to abduct her to the clinic where she was given a complete examination and counseling. This appointment convinced my mother-in-law that she needed help. She has been sobered now for several years, attends Alcoholics Anonymous meetings on a regular basis, and supports people in our family including giving valuable advice to me.

Some grandparents exemplify patience, a wonderful asset that promotes self-restraint and supports harmony. Grandparents can also share advice about setting goals that go beyond doing well in school and the job. A broader perspective enables mental health, family cohesion, and maturity. Children need healthy criteria to define their success that will change over time while helping them achieve further personal development. Having an orientation that clarifies what it takes to succeed in a longevity society can lead parents and grandchildren to view grandparents as valued sources of guidance (Levine, 2023).

Offer Advice About Money

People are reminded by the media to save enough money before retirement so assets will last until the end of life. There is a growing recognition that children also need understanding about money, so personal finances can receive attention needed for wise planning (Haidt, 2024). Because of the extended lifespan and concerns about the long-term solvency of Social Security along with an increasing national debt, there is a common need to seek and give good advice about money (Mather, 2023). In 2013, the federal government formally recognized education in financial literacy was needed, and so a Presidential advisory committee was established led by the Department of the Treasury. According to the Council for Economic Education (2024), 35 states require a course in personal finance for high school graduation. Students benefit from learning to manage a budget, build a credit score, and plan to invest for the long term (Dahl et al., 2024).

Kolluri et al. (2023) have proposed that young adults become informed about the importance of playing the long game, knowing how longevity affects financial planning and caregiving for their future. This recommendation is reinforced by Andy Markowitz (2024) from the American Association of Retired Persons, who warned that the 'Silver tsunami' Baby Boomer population that is now reaching age 65 lacks savings and will largely have to rely on Social Security to meet economic needs during retirement. The United States has never seen so many people reaching retirement within such a short time. An estimated 4.1 million people a year are becoming eligible for Social Security benefits. Well over half of them will find it challenging to maintain their current standard of living (Dahl et al., 2024; Mather 2023).

In most families, grandparents have acquired greater financial wealth than younger relatives. Yet money is seldom a topic for intergenerational discussion. Some grandparents are motivated to avoid being exploited by relatives, so they keep details of their financial affairs secret. However, they may be willing to describe sources they have found helpful in enabling them to attain financial comfort during retirement (Minkin et al., 2024).

Grandparents should encourage younger relatives to gain knowledge that will enable wise management of money.

Ron Lieber (2016) is the money columnist for *The New York Times*. His book titled *The Opposite of Spoiled* is a promise to help children become competent in managing money so they will have a more satisfying future. Grandchildren should become aware of credit card debt, investments, and life insurance. Lieber emphasizes the values and virtues to convey to children for ensuring they will not be spoiled but instead become generous, patient, and resilient. Using those virtues, Lieber guides parents and grandparents about the significance of money, ways to use it wisely, how to spend and save, ways to give, and possible sources for investment.

Principles for Application

1. Everyone should seek help when s/he cannot manage some situation. Early education of grandparents led them to believe independence is the basis of personal success. In contrast, children are taught now to also value interdependence, rely on others at school, home, and work. The merger of independence and interdependence should be part of the education for grandparents so they see why this dual emphasis can help everyone make adjustments.
2. Family advice should be offered even when it is not requested. When grandparents recognize a situation that could present danger or problems unforeseen by others, s/he should tell parents of grandchildren. The possible benefits should outweigh misgivings about whether someone will dismiss advice as unwanted. When some people need help most, they are less inclined to ask for advice.
3. Be seen as someone who gives advice and also asks for advice. Telling loved ones about your worries and fears, acquainting them with your doubts, and expressing indecision calls for self-disclosure. Grandparents who ask relatives for advice gain a larger range of alternatives for solving problems than could be provided by their peers alone.
4. Be willing to risk examination of your advice. Each person can reflect on suggestions and decide whether advice is relevant and should be applied or rejected. However, unless relatives hear your advice, they cannot know what you think is their best course of action.

Conclusion

Giving and seeking family advice are more effective and satisfying when some conditions are met. Grandparents should be willing to talk about financial views during family conversation. It is not surprising that well-informed relatives are the ones parents view as their best sources for advice on raising children. One implication for grandparents is to increase their awareness about obstacles younger relatives face and use this insight as a basis to give relevant counsel. This implicates attitudes such as patience needed to save money. Another shift is to realize that, although children in the past were marginal participants in family discussions, their involvement now includes comments adults need to hear to discover feelings, ideas, and concerns that otherwise might remain unknown.

Children might decide to take another path than the recommendation given by parents or grandparents. This motivates still another change in attitude, accepting decisions that relatives make as a result of deliberation instead of perceiving their contrary choice as an insult. No one should want relatives to always follow advice they are given.

Grandparents should strive to be seen as telling the truth instead of saying only what they believe relatives want to hear. Honesty qualifies a person as someone who can be relied on to describe events and situations in the way they are observed. Grandparents should ask younger relatives for advice about their views as individuals and norms of their age group as a way to demonstrate respect for intergenerational opinions and acquire a broader perspective.

Key Concepts

1. Giving and seeking advice is typical in authentic relationships. Some grandparents refuse to offer advice because they fear it will cause conflict. Those who feel this way should carefully consider whether they currently have a social arrangement or an authentic relationship. A reciprocal expression of feelings and ideas is essential for building a close relationship.
2. Asking younger relatives to give advice is an uncommon sign of wisdom by grandparents. Seeking advice involves taking a risk to enlarge our perspective, find out how others view our situation, and consider the options they see. Willingness to take risks declines with age, but some risks are necessary to ensure the continuation of personal development.
3. Family advice should be offered even when it is not requested. If grandparents recognize that a situation could present danger or a problem, they should tell the parents and grandchildren. When some people need help most, they may be least inclined to ask for advice. If anyone is emotionally upset, they are temporarily unable to access creative thinking to generate practical solutions for personal problems. So being able to recommend courses of action is an important contribution of those who give advice. Being a listener is not enough.
4. All of us should seek help when we are unable to manage any situations. The childhood education of grandparents led them to believe that independence is the basis of personal success. In contrast, students today are taught to also value interdependence and be reliant on others. Merging independence and interdependence should be an important element of grandparent education so that they see why this dual emphasis could help all generations.
5. Feel comfortable offering advice to relatives so they can then decide if suggestions given are practical and add insight or reveal a lack of awareness. No one should believe that when a relative does not follow their advice, this is a sign of disrespect. Instead, personal decision-making after reflection should be the goal that is encouraged for everyone in the family.
6. Adolescents want relatives to offer advice. Many parents and grandparents believe that the adolescent peers have replaced adults as the only important sources of advice. This view leads adults to give up on providing advice, even though teenagers continue to perceive relatives as valued resources. Growing up calls for consulting an ever-widening group of advisors before making personal decisions.
7. People in all age groups benefit from practical advice about money and financial planning. However, many grandparents are secretive about their economic affairs and dislike talking about this topic with children or grandchildren. Individuals should assess their situation and, if mutual trust exists, conversations about money can support more wise decision-making.

8. Black grandchildren consistently identify grandmothers as a valued source of advice they want to continue looking to for help. The influence of Black grandmothers typically lasts longer than for grandmothers in other ethnic groups. Suitable education to match unique conditions of Black grandmothers should be a part of the public policy plan for them.
9. In-laws who sustain a cordial relationship contribute to the well-being of their adult children. Preserving a close relationship with an adult daughter or son while also encouraging success in the husband-wife relationship of their children should become more common. This can be the case when grandparents are aware of the undue stress they may cause by not being able to get along with in-laws.
10. Some grandparents respond to worrisome family problems by praying for relatives. These prayers should also implicate personal development with requests for better communication skills, more trust in those we love, and the ability to recognize possibilities. The willingness to consider changes in ourselves can often be the key for solutions to family problems.

Generational Perspectives Activities

19.1 Discussion
19.2 Conversations With Young Children
19.3 A Scenario: Reasoning and Problem-Solving
19.4 Chapter Review
19.5 Parent and Grandparent Self-Evaluation
19.6 Storytelling

19.1 Discussion

1. Who do the grandchildren in your family turn to most often for advice?
2. What topics do you avoid during conversations with young children?
3. What advice have you been asked for by grandchildren in your family?
4. How do you feel when grandchildren disagree with their parents?
5. When you recognize a relative needs advice, how do you respond?
6. How do you follow-up when a grandchild decides to take your advice?
7. Who has the most influence on your grandchild's behavior and attitudes?
8. Do you ever feel that you just don't want any advice from your children?
9. What advice have you given to a relative that seemed to work out well?
10. Do you ever feel that you don't want to give any advice to relatives?

19.2 Conversations With Young Children

1. If parents give you an allowance, what do you do with the money?
2. How do you feel about waiting to buy things until you have enough money?
3. What lessons have you learned about money from your grandparents?
4. Do you like how much time that your parents spend with you?

19.3 A Scenario: Reasoning and Problem-Solving

Lewis wants to know how his grandchild is learning about money management.

a. Is the child learning about how to use and save money at school?
b. Do parents teach the child about money by taking him shopping?
c. Are parents teaching how to earn money, buy things, and save money?
d. How can I help him learn more about aspects of financial literacy?
e. How much does he actually understand about money management?

19.4 Chapter Review

1. What insights from the chapter will I try to apply in my relationships?
2. What is the most important key concept for me presented in this chapter?
3. What elements of this chapter do I wish I had known about earlier?

19.5 Parent and Grandparent Self-Evaluation

1. The primary sources I rely on for advice include

    a. daughters and sons
    b. grandchildren
    c. peers
    d. in-laws
    e. Other _____

2. How do I think grandchildren feel about me as a source of advice?

    a. they ask for advice and decide whether it is relevant for them
    b. they never ask me to make suggestions about their situations
    c. they would prefer that I keep my opinions to myself
    d. they think I am uninformed about them, so no advice is needed
    e. Other _____

3. What kinds of advice do adult sons and daughters seek from me?

    a. they ask me about financial matters
    b. they ask me about raising children
    c. they ask me about marital problems
    d. they ask me about religious issues
    e. Other _____

4. How do I feel about offering advice to children and their spouses?

    a. I feel comfortable offering advice to them and their spouses
    b. I feel comfortable offering advice to them but not the spouses
    c. I will give advice to any family member only if I am asked
    d. I have not felt that it is my role to advise them about anything
    e. Other _____

5. The relationships between my daughter or son and I include

    a. willingness to help each other

b. honesty in talking about feelings
c. pleasure spending time together
d. difficulty in trying to get along
e. Other _____

6. What sources do I turn to for advice about life as an older adult?

   a. I turn to peers from my age group
   b. I watch television talk shows
   c. I look for answers on the Internet
   d. I read articles, books, and blogs
   e. I seek guidance from my church
   f. Other _____

7. How do I let my children know they do a good job as parents?

   a. By telling them signs of their success that I have observed
   b. I praise my grandchildren, so their parents know I am pleased
   c. I describe their success to my friends but have not told them
   d. It never occurred to me that this is something I should do
   e. I don't tell them because I do not think they do a good job
   f. Other _____

19.6 Storytelling

Historically, storytelling has been a dominant classic and progressive method of teaching around the world. The purposes of a storyteller are to present imaginary or real-life examples showing how some concept applies to a particular situation. People like stories, they pay attention to the procession of events, and usually remember aspects of a story for a long time. Your stories can reinforce the concepts in this chapter for family members and classmates. Please share your stories with them.

References

Borda, M. (2016). *Unselfie: Why empathetic kids succeed in our all-about-me world*. Touchtone.

Cho, J., & Xiang, X. (2023, July). The relationship between volunteering and the occurrence of loneliness among older adults: A longitudinal study with 12 years of follow-up. *Journal of Gerontological Social Work, 66*(5) 680–693. https://doi.org/10.1080/01634372.2022.2139322

Council for Economic Education. (2024, February 26). *Financial education requirements soar in America's high schools*. https://www.councilforeconed.org/financial-education-requirements-soar-in-americas-high-schools/#:~:text=According%20to%20the%20Council%20for,the%20states%20had%20such%20mandates

Dahl, G. B., Kreiner, C. T., Nielsen, T. H., & Serena, B. L. (2024). Understanding the rise in life expectancy inequality. *The Review of Economics and Statistics, 106*(2), 566–575. https://doi.org/10.1162/rest_a_01148

Davis, K. (2023, March 7). *Technology's child: Digital media's role in the ages and stages of growing up*. The MIT Press.

Divecha, D. (2020, October 27). Family conflict is normal; it's the repair that matters: Here's how to navigate the inevitable tension and disconnection in family relationships. *Greater Good Magazine*. https://greatergood.berkeley.edu/article/item/family_conflict_is_normal_its_the_repair_that_matters

Garvey, D. (2023). *Little brains matter: A practice guide to brain development and neuroscience in early childhood*. Routledge.

Goldstein, S., & Brooks, R. B. (Eds.). (2024). *Handbook of resilience in children* (3rd ed.). Springer.
Graydon, S. (2023). *Einstein in time and space: A life in 99 particles*. Scribner.
Haidt, J. (2024). *The anxious generation: How the great rewiring of childhood is causing an epidemic of mental illness*. Penguin.
Harris, J. R. (2009). *The nurture assumption: Why children turn out the way they do*. Free Press.
Harris, J. R. (2023). *The art of risk: What we can learn from the world's leading risk takers*. Simon & Schuster.
Hertz, N. (2021). *The lonely century: How to restore human connection in a world that's pulling apart*. Random House.
Hughes, A. (2023, March 24). New study reveals the typical family only spends just six hours together each week. *Independent*. https://www.independent.co.uk/life-style/family-limited-meal-time-communication-b2306531.html
Kellerman, G. R., & Seligman, M. (2023). *Tomorrowmind: Thriving at work with resilience, creativity, and connection – now and in an uncertain future*. Simon & Schuster.
Kolluri, S., Weiner, J., & Naylor, M. (2023). *Playing the long game: How longevity affects financial planning and family caregiving*. TIAA Institute. https://www.tiaa.org/content/dam/tiaa/institute/pdf/insights-report/2023-10/tiaa-institute-upenn-how-longevity-affects-financial-planning-ti-november-2023.pdf
Levine, A. (2023, September 7). The value of support groups: An overlooked way to increase mental health and emotional well-being. *Psychology Today*. https://www.psychologytoday.com/us/blog/things-to-consider/202309/the-value-of-support-groups
Lieber, R. (2016). *The opposite of spoiled: Raising kids who are grounded, generous, and smart about money*. Harper.
Markowitz, A. (2024, April 19). *Are the last boomers ready for retirement?* American Association of Retired Persons. https://www.aarp.org/retirement/planning-for-retirement/info-2024/peak-boomer-readiness.html
Mather, M. (2023). *Shifts, flips, and blips: Reflecting on 25 years of U.S. population change*. Population Reference Bureau. https://www.prb.org/articles/shifts-flips-and-blips-reflecting-on-25-years-of-u-s-population-change/#:~:text=In%20a%20related%20development%2C%20the,from%2012%25%20to%2017%25
Minkin, R., Parker, K., Horowitz, J., & Aragão, C. (2024, January 25). *Parents, young adult children and the transition to adulthood: Financial independence is a work in progress; few young adults say their parents are too involved in their day-to-day lives*. Pew Research Center. https://www.pewresearch.org/social-trends/2024/01/25/parents-young-adult-children-and-the-transition-to-adulthood/
Peale, N. V. (2003). *The power of positive thinking*. Simon & Schuster.
Pew Research Center. (2020, September 10). *U.S. teens take after their parents religiously, attend services together and enjoy family rituals*. https://www.pewresearch.org/religion/2020/09/10/u-s-teens-take-after-their-parents-religiously-attend-services-together-and-enjoy-family-rituals/
Strom, R. D., & Strom, P. S. (2011). A paradigm for intergenerational learning. In M. London (Ed.), *The Oxford handbook of lifelong learning* (pp. 133–146). Oxford University Press.
Strom, R. D., & Strom, P. S. (2018). Education for grandparents in longevity societies. *Journal of Adult and Continuing Education, 24*(2), 208–228. https://doi.org/10.1177/1477971418810652
Strom, R. D., & Strom, P. S. (2020). Productive aging: Peer influence and retirement. *Educational Gerontology, 46*(11), 678–687. https://doi.org/10.1080/03601277.2020.1807085
Strom, R. D., & Strom, P. S. (2021). Learning throughout life about the needs of all generations: Recognizing and counteracting generational isolation. In M. London (Ed.), *The Oxford handbook of lifelong learning* (2nd ed., pp. 183–206). Oxford University Press. https://doi.org/10.1093/oxfordhb/9780197506707.013.9
Strom, P. S., & Strom, R. D. (2024). *Mental health and relationships from early adulthood through old age*. Routledge.
Sukel, K. (2016). *The art of risk: The new science of courage, caution, and chance*. National Geographic.
Tan, J. (2022). Intergenerational parenting: Managing conflicts between parents and grandparents. *Thoughtfull*. https://www.thoughtfull.world/mental-health/intergenerational-parenting-managing-conflicts-between-parents-and-grandparents#:~:text=Define%20roles%20and%20rules,layout%20each%20other's%20parenting%20values

Chapter 20

Grandparent Strengths and Cultural Diversity

Grandparents want to be seen as a favorable influence by their younger relatives. The purposes of this chapter are to show (a) how strengths and learning needs of individual grandparents can be identified, (b) the methods used to assess progress in grandparent classes, (c) the ways to determine group success in intervention programs, and (d) develop grandparent curriculum to meet the needs of specific cultures. Generational Perspectives Activities present topics to discuss with family members and close friends about grandparent strengths, learning needs, and cultural diversity.

Three-Generational Perspectives of Grandparent Behavior

Experimental and Control Participants

A comprehensive description is presented for the *Grandparent Strengths and Needs Inventory* (*GSNI*), a three-generational instrument developed by Strom and Strom (1993) to reveal strengths and learning needs as perceived by grandparents, parents, and grandchildren. Results from international studies, dissemination of findings, and training programs for volunteer class leaders are explained. Generational and cultural differences are described with implications. Favorable findings from international and immigrant studies have confirmed that grandparents are able to work in cooperative learning teams, and curriculum for them can be adapted to meet different conditions in varied cultures across the globe.

The American Association of Retired Persons (AARP) is as a major advocacy group for seniors in the United States. In collaboration with Arizona State University, a study was conducted by Strom and Strom (1989) with AARP. The purpose was to determine whether grandparents could benefit from an intervention program involving the relationships with grandchildren aged 6–18 years and their parents (Strom & Strom, 2018a). The sample of 400 grandparents represented the national proportion of individuals, ages 50 and older, who identified themselves as Protestant, Catholic, or Jewish. A listing of all churches and synagogues in the Phoenix, Arizona metropolitan area, stratified by religion was assembled with assistance from the Arizona Ecumenical Council (Gallup Foundation, 2024).

In a series of randomly paired drawings within each religious preference, the first church chosen became an experimental site and the second a control site. Selection continued until the sampling needs had been reached. This method avoided the contamination of either group that might have happened otherwise if the experimental and control participants were drawn from the same sites. The 185 grandparents from control sites were not provided any classes, but they were each paid $30 to complete the same schedule of testing as the experimental group.

DOI: 10.4324/9781003534655-26

Each grandparent in the experimental group chose one son or daughter and their 6–18-year-old child who would evaluate changes in attitudes and behaviors of the grandparents. The three generations each completed a separate version of the *GSNI*, developed by Strom and Strom (1993, 1997, 2019). The inventory was administered to participants before classes began, when instruction ended, and three months following the intervention. Grandchildren and parents were assured their responses would not be revealed to the grandparents. The weekly 90-minute classes for 210 experimental participants centered on discussions for topics presented in a guidebook written by Strom and Strom (1991a, 1991b, 1991c, 1992a, 1992b). If someone missed a session at their regular class site, they could consult a list with the full schedule indicating where and when the same session was offered as an option to attend.

Instrument for Evaluation

The *GSNI* consists of 60 items, divided equally into six subsets, with each focused on separate aspects of grandparent development (Strom & Strom, 1997, 2019). Respectively, the subsets evaluated the following grandparent characteristics.

Satisfaction – aspects of the grandparent role that provide satisfaction.
Success – ways in which grandparents successfully perform their role.
Teaching – the scope of family guidance that is expected of grandparents.
Difficulty – problems encountered with the obligation of grandparenting.
Frustration – grandchild behaviors that are upsetting to a grandparent.
Information needs – things grandparents need to know about grandchildren.

Three subsets (satisfaction, success, and teaching) combine to form an index known as grandparent *potentials* on the *GSNI*. The remainder subsets (difficulty, frustration, and information needs) provide an index of grandparent *concerns*. Together the six separate subsets and the two overall index scores offer information that can be used for planning curriculum and guiding instruction (Strom & Strom, 1989, 2019; Strom et al., 1996a, 1996b).

In scoring the *GSNI*, the absolute mean (average) score of 2.5 for either index differentiates favorable and unfavorable performance. A score of 2.5 or higher is recorded as a strength. Conversely, a score below 2.5 suggests further growth is needed. The resulting comparison of how grandparents perceive themselves and how they are seen by younger relatives provides a more reliable perspective of strengths and needs.

GSNI Results for Three Generations With Reliability and Validity

All three generations gave favorable pretest scores to the grandparents on the potentials and concerns indexes. Twelve weeks later, after the intervention, grandparents were assigned higher post test scores from themselves, the parents, and the grandchildren. Grandparents indicated that they experience significant growth in grandparent potentials ($p > .001$) and concerns ($p > .047$). The probability of ($p < .001$) reflects the likelihood a particular result has been attributed to chance. Parents corroborated this view, indicating they saw grandparents make gains in potentials ($p < .006$) and concerns ($p > .019$). Scores from the grandchildren also increased, but these changes were nonsignificant. It is relevant to note that perceptions of grandchildren were significantly more favorable than scores reported by parents and grandparents before the program began and after the intervention. When the *GSNI* was administered a third time several months later, the gains each generational source identified earlier were sustained. In contrast, members of the control group made no gains (Strom & Strom, 1989, 2019).

GSNI potentials and concerns offer a broad view of change but do not reveal contexts where behavior has been modified (Strom & Strom, 1989, 2019). Because the subsets are defined more specifically, they offer more detailed information. The absolute mean score of 25 for any subset distinguishes between favorable and unfavorable ratings. When a higher score than 25 is recorded, the source assigning it has identified a strength; subset scores below 25 reveal behavior or attitudes the grandparent should change.

Grandparents assigned favorable self-impressions on the *GSNI* pretest measures of satisfaction, success, teaching, and ability to manage difficulties and frustrations. At the end of the course, grandparents scored themselves significantly higher on three subsets: satisfaction ($p < .001$), success ($p < .055$), and teaching ($p > .001$). Growth of grandparents as identified by parents showed greater satisfaction ($p < .018$), more active teaching ($p < .005$), and less frustration ($p < .050$). Parent reports of gains for subsets of success and difficulty approached significance. Grandchildren observed similar improvement as shown by higher but nonsignificant gains for every subset on the post test.

The lone subset on which grandparents evaluated themselves unfavorably at the beginning of the program was information needs. Even though scores for these ten items improved on the post test, grandparent self-impressions remained in the unfavorable range. Grandchildren and parents assigned favorable scores but also recorded their lowest ratings on the information needs subset.

When the subset scores for satisfaction, success, and teaching were combined and the difficulties, frustration, and information needs were united, totals for potentials and concerns were favorable if they reached 75. It was found that the grandparents, parents, and grandchildren recorded higher score for potential and concerns following intervention. These findings indicate grandparents improved their influence and became more able to manage family-related problems. Higher ratings for potentials than for concerns indicates grandparents saw their role in a way that was more positive than negative. This is an important distinction because people who enjoy their role can generate optimism when it becomes necessary to cope with difficulties.

The same process is applied to identify progress of grandparents for the items of a subset. To illustrate, grandparents made significant gains on seven of the ten items on the satisfaction subset. Specifically, grandparents became more satisfied by how a grandchild (a) got along with relatives, (b) assumed responsibilities for household chores, (c) set personal goals and priorities, (d) performed at school, (e) shared feelings, (f) showed emotional and social development, and (g) made efforts to stay in contact. Grandparent scores improved for two items on the success subset. They were seen as better at discussing friendships with grandchildren and willingness to express differences of opinion. Four items were implicated on the teaching subset. Grandparents were credited with teaching grandchildren to observe feelings of other people, ways to manage stressful situations, plan for the use of time, to make religious beliefs known, become more patient, and being willing to wait. Two items on the frustration subset reflected progress. Grandparents were less frustrated by the way a grandchild was being brought up by parents and the ability of grandchildren to pay attention. Finally, three items indicated significant progress on the information needs subset. Grandparents needed to know more about the tutoring status of a grandchild, teamwork skills acquired by a child, and what adults should expect of a grandchild at this chronological age (Strom & Strom, 1989).

The *GSNI* reliability and validity were investigated by Collinsworth et al. (1991), who directed factor analytic studies. Responses for 2,012 grandparents, parents, and grandchildren were analyzed to determine if the underlying structure of the instrument fit the hypothesized dimensions suggested by the position of 60 items on six subscales. The pattern of item-to-factor correlation suggested that the 60 items tended to fit the hypothesized pattern of subscales. Empirical evidence supported the presence of six dimensions: (a) satisfaction, (b) success, (c) teaching, (d) difficulty, (e) frustration, and (f) information needs as constructs comprising the six subscales of the *GSNI*.

Spanish Version. Factor analytic studies of the *GSNI* Spanish version conducted by Strom et al. (1997) included three generations. The 402 Mexican American participants included 181 grandparents, 148 parents, and 183 grandchildren. The results revealed differences between English- and Spanish-speaking grandparents. Spanish-speaking grandparents reported a greater need for information than English-speaking grandparents and more frustration when dealing with adolescents than with younger children. All three English-speaking generations agreed that grandparents under the age of 61 experienced more frustration than their older counterparts, and grandparents who spent more than five hours a month with their grandchildren were more effective in their roles than those who spent less time.

Multivariate analysis (an advanced statistical procedure) determined how each of the 11 independent variables influenced the performance of grandparents (Strom & Strom, 2019). Experimental participants performed significantly better when one or more of the following conditions existed: their son or daughter was married, they spent more than five hours a month with a grandchild, lived less than 200 miles from the grandchild, their grandchild was a granddaughter, the grandchild was aged 7–11 years, grandparents were under 70 years of age, and they were grandmothers. The nonsignificant variables included grandparent level of education, grandparent income, grandparent marital status, and whether the grandparent was related to a grandchild through a daughter or son.

Amount of time spent with a grandchild was the factor with the greatest impact on impressions of grandparent success as perceived by all three generations. This research study confirmed a belief that grandparents could benefit from education that implicates their family role (Strom & Strom, 2018, 2019).

Publicity of the AARP Study

Grandparents and their relatives provided favorable reactions to the grandparent education program Becoming a Better Grandparent initiatives which led to public television reports such as in NBC Today, CBS This Morning, and ABC News. The instructional methods for grandparents were reported by *The New York Times, The Wall Street Journal, Newsweek,* and *USA Today.*

More than 90% of the experimental participants completed their course and received a certificate for the *Becoming a Better Grandparent* program from Arizona State University. References for professional journal publications pertaining to the *GSNI* by Strom et al. are available on the website of Auburn University, *parentslearn.auburn.edu.*

Curriculum for Minority Families in the United States

Black Families

Most participants who initially attended the course for grandparents were White and middle class. Adapting the curriculum to Black families required understanding the different conditions of living (Martinez & Passel, 2025). During interviews with families, we found that Black grandparents were described by grandchildren as heroes. The reason for this compliment was because the contributions of Black grandparents to their family goes far beyond expectations typically associated with being a grandparent. Black grandparents are twice as likely as those from other ethnic groups to have grandchildren living with them (Anderson et al., 2024). About 56.7% of Black children compared to 31.34% of Hispanic children and 20.7% of White children also lack the presence of a biological father. Most of these children live with their single mother and grandparents. The grandparents have householder responsibility but without the assurance of financial assistance from relatives who are typically preoccupied with their own economic survival. Even when mothers have the main responsibility for childcare, Black grandparents often provide supervision for children before and after school hours. Black teenagers have a higher rate of pregnancy, school dropout, and involvement with criminal activity than most ethnic groups (Centers for Disease Control and Prevention, 2024).

Watson and Koblinsky (1997) studied 192 working-class grandparents and found a significant relationship between race and interest in taking a grandparent education class ($p >$ .001). A greater percentage of Black grandparents (56%) expressed an interest in taking a grandparent education class than White grandparents (30%) (Watson, 1997). Black grandparent devotion typically results in the development of a close relationship with grandchildren. Most Black teenagers identify grandmother as being a trusted advisor. Because many grandmothers did not complete high school, it might be assumed they lack interest in improving their performance. On the contrary, these grandparents want to succeed and realize education is the key to helping them adjust their goals and methods of parenting to meet the demands of an environment that is more complex and dangerous than during the past.

A study by Strom et al. (1996b) examined *GSNI* performances of Black grandparents, described their family contributions, detected obstacles limiting success, identified the content for a relevant curriculum, and suggested guidelines to build relationships. The three generational sample of 626 non-consanguineous (not blood related) subjects included 204 grandparents of 6–18-year-old grandchildren, 128 parents with 6–18-year-old children, and 294 grandchildren who were 6–18 years old. A nearly equal number of participants were drawn from urban centers in the southeast and southwest regions of the nation. The grandparents ranged in age from 39 to 82 and took care of grandchildren daily. All three generations completed their version of the *GSNI* and credited grandparents for their strengths (Strom & Strom, 1993).

Advanced statistical procedures (multivariate analysis of variance methods, univariate analysis of variance testing, and t-tests) were applied to analyze Black *GSNI* scores, confirm results, and help with the interpretation of data. All three generations described aspects of grandparent success and reported specific realms of learning they felt grandparents should acquire to increase their effectiveness. The analysis of the responses revealed significant main effects for generation, gender of grandchild, age of the grandchild, and amount of time grandparent and grandchild spent together. Considerations were identified for curriculum and instruction to meet the needs of the Black grandparent population (Strom et al., 1996b).

In a study by Steven Heeder (1998), the purposes were to (a) identify perceptions of three generations of females about the influence of Black grandmothers; (b) describe contributions of Black grandmothers, (c) detect obstacles that limit their success, and (d) recommend curricula for programs to enhance success of Black grandmothers. The 253 subjects were Black grandmothers ($n = 76$), mothers ($n = 65$), and granddaughters ($n = 112$). Each generation completed the *Grandparent Strengths and Needs Inventory* (Strom & Strom, 1993). A high degree of agreement among generations revealed that the subscale of teaching was perceived as the greatest strength of grandmothers. The grandmothers' greatest limitation was the need for information about individual grandchildren (Strom et al., 2005).

Mexican American Families

There are approximately 38 million people of Mexican descent living in the United States, making them the largest and most rapidly growing population of Hispanics in the nation (United States Census Bureau, 2024). Strom et al. (1997) collected data at senior centers, public schools, churches, and community organizations located in Phoenix, Arizona. Nearly 40% of the Mexican American grandparent participants had less than an eighth-grade education, and over 60% had not completed high school. The 502 non-consanguineous sample consisted of 181 grandparents, 141 parents, and 173 grandchildren, mostly from lower-income families. Buki (1995) analyzed data on each of the *GSNI* subscales that included satisfaction, success, teaching, difficulty, frustration, and information needs.

Buki (1995) found differences between the English- and Spanish-speaking grandparents. Spanish-speaking grandparents reported a greater need for information about their grandchildren than English-speaking grandparents and more frustration when interacting with adolescents than with younger children. All three generations of English-speaking grandparents agreed that grandparents under the age of 61 experienced more frustration than their older counterparts, and grandparents who spent more than five hours a month with their grandchildren were more effective in their roles than those who spent less time. The possible factors that account for the findings and recommendations to implement a grandparent education program were determined. A factor analysis confirmed the hypothesized underlying structure of the *GSNI*, lending support for use of the six subscales as dependent variables (Strom et al., 1997).

Most schools have not developed partnerships with grandparents, even though some older family members are caregivers of grandchildren and a major source of volunteers in classrooms. Grandparents would perform more efficiently in these roles if they were better informed about what it is like to be growing up now and how the views of parents and the schools have changed since they brought up daughters and sons. Unlike other organizations that link families and schools, grandparent education councils were formed to focus exclusively on the obligations and learning needs of grandparents (Strom et al., 1997). An example of a successful model involved 32 elementary and junior high schools in south Phoenix. Members of each school council included grandparents, parents, a volunteer coordinator, and faculty member, usually the principal. Leadership for the biweekly meetings was assumed by members of the council and professionals who relied on lesson outlines that were developed for them. No school funds or family resources are diverted from the education of children to provide education for grandparents. There is a need for more education efforts to support Mexican American grandparents.

Cooperative Learning for Grandparent Education

Grandparent Education in Assisted Living

The director of a large senior citizen living facility in Phoenix invited Strom et al. (2006) to tour the campus, meet with residents, and initiate plans to introduce grandparent education classes on site. Financial support for this project was provided by Little Debbie of the McKee Foods Corporation. The facility population of 800 residents (average age 81) was primarily female (70%) and widowed (62%). Most of the residents lived independently in their apartment, had their own car, and were required to eat one meal a day in the common dining room to ensure that dietary needs were met. Other residents who were recuperating in the medical unit received care from staff nurses and physicians, and one-third lived in a separate building and were provided complete care because of dementia.

During the tour, residents showed enthusiasm about taking a course focused on their changing family role. In addition, they felt the concept of lifelong learning had left them out by not providing any curriculum related to their needs in old age. Unless these needs could be met, their influence as grandparents was bound to diminish, they would experience greater isolation, and their sense of purpose could be lost. A decision was made to collaborate on condition that enough residents would volunteer for training as leaders of classes made up of small groups.

The goals of the grandparent program were to increase mental stimulation, enrich social relationships, and understand more about younger relatives. The corresponding goals for the university team were to arrange ways for elders to provide indigenous leadership of their own education program, discover suitable methods for teaching this advanced age group, explore procedures to evaluate learning, and provide an educational model that could be considered by other facilities.

Loneliness and Group Peer Support

During the Strom orientation, residents reported that loneliness was a major personal problem, and they seldom had visits from their families. To confront loneliness, Strom and Strom (1997) introduced *cooperative learning* as the method of group instruction and to help participants minimize feelings of isolation and build a social network of friends. The cooperative learning method used for senior adults was well accepted by the grandparents and the volunteer class leaders. Since then, Strom and Strom (2024) have devised guidelines for cooperative learning to be used in grandparent classes.

Twenty women and men, aged 77–91 years, volunteered to be class leaders. Most had earlier careers as teachers, social workers, nurses, or executives in business. They organized a grandparent council to monitor weekly training and handle any problems. Weekly classes attended on average by 65 residents meeting in small groups continued for an entire year. This program demonstrated people of the oldest age who are well can benefit from a cost-free education strategy supported by indigenous leadership focused on learning how to improve family relationships (Strom & Strom, 2016, 2017; Strom et al., 2006).

International Research and Training Leaders

Families are faced with many challenges in this uncertain and ever-changing world. Every country has varied traditions and roles for grandparents. The *GSNI* covers expected beliefs that are naturally held worldwide by grandparents. These include love and protection of grandchildren and enhancing family relationships. The *GSNI* evaluates grandparent satisfaction, success, teaching, difficulties, frustrations, and information needs. By administering the *GSNI*, these grandparent strengths and learning needs can be identified for specific groups (nationalities, races, ethnic and religious affiliations). The curriculum can be shaped to more precisely identify learning needs as well as compliment the grandparent strengths. There are many commonalities worldwide that are shared by all, such as parent and grandparent love and care of their grandchildren, and desire for them to do well.

Additional three-generational studies eventuated into the creation of grandparent courses to meet the needs of specific cultural groups. Workshops using guidebooks and research studies with social workers, psychologists, nurses, and educators have been held in other countries, including England, West Germany, Japan, Hong Kong, Canada, Taiwan, and Sweden (Strom & Strom, 1991a, 1991b, 1991c, 1992a, 1992b). Grandparent education classes continued to be held for grandparents through the Osher Lifelong Learning Institute at Auburn University from 2015 to 2019.

England

The beginning grandparent education initiatives were developed by Strom and Strom (1983). The program was first presented on October 13, 1982, at Homerton College, Cambridge University, Cambridge, England. At the time, while studying gerontology at Cambridge, Robert D. Strom was invited to give a formal presentation to the university faculty and retired members of the University of the Third Age in the community. The presentation included a description of an innovative grandparent education program directed by Strom called Becoming a Better Grandparent, which first began at senior citizens centers in metropolitan Phoenix, Arizona. Grandparents volunteered (without cost) to join the weekly event, participated in the class discussions for 90 minutes for ten weeks and represented various ages, ethnic background, and income levels. The purposes for uniting grandparents in a community setting were to help them gain a better understanding of their rights and responsibilities, share feelings and ideas with family members, improve storytelling as a method for teaching grandchildren, and participate in self-evaluation. Expectations for the changes in the grandparent role were portrayed as a difficult challenge, but the personal growth required would enrich grandparent lives and those of their families.

West Germany

After World War II, Germany recruited foreigners as a temporary source of cheap labor. To emphasize the impermanent status of these newly arrived workers from Greece, Italy, Turkey and Yugoslavia, they were called guest workers. From the beginning it was assumed most would eventually return to their homeland, so no government efforts were made to consider citizenship or integrate children in schools that require understanding of the German language. The alternative was minority populations could provide education in their native language. This supported group pride but did not offer the German language readiness children needed for students to enter higher education. Over half a million guestworker families are still in West Germany (Statistisches Bundesamt, 2024).

The Bavarian Ministry of Education granted permission to conduct a study in 19 public and private schools. Strom et al. (1983, 1984) directed the study and received financial support from the Werner-Reimers Foundation in Munich. The research examined the parents of kindergarten and first-grade students; parents were from West Germany ($n = 155$), and guestworkers from Greece ($n = 106$), Italy ($n = 49$), and Turkey ($n = 60$). To assess parent strengths and learning needs for parents of children aged 3–9 years old, the subjects completed a 50-item instrument called the *Parent As A Teacher Inventory (PAAT)* (Strom, 1984). Before data gathering could begin, a representative from the German as a Second Language Institute at the University of Munich traveled to Arizona to assess the intent of all PAAT 50 items. To ensure comparability of meaning across groups, the PAAT was then translated from English into German, Greek, Italian, and Turkish. Strengths and learning needs for each minority group were described in letters to individual teachers of the children.

Guestworker parents demonstrated a readiness to change traditional child-rearing attitudes by the modification of sex-specific attitudes toward sons and daughters. These changes occurred outside the sphere of formal education. The findings of the study showed that expectations for child gender must keep pace with social change if families were to remain united and productive. Parents and grandparents of each ethnic group were informed about the PAAT results for their ethnic group and implications for child opportunities (Strom et al., 1983; Strom, 1984).

Japan

The purpose of this study was to identify the strengths and needs of Japanese grandparents as perceived by three generations. Three-generation samples in Japan included participants from Tokyo, Yokohama, Osaka, Kobe, and small towns in Tokushima, Japan Prefecture (Strom et al., 1995; Strom, 1996). Many Japanese grandparents believe their status in the family is eroding. They want to be influential, but social policy has not included education for their changing role. Statistical procedures were used to compare perceptions of grandparents ($n = 239$), parents ($n = 266$), and school-age grandchildren ($n = 274$). Grandparents reported more satisfaction, greater success, and more extensive involvement in teaching than was observed by parents and grandchildren. Grandparents experienced greater difficulty and more frustration and felt less-informed to carry out their role than was reported by parents and grandchildren. Significant main effects that influenced responses about grandparent performance were generation, gender of grandchild, age of grandchild, generations living together, frequency of grandchild care by grandparent, and amount of time they spent together. Considerations were identified to improve grandparent behavior and guide the development of educational programs for them.

Hong Kong

From 1976 to 1997, refugees from Laos and Cambodia fled to escape persecution from the communist North Vietnam after it defeated South Vietnam. Most of the 200,000 immigrants came across the China Sea in small boats. In support of these 'boat people,' Hong Kong declared itself a 'port of first asylum,' meaning that no refugees would be turned away. This welcoming attitude differed from other territories like Malaysia, Singapore, and Thailand (Bradley, 2022). Restricted camps were set up to house refugee families outside the city of Hong Kong. In a visit to these camps in 1986, the Stroms were impressed by the coordinated government efforts to keep immigrant families together while preparing them for integration.

A week-long public workshop in Hong Kong was presented by the Stroms regarding the topics of changes in family expectations, understanding play and family development, helping families with stress, watching television and the parent-child interaction, parenting success and failure, supporting parents of mentally handicapped children, identifying single-parent needs, and educating grandparents. These presentations were supported by the Hong Kong Society for Child Health and Development and the Bernard Van Zuiden Charity Trust. Children were taught in their native language while adults received vocational training to join the labor force.

The Stroms returned to Hong Kong in 1991, and the purpose was to train leaders from multiple government units to offer parent and grandparent education. This week-long workshop for social workers, psychologists, nurses, and educators focused on their discussions in small groups as they studied the grandparent curriculum of 12 lessons and methods of self-evaluation (Strom & Strom, 1991c). This workshop was supported by the Hong Kong Society for Child Health and Development.

Canada

This pilot project in Alberta, Canada, was supported by the National Health and Welfare Department of Canada. The purposes were to develop and implement a parent and grandparent education program for immigrants and refugees from Vietnam and Central/South American who had moved to Canada (Strom et al., 1992c, 1992d). Grandparents and parents participated because they were both capable of change, wanted to continue having favorable relationships, and both needed to adjust and build support with the family. Native speakers conducted 60–90-minute interviews with 48 parents and grandparents to identify and prioritize their strengths and educational needs. The results of the interviews were used to formulate a multicultural parent and grandparent curriculum. Classes were presented in Spanish, Vietnamese, or English and met weekly for three months. Each session focused on one of these topics:

- Maintaining your cultural heritage
- Understanding the school system
- Handling independence and freedom
- Supporting socialization of children
- Relationships of siblings
- Spending time with children
- Teenagers, dating, and peer relations
- Language barriers with other adults
- Dealing with bilingualism in children
- Teaching moral and spiritual values
- Day care and early childhood education
- Preventing drugs, alcohol, and smoking
- Monitoring and interpreting television
- Knowing about community resources

Taiwan

A three-generational cross-cultural study by Strom and Strom (Strom et al., 1996c, Strom & Strom, 1998; Strom et al., 1999) consisting of 3,286 non-consanguineous subjects included 751 Chinese grandparents from the Republic of China, Taiwan. From the United States, the sample included Whites (n = 1,086), Blacks (n = 777), and Hispanics (n = 672). Comparisons between generations within each culture and between cultures were the focal points. Findings revealed significant differences in perceptions about grandparents across cultures as well as between the generations within cultures. All three generations identified aspects of grandparent success and issues for consideration. Guidelines and curriculum topics were recommended for education to support grandparent development.

Sweden

A grandparent education workshop for leaders in medicine, psychology, social work, and education was directed by Strom and Strom (1988) with support from the Sven & Dagmar Salén Foundation of Stockholm, Sweden. The workshop agenda included interactive presentations about the rationale for grandparent education, elements of suggested curriculum and instruction, establishing courses for grandparents in Sweden, goals and elements of grandparent education curriculum, and guidelines for facilitators for grandparents and residents of assistance living and long-term care facilities. In Sweden, migrant child education is complemented by training of parents and grandparents. Swedish schools encourage integration of families through a mutual adaptation which familiarizes foreign parents and grandparents with Swedish culture, values, and parental practices. Conversely, immigrant parents are encouraged to interpret their cultural mores to Swedish teachers to achieve mutual understanding and respect. When the family is seen as part of the solution to integration rather than as an obstacle, a more comprehensive and promising strategy becomes more successful.

Recommendations for Grandparents

Support Single Parents of Grandchildren

Over 15 million American single mothers are raising their 22 million children (Anderson et al., 2024). Black, American Indian, Hispanic, and Pacific Islanders account for twice the proportion of White children living with grandparents. Overall, seven million grandchildren live with grandparents. About 60% of householder grandparents are at least 60 years of age. The single-parent mothers of these children also resided with their own parents and grandparents who were householders, owning or renting their property in 80% of the cases. Success can begin when the grandparents and single mother set goals together for a child, mutual reinforcement of lessons taught by each other, and share their observations of child behavior. Grandparent education classes can provide ways to cope with child misbehavior and encourage education opportunities that enhance parenting. Grandparents should be made aware of changes in how public schools operate, challenges students experience, and ways that families should cooperate with teachers to promote progress including involvement of children in tutoring (Strom & Strom, 2011, 2021).

Help Grandchildren Set Goals and Achieve Their Potential

Setting goals is an important asset that should begin before adolescence and initially focus on favorable personality qualities. Children should learn to set goals and acquire a clear sense of self direction supported by perseverance. Such healthy characteristics are modeled by parents and grandparents who demonstrate resilience, optimism, and achievement motivation (Allport, 1963). Boshkova et al. (2018) have drawn to our attention an important teaching procedure called *family reading* which grandparents can use to guide the formation of a child's personality. Many stories are provided from foreign and Russian children's literature about the relationships of grandparents and grandchildren. In the age of information technology, the experiences of grandparents may not seem to be a model for future generations because it is difficult for elders to understand modern life and the interests of the younger generations. Intergenerational relationships are more easily built when the 'family reading' approach is applied for teaching children.

Teach More About Peer Prejudice

Although already rated by younger relatives as good teachers, grandparents can also benefit from greater understanding to help grandchildren cope with peer prejudices (Allport, 1954/1979). Strom et al. (1996b) found that all three generations ($n = 626$) gave Black grandparents highly favorable scores for accessibility to grandchildren, willingness to listen, readiness to provide emotional support, and consistent effort to teach nonacademic lessons about things that children need to know. Even when the grandparents had little formal education, they supported children by teaching respect for the feelings of others, building religious faith, good manners, healthy sense of right and wrong, and benefits of continued learning.

Value Child Fantasy Play and the Power of Imagination

Prowse (2021) explained the long-lasting benefits of childhood creativity that all grandparents and parents of young grandchildren should value to support creative thinking. Using play as a method of teaching honors child strengths and urges them to recognize imagination as a powerful resource. Many grandparents discourage fantasy play because they suppose that it will fail to prepare children for the realities of living in a harsh environment. On the contrary, fantasy can be a valuable defense for confronting adversity with the power of resilience. Play offers choices, enables a sense of what is possible, and motivates persistence needed to succeed in the real world. Children should be encouraged to retain creative abilities so they can generate alternative solutions everyone needs for resolving personal conflicts.

Spend Time Doing Things With Grandchildren

Grandparents should be recognized for the gift of time they share with grandchildren. Studies of child-rearing competence generally emphasize family differences in socioeconomic background and the level of formal education. One common assumption is that advantages in child-rearing are mainly a function of these variables. In our studies of family interaction, the influence of a nontraditional variable has also been examined. This variable is child access to grandparent time. Whereas socioeconomic status and formal education are fixed variables that grandparents cannot control, arranging time for someone else is a variable they can manipulate. Grandparents who spend more time with grandchildren know them better than those who devote less time. Consequently, they set more reasonable expectations for grandchildren who, in turn, are more likely to seek them out as listeners and advisors (Strom et al., 2005, 2018).

Grandparent and Parent Education Classes Should Become Available Worldwide

Many nations are reconsidering their social customs and economic systems that were developed to support conditions of a shorter lifespan. The goal is to design reforms that can fit a longevity of 80 years while improving quality of life (Strom & Strom, 2000, 2017, 2020). In addition to medical care, housing, and financial aid, attention must be given to mental health and well-being. Senior adults want to feel useful so that their lives have purpose. Many express regret that their role seems to have shifted from being the most important members of the family to becoming the least significant. They usually attribute their loss of prominence to advances in technology that have replaced generation, age, and gender as the basis for assigning status. By examining the evolution of these conditions, policymakers can better determine how to ensure that older adults remain valued in the community.

Two factors should be recognized. First, societies that are engaged in global economic competition must assign greater priority to the present and future than to the past. It follows that older adults are no longer considered models in certain sectors of life for younger people. Instead, every generation identifies with well-known individuals in their own or next older age group. Every society that depends on technology has reported a decline in the status of older people. They are seldom considered experts about much of anything except the world of yesterday and the process of growing old (Strom & Strom, 2017).

A second factor to recognize is that intergenerational relationships can enable an outlook on life than cannot be acquired in other ways. Until recently, it was supposed that aging brings perspective. This assumption continues to make sense in cultures where change occurs slowly. But the attainment of perspective in a longevity society requires something else than just getting older. Becoming aware of how other generations see things and feel is necessary to acquire a broad outlook and become responsive to the needs of others. Unless younger generation views are considered, the adult perspective is bound to diminish as they get older. Accordingly, the best method to respect parents and grandparents is to provide education that enables them to stay up-to-date and remain influential members of the family (Strom & Strom, 2020, 2021).

Conclusion

The concepts of parent education and grandparent education should be understood and encouraged by all communities as a way to effectively cope with societal change. This comprehensive approach calls for new traditions that recognize all generations are capable of adjustment through education and include the following:

- Build family expectations that motivate senior relatives to focus learning on self-improvement

- Obligate communities to go beyond advocating for lifelong learning by devising curriculum for culturally diverse populations
- Develop leadership training for volunteers to provide parent and grandparent classes
- Invite retirement community residents to attend grandparent education classes
- Disseminate the concept of parent and grandparent education in other countries

Key Concepts

1. When grandparents receive relevant adult education that focuses on supporting younger relatives, their attitudes and behaviors improve in the estimate of all three generations.
2. Most grandparents are eager to learn how to improve their contribution to the well-being of other relatives, know how to arrange help when a grandchild needs tutoring, and identify higher education opportunities for grandchildren.
3. The *Grandparent Strengths and Needs Inventory (GSNI)* is used to identify the needs of individuals and groups before instruction is provided and track grandparent progress based on an intervention program.
4. Cultural differences in the norms of grandparent behaviors can be gauged and used to shape lessons that match the needs of specific age groups of grandchildren and ethnic groups of grandparents.
5. Society should recognize that older adults need a sense of purpose and meaning to support mental health that can be provided through grandparent education.
6. A new tradition for grandparents should be involvement in classes that enable them to gain respect within the family and community.
7. Religious institutions should assume leadership for providing grandparent education in the community.
8. Volunteer service to nonprofit institutions/organizations is a way grandparents can enrich the life of residents in their neighborhood.
9. Lifelong learning should become a goal to support community mental health in longevity societies.
10. Parents and grandchildren help identify topics suitable for grandparent classes.

Generational Perspectives Activities

20.1 Discussion
20.2 Conversations With Young Children
20.3 A Scenario: Reasoning and Problem-Solving
20.4 Chapter Review
20.5 Parent and Grandparent Self-Evaluation
20.6 Storytelling

20.1 Discussion

1. How could your parents and grandparents benefit from family-related education?
2. What topics would you recommend that older adults should better understand?
3. Why do minority groups express greater willingness to study their family role?

4. How do your parents feel about their current role or potential as grandparents?
5. What are your reactions to formal outcomes attained by grandparent intervention?
6. What are your recommendations for implementing adult education for families?

20.2 Conversations With Young Children

1. What things have you watched grandparents do that you like about them?
2. What are some special things you enjoy about having grandparents take care of you?
3. Are there times when it is disappointing to be around your grandparents?
4. How often do you spend time doing fun things with your grandparents?
5. How do grandparents feel about what you are learning at school?

20.3 A Scenario: Reasoning and Problem-Solving

Janine is the mother of Tricia and the grandmother of 4-year-old LuAnne. Janine and Tricia want to cooperate to build a supportive family environment for LuAnne. What are your suggestions?

a. Set common goals that each of the women is willing to work toward together.
b. Avoid having arguments in front of LuAnne.
c. Provide positive feedback about contributions each of them is observed to make.
d. Talk about how their combined efforts seem to be having the desired result.

20.4 Chapter Review

1. What insights from the chapter will I try to apply in my relationships?
2. What is the most important key concept for me presented in this chapter?
3. What elements of this chapter do I wish I had known about earlier?

20.5 Parent and Grandparent Self-Evaluation

1. What can I do to help my grandchildren cope with racial discrimination?

    a. share my personal experience about ways to overcome bias of peers
    b. tell them to ignore negative messages that come from classmates
    c. advise them to tell the classroom teacher when there is an incident
    d. encourage them to respond in kind toward the peers who offend them
    e. Other _____

2. What goals should I encourage grandchildren to process their coping with racism?

    a. urge selection of personality goals that are key to success in the long-term
    b. recognize that inequity remains a fact of life we will gradually overcome
    c. talk personally to the school principal in charge of all the students
    d. ask the school guidance counselor to provide some recommendations
    e. Other _____

3. How can teachers help students process the racial messages they get from their peers?

    a. teachers can hold class conversations about negative messages of social inequity
    b. teachers should invite discriminated students to describe experiences at school

c. teachers should send a note to all parents about the damage of racial discrimination
   d. Other _____

4. I wanted to find out my grandchild's observations about prejudice at school.

   a. my grandchild recounted incidents that had been seen and heard
   b. the reporting did not include any evidence of bias
   c. my grandchild admitted being a party to racial prejudice
   d. my grandchild reported his observations of an incident to the teacher
   e. Other _____

5. My wish to participate in a grandparent education class.

   a. was not met because the school offered no classes
   b. because district officials said it was an uncommon request
   c. indicated no classes were offered online
   d. found that our community churches had not received any requests
   e. Other _____

6. I want my grandchildren to tell me about racial and religious prejudice they observe at school.

   a. invite the school student council to lead class discussions
   b. conduct an anonymous poll at the school about individual experiences
   c. ask the parent teachers association to decide how adults can help
   d. request that all parents discuss these issues with their family members
   e. Other _____

20.6 Storytelling

Historically, storytelling has been a dominant classic and progressive method of teaching around the world. The purposes of a storyteller are to present imaginary or real-life examples showing how some concept applies to a particular situation. People like stories, they pay attention to the procession of events, and usually remember aspects of a story for a long time. Your stories can reinforce the concepts in this chapter for family members and classmates. Please share your stories with them.

References

Allport, G. W. (1963). *Pattern and growth in personality*. Harcourt College Publishers.
Allport, G. W. (1979). *The nature of prejudice*. Basic Books. (Original work published 1954)
Anderson, L. R., Buck, C., & Hayward, G. M. (2024, February). *Grandparents and their coresident grandchildren: 2021 [P20-588]*. United States Census Bureau. https://www2.census.gov/library/publications/2024/demo/p20-588.pdf
Boshkova, G., Shastina, E., & Shatunova, O. (2018). The role of grandparents in the child's personality formation (on the material of children's literature). *Journal of Social Studies Education Research, 9*(2), 283–294. https://jsser.org/index.php/jsser/article/view/263
Bradley, F. (2022, April 27). *When the boat people came to Hong Kong*. Shanghai United Media Group, Sixth Tone. https://www.sixthtone.com/news/1010214
Buki, L. P. (1995). *Intergenerational perceptions of English speaking and Spanish speaking Mexican American grandparents* (Publication No. 9606201) [Doctoral dissertation, Arizona State University]. ProQuest Dissertations & Theses Global.
Centers for Disease Control and Prevention. (2024). *About teen pregnancy*. Division of Reproductive Health. https://www.cdc.gov/reproductive-health/teen-pregnancy/index.html

Collinsworth, P., Strom, R. D., Strom, P. S., & Young, D. (1991). The *Grandparent Strengths and Needs Inventory*: Development and factorial validation. *Educational and Psychological Measurement, 51*(3), 785–792. https://doi.org/10.1177/0013164491513030

Gallup Foundation. (2024). *How religious are Americans?* https://news.gallup.com/poll/358364/religious-americans.aspx

Heeder, S. H. (1998). *Black grandparents' strengths and needs: A three-generational assessment* (Publication No. 9828182) [Doctoral dissertation, Arizona State University]. ProQuest Dissertations and Theses Global.

Martinez, G., & Passel, J. S. (2025). *Facts about the U.S. Black population*. Pew Research Center. https://www.pewresearch.org/social-trends/fact-sheet/facts-about-the-us-black-population/

Prowse, V. (2021, November 15). The long-lasting benefits of childhood creativity: Creativity is intangible, but has real economic benefits for individuals. *Psychology Today*. https://www.psychologytoday.com/us/blog/work-your-mind/202111/the-long-lasting-benefits-of-childhood-creativity#:~:text=Key%20points,creativity%20also%20boosts%20education%20attainment

Statistisches Bundesamt. (2024). *Current population of Germany*. https://www.destatis.de/EN/Themes/Society-Environment/Population/Current-Population/_node.html

Strom, R. D., Daniels, S., Wurster, S., Betz, M. A., Graf, P., & Jansen, L. (1983). Childrearing attitude assessment as a prelude to integrating foreign families. *Journal of Marriage and Family, 45*(4), 961–963. https://doi.org/10.2307/351809

Strom, R. D., & Strom, S. K. (1983). Redefining the grandparent role. *Cambridge Journal of Education, 13*(1), 25–28. https://doi.org/10.1080/0305764830130107

Strom, R. D. (1984). *Parent As A Teacher Inventory*. Scholastic Testing Service.

Strom, R. D., Wurster, S., Betz, M. A., Daniels, S., Graf, P., & Jansen, L. (1984). A comparison of West German and guestworker parents' childrearing attitudes and expectations. *Journal of Comparative Family Studies, 15*(3), 427–440. https://www.jstor.org/stable/41601511

Strom, R. D., & Strom, S. K. (1988). *Grandparent education*. Sven & Dagmar Salén Foundation Stockholm, Sweden.

Strom, R. D., & Strom, S. K. (1989). *Grandparent development: Final report*. American Association of Retired Persons Andrus Foundation.

Strom, R. D., & Strom, S. K. (1991a). *Becoming a better grandparent. A guidebook for strengthening the family*. Sage.

Strom, R. D., & Strom, S. K. (1991b). *Becoming a better grandparent: Viewpoints on strengthening the family*. Sage.

Strom, R. D., & Strom, S. K. (1991c). *Grandparent education: A guide for leaders*. Sage.

Strom, R. D., & Strom, S. K. (1992a). *Achieving grandparent potential: A guidebook for building intergenerational relationships*. Sage.

Strom, R. D., & Strom, S. K. (1992b). *Achieving grandparent potential: Viewpoints on building intergenerational relationships*. Sage.

Strom, R. D., Johnson, D., Strom, S. K., & Daniels, S. (1992c). Developing curriculum for parent and grandparent immigrants and refugees from Vietnam and Central/South America. *Journal of Instructional Psychology, 19*(1), 53–60. https://www.proquest.com/openview/7095c5aed30d8e379a3f61239fd822ee/1?pq-origsite=gscholar&cbl=2029838

Strom, R. D., Johnson, D., Strom, S. K., & Daniels, S. (1992d). Supporting the adjustment of immigrant families. *International Journal of Sociology of the Family, 22*, 35–43. https://www.jstor.org/stable/23029771

Strom, R. D., & Strom, S. K. (1993). *Grandparent Strengths and Needs Inventory [manual, profile, grandparent, parent and grandchild versions]*. Scholastic Testing Service. https://www.public.asu.edu/~rdstrom/gsnim.html

Strom, R. D., Strom, S. K., Collinsworth, P., Sato, S., Makino, K., Sasaki, Y., Sasaki, H., & Nishio, N. (1995). Grandparents in Japan: A three-generational study. *The International Journal of Aging and Human Development, 40*(3), 209–226. https://doi.org/10.2190/KYFJ-DGWF-WJB8-FLYR

Strom, R. D. (1996). Establishing new traditions for a longevity society: Japan and the United States. *The Journal of Intercultural Studies, 23*, 1–13. Kansai University of Foreign Studies Publications [Osaka, Japan].

Strom, R. D., Beckert, T., & Strom, S. K. (1996a). Determining the success of grandparent education. *Educational Gerontology, 22*(7), 637–649. https://doi.org/10.1080/0360127960220702

Strom, R. D., Strom, S. K., Collinsworth, P., & Strom, P. S (1996b). Black grandparents: Curriculum development. *The International Journal of Aging and Human Development, 43*(2), 119–134. https://doi.org/10.2190/J1WA-WH8G-H6N2-DPQA

Strom, R. D., Strom, S. K., Shen, Y.-L., Li, S.-J., & Sun, H.-L. (1996c). Grandparents in Taiwan: A three-generational study. *The International Journal of Aging and Human Development. 42*(1), 1–19. https://doi.org/10.2190/D7R2-DG1L-DDFY-PTM7

Strom, R. D., & Strom, S. K. (1997). Building a theory of grandparent development. *The International Journal of Aging and Human Development, 45*(4), 255–286. https://doi.org/10.2190/HAVE-HWKU-6BCG-9EY5

Strom, R. D., Buki, L., & Strom, S. K. (1997). Strengths and education needs of Mexican American grandparents. *Educational Gerontology, 23*(4), 359–376. https://doi.org/10.1080/0360127970230405

Strom, R. D., & Strom, S. K. (1998). Education for grandparents in Taiwan and the United States: A three-generational study. *The Journal of Intercultural Studies, 25,* 119–166. Kansai University of Foreign Studies Publications [Osaka, Japan].

Strom, R. D., Strom, S. K., Wang, C.-M., Shen, Y.-L., Griswold, D., Chan, H.-S., & Yang, C.-Y. (1999). Grandparents in the United States and the Republic of China: A comparison of generations and cultures. *The International Journal of Aging and Human Development, 49*(4), 279–317. https://doi.org/10.2190/DQFF-LVRU-U6W9-8Q6L

Strom, R. D., & Strom, S. K. (2000). Meeting the challenge of raising grandchildren. *The International Journal of Aging and Human Development, 51*(3), 183–198. https://doi.org/10.2190/FR92-EGW2-VEVU-P8CR

Strom, R. D., Heeder, S. D., & Strom, P. S. (2005). Performance of Black grandmothers: Perceptions of three generations of females. *Educational Gerontology, 31*(3), 187–205. https://doi.org/10.1080/03601270590900927

Strom, R. D., Strom, S. K., Fournet, L., & Strom, P. S. (2006, August). Cooperative learning in old age: Instruction and assessment. *Educational Gerontology.* https://doi.org/10.1080/0360127970230607 (Original work published 1997)

Strom, P. S., & Strom, R. D. (2011). Grandparent education: Raising grandchildren. *Educational Gerontology, 37*(1), 910–923. https://doi.org/10.1080/03601277.2011.595345

Strom, R. D., & Strom, P. S. (2016). Grandparent education for assisted living facilities. *Educational Gerontology, 43*(1), 11–20. https://doi.org/10.1080/03601277.2016.1231518

Strom, R. D., & Strom, P. S. (2017). Grandparent learning and cultural differences. *Educational Gerontology, 43*(8), 417–427. https://doi.org/10.1080/03601277.2017.1314642

Strom, R. D., Collinsworth, P., Strom, S. K., & Griswold, D. (2018). Strengths and needs of black grandparents. In J. Hendricks (Ed.), *The ties of later life* (pp. 195–208). Routledge.

Strom, R. D., & Strom, S. K. (2018). Raising expectations for grandparents: A three generational study. In J. Hendricks (Ed.), *The ties of later life* (pp. 133–140). Routledge.

Strom, P. S., & Strom, R. D. (2019). Grandparent education: Curriculum, instruction and evaluation. In B. Hayslip, Jr. & C. Fruhauf (Eds.), *Grandparenting: Influences on the dynamics of family relationships* (pp. 331–346). Springer.

Strom, R. D., & Strom, P. S. (2020). Productive aging: Peer influence and retirement. *Educational Gerontology, 46*(11), 678–687. https://doi.org/10.1080/03601277.2020.1807085

Strom, R. D., & Strom, P. S. (2021). Learning throughout life about the needs of all generations: Recognizing and counteracting generational isolation. In M. London (Ed.), *The Oxford handbook of lifelong learning* (2nd ed., pp. 183–206). The Oxford University Press.

Strom, P. S., & Strom, R. D. (2024). *Mental health and relationships from early adulthood through old age.* Routledge.

United States Census Bureau. (2024, June 27). *New estimates highlight differences in growth between the U.S. Hispanic and non-Hispanic populations.* https://www.census.gov/newsroom/press-releases/2024/population-estimates-characteristics.html

Watson, J. A. (1997, Winter). Factors associated with African American grandparents' interest in grandparent education. *The Journal of Negro Education, 66*(1), 73–82. https://doi.org/10.2307/2967252

Watson, J. A., & Koblinsky, S. A. (1997, March). Strengths and needs of working-class African American and Anglo-American grandparents. *The International Journal of Aging and Human Development, 44*(2), 149–165. https://doi.org/10.2190/3NQV-WJQV-0ELF-A4XA

Index

Note: numbers in **bold** indicate a table on the corresponding page.

AACAP *see* American Academy of Child and Adolescent Psychiatry
AARP *see* American Association of Retired Persons
Abbott, R. 209
ABC Mouse 86
abortion 26
Abrahamsson, S. 82
absenteeism 239
abundant and deprived households 64–66
academic achievement 141
accommodation of information 112
achievement motivation 142
achievement scores 173
Action for Children's Television parent advocacy group 125–126
addiction 160, 254, 256; drug 280, 285; screen 123; social media 81–82
addicts as parents 285
adoption of babies and children 27, 63, 283; *see also* orphans and orphanages
advance scheduling 256
advertising: big business 128; truth distorted by 129
advertising aimed at children: beginning of character licensing 124; big business advertising in 128; evolution of 123–124, 132; FCC limits on 126; food preferences and 130; impacts on child health and nutrition 127; legislation for child protections against 127–128; objections to 125–126; parental guidance for child critical thinking about 131; revolution of franchising and 125; teaching children about commercials 130–131; on television 124–125
Alabama: Auburn 272; Montgomery 44; Selma 44; University of Alabama at Birmingham 16
Alabama Law Enforcement Agency 231
Alabbasi, A. 101
Albanese, A. 82
algorithms 15, 82
Allen, D. 186
Allport, G. 216–218, 322
Amber Alerts 236
American Academy of Child and Adolescent Psychiatry (AACAP) 206, 232
American Association of Mental Deficiency 63
American Association of Retired Persons (AARP) 273, 284, 304, 311; AARP Study, publicity of 314
American College Test (ACT) 159
American Educational Research Association 64, 156
American non-profit educational organization *see* Khan Academy
amygdala 30
Anderson, L. R. 281
Annie E. Casey Foundation 1, 9
antisemitism and antisemitic behavior 217–218
antisocial behavior 66, 101, 109, 232
Ardrey, R. 201
Arizona: Mesa 65; Phoenix 311, 316, 318
Arizona Ecumenical Council 311
Arizona State University 3, 311; Becoming a Better Grandparent program at 314; play lab at 58
assimilation of information 112
Assor, A. 190
attachment *see* emotional attachment
Auburn University 3; Osher Lifelong Learning Institute at 318; Strom Website hosted by 103, 314
Australia: immigrants in 190; social media ban for youth in 82
Australian Government Department of Social Services: website *The Australian Parenting Website* 51
autism 51, **219**

babies: 'adoption' by feeble-minded women of 63; attachment by 24, 35; first fears of 234–235; health mothers and normal babies 28; House Guest Experiment on IQ of 63; impact of narcotic drugs in utero on 29; milestones of language development in 49; scientific studies of 2
Baby Boomer generation 205, 304
Bales, D. 287
Barker, J. 249
basic literacy 159
'Battleship' game 116
Baumeister, R. 173–174, 217, 256
Bavarian Ministry of Education 319
Beauvoir, S. de 61
Beaver, N. H. 67
Beckert, T. 184
Becoming a Better Grandparent program 314, 318
Bernard Van Zuiden Charity Trust 320
Binet, A. 111, 117
Black children and doll preference 147–148; see also Doll Study on race
Black families 315–316; see also race
Black grandmothers: Heeder's study of 316
Black grandparents: Strom's study of 322
Black mothers and their children 44; Hess's study of 42
Black preschoolers in Harlem: Deutsch's and Kirk's study of 64
Black preschoolers in Michigan: Weikart's observation of 66
Bloom, B. 64–65, 189
Blossom Experiment 148–149
'boat people' 319
Boomers see Baby Boomer generation
boredom 143, 182; at school 190; common experience of 190; overcoming 189–191; problem of 190
Boshkova, G. 322
Bowlby, J. 25
brain development 24, 30; deprivation and 28; language and 47; playtime and 81, 96
brain function, executive 247, 252
brain scans 27, 255
Braque, G. 112
Bredehoft, D. 285
Brooks, R. 252
Brown, B. F. 156–157
Brown Shoe Company 124
Brown v. the Board of Education 148
Bruner, J. 110
Bucharest Project 28
Buck Rogers character 124
Buffalo Bob character 124–125
Buki, L. P. 316

Bulgaria 265
bully behavior 237; research on 239; school shootings and 233–234
bullying 30, 82, 155, 236–237, 239; establishing anti-bully policies and programs 217, 234; ridicule as 233–234
Burkitt, E. 209
Burundi 265
Bushman, B. 217

Cain, S. 186
Calder, A. 112
California 117; 1986 self-esteem task force 173; 2024 legislation to protect youth from addictive tech 82; Fair, Accurate, Inclusive, and Respectful Education Act (FAIR) 217; Sacramento 65
Campbell, K. 174
Canada 318, 320
Captain Kangaroo character 126
caregivers: of aging relatives 11–12; child adjustment to school and 33; children's imitation of 77; children's play and 209–210; child socialization and 203–204; civil behavior and 201; of disabled children 221; Dunedin longitudinal study and 248; early childhood development and 42; early childhood learning and 3; empathy lessons conveyed by 30; Farran's work on children and 67; grandparents as 205–206, 221, 280–281, 283; impact on early childhood language development of 45; of infants 25; of older relatives 252; non-response by 28; Skeels on orphans and 64; substitute 51; touch and infant stimulation by 27; wages of 29
career goals 143–144
Carlson, M. 26–27
Carlson, S. 250–252
Carr, A. 30
Casey, B. J. 255
Cattaert, C: *Where do Goldfish Go?* 208
Ceausescu, N. 26
cell phones 11, 50, 87, 88, 115, 185; see also smartphones
censorship 103, 208, 209
Centers for Disease Control and Prevention 127, 132
centration 103; see also egocentrism
Centsables, The (television show) 249
Chall, J. 159
Channel One 126–127
Chaplin, C. 124
cheating (in school) 155
child abduction 230–231, 285; see also child kidnapping
child adjustment at school **34–35**

childcare 28–29, 185; family income spent on 205; grandmothers as sources of 283; grandparents and grandparent surrogates as sources of 267, 280–281, 291
childcare centers 65
child custody 232–233
child fantasy play 209; violent or warlike 209
child fears *see* fears of children
child group care 203–204
child health and nutrition 127
childhood *see* goals and priorities in childhood
childhood obesity 127, 132
child kidnapping 230–232
child language development 47
childless couples 232
Child Narcissism Scale 175
child outlook on relationships 283–284
child protection against advertising, legislation for 127–128
children's food preferences 130
children and youth disabilities, types of **219**
child's concern for others **32–33**
child screen time: research on 81; scheduling 81; ways of limiting 128–129
child's sense of hope 233
child sexual exploitation and abuse 231–232
child stages in the comprehension of death 206–208
child thinking and cognitive development 110–121; chapter review 120; conversations with young children 119; discussion 119; generational perspectives activities 119; home schooling and 117; information processing of children 112–113; intelligence and thinking 111–112; key concepts 118–119; parent and grandparent self-evaluation 120; Piaget's stages of cognition **113**, 113–117; scenario (reasoning and problem-solving) 120; storytelling 121; why start school early 110–111
Child Welfare Information Gateway 286
China 12, 51, 321; elementary teachers in 162, 163, 164; Hong Kong 163; Macau 163
China Sea 319
Chugani, H. 27
City College of New York 147
civil behavior and territoriality 201–203
Civil Rights March 44
Clark, K. 147–148
Clark, M. 147–148
Clark, S. 15
cliques 155
Cloward, R. 157
Coalition for Children 235
cocaine addiction 285

cognitive ability 101
cognitive development 28, 62; *see also* child thinking and cognitive development
cognitive flexibility 27
cognitive structures *see* schemas
cognitive tempo 103, 187
College Advising Corps 162
Collinsworth, P. 184
Columbia University 171
commercials and advertising: teaching children about 130–131
Common Sense Media 128
concern for others *see* child's concern for others; empathy
conflicts and learning to get along 201–213; amount of time in group care 203–204; chapter review 212; civil behavior and territoriality 201–203; conversations with young children 211; dominion play 202–203; discussion 211; dominion play guidelines 203; key concepts 210–211; generational perspectives activities 211; grandparents as child caregivers 205–206; the Little Soldier, or talking to your child about war and death 206–210; milestones for 5-year-olds 204–205; parent and grandparent self-evaluation 212–213; scenario (reasoning and problem-solving) 212; storytelling 213
Confucianism 12
Consumer Protection Act (Canada) 128
Cooper, A. 127
cooperative learning 317; inclusion and 220–221
cortisol 26–27
Council for Economic Education 304
Cowdery 217
Cramond, B. 101
Crazy People (film) 130
creativity 60–63, 96; expertise and 101; intelligence and 101; retention of curiosity and 101
credibility of internet sources 79
crime: critical thinking about 232
critical thinking 123; about crime 232; parental guidance for child critical thinking about advertising 131; truth distortion and 129–130

Daniel Tiger's Neighborhood (app) 83
da Vinci, Leonardo 100
day care 3, 27, 29, 88, 115, 183, 191, 201–204
Dearborn Michigan Public Schools 65
Dearing, E. 66

death and dying: child stages in the comprehension of 206–208; race and rates of 16
DeLaune, M. 231
depressed adults 27, 64, 272; grandparents 271, 281
depression 25, 36, 53, 82, 128, 282, 286, 289
deprivation and brain development 28
Deutsch, M. 64
developmental delay **219**
developmental learning and practice 118
developmental psychology 4, 223
disability, disabled students 51; Education for All Handicapped Children Act (1975) 219; grandchildren with 221; learning 64; permanent 210; social exclusion and discrimination against 218–219; types of student disabilities **219**, 219–220
diseases 26; Alzheimer's 302; heart 127; infectious 272; sexually transmitted 232, 256
Disney, W. 124
Divecha, D. 303
divorce 115, 143, 280, 284; childlessness and 232; *see also* parent separation
doll cutout 124
dolls 31, 125, 207
Doll Study on race 147–148
Dominion Play guidelines 203
dose–response relationship 16
Dovidio, J. F. 218
Doyle, W. 67
dropout 239
drug abuse by parents 285
drug overdose by parents 280
Duckworth, A. 171
Duke University 162
Duke University Libraries Exhibits 125
Dunedin Longitudinal Study 101, 232, 248–249
Dunedin University 101
Durkin, K. 67
Dweck, C. 171–172
Dye, H. 63

Early Childhood Mental Health Consultation (ECMHC) 248
early learning at home 75
Economist, The 265
Edison, T. 191
Education for All Handicapped Children Act (1975) 219
ECMHC *see* Early Childhood Mental Health Consultation
egocentrism, of children 31, 103, 143; diminishing 36; Piaget on **113**; in preschoolers 115; reducing 35; in upper elementary grades 116
elder care 12
elders 12, 14, 207, 265, 299, 300; indigenous 317; intergenerational relationships with 322
e-media 11
emotional attachment: Theory of Emotional Attachment 25; trust and 24–25, 35
emotional bonding 25
emotional connection: significance of 26
emotional desensitization 83
emotional development 9, 48, 83, 117, 143–144; milestones of 205
emotional deprivation: nonattachment and 25
emotional dysfunction 30, 143
emotional growth 4
emotional intelligence 24, 247; significance of 29–30
emotional literacy 31
emotional reactivity 84
emotional resilience 3
emotional and social learning 3, 7
emotional stress 221
emotional support 10, 12, 191, 215; peers and classmates as source of 217–217, 219
emotional vulnerability 2
empathy 3, 24, 29, 115, 224; adolescence and 32; child's concern for others and 32–33; fear and 235; fostering 77; lack of 27, 174; limitation of 234; social skills and 30–31; video game use and 83
empathy practice 31
encouragement, limits of 172–173
England 25, 174, 318; Newcastle University 160; Oxford and Cambridge University 163, 176, 318; *see also* United Kingdom
Ericcson, A. 188
expectations, influence of 146–149
Experimenter Bias Effect 148
expertise 101; gender differences in 189; solitude and the development of 188–189

Facebook (Meta) 86, 128
failure *see* student failure
FAIR *see* Fair, Accurate, Inclusive, and Respectful Education Act (California)
Fair, Accurate, Inclusive, and Respectful Education Act (FAIR) (California) 217
families: grandparents and adult education about 14
family abuse 285–287
family advice *see* grandparents giving and seeking family advice
family affairs: encouraging grandparents to be active in 12
family conflict 303

family conversations and child language 42–56; chapter review 54; continued lag in child language 48; conversations with young children 54; discussion 54; electronic versus nonelectronic toys and language 50; generational perspectives activities 54; guidelines for reading to children 51–52; influence of parent and child conversation 42–44; key concepts 53; learning to talk and vocabulary of children 44–48; milestones in language development 49; parent and grandparent self-evaluation 55–56; parents' perception of schooling 43–44; parents' time with children 51; Project Head Start 44; Puzzle Experiment 42–43; scenario (reasoning and problem-solving) 54; storytelling 56; time and teaching methods 49–52
family distancing 13–14
family instability 25
family principles for monitoring success 149–150
family reading 322
family safety rules 235–236
family time 301
Farran, D. 67
fear: good judgement and 234; overcoming 235; universality of 230; value of 218
fears of children 9, 25, 210; denial of 234–235; fantasy as tool to reduce 206; fear of academic failure 240; fear of being alone 240; fear of group differences in school 218; fear of making a mistake 171; fear of punishment 216; fear of peer victimization 239–240; fear of separation from parent 207; fear of strangers 231; fear of uncertainty 239–240; fear of victimization 240; fear of war and death 208, 209; mental health worries of 239; parental responses to 234–237; school-age children's fears 237–241
fears of parents for their children: regarding drugs and online predators 218; regarding the internet 85; regarding mental health 239
fears of parents and children 230–244; chapter review 242; conversations with young children 242; critical thinking about crime 232; discussion 241–242; key concepts 240–241 mental health worries of 239; parent and grandparent self-evaluation 242–244; parent separation and child custody 232–233; safety concerns 230–231; scenario 242; school shootings and bully behavior 233–234; sex offenders 231–232; storytelling 244
Federal Communications Commission (FCC) 126

federal education policy (US) 215, 219; disabled students and 219
federal government (US) 3, 126; employment policies of 219
Fernald, A. 48
Feuchter, M. D. 190
filial piety 12
financial aid from the state 286, 323
financial assistance from relatives 315
financial burdens and difficulties 221, 232, 249; day care as 273; grandparents as substitute carer for children due to 284
financial debt 256
financial literacy 163, 190, 304
financial planning 306
financial status 249
financial support 207
financial support systems (i.e. Social Security) 12, 13
Flash Gordon character 124
Florida 273; Cape Canaveral 156; Department of Education 234; Hope Scholarships 234
Florida State University 173, 256
Flynn Effect 101
food preferences *see* children's food preferences
four foundational harms to children 160
Fox, Nathan 28
frustration 3, 4; cursing to express 247; feelings of 11, 30; preventing 61; at television advertising 129; tolerance for 253–254
frustration effects 183
Frustration Scale 184
frustration tolerance 248

Garcia, E. 46
gay youths 238
gender 31, 47, 50, 82, 101; child 204, 319; grandchild's 315, 319; peers of same age and 182; status and 323
gender differences, in expertise 189
gender equity 273
gender role expectations 149
General Mills 125
generational differences and disagreements 15, 299
Generational Perspectives Activities 4–5, 9, 24, 42, 58, 77, 96, 110, 123, 141, 155, 170, 182, 201, 215, 230, 247, 280, 311
generational reciprocal learning 2
generations: parent and grandparent 16; three-generations perspectives of grandparent behavior 311–314, 315; three-generations studies, various 316, 318–319, 321
Generations United 287
Generation X (Gen X) 205

generativity 272
George Miller Award 223
Georgetown University Center on Education and the Workforce 160
German as a Second Language Institute, University of Munich 319
gerontology 4, 14, 318
Ghertner, R. 285
G. I. Joe character 125
Gill, D. 62
global economy and economic competition 177, 323
global perspectives, era of 190–191
goals 11, 15–16; academic 110; age-appropriate 150; baseline 190; caregiver 27; compassion as 30; happiness as 61; long-term 255; national educational 191; personal 78, 88, 208, 221, 252; personality 9, 143–145, **145**, 146, 237; reasoning and problem-solving as 152; self-improvement 149; self-selected 10; teaching children to set 141–143; tutoring 176
goals and expectations for grandparents 265–278; chapter review 277; conversations with young children 276; discussion 276; generational perspectives activities 276; key concepts 275–276; parent and grandparent self-evaluation 277–278; scenario for problem-solving 276; storytelling 278; traditions and needs for new goals (goals 1–7) 265–275
goals and priorities in childhood 141–153; chapter review 152; conversations with young children on 152; discussion 151; influence of expectations on 146–149; family principles for monitoring success 149–150; key concepts 150–151; parent and grandparent self-evaluation 152–153; personality goals before career goals 143–146; sibling rivalry and the pursuit of autonomy as 146; storytelling 153; teaching children to set 141–143
goal setting and adult success 150
golden years 206
Goldstein, S. 252
Goleman, D. 29, 32
Goodlad, J. 156
Gould, D. S. 262
Goyer, A. 286
grade inflation 165, 177
grandchildren: grandparent education and views of 14–15; grandparents' spending time with 322–323; grandparent views on raising 284–285; helping them set goals 322; supporting single parents of 321; teaching about peer prejudice to 322

Grandfamilies & Kinship Support Network 280
Grandmothers as Mothers Again 287
grandparent behavior: Heeder's study of 316; Strom's and Strom's cross-cultural study of 321; three-generational perspectives of 311–314, 315; three-generational studies, various 316, 318–319, 321
grandparent commitment to raising their grandchildren 280–282
grandparent education: in assisted living 317; cooperative learning for 317; including the views of grandchildren and parents in 14–15; loneliness and group peer support for 317; making available worldwide, need for 323
grandparent education programs and initiatives: Becoming a Better Grandparents 314, 318; in England 318
grandparent goals and expectations *see* goals and expectations for grandparents
Grandparent Information Center 284
grandparents: as child caregivers 205–206; as teachers 12–17
grandparents giving and seeking family advice 297–309: advice about money 304–305; chapter review 308; conversations with young children 307; discussion 307; family respect and giving advice 298–299; generational perspectives activities 307; giving and seeking of advice between generations 300–301; key concepts 306–307; parent and grandparent self-evaluation 308–309; presenting advice with care 303–305; principles for application 305; relying on prayer for guidance 301–302; scenario (reasoning and problem-solving) 308; seeking peer advice 302–303; self-disclosure as necessary risk 299–300; storytelling 309; telling the truth by givers of advice 297–298
grandparents raising their grandchildren 280–294: chapter review 293; conversations with young children 292–293; discussion 292; generational perspectives activities 292; goals to guide family obligations regarding 282; goals for grandparent support groups 287–289; grandparent commitment to raising their grandchildren 280–282; grandparent and parent goal agreement regarding 282–284; grandparent views on 284–285; group communication skills, applying of 289–290; key concepts 291–292; parent and grandparent self-evaluation 293–294; perspectives of grandparents on 281; principles to guide grandparent behavior 290–291;

protection of children from family abuse as a result of 285–287; scenario (reasoning and problem-solving) 293; scope of the challenge regarding 280–281; storytelling 294
Grandparents as Parents group 287
grandparent rights and responsibilities **267–269**
grandparent strengths and cultural diversity 311–326: chapter review; conversations with young children 325; cooperative learning for grandparent education 317; curriculum for minority families in the US 315–316; discussion 324–325; generational perspectives activities 324; key concepts 324; parent and grandparent self-evaluation 325–326; scenario (reasoning and problem-solving) 325; storytelling 326; *see also* grandparent education
Grandparent Strengths and Needs Inventory (GSNI) 311–318; AARP study 314–315; as instrument of evaluation 312, 318; international research and training leaders 317–318; results for three generations 312–314
grandparent support groups: goals for 287–289
grandparent views on raising grandchildren 284–285
gratification: delayed or delaying 3, 171, 247, 255–256; instant 128; patience and delay of 254–255
Greene, R. 247
group communication skills 289–290
group peer support: loneliness and 317
guest workers and guestworker families 318–319
guilt 82, 115, 206, 216; imposing on children of 203; inability to feel 25
Guiney, H. 232
Gunnar, M. 27–28
guns and gun violence in the US 206, 233; *see also* school shootings
Gutierrez, A. 265

Hadani, H. 67
Haidt, J.: *The Anxious Generation* 160
Hannah, D. 130
Harlow, H. 25–26
Harris, J. R. 223, 300
Harris, N. 202
Hart, B. 44–48
Harvard Test of Inflected Acquisition 184
Havighurst, R. 65
Head Start program 3, 44, 65
Heeder, S. H. 316

He-Man and the Masters of the Universe (cartoon show) 126
Henson, J. 125
Hernandez, R. 272
Hess, R. 42–44
Hirsch-Pasek, K. 67
Hispanics 51, 316; *see also* Mexican Americans; race
Holman, C. 250
home and group care 28–29
Homeland Security (US) 236
homeschooling 188
Hong Kong 319–320
Hong Kong Society for Child Health and Development 320
Hopalong Cassidy character 125
House Guest Experiment 63–64
Howdy Doody Time 124
Hughes, A. 301
Huxley, A.: *Brave New World* 13

IDEA *see* Individuals with Disabilities Education Act (US)
identification stage of child development 77
IEP *see* Individualized Education Plan
imaginary or real-life examples, as related by storytellers 5, 20, 39, 56, 71, 93, 108, 121, 136, 153, 168, 180, 195, 213, 228, 244, 260, 278
imaginary friends or companions 185–187
incarceration 66, 239, 284
inclusion: California Fair, Accurate, Inclusive, and Respectful Education Act (FAIR) 217; cooperative learning and 220–221; school inclusion practices 218–219
inclusion classrooms for students with disabilities 219
Individualized Education Plan (IEP) 220
Individuals with Disabilities Education Act (IDEA) 219
infancy: chapter review 37; children as social observers 31–33; conversations with young children 37; deprivation and brain development 28; discussion 37; emotional connection, significance of 26; evaluation of home and group care 28–31; generational perspectives activities 36; importance of touch during 27–28; key concepts 35–36; maternal and social deprivation 25–26; parent and grandparent self-evaluation 37–39; questions and considerations regarding child adjustment at school **34–35**; reporting social skills to parents 34–35; scenario (reasoning and problem-solving) 37; storytelling 39; trust and emotional

attachment 24–25; trust and social awareness 24–39
Infant Schools 155
influence of media on children 123–136; chapter review 134; conversations with young children 133–134; discussion 133; evolution of advertising on children 123–125; generational perspectives activities 133; key concepts 132–133; parent and grandparent self-evaluation 134–135; reflection scenario 134; storytelling 136; *see also* advertising aimed at children
Inhelder, B. 112
instability *see* family instability
Instagram 86, 128
intelligence quotient *see* IQ
intergenerational: conflict 15; conversations 17, 78; discussion 304; opinions 306; relationships 149, 322–323
International Adoption Project 27
international research: training leaders and 317–318
internet *see* credibility of internet sources; young children learn about the internet
internet safety practices 85–88
internet search skills, developing 80
internet skills 86
intergenerational: conflict 15; conversations 17, 78; discussions, about money 304; opinions 306; perspectives 290; relationships 149, 322, 323
interpersonal expectancy 149
IQ 25; Bloom's findings regarding environment and 65, 189; Dweck's experiments with 171–172; Flynn effect on 101; high IQs not tied to future wealth 29; IQ scores less in important than lack of impulsivity regarding future success 249; Kim on creativity and expertise and 101; Marshmallow Experiment results more predictive of SAT results than IQ test 255; nonverbal IQ tests 171; Skeel's experiments with play and orphans with low IQ 63; and wandering 64

Jackson, M. 254: *Distracted: Reclaiming our Focus in a World of Lost Attention* 160
Jacobson, L. 148
Japan 12, 51, 319; Elementary Teacher Training 162
Johnny West character 125
Johnson, L. B. 44; War on Poverty by 65
Jones, C. 280

Kagan, J. 187
Kandinsky, V. 112
Kellerman, G. 272
Kennedy, J. F. 64, 157
Kennedy National Space Center 156
Kenner Products 125
Kerig, P. K. 27
Kermit the Frog character 125
Khan Academy 161
Khan Academy Help Center 161
Khan, S. 161
kidnapping *see* child kidnapping
Kidwell, M. C. 27
Kim, K. H. 101
kindergarten 115; new pre-kindergarten curriculum 67
King, Martin Luther, Jr. 44
Kirk, S. 64
Kiwanis 234
Kloo, M. 234
Koblinsky, S. A. 315
Kolluri, S. 304
Kraizer, S. 235–236
Krznaric, R. 27
Kuppens, S. 285

Landhuis, C. 101
language development *see* family conversations and child language
LeapFrog 86; video games 83
learning disabilities 64
leisure and leisure time 1, 61, 84, 96, 183–184, 188, 281
Leonardo da Vinci *see* da Vinci, Leonardo
Lerner, M. 204
Levine, L. 46, 51
Levitin, D.: *Weaponized Lies* 129
licensing and rights 130; character 124–125
Lieber, R. 305
Lippitt, P. 158
Lippitt, R. 158
Little Debbie 317
Little Orphan Annie 124
Little Soldier, or talking to your child about war and death 206–210
loneliness 185, 191, 235, 301; group peer support and 317
longevity nations and societies 2, 9, 12–14, 304, 323
low-ability children 64
low-income households and families 3; behaviors of elementary students from 182; College Advisory Corps as source of motivation for 162; early intervention programs and 51; discomfort with culture of learning in 79; emotional attachments and behavior issues in school of children from 25; fathers and children from 184; Hess' study of children as students from

42–44; poorly-educated mothers from 48; quality time and 10; Title I schools and 160; underperforming by children from 67, 158; vocabulary and language development of children from 43–45, 48, 52
Lubelfeld, M.: *Student Voice: From Invisible to Invaluable* 218
Lucas, G. 125
Lurye, S. 205
Lustig, S. 252

Madigan, S. 81
Malaysia 319
Mark, G. 254; *Attention Span* 160
Markowitz, A. 304
Marshall (4-year-old child) 202–203
Marshall, T. 147–148
marshals (US air) 236
Marshmallow experiment (delayed gratification) 254–255
Martin, E. W. 237
Matching Familiar Figures Test (MFFT) 187
maternal deprivation 24; social deprivation and 25–26
maternal dialogue with boys 31
maternal employment 114
maternal grandmothers 283
maternal guidance 43
maternal sacrifice 184
maternal separation 25
maternal teaching methods 42
Mattel Toy Company 126
Max Planck Institute for Demographic Research 265
Mayo Clinic Staff 49, 81, 127
McArthur, B. 81
McClelland, D. 141–142
McClelland, M. 251
McDaniel, B. T. 84
McDonald's fast-food restaurant 125; Happy Meals 125
McGowan, M. 284
McKee Foods Corporation 317
McManus, K. 175
meals 44, 82, 87; free for families 286; mealtime 256
media *see* influence of media on children; social media
media messaging 96
mental abilities 142; Piaget on 111, 113, 115
mental age 116
mental deficiencies 111
mental development 2, 26; play and 58, 63–64; positive feedback and 46; stages of 206; talking to children and 48, 52
mental fitness 286

mental health 1–2; attaining 143; benefits to 13; bullying and 233, 236; concerns regarding 128; family 282; misconceptions regarding venting 30; optimism and 149, 170; play and 67; positive thinking and 170; supporting 216; tutoring and home schooling and 117; youth 82; worries regarding 239; worrying and 237
mental health and development 42, 199
mental illness 280
mental processes 78; child 77–79
mental state(s) 31, 192
Mexican American families 316
MFFT *see* Matching Familiar Figures Test
Mickey Mouse character 124
milestones: for 5-year-olds 204–205; evidence-based 219; of language development in babies 49
military deployment or service 280, 284
military personnel 27
military-themed games 206
Millar, G. W. 101
millennial parents 205
Miller, G. 223
Miro, J. 112
misbehavior in school 247–248
Mischel, W. 254–255
missing children 230–231; *see also* child abduction
Miss Piggy character 125
Mitra, S. 160–161
Mobilization for Youth initiative 157
money 63; dreaming of winning the lottery 189; fear of not having enough 235; offering advice about 304–305; saving 256
money management 249
monkeys 25; experiences of lack of fairness by 274; Harlow's monkeys and mothers experiment 25
Moore, D. 130
mother-daughter conflict 283
Mott Children's Hospital national survey 16
Moullin, S. 25
Munsch, J. 51
Muppets 125
Murthy, V. 82

NAACP *see* National Association for the Advancement of Colored People
NAEP *see* National Assessment of Educational Progress
name-calling 218, 233
narcissism 174–175; childhood self-impressions and 174
Narcissistic Personality Inventory 174
Narcissus 174

National Assessment of Educational Progress (NAEP) 159–160
National Association for the Advancement of Colored People (NAACP) 147
National Center for Missing and Exploited Children (US) 230–231
National Council of Youth Sports 249
National Health and Welfare Department of Canada 320
National Threat Assessment Center of the U.S. Secret Service 230
Nation's Report Card 46, 159
Nelson, C. 26
Neyer, W.-U. 171
Ng, F.172
Nickow, A.: *PreK Tutoring Programs and Student Learning Outcomes: A Systematic Review and Meta-Analysis of the Experimental Evidence* report 164
noncustodial grandparents 283
noncustodial parents 230, 233; father 232
non-graded elementary schools 156–157
Norwegian Education Act 82

obesity: failure of willpower and 252; *see also* childhood obesity
O'Bryan, E. 256
Office, The (television show) 31
optimism: constructive behavior and 287–288; employee value and 282; importance of 170–171; sharing 271–272
optimistic attitude 149
orphans and orphanages: Iowa (US) 63–65; Little Orphan Annie 124; Romanian 26–28
Orwell, G.: *1984* 13–14
Osher Lifelong Learning Institute 318
Ovid: *Metamorphoses* 147

PAAT *see* Parent As A Teacher Inventory
Packer, J. 127, 130
parental substance abuse 285
Parent As A Teacher Inventory (PAAT) 319
parent environment influence 188
parent and grandparent generations: learning more and living longer 16
Parent Observations of Child Internet Learning Skills 84, **85**
Parent Overvaluation Scale 175
parent separation: child custody and 232–233
parents and grandparents as partners 9–20; chapter review 19; conversations with young children 19; discussion 18; generational perspectives activities 18; grandparents as teachers 12–17; key concepts 17–18; parent and grandparent self-evaluation 19–20; parents as teachers 9–12; scenario (reasoning and problem solving) 19; storytelling 20

parents' perception of schooling 43–44
parents as teachers 9–12
Parent Success Indicator (PSI) 51, 184
parks 182
patience: delay of gratification and 254–255; *see also* gratification; self-control, patience, and resilience; willpower
Peale, N. V. 170
pedophiles: internet 231
peer influence 224; power of 223
peer prejudice, teaching more about 322
peer pressure protectors 221–223; parent as 222–223; teacher as 221–222
peers: affluent 11; child reliance on 10; income and learning 48; learning from 4; learning with 287; playground 45; play time with 58; raising expectations of 149; unique lessons from 215–216; *see also* emotional support; relationships with parents and peers
peer teachers/tutors 155–158; outcomes 157–158; training peers as 158
Perron, B. 83
personal goals and limitations 144–145
personality goals and achievements 143–144, **145**
Phantom, The (fictional character) 124
Piaget, J. 110–118; Concrete Operational Stage of Thinking for children of ages 6–11 115, **116**; information processing of children as understood by 112–113; Preoperational Thinking Stage of Young Children **113**; qualitative differences in thinking in children as understood by 111–112; schemas of 112; stages and Stages of Cognition of 113–117
Picasso, P. 112
PISA *see* Program for International Student Assessment
play: abundant and deprived households and 64–66; allowing time for 17; how to respond when a child asks a parent to play 58–59; importance of parent's influence during 59; importance of watching one's child play 60; long-term effects of creative play with one's child 62–63; making time for 58; mental development and 63–67; parent-child 58
play activities: parent and child 51
play and child development 58–71; chapter review 69; conversations with young children 69; discussion 69; generational perspectives activities 68; key concepts 67–68; parents as partners in pretend play 60–62; parent and grandparent self-evaluation 69–71; parent questions about the benefits of child play 58–60; relationship of mental development to

play 63–67; scenario (reasoning and problem-solving) 69; storytelling 71
play curriculum 66–67
playground and playroom 32, 45, 47
playing by oneself (on the importance of solitude) 182–195; chapter review 194; conversations with young children 193; discussion 193; generational perspectives activities 192–193; key concepts 191–192; overcoming boredom 189–191; parent and grandparent self-evaluation 194–195; parent monitoring of family time 182–185; scenario (reasoning and problem-solving) 193; solitude and the development of expertise 188–189; storytelling 195; value of solitude 185–188
play partners and playmates 9, 31; fantasy 1
play sessions 50
playthings 50, 128, 209
playtime 50, 59; unstructured 81, 96
Pollock, J. 112
Pool, R. 188
Polgár, J. 188
Polgár, K. 188
Polgár, L. 188
Poulton, R. 248
praise 172; myth of linking self-esteem to 173–174
prayer 301–302
Preckel, F. 190
pregnancy 51; Black teen 315; teen 283, 315; unplanned 248; unwanted 256
pregnant women: smoking and drinking to be avoided by 28–29, 36
prejudice: Allport on 216, 218; anti-Black 147; bullying and 239; ideational 221; middle-school 224; peer 322; social 216–217
pre-kindergarten curriculum, new 67
preschool suspension 248
Probation Information Network 231
productive aging 13
professional families (i.e. families headed by parents with white-collar jobs) 46
professional parents (i.e. parents with white collar jobs) 46, **47**, 48
professional volunteers 287
Program for International Student Assessment (PISA) 163–164
Prowse, V. L. 62, 322
Puzzle Experiment 42–43
Pygmalion 147
Pygmalion Effect 149
Pygmalion (Shaw) 147

qualitative differences in thinking in children 111–112
quality of life 217
quality-of-life criteria 190
quality time 10, 51
quiet time for children 182

race (Blacks, Whites, Hispanics): data analysis factoring in 16, 44–46, 50–51, 183–184, 239, 281, 284, 315, 321; Doll Experiment on 147
race and education: life expectancy and 16
racism 143
Radesky, J. S. 84
Raffoul, A. 128
Rapa, L. 233
reading 256
reading deficiencies 158–159
Reagan, R. 126
reciprocal learning 15
refugees 206, 319–320
relationships with parents and peers 215–228; chapter review 226; conversations with young children 226; discussion 226; experiences of belonging and rejection via 216–221; generational perspectives activities 225; key concepts 224–225; parent and grandparent self-evaluation 226–227; scenario (reasoning and problem-solving) 226; storytelling 228; unique lessons from peers 215–216; *see also* peer influence; peer pressure protectors
remedial instruction 88
report card grades 157, 176
reports to parents about child social skills **34–35**
research and training leaders in other countries by Strom 317–321; Canada 320; Cambodia 319–320; England 318; Greece 319; Hong Kong 319–320; Italy 319; Japan 319; Laos; 319–320; Sweden 321; Taiwan 321; Turkey 319; West Germany 318–319
resilience 1, 29, 143, 149; age and 252–253; chapter review 259; conversation with young children 258; discussion 258; emotional 3; generational perspectives activities 258; key concepts 257–258; misbehavior in school and 247–248; parent and grandparent self-evaluation 259–260; relationships and 253; scenario (reasoning and problem-solving) 258; self-control and patience and 247–260; storytelling 260
restaurants 83, 206; fast-food 125, 128; *see also* McDonald's; Wendy's
retirees 15; benefits collected by 266; protection for 11; traditional norms to be replaced by more mature goals for 13; *see also* AARP

ridicule 102; as bullying 233–234, 239; fear and 235, 240
Riehm, K. 82
Riessman, F. 157
risk: behaviorally at-risk students 253; children's views of 34; growth-oriented 189; health risk behaviors 232; internet as risk to mental health 82; low-risk settings, exposing children to 142; mortality 16; of overscheduling children 247; teaching children how to assess 232, 240
risk assessment: help sources and 230–231
Risley, T. 44–48
Roberto, C. 130
Robertson, L. 101
Rosenthal, R. 148–149
Roosevelt, T. 265–266
Roy, B. 16
Ruffman, T. 30
runaways 230
Runco, M. 101

safety practices 77; internet 85
safety rules *see* family safety rules
Sahlberg, P. 67
Saroyan, W.: "The Sunday Zeppelin" 129–130
Saturday morning television programming 125–126, 249
schemas 112; *see also* Piaget, J.
school achievement *see* tutoring for literacy and school achievement
school inclusion practices 218–219
School in the Cloud 160–161
school shootings 233–234
Schwartz, D. 217
screen time *see* child screen time
Second Time Around Parents 287
Seinfeld, J. 132
self-control, patience, and resilience: age and 252–253; chapter review 259; conversation with young children 258; discussion 258; emotional 3; generational perspectives activities 258; key concepts 257–258; misbehavior in school and 247–248; parent and grandparent self-evaluation 259–260; relationships and 253; scenario (reasoning and problem-solving) 258; storytelling 260
self-control, as predictor of health and wealth 248–251
self-control skills, teaching of 251–252
self-disclosure 288–289
self-esteem: praise and 173–174; self-evaluation and 175–176
self-evaluation 288–289; self-esteem and 175–176
self-fulfilling prophecy 146–147

self-selected goals 10; *see also* goals
Seligman, M. 272, 282
Selma, Alabama *see* Civil Rights March
seniors in the US *see* AARP
sex offenders, awareness of 231–232
sex scenes, exposure of children to 103
sex-specific attitudes towards sons and daughters 319
sexual content online 82
sexual exploitation and abuse *see* child sexual exploitation and abuse
sexually transmitted diseases 256
Shaw, G. B.: *My Fair Lady* 147; *Pygmalion* 147
Shirley Temple dolls 124
'Shut Up' toy 83–84
sibling rivalry 146
silent screen era 124
'Silver Tsunami' 304
Singapore 162, 163, 190, 319
single mothers 42, 161, 315, 321; Black families headed by 44
single parents 248, 280, 302, 320; children of 208; of grandchildren 321–322
Skeels, H. 63–66
skim reading 159
Skodak, M. 63
'smart kids' 171
smartphones 82–84; student performance and 160
Smurfs 125
social competence 203; importance of 204
social incompetence 204
social media 82, 110, 128–129; child reliance on 10
social media addiction 81–82
social media ban for youth, Australia 82
Social Media and Youth Mental Health (US) 82
social prejudice, beginnings of 216–217
social rejection 216
Social Security (US) 13, 265–266
social workers 286
solitude 182–183, 191, 222; development of expertise and 188–189; value of 185
Sosa, A. 50
South Korea: tutoring in 162–163
Sparling, J. 27
sports 249–250
Stanford-Binet Intelligence Scale 111
Steamboat Willie (film) 124
Stevenson, R. L.: *Land of Counterpane* 186
'stranger danger' 230
Strom, P. S. 30, 203; brief biography of 3; cross-cultural studies by 58; on curiosity and creativity in beginning students 102; on link between time and learning 254; online polling study about tutoring 176; Parent

Observations of Child Internet Learning Skills 84, **85**; *Parent Success Indicator* 51; on peer assessment of special education students 220; secondary school polls developed and administered by 99; on solitude and teaching children about solitude 183; on stories on peer mistreatment 218; studies by 3, 58; on waiting for children to respond to questions 103

Strom, R. D. 30, 203; brief biography of 3; cross-cultural studies by 58; on curiosity and creativity in beginning students 102; on link between time and learning 254; online polling study about tutoring 176; Parent Observations of Child Internet Learning Skills 84, **85**; *Parent Success Indicator* 51; secondary school polls developed and administered by 99; on solitude and teaching children about solitude 183; studies by 3, 58; on waiting for children to respond to questions 103; *see also Grandparent Strengths and Needs Inventory; see also* research and training leaders in other countries by Strom

Strom Website, Auburn University 103

stories 96, 127, 144, 150, 187; crime 232; foreign, about grandparents and grandchildren 322; sad 218; sharing of 20, 39, 56, 71, 93, 108, 121, 136, 153, 168, 180, 195, 213, 228, 244, 260, 278, 294, 309, 326

storytelling 4, 5, 20, 39, 56, 71, 93, 108, 121, 136, 153, 168, 180, 195, 213, 228, 244, 260, 278, 294, 309, 318, 326

student disabilities: types of **219**, 219–220

student failure 172

student progress: teacher expectations and 148–149

student recognition of learning deficiency 176

suicide or attempted suicide 232, 239

Support Grandparents Raising Grandchildren Act (US) 280

Sven & Dagmar Salén Foundation of Stockholm, Sweden 321

Sweden 321

Taiwan 12, 51, 162, 164, 318, 321
Take a Stand program 236
taking turns 256
Tarzan 124
teacher expectations: student progress and 148–149
Teamwork Skills Inventory 220
technoference 84
Technology Entertainment Design (TED) 160–161

TED *see* Technology Entertainment Design
teenagers 14, 51; advice given to parents by 300; juvenile delinquency and 25; math tutoring by 157; unwed pregnancy in 283, 315
television *see* advertising; watching television with children
Temple, S. 124
tempo: cognitive 103, 187; impulsive 103, 187; reflective 103, 187
Templeton, T. N. 129
Terman, L. M. 111
territoriality: civil behavior and 201–203
texts and texting 11, 88, 159, 177, 270
Thailand 319
Thoreau, H. D.: *Walden* 30
TikTok 128
time: and learning, link between 254; teaching methods and 49–52
time management 11, 17, 184, 301
Title I schools 286
Torrance, E. P. 101
Torrance Test of Creative Thinking 101
touch, importance of 27–28
Tracy, E. 281
transparency, importance of 5
truancy 239
truth distortion: by advertising 129–130; critical thinking and 129–130; on the internet 79
Tsujimoto, M. 162
Turkle, S. 32, 185; *Alone Together: Why We Expect More from Technology and Less From Each Other* 185
tutoring 3, 114; home schooling and 117
tutoring for literacy 155–168; chapter review 167; conversations with young children 166; discussion 166; generational perspectives activities 166; key concepts 165; parent and grandparent self-evaluation 167; peer teachers/tutors in school 155–158; scenario (reasoning and problem-solving) 166; storytelling 168
tutoring for reading 158–162; focus on individual learning 160; National Assessment of Educational Progress (NAEP) 159–160; school in the cloud 160–161; smartphones and student performance 160; *see also* College Advising Corps; Khan Academy
tutoring in various countries 162–164; Japan 162; PISA assessment of 163–164; South Korea 162–163; United Kingdom 163; United States 164
tweeting 159
Twenge, J. 174
Twitter 86, 128

Unfrosted (film) 132
United Kingdom: salt consumption in 127; tutoring in 163–164
United Nations 28
United States (US): average lifespans in 266; *Brown v. the Board of Education* 148; Education for All Handicapped Children Act 219; establishment of public schools in 156; Individuals with Disabilities Education Act. (IDEA) 219; numbers of children being raised by grandparents in 281–282; Social Security in 13, 265–266; Support Grandparents Raising Grandchildren Act 280; tutoring in 164; *see also* Johnson, L. B.; Kennedy, J. F.; Roosevelt, T.
United States Census Bureau 265; *Household Pulse Survey* 117
United States Department of Health and Human Services 280
United States Office of Education's Division of Handicapped Children 64
United States Secret Service: National Threat Assessment Center 230
United States Supreme Court 148
University of the Third Age 318
U.S. News & World Report 217

video game involvement 82–83
Vietnam 319–320
violence 82, 232; bullying and 234; in cartoons 126; death and 208; domestic 256; interpersonal 235; school-related 233; self-esteem and 173; on television 103; too much screen time linked to 127; in video-game 83; *see also* guns and gun violence in the US
violent behavior 254
violent toys 206, 209
Vohs, K. D. 174

Waal, F. de 102, 201, 274
waiting: for children to respond to questions 103; opportunities to practice 255–256
wandering IQ 64; *see also* IQ
War on Poverty 65
Warren, E. 148
watching television with children 1, 3, 9, 31, 81, 59, 88; asking children questions about television 96–108; chapter review 106; conversations with young children 105–106; curiosity and creativity and 100–103; discussion 105; family challenges of television 96–100; generational perspectives activities 105; key concepts 104–105; parent and grandparent self-evaluation 106–108; parent questions for their children about television 102–103; questions to stimulate parent-child conversations on television 97–99, **99–100**; restricting time for child viewing 101; scenario (reasoning and problem-solving) 106; storytelling 108; waiting for children to respond to questions on television viewing 103
watching your child play 60, 62
Watson, J. A. 315
Wechsler Preschool and Primary Scale of Intelligence 111
Weinberg, R. S. 250
Weisleder, A. 48
Weiss, E. 46
Wendy's hamburger franchise 125
West Germany 318–319
Whittle, C. 126–127
Williams, P. G. 204
willpower and self-control 256–257; failure of 254; as predictor of achievement 247; tests of 255
Wolf, M. J. P. 83
working-class grandparents 315
working-class mothers 46
working-class parents **47**, 48
World War II 318
Wyatt, S. 67

Yamasaki, Y. 162
Yeon-Woo, L. 163
Yoon, H. S. 129
young children learn about the internet 77–93; benefits for children of 77–79; chapter review 91; conversations with young children 90–91; credibility of internet sources, learning about 79; discussion 90; focus on child mental processes 77–79; generational perspectives activities 90; internet safety practices 85–88; key concepts 89–90; parental evaluation of child's internet learning skills 84, **85**; parent and grandparent self-evaluation 91–93; parent guidance for teaching their children about 80–85; protection from social media addiction 81–82; scenario (reasoning and problem-solving) 91; storytelling 93; 'Shut Up' toy 83–84; video game involvement 82–83
youth culture 10
youths: blue-collar 11; gay 238; Mobilization for Youth initiative 157; peer pressure on 221; screen addiction among 123; social development of 14; social media and 128; Social Media and Youth Mental Health 82; video games and 83

Zeanah, C. 28
Zelazo, P. 250–252
Zinsser, K. 204
Zubler, J. 219

For Product Safety Concerns and Information please contact our EU representative GPSR@taylorandfrancis.com
Taylor & Francis Verlag GmbH, Kaufingerstraße 24, 80331 München, Germany